The 80th Division in World War I

  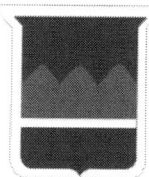  

Into The Meuse-Argonne
Sept.-Nov. 1918

Maj. Gary Schreckengost (U.S.A., ret.)

80thdivision.com

To Our Departed Comrades
And Their Families.
The 80th Division Only Moves Forward!

Copyright © 2016 Gary Schreckengost
All rights reserved.
All photographs either belong to the 80th Division Veterans' Association or the U.S. Army Signal Corps.
Frontispiece: 317th Inf. M.G. Squad Advancing in the Meuse-Argonne, Oct., 1918.

80th Division Association
www.80thdivision.com
Amazon.com

CONTENTS

Preface, 4.

Chapters

1. The Meuse-Argonne Offensive: Preliminary Moves (Sept. 16-25, 1918), 25.

2. The Battle for *HAGEN* (Sept. 26), 70.

3. The Battle for *GISELHER* (Sept. 27-30, 1918), 121.

4. Combat in *Bois Brieulles* (Oct. 1-3, 1918), 156.

5. The Hell of *Bois d'Ogons* and *KRIEMHILDE* (October 4-6), 177.

6. The Battle for *Ferme Madeleine* and Recovery (Oct. 7-31, 1918), 209.

7. The Battle for Buzancy and *FREYA* (Nov. 1-2). 278.

8. In the Open: The Battle for Fontenois (Nov. 3, 1918), 306.

9. The Battle for *Ferme Polka* (Nov. 4, 1918), 316.

10. The Final Drive, Relief, and Cease Fire (Nov. 5-11, 1918), 327.

11. The Long Walk Home (Nov. 12, 1918-June 9, 1919), 359.

12. America's Blue Ridge Infantry Division Today (1938), 391.

Bibliography, 396.

About the Author, 398.

Preface

America's 80th "Blue Ridge" Infantry Division was constituted on August 5, 1917, as part of the National Army (today's Army Reserve), with headquarters at Camp Lee, Virginia. The division itself consisted primarily of drafted men or "Selectees" from Virginia, West Virginia, and Pennsylvania and adopted the now-famous moniker "Blue Ridge Division," as the wondrous Blue Ridge Mountains of the Appalachian chain connected all three states and its peoples. When thrown into combat during the bone-crushing and war-ending Meuse-Argonne Offensive of September-November 1918, the 80th Division was also *the only American division to breach all four of the vaunted German Hindenburg defensive lines during the Meuse-Argonne Offensive* (*HAGEN, GISELHER, KRIEMHILDE,* and *FREYA*). In fact, the place where it breached *KRIEMHILDE*, the strongest of the lines, there now sits America's largest Soldier cemetery in France, standing as stoic reminder of the 80th Division's desperate and heroic actions. Because of its operations and the operations of many other American divisions, the Associated Powers (the Allies plus the United States) were finally able to smash the near-impregnable German defenses and push north to the outskirts of Sedan, ultimately ending the war with a German defeat. All told, the 80th "Blue Ridge" Division advanced some twenty miles across the most-heavily defended place on the earth at the time, suffered over 6,000 casualties—over half of its infantry strength—and killed or captured thousands of German soldiers in order to achieve ultimate victory. Their actions so inspired their Regular Army division commander, Maj. Gen. Adelbert Cronkhite to loudly proclaim: "The 80th Division Always Moves Forward!"

One of the missions of the 80th Division Association is to try to help Blue Ridge Division Soldiers, family members, and interested parties better understand "what it was like" for its Soldiers in the service of America's Blue Ridge Division.

This book is an effort to fill that need.

As such, *this is the historically accurate story* of a representative Dough Boy who served with America's Blue Ridge Division during World War I: Automatic Rifleman Joe Riddle of Company B, 1st Battalion, 318th Infantry Regiment, 159th Infantry Brigade. In Volume 1, read how and why Joe joined the Army in 1917, what training was like at Camp Lee, Virginia, how he was shipped to France, what it was like serving with the British in Artois and Picardy, France, and what the division did during the American First Army's first offensie of the war: the Saint Mihiel Offensive.

This book is actually part of a series. The heart of the series revolves around Volumes 1 and 2. While Volume 1 deals with the assemblage and the training of the division at Camp

Lee, Virginia, its service with the British in the Somme, and its participation in the Saint-Mihiel Campaign of 1918, Volume 2 is about the division's heavy combat in the Meuse-Argonne Offensive, its aftermath, and coming home. This volume is a truncated version of Volume 2.

I'd like to acknowledge the people who helped me complete this project. First, I'd also like to acknowledge my 80th Division Association brothers and sisters who helped me with the research, gathering of pictures, and who said "do it Schreck," in no particular order: Capt. Lee Anthony (U.S.N., ret.), the 80th Division Association's "World War I Historian" and editor of Sergeant Stultz's tome about the division's history during the Great War for Civilization, Maj. Gen. John P. McLaren (U.S.A., ret.), commander emeritus of the 80th Division Association and my commanding officer in Iraq, Mr. Ben Jarratt of the Association who meticulously proofed my manuscript and helped improve it, Mr. Andy Adkins, the Association's "World War II Historian" and author of *You Can't Get Much Closer Than This: Combat with the 80th "Blue Ridge" Division in World War II Europe*, Maj. Dean Dominique (U.S.A., ret.), the author of *One Hell of a War: Patton's 317th Infantry Regiment in WWII*, and Mr. Jeff Wignall, the 2015 National Commander of the Association and author of *Farebersviller 1944*.[1]

Maj. Gary Schreckengost (U.S.A., ret.), 80th Division Association
Cold War, Homeland, Bosnia, and Iraq

---

[1] www.80thdivision.com. The Association consists not only of veterans of the division, but also family members of those who served in the division. Lee Anthony's and Ben Jarratt's ancestors, for example, served in the division during World War I.

1-2

HEADQUARTERS EIGHTIETH DIVISION.

AMERICAN EXPEDITIONARY FORCES.

France, 11 November, 1918.

GENERAL ORDER No. 19.

To the Members of the 80th Division:

The 80th Division Only Moves FORWARD.

It not only moves forward against the enemy, but it moves forward in the estimation of all who are capable of judging its courage, its fighting, and its manly qualities.

In the operations for the period of November 1-5, the division moved forward fifteen and five-eighths miles in an air line.

It always led.

It captured two Huns for every man wounded.

It captured one machine gun for every man wounded.

It captured one cannon for every ten men wounded, besides large quantities of munitions and other stores.

It accomplished these results of vast importance to the success of the general operation, with a far smaller percentage of casualties than in any other division engaged.

It has learned from hard training and experience.

The appreciation of the corps and the Army commanders is expressed in the following:

2-2

Telegram from the Commanding General, First Army (dated Nov. 1):

"The Army Commander desires that you inform the Commander of the 80th Division of the Army Commander's appreciation of his excellent work during the battle of to-day. He desires that you have this information sent to all organizations of that Division as far as may be practicable this night. He fully realizes the striking blow your division has delivered to the enemy this date."

Telegram from the Commanding General, First Army Corps (dated Nov. 1):

"The corps commander is particularly pleased with the persistent, intelligent work accomplished by your division today which has borne the brunt of the burden."

Letter from the Commanding General, First Army Corps, A.E.F. (dated Nov. 11):

The corps commander desires that you be informed and that those under your command be informed that in addition to other well deserved commendations received from the Army commander and corps commander, he wishes to express his particular gratification and appreciation of the work of your division from the time it has entered under his command."

It is necessarily a great honor to be allowed to command an organization which earns such commendation.

It is likewise a great honor to belong to such an organization.

I do not know what the future has in store for us.

If it be war, we must and shall sustain our honor and our reputation by giving our best to complete the salvation of our country.

If it be peace, we must and shall maintain our reputation and the honor of our division and the Army, as soldiers of the greatest country on earth, and as right-minded, self-respecting men.

The 80th Division Only Moves FORWARD.

CRONKHITE, Major-General.

1-2

France, 18 March, 1919.

GENERAL ORDERS NO. 12.

The 80th Division, having been instructed to prepare for return to the United States, will pass from the command of this Army Corps on 20 March, 1919.

The 80th Division arrived in France about June 5, 1918. This Division trained with the British Troops and was on active duty with them in the Artois Sector near Arras in July. The Division was in reserve at the battle of ST. MIHIEL, except the 320th Infantry and 315th Machine Gun Battalion, which took part in the operations of the II French Colonial Corps. From September 26 to 29, inclusive, the Division attacked at BETHINCOURT with the III American Corps and advanced nine kilometers in two days. The Division was withdrawn from the line for five days and again attacked on October 4 at NANTILLOIS. In 9 days of heavy fighting through the BOIS DE OGONS an advance of four kilometers was made. The Division was withdrawn from the line October 12 for re-equipment and replacements. The Division moved forward on October 29 and 30 and re-entered the line at ST. JUVIN.

The 80th Division passed under the orders of the I Corps on October 23. On November 1, the Division attacked as the right division of the I Corps and in six days advanced a depth of 24 kilometers. The Division was relieved from the line on November 6, with its patrols on the west bank of the Meuse. From 18 November to 1 December, the Division marched 221 kilometers to the 15th Training Area at Auey-le-Franc. The artillery of the Division was part of the time detached from the Division and was in action at all times from September 26-November 11.

2-2

The Division has remained in the 15th Training Area until its present order to prepare from embarkation to the United States.

The 80th Division was given the difficult tasks on the front line and in accomplishing them made a splendid record. The corps commander desired particularly to express his appreciation for the soldierly achievements of this division during the time it served with the I Army Corps. After returning to the training area where living conditions were not easy and often difficult the spirit of the division has been excellent and has been manifest at all times. The division leaves on the first part of its journey with the corps commander's congratulations for its excellent record and his wishes for a speedy return to the United States and a successful future.

By command of Major-General Wright.

W.M. FASSETT.

Chief of Staff.

OFFICIAL.

Lt.-Col. A.G.D. Adjutant.

HEADQUARTERS EIGHTIETH DIVISION.

AMERICAN EXPEDITIONARY FORCE.

France, 14 May, 1919.

BULLETIN # 113.

The following letter has been received from Lieut. Gen. Robert Lee Bullard, U.S.A., in command of the III Corps, A.E.F., during the Meuse-Argonne Offensive:

"Under the pressure of great events I, at that time commanding the III Corps to which the 80th Division then belonged, failed to cite the gallant conduct of the division in making three successive assaults with great bravery and finally taking and driving the enemy from Bois Ogons in the great battle of the Meuse-Argonne. I cite it now. It was truly admirable. We see it now more plainly in the light of the results that followed. I ask that this be communicated to your gallant division."

The 80th Division was the only A.E.F. division which went into line in the Meuse-Argonne Offensive three times.

By command of Major General Cronkhite:

W.H. Waldron,

Col., General Staff,

Chief of Staff

The 80th Division officially participated in four campaigns during World War I ("The Great War for Civilization") and suffered 6,101 casualties (217 K.I.A. and 5,884 W.I.A.) out of around 28,000 assigned (22% casualty rate, 2% K.I.A., 20% W.I.A.). We were present at the Saint-Mihiel campaign, too, but the Army didn't officially recognize it as a division battle, as only one regiment, the 320th Infantry, was sent into it. The infantry battalions, of course, suffered far greater casualties. The 3/320th Infantry, for example, suffered 600 casualties out of 840 men (71%), which breaks down to 91 K.I.A. (11%) and 509 W.I.A. (60%). By operation, the casualty figures are as follows:

1918 Somme Offensive: 427 casualties (7 K.I.A., 420 W.I.A.).

1918 Meuse-Argonne (Phase I): 1,064 casualties (27 K.I.A., 1,037 W.I.A.) .

1918 Meuse-Argonne (Phase II): 3,551 casualties (1,154 K.I.A., 2,397 W.I.A.).

1918 Meuse-Argonne (Phase III): 1,059 casualties (44 K.I.A., 1,015 W.I.A.).

As for decorations, citations, and awards, the 80th Division received a total of 619, as follows:

Distinguished Service Crosses: 59

Distinguished Service Medals: 20

General Headquarters, A.E.F. Citation: 41

War Dept. Citations: 31

Division Citations: 35

Brigade Citations: 345

Meritorious Service Certificates: 34

Maj. Gen. Adelbert Cronkhite, our beloved division commander. He was the Regular Army coast artillery officer in charge of the Panama Canal Zone before the war.

Cronkhite's primary staff. Col. William Waldron, the division chief of staff, is top center.

Brig. Gen. Charles S. Farnsworth, 159th Inf. Brig. commander and his principal staff (317th and 318th Inf.). He was later promoted to command the 37th "Buckeye Division" in France.

Col. George H. Jamerson, 317th Inf. commander and his principal staff. Most of the 317th Regiment came from western Virginia.

Col. Briant H. Wells, 318th Inf. commander and his principal staff. Most of the 318th came from eastern Virginia.

Brig. Gen. Lloyd M. Brett, 160th Inf. Brig. commander (319th and 320th Inf.). Arguably the best brigadier in the entire A.E.F. Medal of Honor recipient for actions during the Geronimo Campaign, cited for gallantry during the War with Spain, the Philippines, and the Punitive Expedition under Pershing, Superintendent of Yellowstone Nat'l Park, commander of the 4th Cav. Reg't. when war was declared.

Col. Frank S. Cocheu, 319th Inf. commander and his principal staff. Most of the 319th Regt. came from Pittsburgh. Maj. Montague's 3/319th was the most engaged and most successful battalion of the division.

Col. Ora E. Hunt, 320th Infantry Commander and Staff. Most of the 320th Inf. came from the counties surrounding Pittsburgh.

Brig. Gen. Gordon G. Heiner, Commander of the 155th Arty. Brig. and his principal staff. Units from our artillery brigade spent more days in combat than any other of the Blue Ridge Division.

Col. Charles D. Herron and 313th Arty. Staff.

Col. Robert S. Welsh and 314th Arty. Staff. Welsh will eventually command the 155th Arty. Brig.

Col. Russell P. Reeder and 315th Arty. Staff. This was the division's "heavy" artillery regiment.

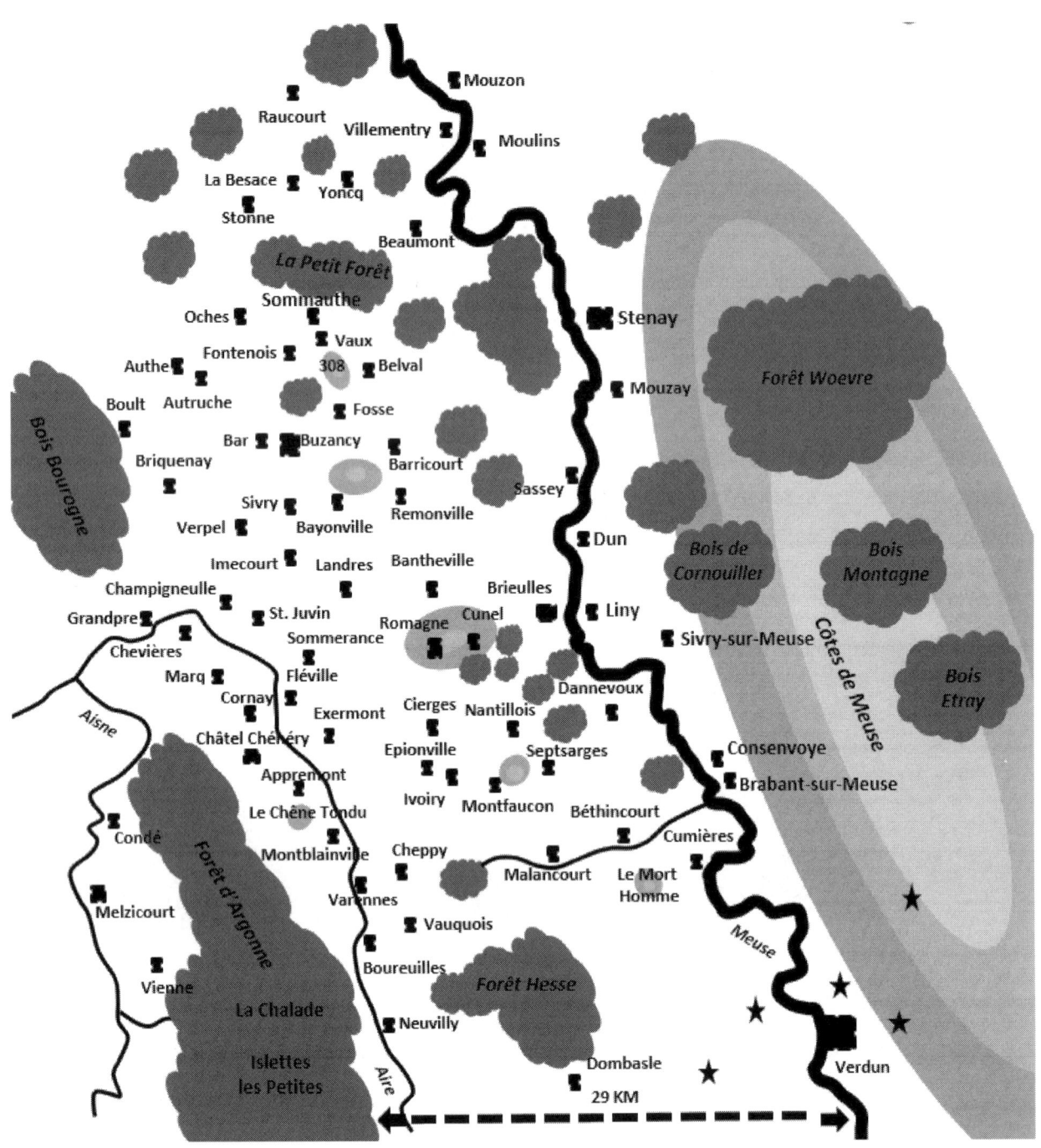

80th Division Operations in the Meuse Argonne, Sept.-Nov., 1918. The Meuse River is on the right and the Argonne Forest is on the left. The division mostly operated in the vicinity of Béthincourt, Septsarges, Dannevoux, Nantillois, Cunel, Sommerance, Sivry, Buzancy, Sommauthe, and Yoncq.

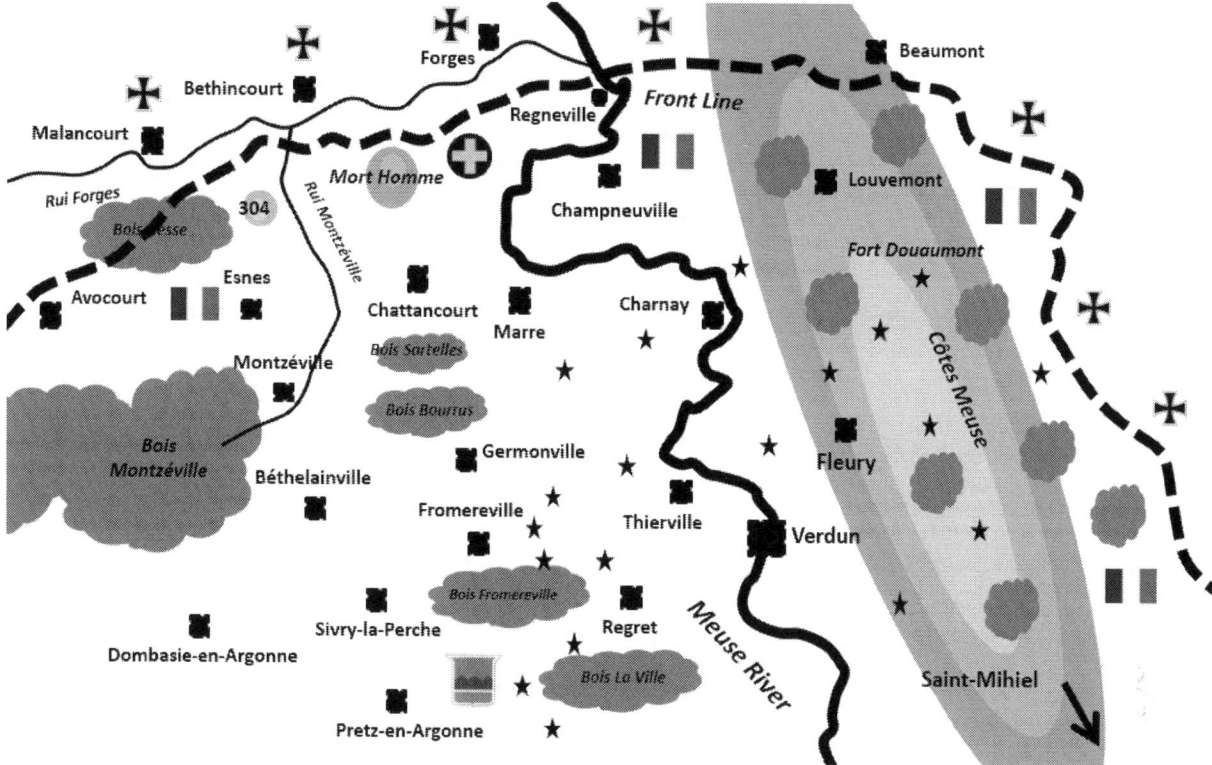

Advance to the Meuse-Argonne Sept. 16-25, 1918. The star icons represent the forts of the area.

"Barber Shop and a dug-out in the front lines 9-11-18" (L) and "Water Cart near Germonville, 9-25-18." This company water buffalo is being filled by a Q.M. water tanker (R).

"The gate at Verdun" is said to have been the inspiration for the insignia of the U.S. Corps of Engineers (L) and *Général de France* Robert Nivelle, the man who famously coined the phrase at Verdun: "They shall not pass!" (R) He also infamously led the abortive 1917 "Nivelle Offensive" which drove much of the once-proud French Army to mutiny. Pershing argued that if we would have sent 500,000 trained Americans to France in 1917, the British and French may have broken through.

German *General der Artillerie Max Karl Wilhelm von Gallwitz*, Pershing's opposite in the Meuse-Argonne (L) and "Field apothecary, 317th Inf., 80th Div., Sept. 19, 1918" (R).

Riding in the back of a steel-wheeled *camion* was not easy (L) and engineers working on a road in the muddy Meuse-Argonne Sector (R).

"On the War Path" with the 318th Inf. (L) and "American Troops Passing Through Chattancourt" (R).

"Road Scene at Esnes, an Important Road Center During the Meuse Argonne Operation" (L) and French *Poilu* or "Hairy Ones" in the trenches of the Meuse-Argonne (R).

Blue Ridge P.C. in the Meuse-Argonne (L) and Brig. Gen. Fox Connor, Pershing's Operations Officer. "The Man Behind the Curtain" at the Meuse-Argonne (R).

Blue Ridge Infantry Division Doughs advancing "Up the Line" in the Meuse-Argonne.

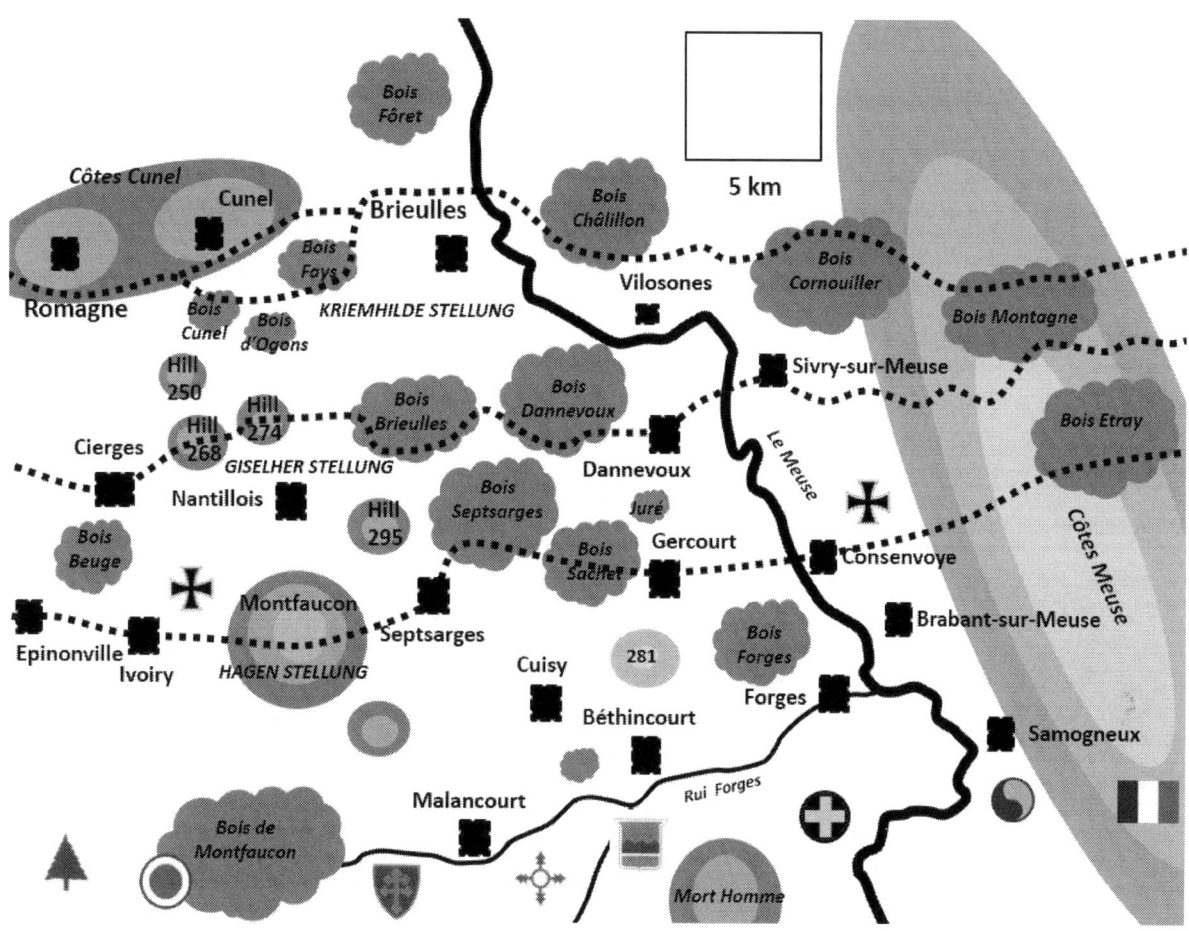

The eastern half of the Meuse-Argonne sector, Sept. 24, 1918. The 80th Div.'s axis of advance: Béthincourt-Gercourt-Dannevoux.

Engineers working on a road in the Meuse-Argonne Sector (L) and Maj. Gen. Robert Lee Bullard, Commander, American III Corps (R).

Gun squad from the 313th Arty. "in readiness." Note how the crew has used tree limbs to help camouflage the guns from aerial observation.

"Camouflaged Road Near Forges" (L) and the forward lines just south of Forges Creek. We were actually quite surprised by how primitive the forward trenches were in this zone.

Doughs from the 160th Inf. Brig. assemble near Forges Creek, Sept. 25, 1918.

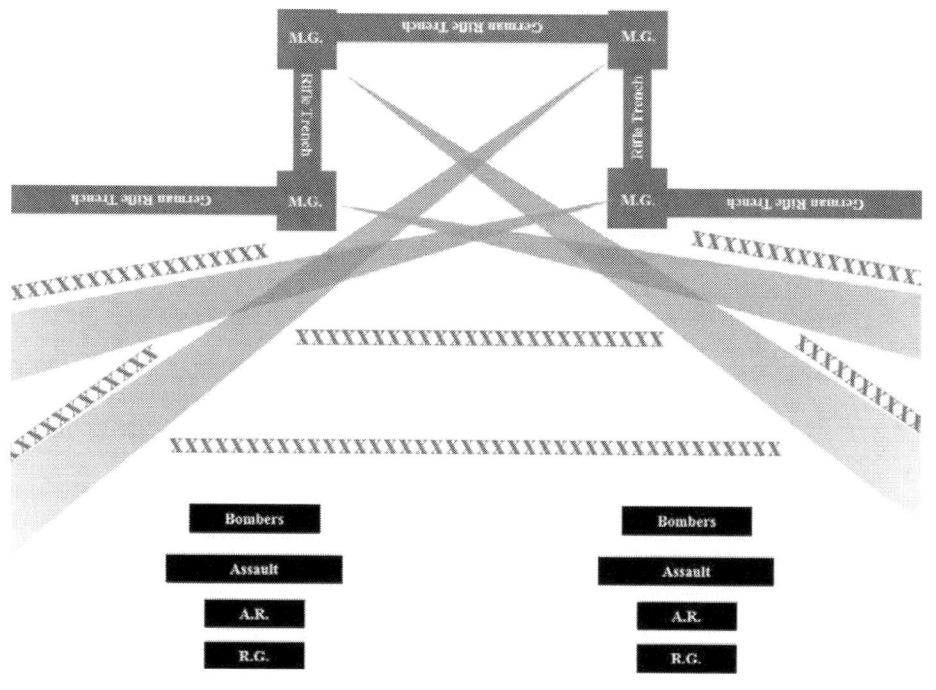

Basic platoon drill to take out German M.G. nests. As the dug-in M.G. nests were protected by interlocking fields of fire, getting shot from the flank or in enfilade, was our biggest concern. While the M.G.s fired up a line of barbed wire at an angle, squads of Hun infantry, armed with rifles and hand grenades, would usually fire straight on, protecting the flanks of the M.G.s. On the top, it shows how our infantry companies usually advanced in two platoon columns with squads stacked, one behind the other. On the bottom, as the bomber squad neared the target and were stopped by well-placed Hun M.G. fire, the A.R.s would maneuver and suppress the M.G.s to their right or left. Behind them would come the R.G.s, who would shoot W.P. smoke grenades at the M.G. nest embrasures.

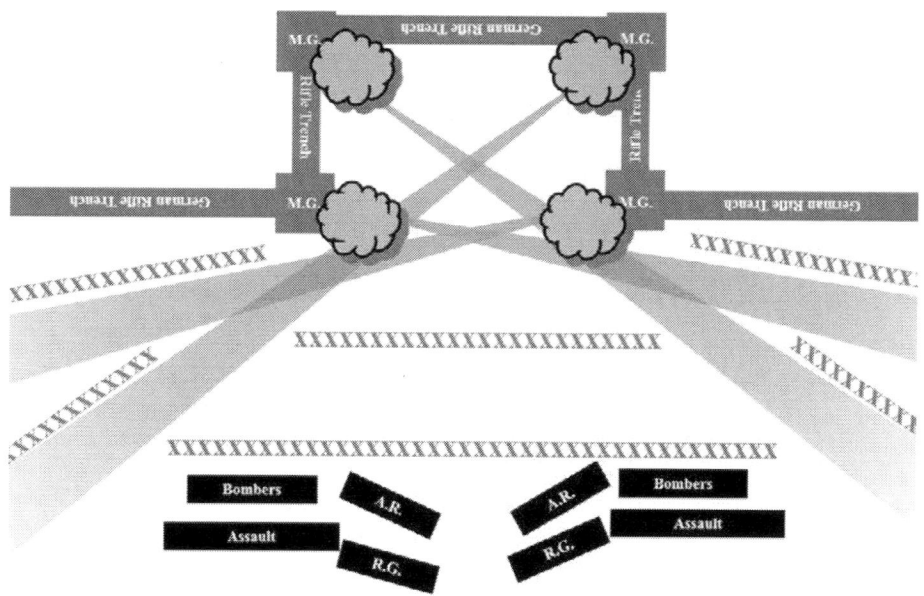

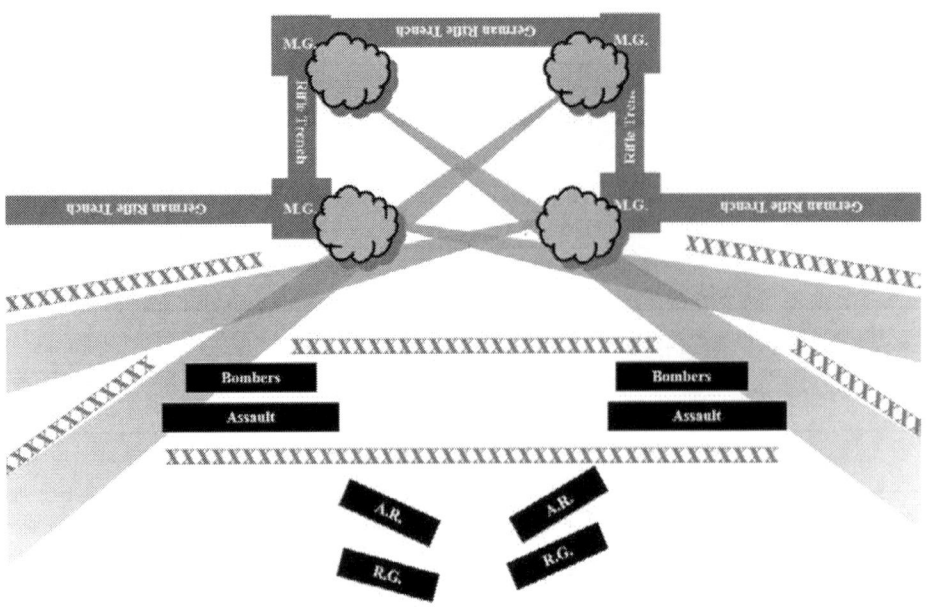

Gaining fire superirority was the key (top). If his platoon was not gaining it, the P.L. would send a patrol back to bring up an M1915 M.G. or an I.G. Once it was determined that the platoon had in fact achieved fire superiority, the P.L. would lead the assault squad through the bombers (bottom) and charge the enemy position, taking the Hun M.G. nest in flank and rear. Once the assault is launched, the P.G. would lead what was left of the bomber, the A.R., and R.G. squads to hold the position. Immediately behind these two platoons were two more platoons from the same company and behind them were four more platoons from another company in the same battalion. The key was to always keep the attack moving forward.

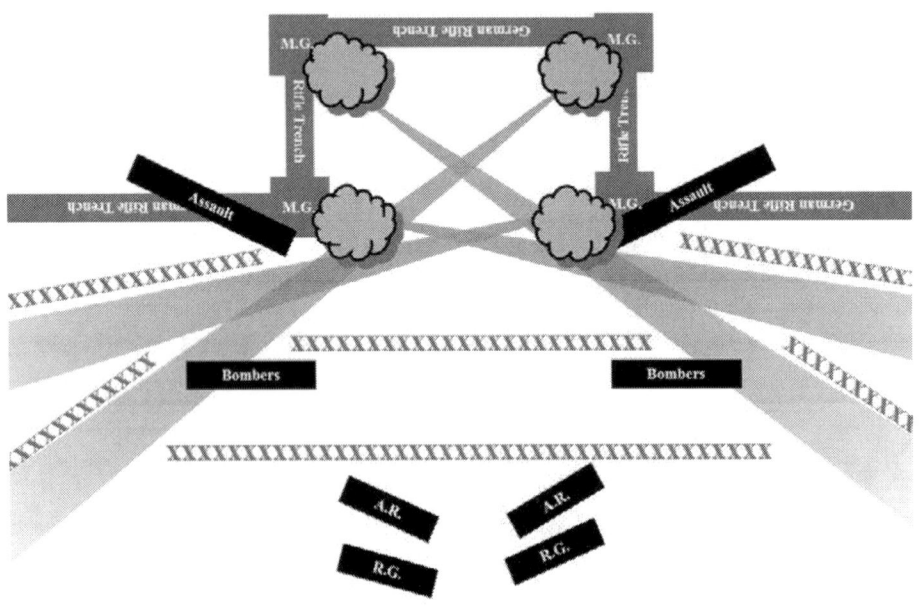

Chapter 1

The Meuse-Argonne Offensive: Preliminary Moves (Sept. 16-25, 1918).

I was drafted into the Army in August, 1917 from Petersburg, Virginia, and reported right next door to Camp Lee. There myself and thousands of other Selectees (as we were called) were turned into hardened American soldiers ready to beat the Imperial German Government in order to help "Make the World Safe for Democracy."

I was assigned to Company B, 1st Battalion, 318th Infantry Regiment, 80th Infantry Division, Maj. Gen. Adelbert Cronkhite, commanding. I'm glad that I was. Cronkhite named us the "Blue Ridge Division" because it was built around Selectees (or draftess) from Virginia, West Virginia, and Pennsylvania. The one thing that connected them all—timelessly—were the beautiful Blue Ridge Mountains of the Appalachian Range. I had never seen the mountains before, but I certainly liked the design. For our division motto, Cronkhite chose *Vis Monitum* or "Strength of the Mountains."

From Sept. 1917 until June 1918, the division was assembled, trained, and equipped at Camp Lee for shipment overseas. In July, we crossed the great Atlantic and by August 1917, the infantry brigades (159th and 160th Infantry Brigades) of the division were training with the British in Artois and Picardy. The division's artillery brigade, the 155th Artillery Brigade, trained near the coast at Redon with the French. It had two light artillery regiments that were armed with French 75mm Field Guns and one heavy artillery regiment, which was armed with French 155mm Howitzers. While with Maj. Gen. Julian Byng's Third British Army near Albert, the infantry brigades participated in the Somme Offensive of 1918. This was my first action against the hated Hun. I was an Automatic Rifleman (A.R.) who fired an M1915 Chauchat. My assistant gunner (A.G.) and good friend was Earl Getz.

In Sept. 1918, infantry brigades of the division were sent south to help collapse the Saint-Mihiel Salient with General John "Black Jack" Pershing's First American Army. Because the operation was such a success, most of the division was held in reserve. My regiment, the 318th Infantry, saw no real action during this offensive.

After this, the entire 80th Division—including its artillery brigade—was slated for the bone-crushing and war-ending Meuse-Argonne Offensive. For this offensive, we were attached to Maj. Gen. Robert Lee Bullard's American III Corps. The Meuse-Argonne sector was just north of the fortified city of Verdun, where the French famously stopped the Germans in 1915-16 ("They Shall Not Pass!"). Since then, the area had remained a hellhole—a place where neither man nor beast should live. Both the French and the Germans were dug in deep in this sector. It was called the Meuse-Argonne Sector because it was between the deep *Forêt d'Argonne* to the west and the great Meuse River to the east with *les Côtes de Meuse* (Heights of the Meuse) overlooking the entire area from the east.[2] Neither side had really attacked the other since 1916 because the area was deemed impenetrable given the dominance of the terrain and the man-made defenses that complemented it.

General "Black Jack" Pershing's American First Army was to advance northward between the Meuse River and the Argonne Forest, supported on its left by the French Fourth Army, which was just west of the forest. To the left of the French Fourth Army, northeast of Paris, the French were to force the Germans back from the Aisne River while farther north, French, British, and Belgian divisions, reinforced by some American divisions, were to continue the attack east toward Brussels, Liège, and Aachen.

The significance of the American First Army's northward drive up the Meuse-Argonne toward Sedan in this up-and-coming campaign lay in the fact that, if carried far enough, it would gain control of the lateral railways and divide the German Army in northern France and Belgium. If we captured Sedan, the "Hun with the Gun" would be unable to maintain his forces in France and Belgium, since communications between his two wings would be practically impossible except by the circuitous route through Liège. Furthermore, the capture or defeat of German armies west of Sedan would be practically certain because, under the powerful attacks by which the British and the Allies were currently delivering in Flanders, the Huns would not be able to conduct an orderly withdrawal through Liège.

It was evident to both sides, therefore, that it was south of Sedan that the Germans could least afford to lose ground.

And that was the very place we Americans resolved to take.

Along most of the Western Front, the Germans had prepared several defensive lines to the rear of their first position (i.e., a classic defensive-in-depth). Northwest of the Meuse-Argonne Sector, the loss of ground to the Germans would have had no decisive effect as their defensive lines or belts were separated by several miles. In the Meuse-Argonne, however, where the important railways and Sedan lay comparatively close to the first line, the second and third lines were built close to the first position, forming a practically continuous defensive zone about ten miles deep. Each line had a code-name like "*HAGEN*" or "*KRIEMHILDE*," etc.

The other factor to understand is that the Meuse-Argonne was ideal for defensive fighting. The heights just east of the Meuse constituted a formidable natural barrier and furnished splendid observation sites for the Hun. These heights and the broken hills of the

---

[2] *Forêt d'Argonne* is pronounced "Fore-et-dar-gone" and *Les Côtes de Meuse* is pronounced "Lay Coat day Mooz-ah."

sector had been organized by the Germans into almost impregnable defensive positions or *Stellung*. Between the Meuse and the Argonne Forest, for example, lay the dominating hill of *Montfaucon* (Mount Falcon), which afforded the Germans perfect observation. During the Battle of Verdun in 1916, the Crown Prince of Prussia even built a a reinforced tower atop the hill and the Germans called it "Little Gibralter."[3]

In the sector, numerous east and west running ridges lent themselves to the construction of defensive lines which connected the Heights of the Meuse, in the east, with the Argonne Forest, in the west. In organizing these lines, the Germans made extensive use of barbed-wire, trenches, concrete M.G. emplacements, and prepared artillery positions—all mutually supporting. The comparatively narrow front and the great depth of the German defenses therefore made our task an extremely difficult one. The only feasible method of breaking through such defensive strong lines (and at great cost) was to drive salients into them by launching wave after wave of frontal assaults and then roll up Germans' flanks from the salients.[4]

The defensive positions we would be facing were all on the forward crests of ridges. According to Col. Moss, these types of positions had the following strengths and weaknesses:

Strengths—the enemy can generally see better what is going on to their front and flanks and the men have a feeling of security that they do not enjoy on low ground, the enemy can generally reinforce the firing line better and the dead and wounded can be removed more easily, and the enemy's line of retreat is better.

Weaknesses—plunging fire of a high position is not as effective as a sweeping fire of a low one and it is not as easy to conceal their position.[5]

Of course we planned to exploit the weaknesses and talked about how we would move under their fire and through their wire.

The movement of men and *matériel* into the Meuse-Argonne was conducted with utmost secrecy, entirely under cover of darkness. Consequently, at night the overloaded roads overflowed with intermixed infantry, artillery, and service of supply (S.O.S.) units. Motor lamps, fires, or even cigarette, cigar, or pipe smoking was strictly forbidden. During the day, the roads and fields were to be clear so that German aerial scouts could not identify movement into the

---

[3] *Stellung* is pronounced "Stel-loong" and *Montfaucon* is pronounced "Mon Fack-own."

[4] A *salient* is a wedge in the line—either in or out.

[5] *M.M.T.* 1161.

sector. To further mask our movement, French infantry (*Poilu*—or "Hairy Ones") remained in the forward positions.

In all, about 220,000 French soldiers were moved out of the sector and approximately 600,000 Americans were moved into it—a Herculean task. The fact that it was performed with such relative smoothness and precision, and without gaining much attention from the enemy, is a striking tribute to the ability of the American First Army and its staff. Maj. Gen. James Harbord, the commander of the S.O.S., later remembered:

> *General Pershing's immediate problem was the secret transportation over inadequate highways of approximately half-a-million men comprising fifteen full-strength divisions, most of them just out of a major engagement at St. Mihiel, and some thousands of Army troops. They had to be in place for the coming battle. Necessarily it meant night movements by marching, by rail and by trucks...As the sector to be occupied by the American First Army was held by the French, it had to be vacated by them before the Americans could move in. Approximately 220,000 men were moved out and some 600,000 took their places, making a total of 820,000 troops handled. The work of the American Staff has received the commendation of more than one Allied authority.*[6]

To get to our concentration area just south of Meuse-Argonne, we marched during the night on muddy, dark roads—roads that most of us could not identify on a map even if our lives depended on it ("Join the infantry and see the world...on foot...and in the dark!"). We would march from one wood to the next and wait out the day under cover. During the day, movement was restricted to groups of two with 200 yards between groups, the parking of vehicles in formation was prohibited, and vehicles had to be kept either under the cover of trees or close to a building and camouflaged. Animals were also to be kept under cover, with their watering limited to groups four, and then only after 7:15 P.M. Cronkhite ordered that "Every man on the firing line or in any other part of the area must avoid being seen by the enemy. A single observation of the change in the color of the uniform will give important information."[7] Finally, about six km southwest of Verdun, near Regret, we were ordered to halt and stand by for several days in *Bois La Ville*, where the entire 80th Division was concentrated for the first time since we left Camp Lee.[8]

---

[6] Harbord, 430.

[7] As cited in Stultz, 347.

[8] *Regret* is pronounced "Re-gret" and *Bois La Ville* is pronounced "Bwa La Veal."

The northern edge of *Bois La Ville* contained a large French ammunition dump (*Dépôt Munitions*), which, together with the many French and American artillery batteries, made attractive targets for German airmen.[9] Several aerial bombing raids were in fact made while we were concentrated here, but we suffered no casualties. Aerial bombardment wasn't so bad because an aeroplane can only drop so many bombs on one's head before it had to fly off. But a battalion or brigade-sized artillery strike, that's just down-right deadly.

Bois La Ville or "Camp Gallieni" had long been a permanent rest center for French troops entering and leaving the lines around Verdun. The undergrowth in the woods had been cleared away and barracks, huts, or tents were scattered over the area. While several units occupied the camp's makeshift barracks, the bulk of the command (especially the infantry!) was quartered in tents. The men found the new area comparatively pleasant, since duties were light and they could visit friends in other units of the division. Another highlight of our brief stay at Camp Gallieni was a Y.M.C.A. show with an American woman as the feature attraction (I don't remember her name—but she was pretty). Our most-utilized diversion, however, was in reading or writing letters. One soldier from 3/320th Infantry remembered: "Most of the men wrote home every day during that short period, since each day might be the last chance in this life. Some letters were also written to be mailed only in case the writer was killed, but I don't think that there were too many of these. Because each letter home had to be censored by our platoon leader, the company's lieutenants spent most of their time reading through (and censoring) our letters. If we wrote about our location, size of our unit, troop morale, or anything that may tip the enemy off about our fighting power, it was cut right out of the letter and we received a tongue-lashing not to do it again because "letter writing is a privilege in the Army and not a right."[10]

It was here at Camp Gallieni where we received our pre-battle instructions and issues of new equipment, including repeating shotguns that we generally called "trench brooms." The most common model was the Model 12 Winchester, an upgrade of the M1897 that was used in the Philippines to combat insurgents. The M12 is a .12 gauge weapon that uses a pump action in combination with an attached tubular magazine (under the barrel) that can spray loads of .32 cal. pellets over an area with deadly speed.

"Sha-Clack."

"Boom!"

"Sha-Clack."

---

[9] *En Dépôt Munitions* is pronounced "Dep-oh Mune-it-ee-own."

[10] As cited in Stultz, 349-50.

"Boom!"

"Sha-Clack."

"Boom!"

Some of the trench brooms were even fitted to take a M1917 Enfield Bayonets, and together, we called them "combat trombones." The only drawback to the weapon, aside for its close range, was that its shell casings were made from cardboard and cardboard sucks up moisture really fast. Other equipment was given a last inspection, gas masks were again tested, and large quantities of grenades of various types were issued and demonstrated (e.g., the M2 "Pineapple Grenade"). With all of this equipment, our infantry platoons packed more of a combat punch than that of our enemy.

Pyrotechnics with a code for their use were distributed to company commanders and platoon leaders and were demonstrated by French officers. These pyrotechnics included day and night rockets and flares (e.g., *Véry* Lights). Battle maps were issued to all officers, with known German positions and the pre-planned artillery barrage lines noted. Letters, diaries and other identification were ordered destroyed before entering the front lines.

We all knew that the 1916 battle of Verdun was one of the biggest and bloodiest battles of the war thus far. It was when the German General-in-Chief at the time, *Generalfeldmarschall Erich von Falkenhayn*, ordered the Prussian Crown Prince Wilhelm's German Fifth Army to attack the strong French defenses of the *Région Fortifiée Verdun* (R.F.V.) and those of the French Second Army on the right bank of the Meuse. Falkenhayn intended to capture *les Côtes de Meuse* from which Verdun could be overlooked and bombarded with observed artillery fire.[11] Once taken, the French would no doubt be *provoked* into trying to retake the decisive heights and as the did so, they would be smashed and bled white by superior German fire power.

On February 21, 1916, Falkenhayn's great offensive (code-named *Unternehmen Gericht* or "Operation Judgment") against Verdun began and in fact drove the French back upon *Côtes Meuse*.[12] By March 6, 1916, some twenty French divisions were committed to the defense of Verdun, which defended an ancient crossing of the Meuse. *Général de France Philippe Pétain* ordered that no withdrawals were to be made and that counter-attacks were to be conducted, despite exposing French infantry to German massed artillery. To better communicate this

---

[11] *Generalfeldmarschal* Erich von Falkenhayn is pronounced "Gen-er-awl Feld-marshall Er-eek von Falk-en-highn" and *Région Fortifiée Verdun* is pronounced "Rage-on Fort-ee-fay Ver-done."

[12] *Unternehmen Gericht* is pronounced "Oon-ter Nay-men Ger-rickt."

directive, *Général de France Robert Nivelle,* one of Pétain's loyal lieutenants, coined the phrase: *"Ils ne passeront pas!"* or "They Shall Not Pass!"[13]

The road from Bar-de-Luc in the south to Verdun in the north was called *le Voie Sacrèe* ("The Sacred Way") and it kept the French soldiers there supplied with food, water, and ammunition.[14]

By April, French artillery on the west bank of the Meuse finally reached parity with the Germans, and the French started to inflict thousands of casualties on the Hun atop the Heights of the Meuse.

To change the dynamic, Falkenhayn shifted his attacks into the Meuse-Argonne Sector, which was on the west bank of the Meuse in order to flank Verdun from the north. French reinforcements contained the attacks, however, especially atop a steep elevation, which came to be called *Côtes de Mort Homme* ("Dead Men Hill") that is just southeast of *Béthincourt*.[15] To support the French at Verdun, the British launched a massive (and failed) offensive up the Somme River in July (Somme Offensive, 1916) and it became one of the most bloody offensives of the war. Although the British failed to break through all of the Germans' defensive lines in the Somme, they were able to draw enough German forces away from Verdun to enable the French to stabilize the line there. We were told that both sides lost around 500,000 at the Battle of Verdun, an average of about 80,000 casualties for each month of the battle. Ever since then, the fighting in the area had been desultory at best, because it was one of the most difficult to take—for both sides. According to Maj. Gen. Robert Lee Bullard, who commanded the American III Corps in the Meuse-Argonne:

> *To what nature had, perhaps without design, created in the way of defenses, military art had contributed every device known to modern war. Old, rusty, new, twisted, straight, netted, crossed and overlapping barbed wire was getting strung in endless miles with fortified strong points, dugouts, concrete M.G. emplacements, skillfully selected natural M.G. sites, and many lines of trenches flanking and in parallel depth. It was probably the most comprehensive system of leisurely prepared field defenses known to history.*[16]

---

[13] *Général de France Robert Nivelle* is pronounced "Gin-air-awl day Frawnce Row-bear Row-bear Nee-veal" and *Ils ne passeront pas* is pronounced "Eel nee Pass-or-awn Pa."

[14] *Le Voie Sacrèe* is pronounced "Lay Vwa Sack-ray."

[15] *Côtes de Mort Homme* is pronounced "Lay Coat day More Oam" and *Béthincourt* is pronounced "Beth-awn-core."

[16] As cited in Bullard, 433.

All told, the 80th Division spent five days in *Bois La Ville* hiding out by day and training by night. One soldier from 3/320th Infantry remembered:

We knew that we were on the verge of a big drive, and had frequent conferences, at which, thanks to the wisdom of the major, the sergeants who commanded the platoons, as well as the officers, were present. Our stay at here is chiefly remembered by the men for one evening when the whole regiment was led on a sort of "follow the leader" stunt through the woods. The object was to see if we could keep "closed-up" and avoid splitting up and losing part of the outfit, and it was a thorough enough test, for we had double-timed through the woods, jumped logs and turned sharp corners aplenty before we finally regained the main road and reorganized the column.[17]

Also during this time, many reconnaissance missions were conducted by our officers to the jump-off lines, which were currently thinly held by units of the French Army and the American 33rd (Prairie) Division. As was already stated, America's Blue Ridge Division was transferred to Maj. Gen. Robert Lee Bullard's American III Corps, which was to be centered around Mort Homme. It was to be used as part of the supporting effort to break through the strong German lines in the vicinity of Montfaucon.

Bullard was a Pershing favorite. He was a tall, athletic, 57-year-old Regular Army officer from Alabama who had commanded the American 1st Division at Cantigny. He had drive, and in our opinion, a ruthless disregard for losses.

But how else was he supposed to feel?

The day before the big attack began, for example, Bullard sternly instructed his division commanders (like our very own Cronkhite) not to worry about their flanks. "In every previous fight," he told them, "I heard division, brigade, and regimental commanders excuse their failures to continue the advance by blaming the units on their right or left for failing to come forward with them." In this battle, he would "take no such excuse...each of your divisions maintains its reserve for the very purpose of protecting its flanks."

There would be no excuses—this time, they would attack, whatever the cost.

And we ground pounders were the cost.

As far as "forget about the flanks" goes, Bullard was right. We found that each brigade, battalion, company, or platoon should in fact advance as far as it could without worrying about the unit to their left or right.

---

[17] As cited in Stultz, 347-48.

Should each unit defend its own flanks? Absolutely! But the message was to stick as many knives into the German hog as possible, creating salients in their lines—making them react to us and not us reacting to them.

So each corps, division, brigade, etc., was to advance to their assigned objectives without waiting for their flanks to be secure. This meant that we had to maintain 360° security at all times, especially in the woods, in order to prevent getting hit in flank or rear.

The advance to the American First Army's initial objective, *Côtes de Cunel*, however, was to be paced by Cameron's V Corps, which was in the center of the Army axis of advance with the 79th Infantry Division. *HAGEN, GISELHER* and *KRIEMHILDE* were expected to be breached on the first day (!), and *FREYA* the next. As we shall see, many days and nights—and weeks—were to pass before this goal was attained.[18]

The fact that Pershing or Foch even expected us to breach one of these lines in one day was either cruel, arrogant, or sly. Pershing would often say to his corps and division commanders during the offensive: "You're behind schedule! You're behind schedule!" It's like saying that I should be able to drive from Richmond to San Fransisco in one hour. Every hour above that, I'd be late.

It's a ridiculous assumption—but a motivator.

The first unit of America's Blue Ridge Division to move north from *Bois la Ville* to the front line was 3/319th Infantry. It marched during the night of Sept. 21-22 to *Bois Bourrus*, where it relieved 3/131st Infantry, 33rd (Prairie) Division, which held a reserve position in the Béthincourt sector. The Prairie Division had occupied the support line with only a thin line of French troops remaining in the forward positions south of *Ruisseau Forges* (Forges Creek) to screen the relief.[19]

The 80th Division's mission was to punch through the German outpost line at *Béthincourt* (code-named "Wiesenschlecken"), breach the first line, *HAGEN*, at *Gercourt*, and advance up to *Village Dannevoux*, which was about 8 km north of Forges Creek, was the corps' designated Line of Departure (L.D.).[20] From there, we were to break through the *GISELHER, KRIEMHILDE*, and *FREYA* (*KRIEMHILDE* being the strongest along Côtes de Cunel) in

---

[18] *Côtes de Cunel* is pronounced "Coat day Que-nel." According to Germanic legend, *Hagen* was the German Burgundian knight who killed his supposed friend Siegfried by stabbing him in the back, *Giselher* was the King of Burgundy who Siegfried helped to marry *Brünhilde* (Siegfried had to climb a mountain, go through a ring of fire, and awaken *Brünhilde* from a spell with a kiss, i.e., "Sleeping Beauty"), *Kriemhilde* was Siegfried's wife and *Giselher's* sister and *Freya* was *Wotan's* wife (*Wotan* is King of the Gods) and *Freya* is the Goddess of Love, Sexuality, Beauty, Fertility, Gold, etc.

[19] *Bois Bourrus* is pronounced "Bwa Borrows" and *Ruisseau Forges* is pronounced "Reese-sew Forge."

[20] *Gercourt* is pronounced "Geyr-core" and *Village Dannevoux* is pronounced "Veal-awg Dan-ev-voo."

conjunction with other American First Army units and continue the advance "in the open" toward Sedan until the Germans surrendered. The division sector was be about two km wide (each attack battalion covering one km and each attack company 500 meters), or about one km on each side of the ruins of *Béthincourt* south of *Rui Forges*.[21]

As per Army doctrine, Cronkhite directed the Blue Ridge Division to attack in column of brigades, the 160th Brigade leading. The infantry regiments were to be side-by-side in column of battalions—Col. Frank Cocheu's 319th Infantry on the right and Lt. Col. Ephraim G. Peyton's 320th Infantry on the left. Each regiment would then attack in column of battalions: assault, support, and reserve. Each company would then attack with two platoons up and two in back. The support battalion would "mop-up" postions by-passed by the assault battalion and protect the regiment's flanks while the reserve battalion provided ammunition and supply details for the assault battalion. Once the assault battalion shot its bolt, it would be replaced by the support battalion, etc. And once the attacking brigade was beaten into pulp, the other brigade would come up behind it and repeat the process.

We all knew that the only way to break these strong defensive lines would be to "attack in depth" and the way the A.E.F. divisions were purposely organized, depth would be achieved.

The advance was to proceed at a rate of one hundred meters every four minutes through the enemy outpost line about a km north of Béthincourt, then through HAGEN at Gercourt, and up to Côtes Dannevoux and GISELHER. It was important for the infantry to get from "Point A to B" at exact times in order to maintain artillery support, which was rigidly pre-planned. Cronkhite's battle orders stated, in part:

It is directed that the attack be pushed with vigor and that each leading battalion continue the advance until slowed down, when it will be passed by the next battalion in rear as directed by the brigade commander. It is not intended to use more than one brigade to [breach HAGEN und GISELHER]. When the objective has been attained, the troops occupying it will at once reform and take up the organization of the ground for defense in depth and the police of the battlefield.[22]

To the surprise of the men of 3/319th Infantry (Blue Squares), the trenches that the soldiers of the 33rd (Prairie) Division were holding were not solid. They were more like company-level strong points that over-looked Forges Creek and the broad plain to the north.

---

[21] *Rui Forges* is short for Forges Creek. It is pronounced "Roo Four-jez."

[22] As cited in Stultz, 365.

The plan was that as other units of 160th Inf. Brig., 80th Division, came forward into their zone, the 33rd Division would yield their positions and stack up further to the right, in their assigned attack zone. Interspersed throughout the area were still a few errant French artillery or S.O.S. units.

September 23, 1918.

On the night of Monday, Sept. 23, we in the 159th Inf. Brig. received orders to proceed north by marching from *Bois La Ville* to *Bois Fromereville*.[23] After a couple of hours on the march, however, word was received to "hold in abeyance." No one present, from the colonel on down, knew what that meant, exactly. We took it to mean, "Halt and be ready to move out at a moment's notice because something is screwed up ahead." Waiting in the open is hard on the troops, especially when they have to stand in the mud in a cold, drizzling rain. It wasn't until three hours later, well-past midnight, that we received word to "disregard and keep moving."

Typical!

In the meantime, significant players of the division (brigade, regimental, and battalion commanders) were sent north to conduct a reconnaissance of the forward positions to ensure that their unit got to the right place at the right time. Maj. Ashby Williams of 1/320th remembered:

> *I am pretty sure it was Sunday morning (Sept. 22) that word came that our brigade (the 160th) would go up into the line in a day or two to take part in a great offensive. Those were indeed exciting times that made the heart beat fast. These were not rumors, but orders, and here were the maps showing where we were to go over the top at the foot of Dead Man's Hill, our regiment to be shock troops. The regimental commander decided that the battalion commanders should go up to the front at once and make a thorough reconnaissance of the line where we were to go over the top. Shortly after lunch, therefore, Maj. Holt, Maj. Emory, and I started out for the front in the colonel's car. We passed, I think, through Sivry, Bethelainville and Montreyville and left our car in the town of Chattancourt and went on foot from there. It must be remembered that the road along which we passed was just to the left of Verdun and these little towns through which we passed had suffered the usual fate in the greatest*

---

[23] *Bois Fromereville* is pronounced "Bwa Frum-are-ah-veal."

battle, probably, in the history of the world and they were merely piles of stone with a wall or a roof here and there. From Chattancourt we walked northwest, and when on the ridge above the town we could see to the right-front the great Dead Man's Hill (Mort Homme) where many thousand Frenchmen died for France, and to our left-front the historic Hill 304 which changed hands so many times in the great battle of Verdun. To our front were the ruins of the little town of Bethincourt by the Forge's Creek in no man's land between the Boche and Americans. The whole landscape was a barren waste with hardly a spring of living stuff and not a living soul in sight. Wherever you looked the ground was pock-marked with shell-holes. We lost no time in contemplating this spectacle because more important business was in hand. We descended at once the road leading toward Bethincourt between Dead Man's Hill and Hill 304 until we reached the trench system of the America line. After some difficulty we located an officer of one of the companies of the 33rd Division, they holding the line, and he took us down in his dugout and we went over the map of all the positions and he explained them to us in detail. I remember when we came out of the dugout it was pitch dark and I had great difficulty in keeping up with the guide. We went over the whole system, however, even down to and including the outpost system of trenches within a few hundred yards of the Boche line. I remember how we got out of the trenches on the outpost line and strained our eyes in the darkness trying to visualize the lay of the land and especially to see what obstacles we might be expected to meet in going over the top.[24]

Included in the reconnaissance were scouts from Heiner's 155th Arty. Brig. They were sent forward to the vicinity of Mort Homme in order to conduct a Reconnaisance, Selection, and Occupation of Position (R.S.O.P.) so they could guide the guns forward under cover of darkness the next night. According to Army Regulations, while the commander of the maneuver forces (i.e., infantry or cavalry) "determines the object of the action.... the determination of the way in which the artillery is to attack them are the province of the artillery commander," *viz.*:

A.D.R. 1072. The commander of the troops [i.e., infantry or cavalry] determines the object of the action, fixes the extent of the artillery support to be furnished the larger units, and indicates important objectives for special attack. The distribution of objectives and the determination of the way in which the Artillery is to attack them are the province of the artillery commander.

---

[24] As cited in *1/320th Infantry*, 72.

A.D.R. 1073. At the beginning of the action, the artillery brigade commander, knowing the objective of the infantry, what troops are designated to attack these objectives, and the degree of support for the different attacks, distributes the artillery at his disposal so as to best accomplish the desired results. He designates the organizations that are to support a particular attack and those that are to be held in observation or in readiness to meet the developments of the action. He makes clear to his subordinates the mission that each is to accomplish. As the combat progresses he keeps himself informed of the progress of the different attack and if necessary modifies his initial orders. He keeps his subordinates informed, as far as possible, of the situation and of changes in the general plan.

A.D.R. 1074. The artillery regimental commander causes his unit to take position and assigns sectors to the battalions in accordance with the orders he has received. He keeps himself constantly informed as to the dispositions both of the enemy and of the troops with which his regiment is cooperating. He takes steps to insure an adequate supply of ammunition. In certain cases, as, for example, when it may be necessary to concentrate the fire of his entire regiment against a comparatively narrow front, the regimental commander may have to direct the fire in detail. In general, however, he indicates the portions of the enemy line upon which fire is to be delivered, leaving the details of fire direction to is battalion commanders.

A.D.R. 1418. The duties of the artillery battalion commander are mainly tactical. He informs the battery commanders as to the tactical situation, the mission of the battalion, and the role of each battery. The more detailed this information the more surely may the major rely upon correct initiative by his captains when communication fails.

A.D.R. 1075. The artillery battalion commander directs the fire by assigning targets to the batteries and by furnishing them such information and data as will tend to increase the efficiency of their fire. To this end he transmits to them such information concerning the nature of their targets, ranges, confirmation of the ground in the vicinity of the objectives, etc., as may become available from maps, reports, and orders received, from his personal reconnaissances, or any other sources. The battalion commander must keep himself constantly informed as to the effect of the fire.

A.D.R. 1076. The battalion commander designates targets and assures himself that they are identified. Technical details are ordinarily left to the battery commanders...Fire direction is the function of battalion commanders, who exercise it in detail by assigning targets to particular batteries, and conduct of fire is the function of battery commanders.

A.D.R. 1419. The role assigned to a battery should be given broadly, leaving to the captain within his sphere a full power of initiative and fixing upon him a definite responsibility.

A.D.R. 1420. The major should conserve his force by assigning to a particular task only so many of his units as should accomplish it with their maximum power. He may thus be able to retain at his disposal other units to meet contingencies not yet developed.

A.D.R. 1077. Sudden changes in the tactical situation may cause the battalion commander to take under the fire of his batteries targets not originally assigned to his unit. He will at once report the fact to his immediate superior.

A.D.R. 1423. In general, the major will devote his attention principally to the assignment of targets, to the observation and study of the terrain and of the situation; to the digestation of information received from higher commanders, freiendly troops and auxiliary observers; to reports of the regimental commander regarding changes of the situation; to amplifying the information already furnished to his subordinates and to rendering them every possible assistance; to keeping open lines of communication; to preparation for the effectiveuse of unengaged batteroies; to maintenance of the supply of ammunition.

The plan was to switch out French artillery with American, and then, no later than Sept. 25, to do the same with the infantry. We wanted the Germans to believe that the front was in fact not being reinforced for the big push that was set for dawn, Sept. 26, 1918. According to Cronkhite's concept, Brett's 160th Inf. Brig. would lead the attack with the 319th Infantry on the left and the 320th on the right in column of battalions (attack, support, and reserve), Jamerson's 159th Inf. Brig. would be held in reserve, and Heiner's 155th Arty. Brig., (+) would conduct counter-battery, interdiction, infantry support, or accompanying missions. Of these, Maj. Frank J. Dunigan's 1/313th Artillery was assigned the duty of "accompanying artillery." After consulting with Lt. Col. Otto L. Brunzell, commander of the 313th Artillery, General Brett decided to attach a pair of 75mm field guns to each attack Infantry battalion in the 160th Inf. Brig. (a total of four guns, or an entire battery) and kept two batteries with him limbered near the brigade H.Q. to reinforce the breakthrough. Remember, according to the *F.S.R.*, "the leader of each Infantry unit to which artillery support has been assigned will, in both the attack and defense, make known to the artillery commander his plans and their expected development and will, throughout the action, keep the artillery representative accompanying him fully informed of the needs of the Infantry in the matter of artillery support":

> *F.S.R. 124. Artillery.— The artillery is the close supporting arm of the infantry in combat and its duties are inseparably connected with those of the infantry. Its targets are those units of the enemy which, from the infantry point of view, are most dangerous to the infantry or that hinder infantry success. The greater the difficulties of the infantry the more powerful must be the artillery support. In order to insure close cooperation of the artillery with the Infantry in combat, the leader of each infantry unit to which artillery support has been assigned will, in both the attack and defense, make known to the artillery commander his plans and their expected development and will, throughout the action, keep the artillery representative accompanying him fully informed of the needs of the Infantry in the matter of artillery support. The security of the artillery in combat must be provided for either by the distribution of the other arms or specifically in orders.*

Maj. Frank Dunigan's 1/313th Artillery would therefore not participate in firing the barrage that was to precede the attack. It was to instead advance with the infantry as fast and as far as possible and "be ready to assist them with direct fire from hastily chosen positions as soon as the infantry should meet strong enemy resistance." In order to accomplish this mission, Maj. Dunigan would have to decide which roads his battalion would take in order to keep pace with the attacking infantry. This is the essence of R.S.O.P.

Accordingly, Maj. Dunigan, his adjutant, Capt. Shelton Pitney, the three battery commanders of the battalion, Lt. Joe Peppard (A), Capt. Robert Perkins (B), Capt. George Penniman (C), and the Regimental Telephone Officer, Lt. Thomas Crowell, set out from Bois de Ville at 1:00 A.M., Sept. 24, in General Brett's limousine. By 3:00 A.M., they arrived to what had once been Chattancourt, a village that had been reduced to simple but ugly and bleak piles of brick and mortar.[25] A study of military and "Michelin" maps had shown that there were but

---

[25] *313th Artillery*, 19. *Chattancourt* is pronounced "Chat-an-core."

three roads leading north within the division sector.[26] One of these roads ran from *Chattancourt* over the eastern slope of *Mort Homme* and seemed to be the least promising of the three for the reason that it was shown as being "unimproved" for more than half of the distance to *Rui Forges*, the 80th Division's designated L.D. The second road passed over the western slope of *Mort Homme*, and the third led north from *Esnes*, converging with the second one just south of *Béthincourt*. The most important discovery, however, was that the only bridge over Forges Creek in the division's sector, as shown on the Michelin map, was the one leading into *Béthincourt*. It could only be reached by either of the last two roads mentioned.[27]

Taking the center road, the one just to the left or west of Mort Homme, Maj. Dunigan led the way north for perhaps a km. As he tells it, on either side of the darkened road were old shell craters that were about one meter deep and and one meter in diameter, each one giving way to another in such perfect continuity that there was never room for more than a single person to pass between them. Usually each crater was composed of two or more smaller ones. Although the road was still passible for light artillery (e.g., 75mm guns), the adjoining farm fields, which had been totally cratered, were not. In addition, Maj. Dunigan's artillery scout passed two old trench systems and two belts of barbed wire, the latter were loose and rusted, remnants of the horrific battle that had occurred here in 1916.[28] Clearly, the light batteries of the 155th Arty. Brig. could not use this route to advance during the attack.

Finding this area unsuitable, the artillery scouts retraced their route through the dark and the drizzle, returned to *Chattancourt*, and drove up to the summit of *Mort Homme*, which was only thinly held by troops from the Prairie Division. Like Maj. Williams of the 320th Infantry, the artillerists were impressed by the total destruction of the area, which had been "ploughed by continuous shell fire, with not a sign of vegetation except a solidary blood-red poppy here and there, its dome resembling in some respects a human skull, this hill presented a picture of desolation, where in 1916 [thousands of] lives were sacrificed in less than 24-hours in the attempted taking of Verdun. Here the French, with the determined words of '*Ills ne passeront pas*,' made their effective stand and compelled the enemy to entrench themselves on Hill 281."[29]

---

[26] "Michelin Maps" were travel maps created by the Michelin Tire Company. Yes, we used them.

[27] *Esnes* is pronounced "Es-nay."

[28] *313th Artillery*, 20.

[29] As cited in *314th Artillery*, 50.

Atop *Mort Homme*, the 313th Artillery scouts were directed to an abandoned telephone dugout where they could light a lantern and consult the map. From there, they descended southern slope of the hill to find firing positions for the batteries while Lt. Crowell determined where the telephone wires should be laid (the telephone wires back then had cloth and not rubber coating, and were therefore not nearly as reliable as they are today). Maj. Dunigan himself selected the site for a potential battalion *Poste de Command* (P.C.). After stumbling about for about an hour across the churned-up hill, Dunigan held another conference in one of the many holes to discuss the initial deployment of the guns that were to support the attack of the 160th Inf. Brig.[30]

Dunigan decided that the brigade's howitzers (i.e., high angle, 155mm guns) should be posted south of the haunted hill and that the brigade's light field guns (i.e., 75mm cannon) should be posted to the west, out toward Esnes and the assigned western boundary of the division. Because of its range, artillery doesn't have to be directly behind the infantry or cavalry units its supporting. Artillery can, in fact, shoot diagonally across a battlefield in order to engage targets. This was one of the great advantages of indirect artillery fire, a technique and technology that was generally new to the world in 1914.

This first artillery scout showed a few things. First, that the eastern road over *Mort Homme* was not feasible for an advance by artillery. Second, a night without moon or stars is a poor time to conduct a reconnaissance, and third, and most importantly, it provided some basis to what Pershing was saying to us all along: "Don't necessarily rely upon supporting arms to move forward." It wasn't because he was against supporting arms—on the contrary. It's because he knew that the conditions on the Western Front (i.e., cratered moonscape with trenches) would make it very hard in bringing up direct-fire supporting arms like machine guns (M.G.s), 37mm Infantry Guns (I.G.s), let alone direct fire 75mm artillery or tanks. Granted, the roads were "clear," but the Germans would certainly have them zeroed in—and not just in one spot—but across an entire strip of some 200-300 meters at a time.

Dunigan's artillery scouts eventually made it over to Esnes, dismounted, and walked as far north as they could. They knew that once they reached *Côte 304* (Hill 304), which was in "No-Mans-Land," Béthincourt, the division's first objective, would lie in a valley a little more than a km to their front. The problem was, once the scouts topped the hill, they could not see Béthincourt. Were they lost? Was the map wrong? The fact is that neither was true. Béthincourt was there, but could not be seen as it was, in fact, blown into bits.

---

[30] *313th Artillery*, 20-21.

Understanding that they had gone as far north as they dared—as they were now in range of Hun M.G. or rifle fire—the Red Legs chose to exfiltrate *Côte 304* in true infantry fashion: on their bellies. With full equipment, which consisted of field glasses, respirator bag, haversack containing "Iron" or "Emergency" Rations (chocolate bars and crackers), etc., map case, belt with spare automatic pistol cartridges, first aid pouch, overcoat, and helmet, each man started to crawl on his empty belly through the tall, wet grass or slimy mud, hopping or rolling from hole to hole, in search of a communication trench. According to Capt. Shelton Pitney of 1/313th Artillery: "All appreciated that real endurance was required and [pitied] the plight of the Doughboy." [31]

As Dunigan's patrol moved further, an explosion was heard from the direction of the German lines. One of the scouts, who had received special training in firing gas shells (they're more fragile than H.E. or shrapnel) and whose words therefore carried much weight with the others who had no experience on the line, shouted, "Gas!"

With that, off came the helmets and out came the gas masks from the respirator bags. For some, including Capt. Pitney, it took a full five minutes to properly seat the mask. The patrol then moved south and after "an interminable time," a point was reached whence it was thought safe to remove the masks and to make a dash for the nearest French or American-held trench. Good thing the gas attack was in fact a false alarm—the first of many. According to Capt. Pitney, "training was worth a tenth—experience the other nine." [32]

We all knew this tenant to be true, especially after our time "Up the Line" in Picardy.

After this scout, Maj. Dunigan determined that the only reasonable artillery firing positions for the light battalions to support the attack of the 160th Inf. Brig. lay along the road from Esnes to Béthincourt, using Hill 304 as cover. As per regulations, a basic map overlay was created that included a rough plan of laying telephone wire from the battery positions to the observation posts (O.P.s) that would be located atop Hill 304. Cronkhite later agreed to attach a company of engineers on D-day to C/1/313th Artillery to help it get its guns, limbers, and caissons across the creek at the appointed hour.

Once the battery got across the creek, its 1st platoon (two guns) under Lt. Edwin Morgan would join the attack battalion of the 319th Infantry and its 2nd Platoon, under Lt. George Penniman, would join the attack battalion of the 320th Infantry. The rest of 1/313th Artillery, Batteries A and B, would remain limbered "in readiness" near Hill 304 while 2/313, in

---

[31] As cited in *313th Artillery*, 22.

[32] *Ibid.*

conjunction with the battalions from the 314th and 315th Artillery, would be in battery, firing pre-plotted fire missions from behind Hill 304 or Mort Homme, respectively. On order, they'd move forward to assist the attacking infantry battalions with direct fire, just like C/1/313.

While Dunigan's 1/313th Artillery advanced with the 160th Inf. Brig., Maj. John Nash's 2/313th Artillery was assigned to be part of the barrage. Its barrage front extended from a point in the town of Béthincourt on the Béthincourt-Gercourt Road west for 600 yards, this being the approximate center of the divisional sector. The barrage zone extended in a northerly direction over Hill 281 and on out to the range limit of one km short of Bois Sachet. The rate of fire was to be one hundred rounds per gun per hour. As per Dunigan's scout, the O.P. for 1/313th Artillery would be established atop Hill 304 and the O.P.s for 2/313th Artillery and Col. Robert S. Welsh's 314th Artillery would be established atop Mort Homme.[33]

As the artillery commanders completed their initial deployment plans, the 315th Artillery (H), was still struggling to make its way north through the traffic jams. It was in fact so bad that it was forced to halt in *Bois des Sartelles* where it remained until the evening of Sept. 23. During the night of 23-24 Sept., D minus two, they completed their march north through Fromereville, Bethelainville, Vigneville, and Montzeville to their positions southwest of *Mort Homme*. The regimental P.C. was established in a dugout on the Montzeville-Chattancourt Road, formerly occupied by the French. One soldier from the 315th Artillery remembered:

The worst problem, which in turn complicated all other problems, was that of transportation. There was always a crisis of transportation in the Argonne. To begin with, there were very few roads and those were always crowded on account of constant use, and always out of order. No sooner did the engineers repair them than the autumn torrents came and turned them into bottomless bogs, or shells came and blew them up to heaven, together with all the traffic and the road-menders thereon. "Split Your Convoy" was the sign that was posted every hundred yards on the shell-torn thoroughfares leading into the sector. Even with the utmost prudence, maintaining a distance of fifty yards between vehicles; changing the heavy motor lorries for lighter horse-drawn trucks; keeping on hand a constant supply of spare teams; road-menders and tractors for mired down wagons; maintaining one-way roads exclusively for in-traffic and out-traffic—still all these and a score of other things failed to prevent blockades in the face of the constant shelling and rain and mud.... In addition, there was an acute shortage of horses. There had not been enough to

---

[33] *313th Artillery*, 27 and *314th Artillery*, 50. *Bois Sachet* is pronounced "Bwa-Sa-chet."

begin with, and those in use were second-rate, broken down by the brutal strain. In the back area, motor lorries could be used, but close up behind the lines only pack mules and horses could negotiate those uncharted wastes of slush. Horses died by the hundreds, the woods were filled with their carcasses.... With the supply train stalled behind them on the road, mired hub deep in an indescribable congestion of artillery, motor lorries, ambulances, field kitchens, water carts and dragged-out pack mules, the men drank the water from the shell holes where dead horses lay.[34]

To complement the artillery barrage, the Division Machine Gun Officer (D.M.G.O.), Lt. Col. Oscar Foley, late commander of the 313th M.G. Battalion, was directed by Cronkhite to order the M.G. battalions of the division various missions, much like one would an artillery unit. As such, "x" platoons were assigned to complement the artillery barrage with indirect fire and "y" platoons were assigned to be "accompanying batteries" for the infantry. The sections of the 314th M.G. Battalion, which were motorized, would be used by Cronkhite to help "weigh the main effort." In other words, if we saw motorized M.G.s approach, we knew that we were in for it as this was the hottest point in the line. As such, Foley and his battalion and company commanders also conducted an R.S.O.P. of their own atop *Mort Homme*. They interfaced with artillerists, surveyed their assigned targets, located positions for their M.G.s., and figured out the firing data for the inclinometers.

In true form, our M.G.ers were morphing into a cross between artillery and infantry. They always kept in the back of their minds that they were the Army's "suicide squads," however, and were very sensitive to where and when they opened fire.[35] The key to accurate indirect M.G. fire is to ensure that the gun's tripod is firmly seated once the inclinometer is set. During firing, a M.G., due to the indisputable laws of physics, will bury itself deeper into the ground, changing the trajectory of the cone and thus increasing its range. For example, one mil to the left or right, up or down at a hundred meters is negligible. At one thousand meters, however, it will add one meter of range, at two thousand meters, two meters, etc. As for overhead clearance, the British suggested to our gunners to fire at least ten meters over the troops at a hundred meters and rising to fifty meters of clearance at a range of two thousand meters.

---

[34] As cited in Stultz, 398.

[35] *314th M.G.*, 25-26.

To sum up, we in the 80th Division generally attacked with one infantry brigade up and one behind. The attacking infantry brigade was divided in two by two regimental attack axes. While one infantry regiment attacked up the left of the division boundary, the other attacked up the right. Each infantry regiment attacked in three battalion waves: attack, support, and reserve. All of the M.G. battalions were commanded by D.M.G.O. Foley and he either fought them as a unified force or attached them to the division's two attack battalions.

As such, no M.G.s were ever held in reserve.

As far as the division's artillery brigade was concerned, it also fought as a full brigade with its guns engaging targets in support of the assigned infantry attack battalions. Some of its units were sent forward as "accompanying artillery," however, to support the attacking infantry battalions with direct fire.

In this way, the artillery, like the M.G.s, was never held in reserve.

When an attack infantry battalion ran out of steam, it was replaced by the support battalion, which became the new attack battalion and the old reserve battalion became the new support battalion. The shot-up attack battalion thus became the new regimental reserve battalion.

This is how the forward motion of the attack was maintained.

September 24, 1918.

Weather: Clear

Roads: Heavy

Throughout the day of Sept. 24, most of the 80th Division, as well as Pershing's entire American First Army, stayed under cover in the scattered woods between *Mort Homme* and *Bois La Ville*, preparing for the final move north to the L.D. under the cover of darkness. Meanwhile, army, corps, and division staffs worked feverishly to get as many follow-on units to the front as quick as possible. This was a daunting task. They used planning tables from the *F.S.R.* to help them. For example, an infantry division of 22,000 men, 7,500 draft animals, and 900 motor vehicles was supposed to take up 10.3 miles of road space![36] Mississippi-born Brig. Gen. Fox Connor, Pershing's Operations Officer (and later, Chief of Staff), orchestrated this complex move in conjunction with the operations officers at corps, division, and brigade levels.[37] The Operations Officer or G-3 for the 80th Division at the time was Col. John B. Barnes.

---

[36] *F.S.R.*, 172.

[37] Fox Connor, West Point Class of 1898, was commissioned into the Field Artillery. Currently (1938), he commands the First Army, which is H.Q.'d here in the States.

In order to move several ten mile long units along tiny secondary roads, timing and orchestration is key.

At 7:00 P.M. Sept. 24, the division continued its march north. Heiner's 155th Arty. Brig. led, followed by Brett's 160th Inf. Brig., followed by Jamerson's 159th Inf. Brig., followed by Hamilton's 305th Trains Brigade. Maj. Ashby Williams of 1/320th Infantry remembered:

> *When darkness came [we moved north to another staging area]. It was not only dark, it was black, so that men could not see each other in the road, and the road out of the woods was winding and difficult to follow. I remember on this occasion I used to the fullest extent the system of connecting files to keep in touch with the column ahead, using for that purpose at times as many as a whole platoon in addition to my runners...The moon came up at about 9:00 P.M. I remember when we sat down to rest, its light was shining upon the crosses on a grave yard to the right of us. I remember, also, as we sat there trucks came by us from the direction of the front and passed into the graveyard. The foul odor of the trucks as they passed and their destination and evident mission sent a thrill of horror through me that I never felt before or since that time, although I have seen many horrible sights. We passed that night great lines of transports and artillery upon artillery bound to the front. In fact, for many km the roads were so congested with traffic of that sort that we had to parallel the wagons and guns along the roads. At Fromereville, Jerry sent over a few shells but none fell close enough to us to do any harm. We passed on through Fromereville and about midnight reached the Bois de Borrus, a great woods not far from the Meuse northwest of Verdun. An officer who had been sent ahead by the division met us at the base of the hill and took us up into the road into the woods and showed me the area assigned to my battalion. It was late and the men wrapped themselves up in their blankets and went to sleep. I tried to sleep but could not because my feet were so cold.*[38]

The first units from the division to arrive to their designated attack positions were in fact from Heiner's 155th Arty. Brig. With the R.S.O.P. complete and the scouts and markers set, Welsh's 314th Artillery went into battery along the southern or reverse slope of *Mort Homme*, posting its O.P.s on the crest.[39] Meanwhile, 1/313th Artillery went into battery in the open near

---

[38] As cited in *1/320th Infantry*, 75.

[39] *314th Artillery*, 38.

Esnes, with A and B Batteries about 800 meters north of the town and masked by Hill 304 and C/1/313 just off the Esnes-Béthincourt Road about one km northeast of Esnes "in readiness" (i.e., guns limbered). 2/313th Artillery moved into old French gun emplacements some 400 meters north of the Montzéville-Chattancourt Road about midway between the two towns and in rear of *Mort Homme* (Hill 295), near what was called "Trench Kleber."[40] There the firing batteries camouflaged themselves, including the caissons and the regimental ammunition trains. On "Night Firing," Army Regulations state the following:

> *A.D.R. 1429. Preparation of fire will be most reliable if the battery, or at least oart of the guns, can be placed in position before dark. If this is not possible, the necessary measurements and calculations must be made during daylight with the greatest possible accuracy.*
>
> *A.D.R. 1433. For night firing, stakes carrying lanterns may be provided as aiming points. Similar stakes may be used by observers to fix the directions to targets. Sights must be illuminated.*

My brigade, Jamerson's 159th Inf. Brig., marched north through *Fromereville* and *Germonville* and into *Bois Bourrus*, a distance of about five km.[41] Fromereville, which is due west of Verdun and atop a ridge that overlooks the Meuse, was corked shut by a massive traffic jam that night.

---

[40] Named after Lt. Kleber DuPuy's platoon of the French 7th Infantry Regiment which held this position against a German onslaught on July 12, 1916, helping to save the battle the battle of Verdun.

[41] *Fromereville* is pronounced "Froam-ray-veal," *Germonville* is pronounced "Cher-mon-veal," and *Bois Bourrus* is pronounced "Bwa Bore-roo."

I have never seen, nor will I ever see, that many people, mud, motor cars, horses, mules, or other beasts of burden in one place in my life. It was sheer pandemonium and so close to enemy lines! Everything and everybody was trying to move up this narrow, muddy road and push through a tiny, blown-up town at the same time: infantry, artillery, ammunition and supply motor trucks and wagons, command cars, motorcycles, you name it. If it had wheels, hooves, or feet, it was on this road that night. We saw only two poor M.P.s trying to direct traffic, and they were swamped. Had the Hun had an O.P. nearby with communications back to a gun line, many Americans would have been killed that night. But, as Germany's "Iron Chancellor," Otto von Bismarck reportedly once said: "The Lord takes care of babes, fools, and the United States."

On the eve of the great battle, the command and staff of the American 80th "Blue Ridge Division" was as follows:

80th Division Command and Staff

Div. C.O.: Maj. Gen. Adelbert Cronkhite
C.o.S.: Col. William H. Waldron
G-1: Col. Sherburne Whipple
G-2: Maj. Cuthbert P. Noland
G-3: Col. John B. Barnes
G-4: Maj. James F. Loree
Adj.: Maj. Charles M. Jones
Surg.: Col. Thomas L Rhoads
I.G.: Maj. Albert G. Goodwyn
J.A.G.: Maj. Clifford V. Church
Ord.: Maj. Earl D. Church
French Liaison Off.: Capt. Michael Godechaux

305th Engineer Regt.: Col. George R. Spalding
305th Field Signal Bn.: Maj. E. E. Kelly
D.M.G.O.: Lt. Col. Oscar S. Foley
313th Machine Gun Bn.: Maj. Prescott Huidekopper
314th Machine Gun Bn.: Maj. Robert H. Cox
315th Machine Gun Bn.: Maj. Leland B. Garretson

305th Trains Brigade
Col. George F. Hamilton
305th Sanitary Train Bn.: Lt. Col. Elliot B. Edie
305th Motor Transport Train Bn.: Maj. J. W. O'Mahoney

155th Artillery Brigade
Brig. Gen. George G. Heiner
305th Ammunition Train Bn.: Lt. Col. Orlo C. Whitaker
305th Trench Mortar Battery: Capt. Paul B. Barringer
313th Artillery: Lt. Col. Otto L. Brunzell
1st Bn.: Maj. Francis J. Dunnigan
2nd Bn.: Capt. John Nash
314th Artillery: Col. Robert S. Welsh
1st Bn.: Maj. Howard Eager
2nd Bn.: Maj. Granville Fortescue
315th Artillery: Col. Carroll I. Goodfellow
1st Bn.: Maj. R. W. Barker
2nd Bn.: Maj. Lloyd C. Stark
3rd Bn.: Maj. Otis L. Guernsey

<u>159th Infantry Brigade</u>
Brig. Gen. George H. Jamerson
317th Infantry: Col. Howard R. Perry; Lt. Col. Charles Keller
1st Bn.: Maj. Powell Glass
2nd Bn.: Maj. C. C. Clifford
3rd Bn.: Maj. Walker H. Adams
318th Infantry: Col. Ulysses Grant Worrilow; Lt. Col. Chas. Mitchell

1st Bn.: Maj. Charles Sweeny

2nd Bn.: Maj. Jennings C. Wise

3rd Bn.: Maj. Henry H. Burdick

<u>160th Infantry Brigade</u>
Brig. Gen. Lloyd M. Brett

319th Infantry: Col. Frank S. Cocheu; Lt. Col. Gordon R. Catts

1st Bn.: Maj. Hugh H. O'Bear

2nd Bn.: Maj. James L. Montague

3rd Bn.: Capt. Gerald Egan

320th Infantry: Col. Ephraim G. Peyton; Lt. Col. William M. Gordon

1st Bn., Maj. Ashby Williams

2nd Bn., Maj. Harry P. Holt

3rd Bn., Maj. German H. H. Emory

<u>September 25, 1918.</u>

Weather: Clear.

Roads: Heavy.

On Sept. 25, Brett's 160th Inf. Brig. marched into *Bois Sartelles*.[42] The division order of march was H.Q./160th Inf. Brig., the 319th Infantry (-), the 314th and 315th M.G. Battalions, the 320th Infantry, division H.Q., units from the 305th Trains Brigade, H.Q./159th Inf. Brig., the 317th Infantry, the 315th M.G. Battalion, and the 318th Infantry. The order of march for the 318th Infantry was H.Q. Company, 1st Bn., 318th M.G. Company, 2nd Bn., 3rd Bn., and then Supply Company.[43] That was pretty much the standard order of march for an infantry regiment.

---

[42] *Bois Sartelles* is pronounced "Bwa Zar-tell."

[43] *318th Infantry*, 169. (-) means that the unit is smaller than normal due to its detachments and (+) means that the unit is bigger than normal due to attachments.

The 160th Inf. Brig., meanwhile, waited for dusk to conduct its passage of lines with respective units from the 33rd Prairie Division, relieving them of their duty on this part of the line and allowing them to concentrate father to the east, along the Meuse itself. The 319th Infantry, which was to attack up the right side of the division axis, adjoining with the Prairie Division's left, established its regimental P.C. on the northern slope of *Mort Homme*, near O.P.s of the 314th Artillery.[44] D.M.G.O. Foley arrayed the divisional M.G. battalions along the south side of the creek in conjunction with the light artillery batteries.[45]

We prayed that a German air reconnaissance squadron would not break through our counter-reconnaissance air squadrons, because if they did, they'd be able to direct their artillery upon our vulnerable assembly areas. But as luck (or fantastic planning and execution by our air counter-reconnaissance) would have it, we received no enemy shelling. The zone was, in fact, very quiet—almost too quiet. Granted, there was a bevy of American activity in getting hundreds of thousands of men, machines, and beasts of burden to the front, but there was actually little-to-no shelling on Sept. 25, the day before the big push.

Cronkhite established division H.Q. in *Bois Bourrus*, Jamerson located the 159th Inf. Brig.'s P.C. at *Fromereville*, Brett located the 160th Inf. Brig. P.C. on the outskirts of *Germonville*, and Brig. Gen. Heiner located his 155th Arty. Brig. P.C. near that of the division's in *Bois Bourrus*. From these positions, the major players of the division issued their final orders and conducted their final inspections.[46]

Attached to Heiner's 155th Arty. Brig. to help with the initial bombardment was the American 2/76th Artillery (L), the French 228th Artillery (L), and the French 1/289th Artillery (H). Against us, the Hun had 77mm, 88mm, 105mm, 150mm, 210mm, 305mm, and 420mm guns. The up-and-coming artillery bombardment, according to French and British fighting doctrine, would be the key to success. The fire support plan was as follows: From H-minus-6 to H-minus-3, army and corps heavy artillery was to deliver harassing or interdiction fire upon the enemy's rear areas. From H-minus-3 to H-hour, divisional heavy artillery (e.g., 155mm guns from the 315th and 289th Artillery) was to join the army and corps artillery in counter-battery and destructive fire missions.

At H-hour, light artillery (e.g., 75mm guns from 2/76 and the 228th, 313th, and 314th Artillery), in our zone anyway, was to lay down a standing barrage on the Germans' front lines between *Rui Forges* and *Béthincourt*. This barrage was to be maintained at the rate of 100

---

[44] *319th Infantry*, 22.

[45] *314th M.G.*, 26.

[46] *Bois Bourrus* is pronounced "Bwa Boar-row."

rounds per gun per hour from H-hour to H-plus-24-minutes during which time the attacking infantry battalions of the 160th Inf. Brig. were to advance to it. After that, the barrage was to become a rolling one and advance at the rate of 100 meters every four minutes and sweep through *HAGEN*.

Once *HAGEN* was taken in the vicinity of Gercourt, the light batteries of the 313th and 314th Artillery, covered by the heavy batteries of the 315th Artillery, were to advance to new positions in order to better support the attacking Infantry as it moved on to the next line, *GISELHER*, which was just north of Dannevoux. According to the *F.S.R.*:

> *127. The limited mobility of heavy field artillery renders its use inadvisable in any position from which the conditions of combat may require its hasty withdrawal. For that reason it has no place in an advanced guard; in an outpost, unless occupying a position in which the action is to be fought to a decision; in advanced positions or posts; in the reconnoiter; or in delaying actions, unless its loss is justifiable.*
>
> *128. On the offensive, heavy field artillery finds its function in firing upon supporting points in the hostile line; upon covered positions occupied by large bodies of the enemy, particularly his reserves; in the destruction of material objects, as buildings, bridges, etc.; and, in general, against a position that has been deliberately taken up and strengthened by the enemy.*
>
> *129. On the offensive, heavy field artillery finds its uses in compelling the deployment of the enemy's columns at long distances from the defensive line, against any large formed bodies of the enemy, and against those parts of his matériel or material objects within his lines that offer an important target. Due to its long range, it is profitably used in both offensive and defensive combat in restricting the field of activity of the enemy's shorter-range artillery. It can also be used to advantage in the destruction of the enemy's field artillery matériel.*
>
> *130. The use of the heavier types of field artillery pre-supposes an offensive, where reconnaissance of the enemy's position has been thorough and where the attack has been carefully planned; or a defensive, where there has been time to deliberately select and strengthen a position. Until the use of the heavier field artillery under the conditions given can be clearly foreseen, its position is well to the rear of all the combatant units.*

To ensure better command-and-control of the artillery, units were combined into three caliber-similar groups. Group I consisted of the 75mm guns of the 313th and 314th Artillery and it was commanded by Lt. Col. Otto Brunzell of the 313th Artillery. Group II consisted of the French 75s, and Group III of the 155s. Col. Welsh of the 314th Artillery was assigned as General Heiner's important brigade operations officer. Lt. Col. James F. Walker took his place.[47]

As was already stated, Maj. Gen. Robert Lee Bullard's American III Corps was posted on the right of the American First Army's axis of advance and the 80th Division was posted in the center of the III Corps. In the III Corps area, there were three divisions on line. The 33rd (Prairie) Division was on the right, the 80th (Blue Ridge) Division was in the center, and the 4th (Ivy) Division was on the left.[48] Bullard's III Corps's front extended from the Meuse River on the right (or east) to Montfaucon on the left (or west), adjoining with the American V Corps under Maj. Gen. George Cameron and 79th Infantry Division. Cronkhite's 80th Division's attack axis ran north from Béthincourt to Dannevoux, which was situated near the west bank of the Meuse. In between Béthincourt and Dannevoux there were two wood lots (or *bois*): *Bois Sachet* and *Juré*.[49]

On the east bank of the Meuse, attacking along the heights and trying to protect our exposed right flank, were the American 29th (Blue and Grey) Division, the French 18th and 26th Divisions, and the French *Division d'Infanterie Coloniale 10* (West African). To the left or west of the 4th Division were the American 79th (Cross of Lorraine), 37th (Buckeye), 91st (Pine Tree), 35th (Sante Fe), 28th (Keystone), and the 77th (Metropolitan) Divisions. The general plan for the 80th Division was to break through the German out-post line, code-named *Wiesenschlenken*, which ran through Béthincourt, breach *HAGEN* in the vicinity of Gercourt, and push north to Dannevoux.[50] After that, we were to break through *GISELHER* and then the prize, *KRIEMHILDE*, which connected Brieulles, Cunel, and Romagne along a nice, fat, somewhat wooded ridgeline. *KRIEMHILDE* was the main line of resistance of the vaunted *HINDENBURG STELLUNG* in our sector. After *KRIEMHILDE* was the last line, code-named *FREYA*, and it was anchored along *Côtes Barricourt*.[51] After that, we would engage in "pursuit" or "open warfare" operations all the way north to Sedan, endangering the entire Hun line in Belgium! General Bullard remembered:

---

[47] *313th Artillery*, 26 and *314th Artillery*, 38.

[48] While the American 4th Infantry Division consisted of the 39th, 47th, 58th, and 59th Infantry Regiments; the 33rd Division consisted of the 123rd, 130th, 132nd, and 136th Infantry Regiments.

[49] *Bois Sachet* is pronounced "Bwa Sach-et" and *Juré* is pronounced "Jur-ah."

[50] *Division d'Infanterie Coloniale* is prononounced "Dee-vis-ee-own Din-fan-tree Call-own-ee-awl." It means "Colonial Infantry Division." *Wiesenschlenken* is pronounced "We-zen-shlenk-en."

[51] *Côtes Barricourt* is pronounced "Coat Bar-ee-core."

The force with which General Pershing was to start his fight in the Meuse-Argonne was as typically American as our country itself. The three Army corps H.Q.s which had fought at Saint Mihiel had come for the Meuse-Argonne battle, but with a different assignment of divisions. The nine divisions used to be in the initial attack had not been engaged at St. Mihiel. Four of them, the 35th, 37th, 79th, and 91st, had not yet been in battle... Named in the order in which they stood from left to right when they went over the top at dawn on September 26th, they were the 77th, 28th, and 35th of the I Corps, under the experienced and wise [Maj. Gen. Hunter] Liggett; the 91st, 37th, and 79th of the V Corps, under Maj. Gen. George H. Cameron, who had been director of the War College [at Fort Myer] when I attended it; the 4th, 80th, and 33rd of the III Corps, under Maj. Gen. Bullard, a graduate commander from the veteran 1st Division. [Six] of these divisions, the 4th, 28th, 33rd, 35th, 77th, [and 80th] had been trained with the British. The 4th was a Regular Division. The 28th, 33rd, 35th, and 37th were National Guard in origin. The rest were of the National Army—made up of Selectice Servive men. The 4th, under John L. Hines, was all-American in geographical origin. Metropolitan New York furnished the 77th, made up of all the racial strains which characterize that great city, and its commander was Robert Alexander. Practically pure Pennsylvanian was the 28th, commanded by Charles H. Muir. My native state of Illinois contributed its National Guard to make up George W. Bell's 33rd Division. The 37th under Charles S. Farnsworth [former commander of the 159th Inf. Brig., 80th Division] was a National Guard Division from Ohio. Men of the National Guard of Kansas and Missouri manned the 35th under Peter E. Traub. Joseph E. Kuhn commanded the 79th, Selective Service men from [D.C., Maryland, Delaware, and eastern Pa.]. The 91st, which was under William H. Johnston, came from the Pacific slope states of Montana, Idaho, Washington, and Oregon, and was National Army. This battle was not based on any particular fitness of a division for the duty expected it. Each took its turn. The most distant and perhaps most difficult objective in this attack was given the 79th, which had never been under fire. Such things had to be.[52]

The worst part about our attack axis was that it was flat—across some of the best (at one time) farm land in the world—criss-crossed by dug-in Hun M.G.s and backed by copious artillery support. On top of that, it was cratered, and I mean cratered. To our distant front was

---

[52] As cited in Bullard, 434-35.

Côtes Romagne, from which the enemy could easily observe and pulverize any movement to their front.⁵³ In fact, if their M.G.s had the range, they could have simply murdered us all with enfilade fire, especially around *Nantillois*. According to Army Regulations, we were supposed to follow the tenants of what is called "Deployment for Attack":

> *To deploy means to extend the front. When does a column extend its front or prepare to fight? When open terrain, which will probably expose the troops to hostile artillery fire, is reached. This place may be two or more miles from the enemy. What is done? Strong patrols are sent out to clear the foreground of the enemy's patrol. The plan of the attack is inaugurated. Extra ammunition is issued. Each organization is assigned its task. The organizations in the firing lines are assigned objectives and move out, followed by local supports and reserves. Don't understand that they go "as skirmishers." They usually march in column of squads. Strong combat patrols are sent out to protect each flank. This is very important even with small commands.*⁵⁴

We were told that we were pitted against the Prussian 7ᵗʰ Reserve Division (*7. Preussisches Reserve-Division*), Fifth German Imperial Army (*5. Deutsches Reischsarmee*), which was commanded by *General der Artillerie Max von Gallwitz*. Most of the men from this particular division hailed from either the Kingdom of Saxony or the Duchy of Anhalt (i.e., northern Germany). Much like the French after 1915, most German (i.e., Prussian and Bavarian) divisions consisted of three infantry regiments of three battalions each and each battalion had four rifle companies with supporting arms assigned. But unlike the French, the Germans also maintained an infantry and artillery brigade H.Q.s. The Germans also had, like we Americans, T.M. (*Minenwerfer*), sanitary, quartermaster, ordnance, and provost units:

---

⁵³ *Les Côtes Romagne* is pronounced "Lay Coat Rome-awn-yah."

⁵⁴ *P.M.*, 244.

<u>Prussian 7th Reserve Infantry Division.</u>
1/1st Reserve Cavalry
307th Reserve Engineer Battalion
71st M.G. Battalion
207th Reserve T.M. Company
<u>14th Reserve Infantry Brigade</u>
36th Reserve Infantry Regiment
66th Reserve Infantry Regiment
72nd Reserve Infantry Regiment
<u>95th Reserve Artillery Brigade</u>
7th Reserve Artillery Regiment (L)
52nd Reserve Artillery Regiment (H)

Behind the Prussian 7th Reserve Division, coming from across the Meuse, was the Bavarian 5th Reserve Division. This division consisted of the 11th Bavarian Reserve Inf. Brig. with the 7th, 10th, and 12th Bavarian Reserve Inf. Regts., the 17th Bavarian Reserve Arty. Brig. with the 5th Bavarian Reserve Art. Regt., the 17th Bavarian Art. Regt., and the 2/19th Saxon Artillery. Included was an engineer battalion as well as a cavalry squadron. The German Empire at the time was actually a loose confederation of several kingdoms, duchies, principalities, or free cities, the Kingdom of Prussia (*Königsreich Preussen*) being the strongest and the home of the German Emperor (*Deutsches Kaiser*), the man who tied all of the German kingdoms (and thus the German people) together.[55]

The two German kingdoms who fielded their own armies during the war were Prussia and Bavaria. During the 1860s, Saxony, Württemberg, Baden, Brunswick, Hessia, Mecklenberg, and Oldenburg rolled their regiments into the Prussian Army establishment. It was an accepted fact that while regiments from Prussia, Saxony, Hessia, and Baden were the strongest and most deadly of the German Army (especially the Prussian Guards units), ones from Bavaria weren't as dangerous (sorry Bavaria!). Joe Latrinky told us that the American I and V Corps, to our left, had to in fact face the crack Prussian 5th Guards Division.[56]

Highlighting Bullard's order to attack at all costs, Cronkhite met with brigade, regimental, and battalion-level officers of Brett's 160th Inf. Brig. at 5:00 P.M. on September 25 at Brett's P.C. near *Mort Homme*. Maj. Ashby Williams of 1/320th Infantry remembered:

---

[55] *Königsreich Preussen* is pronounced "Koo-nigs-rike Proy-sen" and *Deutsches Kaiser* is pronounced "Doitsch-es Kye-zer."

[56] "Joe Latrinksy" is a fictitious soldier who spreads rumors.

Maj. Gen. Cronkhite sat at the head of the table and Brig. Gen. Brett at his right, Col. Spaulding, the division engineer, sat at the foot of table and I sat at his right, and then Maj. Holt, Lt. Col. Peyton, Maj. O'Bear, Maj. Emory, and many others. When we all got seated at the table there was a moment or two of suppressed excitement, a calm before the storm, as we waited to hear what Maj. Gen. Cronkhite was about to announce. "Gentlemen," he said, "H-hour is 5:30 tomorrow morning." I think every man's heart beat a little faster at that announcement. At least mine did. It was especially unsettling to have to listen to the silence that followed the announcement. That meant we were going over the top at 5:30 A.M. the next morning...General Cronkhite went over with us the question of our preparations; he spoke of the extent and purpose of the offensive and our part in it; and he spoke particularly about the nature of the barrage and the reasons for it. The big guns were to begin at 11:30 P.M. that night, but the small ones (that is, the division artillery of three and six-inch pieces) were to open up only a short time before "H" hour so as not to give the Hun a chance to locate their positions. When he finished he turned to General Brett and said, "Brett, I do not ask if you are ready. I know you are. Have you anything to say?" General Brett had nothing to say. General Cronkhite then took out his watch and said, "Gentlemen, I have synchronized my watch with corps. It is now four minutes after five." There was a tense silence that followed as each officer took out his watch and set it by the general's time. After that General Cronkhite said: "gentlemen, we have reached the time we have all been looking for, we are about to engage in the most serious business ever undertaken by man, and no one can tell who will come out of it. Gentlemen, may God be with you."[57]

At 11:30 P.M., long-range corps and army heavy artillery opened harassing and interdiction fire on *les Boche*.[58] Key targets were known enemy M.G. nests, artillery positions, crossroads, Hill 281, and *Bois Forges* and *Sachet*, where the enemy clearly kept a reserve. According to Capt. Francis "Frank" Crandall of E/2/313th Artillery, who was positioned near Hill 304 with his command: "From the forward battery positions the effect was as of an intense electric storm accompanied by continued thunder claps. The horizon in the rear was clearly

---

[57] As cited in *1/320th Infantry*, 77.

[58] *Les Boche* is the French term for the Hun. It's pronounced "Lay Baash."

outlined by a quivering glow reaching up into the sky. The volume of sound became a roar rising and falling in tone."[59]

At 2:30 A.M., Sept. 26, the great war-ending Meuse-Argonne Offensive was inaugurated for us in the Blue Ridge Division when the big 155mm howitzers from Goodfellow's 315th Artillery and its French attachments commenced fire upon known Hun trench systems and battery positions (thanks, in large part, to aerial photography). In fact, the artillery firing area behind Dead Man's Hill and Hill 304 was lit so brightly during the remainder of the night by the flashes from the muzzles of the guns that it almost seemed like day break for those who were in the area.

This preliminary bombardment—orchestrated by Pershing himself—began over a 65 km front and some 3,700 artillery pieces took part in the rain of steel upon the German lines! It was awe-inspiring and frightening at the same time and I'm glad that we weren't on the receiving end! We knew that we were in the presence of the most terrific bombardment yet witnessed in the annals of war. For six hours the fire from all available guns continued, increasing in intensity, if that was possible, as the night wore on into morning. According to Capt. George C. Penniman of C/313th Artillery: "At about 2:00 A.M., the barrage was at two-thirds strength—at 5:00 A.M., at full strength, with every French and American gun of large and small caliber firing at deathly speed."[60]

Although the Germans answered, they did not do so in kind. In our zone, for example, "the Hun with the Gun" only really targeted *Mort Homme* or targets just south of *Béthincourt*. Lt. Edward Lukens of 3/320th Infantry, posted just to the left of *Rui Montzéville* in a small patch of woods, experienced his first "real war" experience by surviving a Hun artillery strike, which killed man a man in his regiment:

The men were drinking their coffee, lying on the ground in little groups, and trying to get sleep before we started off. Without an instant's warning, Hell cut loose! C-r-r-ash! A big H.E. came tearing through the trees, and landed within a few yards of battalion headquarters. Another followed in about thirty seconds; it landed square in midst of a meeting of L Company N.C.O.s and killed or wounded every corporal and sergeant in one of its platoons. More followed, striking in different places all over that corner of the woods, until it was a perfect pitch-dark maelstrom of flying shell fragments and pieces of trees, with

---

[59] As cited in *313th Artillery*, 28.

[60] *Ibid.*, 35.

men running about frantically trying to get out of the way, and wounded men crying for help on all sides.... There were, I believe seventeen killed and over fifteen wounded in all, most of them from our battalion. When a final search was made at daylight, heads and limbs and torsos were seen scattered all over the ground where Company L had been, one of the fellow's body being smeared on a kitchen wheel as if the spokes had been a part of his own skeleton.[61]

As the artillery roared, at 3:30 A.M., the battalion commanders of the 318th Infantry read the following message from our division commander, General Cronkhite, to their men:[62]

---

[61] *3/320th Infantry*, 58.

[62] As cited in Stultz, 373.

HEADQUARTERS.

EIGHTIETH DIVISION.

AMERICAN EXPEDITIONARY FORCES.

FRANCE, 23 SEPTEMBER, 1918.

To the Members of the 80th Division:

For over a year we have been learning how to fight.

Within the next few hours, we shall have a chance to apply what we have learned.

We form part of a vast army, consisting of over 300,000 Americans and an equal number of our French Allies.

No enemy can withstand you, men from Pennsylvania and West Virginia and Virginia.

You are fighting for everything that makes life worth living, the safeguarding of your families and homes, and that personal liberty so dearly earned and so tenaciously maintained for over a century.

Go at them with a yell, and regardless of obstacles or fatigue, accomplish your mission.

Make the enemy know that the 80th Division is on the map: make him know, when he faces you in the future, that resistance is useless.

A. Cronkhite,
Major-General.

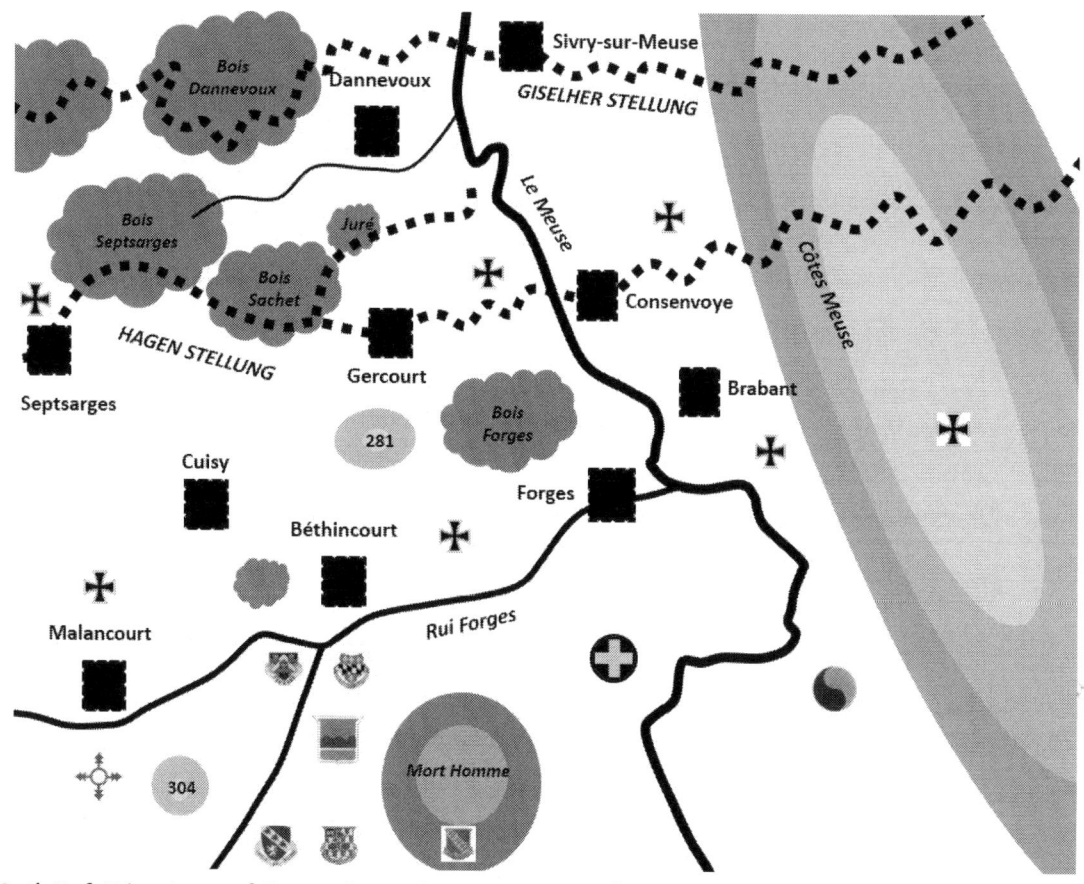

80th Inf. Div. Area of Operations, Sept. 26, 1918, dawn. The 320th Inf. is on the left and the 319th Inf. is on the right. The artillery of the division is deployed between Mort Homme and Hill 304 and behind the guns are the 317th and 318th Infantry Regiments, in support.

What we had to fight through. The little dots in the ditches on the left were us.

The M1917 French Schneider 155mm Howitzer was used in place of the U.S. M1908 Howitzer in France (L). It is posted "in immediate action, in the open" (L) and 155mm howitzers firing in the Meuse-Argonne (R). The 315th Arty. was armed with these types of howitzers. These guns are posted "in observation, masked" (R).

Looking north—attack axis of the 319th Inf. "The Hun with the Gun" was dug-in deep along the ridge line. Note the wide open fields of fire—a defender's dream.

"Ruins of Bèthincourt, 9-26-18. Held by the Germans and captured by the Yanks in the Argonne Offensive."

"'H' Hour troops at the Forges River at daybreak. Jumping off place of the Argonne Drive. Company 'B' Bridge. Bethincourt, 9-26-18" (L). These troops were from B/1/305th En. and the 160th Inf. Brig. "Company 'B' Bridge at Bethincourt, 9-26-18. Bridge over the Forges River constructed by the 305th Engrs. while under shell fire" (R). Shown is a caisson squad from one of the light batteries of the division.

A gun from Capt. Perriman's C/1/313th Artillery crossing the "Engineer Bridge" at Béthincourt Sept. 26, 1917.

Hun outpost M.G. team (L). This is what the combat groups of the 160th Inf. Brig. dealt with in the early phase of the offensive. "German inf. firing with telescopic sights" (R).

"Toll of one shell: 14 horses and one man killed by one shell; Bethincourt, 10-2-18" (L) and Doughs advance through German lines in the Meuse-Argonne (R).

While R.G.ers lay down smoke and A.R.men suppress Hun M.G. nest embrasures, Bombers "contain" the targeted Hun M.G. nest and the Assault Squad over-runs the position (L). Bombers (R) throw their grenades while A.R.-men, to their left, lay down suppressive fire in the prone position. Most of the time A.R.-men had to kneel in order to better suppress the target.

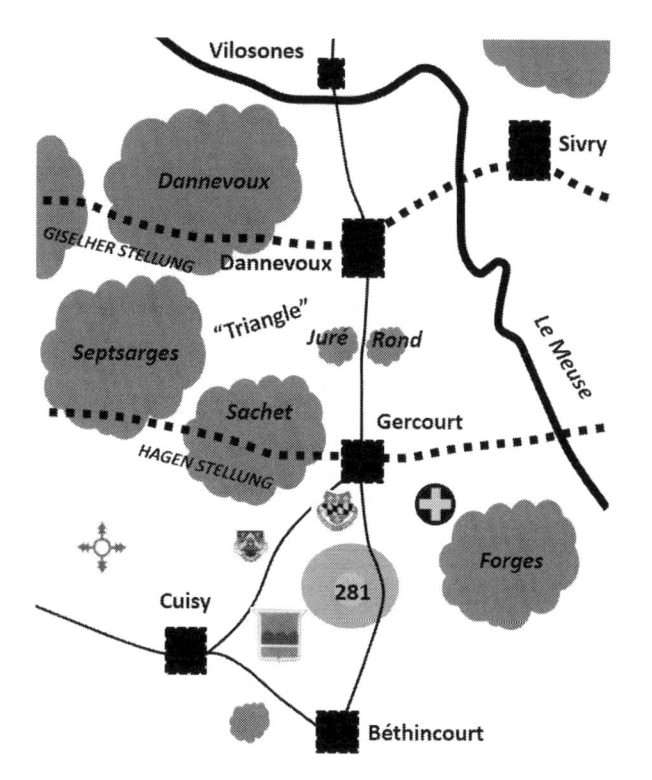

80th Inf. Div. Area of Operations, Sept. 26, 1918, Noon. The Yellow Cross icon represents the 33d Division and the circle with four lines represents the 4th (Ivy) Division. The 319th Inf. attacked up the right and the 320th Infantry attacked up the left of the 80th Division axis of advance toward Dannevoux.

"Jerry Guns. Part of the 5,000 captured. Béthincourt 9-28-18."

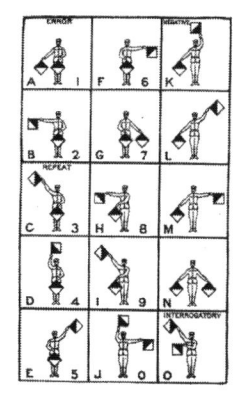

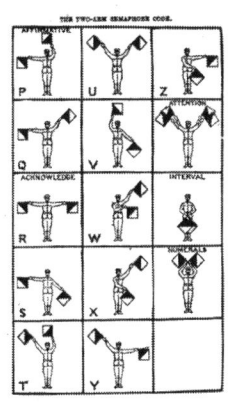

Dough Litter Team in action (L). The Litter Teams of the 319th Inf. transported men south through Gercourt. Semaphore Wig-Wag Signals (R). Note that some of the letters also meant things like "Error" or "Negative."

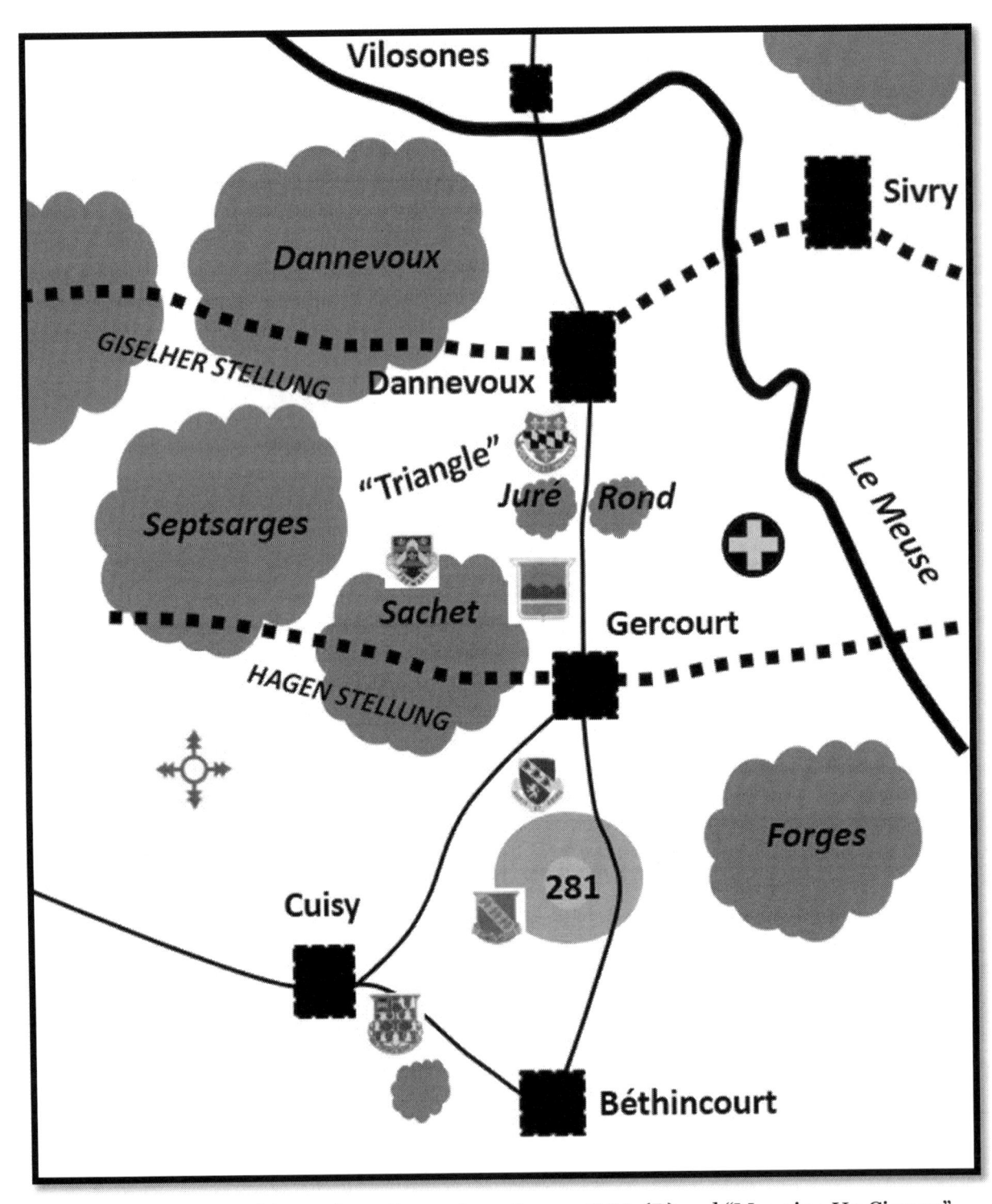

80th Inf. Div. Area of Operations, Sept. 26, 1918, 5:00 P.M. (R) and "Mopping Up Cierges" by Wallace Morgan. This captures what it was like for the 319th Inf. as it pushed through Gercourt and Dannevoux on Sept. 26, 1918 (below).

A.E.F. advances north up the Muese-Argonne.

Typical Hun wire entanglements and trench works along *GISELHER*. Note the beautiful (and deadly) fields of fire.

Looking north into Dannevoux (L). The 319th Inf. attacked up this road and took the village on the evening of Sept. 26, 1918. *GISELHER* was along the ridge in the background. Looking northwest into Côtes Dannevoux (R) where the 319th and 320th Inf. Regts. adjoined and where *GISELHER* was situated.

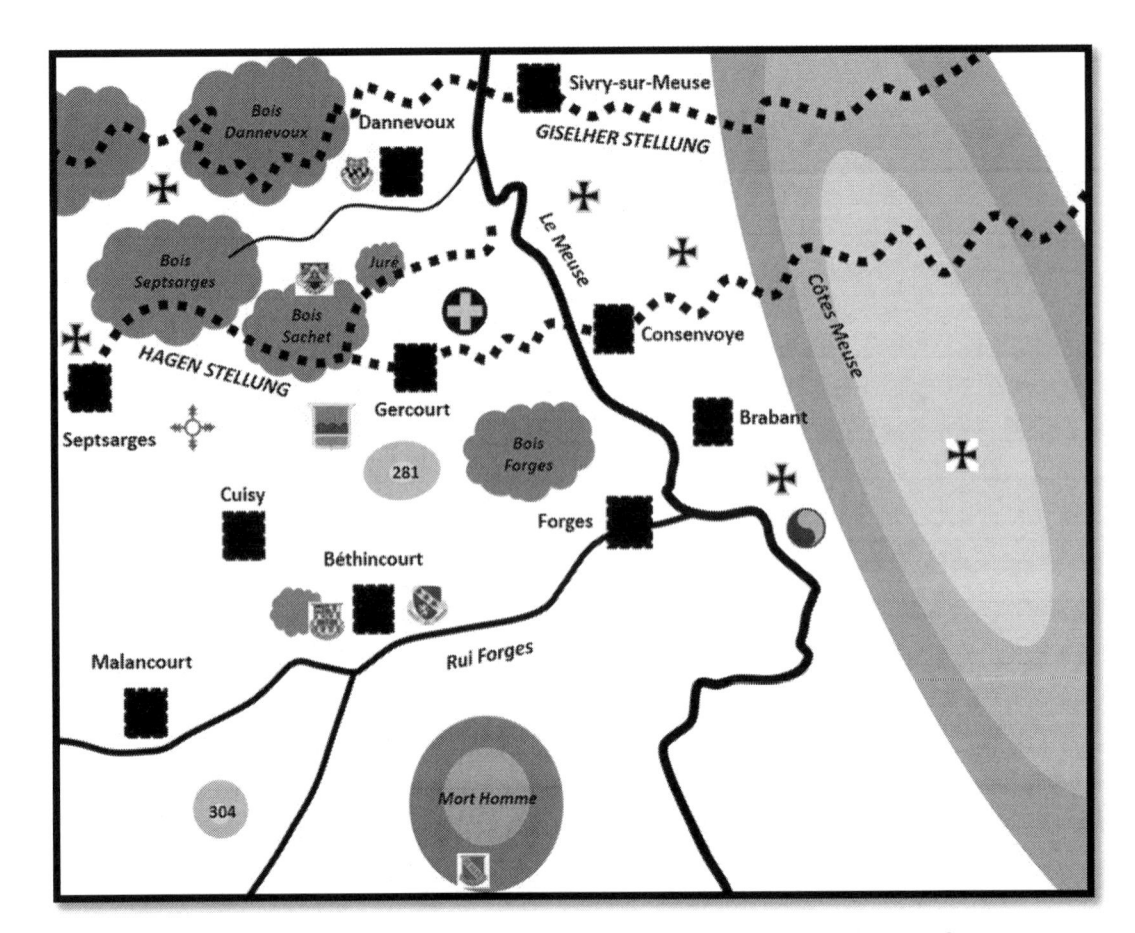

80th Inf. Div. Area of Operations, Sept. 26, 1918, 10:00 P.M. The swirl icon on the right represents the American 29th Division. In the 80th Division's zone, the 319th Inf. is in and around Dannevoux, the 320th Inf. is in Bois Sachet, the 317th and 318th Inf. Regts. of the 159th Inf. Brig. are around Béthincourt, and the division's 155th Arty Brig. is massed between Mort Homme and Hill 304.

(L) Looking east—the 319th Inf. attacked from right to left. *Dannevoux is* in the center and *Côtes Meuse* is in the background. (R) looking south from *GISELHER*. The 319th Inf. attacked from the background and into the foreground on the first day of the Meuse-Argonne Offensive. Dannevoux is on the left and Bois Juré is on right.

Water service train in the Meuse-Argonne.

Ration party moving forward. Note the loaves of bread slung across a pole.

Chapter 2
The Battle for *HAGEN* (Sept. 26).

September 26, 1918.

Weather: Rain.

Roads: Poor.

At 4:30 A.M., Sept. 26, "H-Hour-minus-one," just as the drizzle escalated into light rain during the early morning darkness, sappers from the 305th Engineers, reinforced by soldiers from the reserve battalions of the 160th Inf. Brig. (e.g., A/1/320th Infantry), began the great war-ending offensive by crawling forward from the out-post line, through the rusty barbed wire, and into the corpse-lain swamp, marking paths with white engineer tape for the infantry to follow at daylight.

They were covered by the artillery, which was now firing a walking barrage forward from the creek.

The engineers and their infantry supports removed mines, cleared strands of wire, laid duckboards, and emplaced *fascines* ("cylindrical bundles of brush, closely bound") in *Rui Forges* and its associated rivulets and bogs.[63] And instead of returning to their lines at daybreak, they stayed in the swamp with their makeshift bridges to help the men of the 160th Inf. Brig. move forward. Lt. Edward Lukens of 3/320th Infantry, posted in the "support battalion" position on the division's left, remembered the scene just before the main attack commenced at H-hour:

> We deployed in an open field in front of Dead Man's Hill, guiding the moppers-up on the support companies of the battalion ahead. We had about six squads, which we placed at intervals with the corporal in charge of each one, while Lt. Titus and I each took command of three squads. Less than an hour remained after we had completed our dispositions until the advance should begin. Titus and I sat down together for a few minutes and shared a jelly sandwich that I had carried with me for the last two days and shook hands to our mutual luck; then we went to our our own sections, and I attached myself to the middle squad of the three, as it was too dark to hope to see them all.[64]

At 5:30 A.M., H-Hour, the artillery switched over from firing a standing barrage north of the creek to a rolling one in conjunction with those M.G.s that were firing indirect fire

---

[63] *Fascines* is pronounced "Fash-een."

[64] As cited in *3/320th Infantry*, 59-60.

missions.[65] With the paths secured and the artillery and M.G. rolling barrages advancing, Majors O'Bear and Holt, the respective commanders of the attack battalions of the 319th and 320th Infantry, 160th Inf. Brig., blew their whistles. They were echoed by the company commanders and the platoon leaders, all who were holding Browning .45 caliber automatic pistols in hand, and yelling, "Over the top lads! Over the top!" just like our British brethren had in Picardy.

The companies crossed the L.D. in "Indian files," conducted a passage of lines with the Engineers, and moved up the division's axis of advance "on line" and into the jaws of 7.92mm German M.G. and 7mm rifle fire near *Béthincourt*.[66] They moved about 100 yards every four minutes through the thick fog, around or through the craters, following the prescribed rolling barrage. Red hot enemy M.G. bullets whizzed over their heads and shells screeched in—landing all around them.

Supporting Artillery.

I.D.R. 421. In attack, artillery assists the forward movement of the infantry. It keeps down the fire of the hostile artillery and seeks to neutralize the hostile infantry by inflicting losses upon it, destroying its morale, driving it to cover, and preventing it from issuing its weapons effectively. In defense, it ignores the hostile artillery when the enemy's attack reaches a decisive stage and assists in checking the attack, joining its fire power to that of the defending infantry.

I.D.R. 422. Troops should be accustomed to being fired over by friendly artillery and impressed with the fact that the artillery should continue firing upon the enemy until the last possible moment. The few casualties resulting from shrapnel bursting short are trifling compared with those that would result from the increased effectiveness of the enemy's infantry fire were the friendly artillery to cease firing. Casualties inflicted by supporting artillery are not probable until the opposing infantry lines are less than two hundred yards apart.

I.D.R. 423. When the distance between the hostile infantry lines becomes so short as to render further use of friendly artillery inadvisable, the commander of the infantry firing line, using a pre-concerted signal [a four-foot white and red regimental signal flag] , informs the artillery commander. The latter

---

[65] "H-Hour" is the appointed hour to begin an attack. "H-Plus-One" means "At one hour past the kick-off, this or that is supposed to happen."

[66] *3/320th Infantry*, 60.

usually increases the range in order to impede the strengthening of the enemy's foremost line.

The attack battalions advanced with two companies up and two behind, with the medical, signal, and transportation detachments sprinkled throughout the column. The regimental heavy weapons detachments were deployed between the front and rear companies of the attack battalions. The infantry gun (I.G.) detachment consisted of one sergeant, one wagoner, and about five men per gun. The gun itself was pulled by a donkey and a limber or, when the going got tough, was hauled forward disassembled by hand. The Stokes Mortar detachment, which had two or four 81mm mortars, consisted of one sergeant, one corporal, and around five privates per gun. Some battalions, like 1/320th Infantry, also had a "Snipers, Observers, and Scouts" section. We in 1/318th did not as we figured that any squad could do that job if assigned the task.[67]

To hear the men of Brett's 160th Inf. Brig. tell it, as dawn broke that fateful morning, they moved through the pitted, corpse-infested swamp about 200 meters to their front (they couldn't believe it—corpses in varied stages of rot, mostly from months or years before, lay there tangled in the rusted barbed wire, both French and German) with the attack companies of the 319th Infantry on the right and the 320th Infantry on the left. For whatever reason, the men of the 160th Inf. Brig. were ordered to advance with "light packs only," which meant only a slicker and two days' emergency rations (E-rats).[68] We in the 159th Inf. Brig., however, were ordered to advance with "full packs."

I'm glad we were.

Although there are advantages to turning in one's blanket, shelter-half, etc. to the company supply sergeant (less weight), what happens if the company supply wagon gets lost, blown-up, or just can't plain make it to where you are? Then what? I preferred to keep my pack with me and if I chose to unhook it from my person, then that was my cross to bear and not somebody else's. The weakness of this method, however, is in having one's troops' packs festooned across the battlefield like Easter Eggs, making it near impossible to recover them later. The *I.D.R.* did state that we should keep our packs on, as it helped "defend against shrapnel," which, I'm sure, is only according to Joe Latrinsky because the only thing that could stop shrapnel, in my opinion, is if we carried boiler plates on our backs.

---

[67] *1/320th Infantry*, 153.

[68] *3/320th Infantry*, 58.

I.D.R. 368. The complete equipment of the soldier is carried into action unless the weather or the physical condition of the men renders such measure a severe hardship. In any event, only the pack will be laid aside. The determination of this question rests with the regimental commander. The complete equipment affords to men lying prone considerable protection against shrapnel.

Shell holes, filled with dense stews of water, mud, rotten equipment, and human and animal remains were topped with dense coatings of scum and vegetation. Rusty barbed wire, broken rifles, M.G.s, unexploded grenades, tattered clothing, and human bones—remnants of an unsuccessful French attack two years before—lay about everywhere. Yet unseen to the men of the 160th Inf. Brig. were German M.G. teams, carefully concealed behind tufts of swamp grass. And behind them was the blown up village of *Béthincourt* which no doubt acted as a German battalion H.Q.

On the division right with the 319th Infantry, Maj. Hugh O'Bear's 1/319 was the attack battalion, Maj. James Montague's 2/319 was support, and Capt. Gerald Egan's 3/319 was reserve (Maj. Oliver L. White was too sick for duty). In O'Bear's battalion, Capt. Charles Muse's Company A was on the right and Lt. Ralph Johnson's Company C was on the left. They were followed by Capt. Erskine Gordon's Company D and Capt. Henry Jones's Company B, respectively.[69] On the division left, with the 320th Infantry, Maj. Holt's 2/320 was the attack battalion, Maj. Emory's 3/320 was the support battalion, and Maj. Williams's 1/320 was the reserve battalion. As the reserve battalion commander, Maj. Williams was tasked with detaching some of his companies to specified regimental duties. Company A, for example, was sent forward to help the engineers and Company D was assigned to be ammunition carriers in support of the M.G.s, I.G.s, and mortars, which were up front with Maj. Holt's attack battalion. That left him with only two companies, B and C, to actually serve as reserve companies.[70]

As 1/319 and 2/320 advanced up the division's attack axis, using all of the fire and maneuver skills taught to them since the training days at Fort Lee, they over-ran several Hun M.G. positions in the swamp. Because of the fog and the nature of the terrain, proper distances between battalions, companies, or even platoons were not kept. Units in fact became mixed. But in general terms, the rifle companies of the 160th Inf. Brig. attacked with the bomber and assault squads up front, followed by the A.R. and R.G. squads. For being relative novices, they actually

---

[69] *319th Infantry*, 23.

[70] *319th Infantry*, 23 and *1/320th Infantry*, 78.

stayed close behind the rolling barrage, which advanced 100 yards every four minutes. Capt. Josiah C. Peck, the Regimental Intelligence Officer of the 319th Infantry remembered:

> *Immediately the attacking battalion had reached the swamp in front, which was found to be easily passable, in many places, a feeling of confidence came to officers and men alike. The counter-artillery fire of the enemy was not heavy and at this point his rifle and M.G. fire not especially effective. The swamp was crossed and the attack swept on, up the rising ground beyond, to the enemy's first position, which was taken without difficulty.*[71]

Lt. Edward Lukens of 3/320th Infantry similarly reported:

> *We came to a gully about ankle deep in water, and crossed it in a leap. We didn't know that this was Forges Brook, which we had been told was deep enough to require bridges, and kept on wondering when we would come to it. Some of the engineers made the same mistake, for we had gone several hundred yards beyond it when there loomed up out of the fog, going diagonally, a crowd of about twenty men carrying a bulky wooden structure which they told us was a bridge for Forges Brook. Soon we began to meet parts of other outfits, generally striking on slightly different angles from our own, for very slight compass errors make a big difference when a little distance has been passed. It became apparent that the different companies had already become pretty badly intermixed, and as for the moppers-up, I didn't have the slightest idea where any of my other squads were. The smoke and fog were fatal to any hope of keeping organizations in their proper place and formation, but in spite of that it was a tremendous life-saver, for the front waves had gone over and flanked the first row of M.G. nests before the Boche gunners had hardly a chance to fire a shot, and our casualties were almost nothing as long as we were hidden.*[72]

We had been warned by our British advisors that our offensive operations would be, at best, platoon-level operations when all was said and done. As such, we quickly realized that every man jack in the platoon should have at least a terrain sketch or his axis of advance with a compass bearing noted. While at Camp Lee and in Artois, we were taught the basics of orienteering (the science of knowing where you are on a map) and how to get from point "A" to point "B." In retrospect, we should have also done this training at night, because battlefield

---

[71] *319th Infantry*, 24.

[72] As cited in *3/320th Infantry*, 60-61.

conditions will almost blind a soldier, even during the day. According to the Army, we were to use the following combat principles during offensive operations:

The Advance.

I.D.R. 212. The advance of a company into an engagement (whether for attack or defense) is conducted in close order, preferably column of squads, until the probability of encountering hostile fire makes it advisable to deploy. After deployment, and before opening fire, the advance of the company may be continued in skirmish line or other suitable formation, depending upon circumstances. The advance may often be facilitated, or better advantage taken of cover, or losses reduced by the employment of the platoon or squad columns or by the use of a succession of thin lines. The selection of the method to be used is made by the captain or major, the choice depending upon conditions arising during the progress of the advance. If the deployment is found to be premature, it will generally be best to assemble the company and proceed in close order. Patrols are used to provide the necessary security against surprise.

I.D.R. 219. The advance in a succession of thin lines is used to cross a wide stretch swept, or likely to be swept, by artillery fire or heavy, long-range rifle fire which can not profitably be returned. Its purpose is the building up of a strong skirmish line preparatory to engaging in a fire fight. This method of advancing results in serious (though temporary) loss of control over the company. Its advantage lies in the fact that it offers a less definite target, hence is less likely to draw fire.

I.D.R. 220. The above are suggestions. Other and better formations may be devised to fit particular cases. The best formation is the one which advances the line farthest with the least loss of men, time, and control.

Advancing the Attack.

I.D.R. 453. The firing line must ordinarily advance a long distance before it is justified in opening fire. It can not combat the enemy's artillery, and it is at a disadvantage if it combats the defender's long-range rifle fire. Hence it ignores both and, by taking full advantage of cover and of the discipline of the troops, advances to a first firing position at the shortest range possible. Formations for crossing this zone with the minimum loss are considered in paragraphs 212 to

220, inclusive. These and other methods of crossing such zones should be studied and practiced

I.D.R. 454. The best protection against loss while advancing is to escape the enemy's view. Formations for crossing this zone with the minimum loss are considered in paragraphs 212 and 220 inclusive. These and other methods of crossing such zones should be studied and practiced.

I.D.R. 455. Each battalion finds its own firing position, conforming to the general advance as long as practicable and taking advantage of the more advanced position of an adjacent battalion in order to gain ground. The position from which the attack opens fire is further considered in paragraphs 306 to 308, inclusive.

I.D.R. 457. In advancing the attack, advanced elements of the firing line or detachments in front of it should not open fire except in defense or to clear the foreground of the enemy. Fire on the hostile main position should not be opened until all or nearly all of the firing line can join in the fire.

As the attacking infantry battalions advanced through the smoke and fog, they were followed by division M.G. sections that were assigned to move forward with them. According to Lt. Herman Furr of the 314th M.G. Battalion:

Each M.G. platoon leader, under the direction of the company commander, was allowed to choose his own route in leading his platoon forward, it being his duty to get anywhere the infantry might be held up, thus assisting the infantry in getting forward by applying direct or indirect fire on strong points of M.G. nests. Each platoon leader knew from the map what the final objective was, and where his guns were to be placed when that objective was reached.[73]

While motorized platoons from the 314th M.G. Battalion advanced north toward Dannevoux in "Specials" behind the advancing 319th Infantry, those from the 313th or 315th M.G. Battalions were to advance as far as they could with their mule or donkey-drawn carts, each cart carrying one M.G. and several cans of ammunition. Remember, one can of 250-round belt ammunition was spat out in but thirty seconds. If the M.G.ers couldn't advance any longer with their carts or Specials, then their platoon leader would order them to continue the advance on foot in the manner previously explained.

---

[73] *314th M.G.*, 28.

At this point, Capt. George Penniman's C/313th Artillery, assigned as the 160th Inf. Brig.'s accompanying battery, moved up the Esnes-Béthincourt Road in the wake of the advancing infantry. While the 1st and 2nd (Gun) Sections and the 5th (Caisson) Section commanded by Lt. Edward F. Morgan were to support O'Bear's 1/319th Infantry, the 3rd and 4th (Gun) Sections and the 6th (Caisson) Section, commanded by Lt. John A. Penniman, were to support Holt's 2/320th Infantry. Penniman's battery didn't proceed far, however, when it was held up by a battalion of French 75s firing directly across the road. Because of the intricate trench system, it was impossible to skirt them and go ahead. The French artillery was firing a rolling barrage at the rate of one round per gun every thirty seconds, covering the infantry's advance, and could not cease firing.[74]

After some delay, it was decided that the French battalion would fire all of its guns at once and during the thirty-second wait time, Penniman would scoot one limber or caisson across its front and up the road and into *Béthincourt*. As the men waited for the apportioned time, they watched "with horror" as the French artillerists broke several rules of the *A.D.R.* For example, the French had no more than one N.C.O and four men manning each gun, and the men were taking turns eating while the remaining doubled up on the duties of the crew. According to Capt. Penniman: "The nonchalance and ease with which the French smoked, ate, and talked as they fired caused our then green, muchly fed-on-drill-regulations men to look aghast. They almost shouted in protest when they saw a shell stick on entering the breach and beheld the No. 2, instead of carefully extracting it with the ramrod, pick up another shell and with its base drive home the stuck shell."[75]

Once his guns were across, Capt. Penniman, who was on horseback, led his battery up the road until he was again stopped—this time at the bridge site. The engineers and attached Doughs of Brett's 160th Inf. Brig. had not yet completed building the bridge across the creek because the pre-fabricated parts that they needed, which were being brought forward by mules, had not arrived.[76]

Again, Pershing was right: the infantry must be ready to advance on its own volition.

At 5:54 A.M., as Penniman waited at the bridge site, the artillery and M.G. barrages rolled north across Hill 281, further churning the ground into a slushy brown mess. The barrage

---

[74] *313th Artillery*, 35.

[75] As cited in *Ibid*, 36.

[76] *Ibid*.

then slinked farther north at a pace of fifty yards every two minutes (called a "creeping barrage").

Blam!

Blam!

Boom!

The assault battalions of Brett's 160th Inf. Brig. moved ahead at the same rate, following the curtain of H.E. and cones of M.G. bullets which kept the Huns' heads down in his dugouts, masking their advancing line from the German M.G.s and O.P.s.[77] One captured German officer commented that this M.G. barrage, which "landed without warning or sound," was "the most effective he had encountered in his four years of service."[78] Maj. Ashby Williams, in command of the reserve battalion of the 320th Infantry, on the division's left, remembered:

The attack was to proceed by a regular schedule. The barrage, which was laid down in front of Bethincourt, was to creep forward at a rate of 100 meters every four minutes until it reached the second position where it was to remain down thirty minutes and then creep forward. The front line battalion, under command of Maj. Holt, was to follow the creeping barrage at a safe distance, but close enough to prevent the Boche from coming out of his shelter after the barrage and before the arrival of our troops. The support battalion under the command of Maj. Emory was to follow the support battalion at six hundred yards. I was to follow the support battalion at eight hundred yards. One of my platoons, under command of Lt. Worboy, preceded me for the purpose of mopping up the trenches north of Bethincourt in the second German line of defense. Just at the Forges Brook that runs before the town three of the platoons of Company D and some of the men of Company A had gone out, if you remember, the night before, to place the bridges across the brook joined me. We crossed the stream on the foot bridges that had been laid and passed into the town. I remember that Lt. Preston and I were in the lead, he with a map and I with a compass, endeavoring to find the way through the fog and over the grown up debris of the town... We came to the north edge of the town and turned to the left upon what was shown upon the map to be a road but what was now a mere path. This area had been No-Man's-Land since the great battle

---

[77] *313th Artillery*, 28.

[78] As cited in *314th M.G.*, 38.

of Verdun and weeds and grass have overgrown the streets and roads, and it was no easy task to find the way. At length, with the use of map and compass we picked the right the right course and started out. There seemed to be a lull after the great storm and hardly a shot was heard, except now and then a stray bullet hit the ground around us. I remember one struck a piece of corrugated iron close to my side. On the edge of town we encountered fifty or sixty German prisoners, Prussians and Bavarians for the most part, coming towards us holding up their hands. They took off their hats and seemed to be very happy when I told them in what little German I knew to pass on to the rear... We went forward with the [Béthincourt-Cuisy] Road as our guide and I sent out runners to maintain contact with the troops ahead. We reached the great system of shelters in the ridge east of Cuisy, from which the German prisoners had been taken. It was a smoldering ruin battered to pieces by our artillery.[79]

When the sun fully rose above the Heights of the Meuse to the east at around 6:30 A.M., scores of German troops poured out from their swampy lairs and surrendered to the advancing units of the 160th Inf. Brig. and blown-up *Béthincourt* was taken with ease. We figured as much as it was simply the Huns' outpost line. The real work, it was thought, would only begin when the attack battalions of the 160th Inf. Brig. hit *HAGEN*, which was built through *Bois Sachet* and *Gercourt*. It was critical for the 80th Division to breach *HAGEN* in *Bois Sachet* so the 4th (Ivy) Division, operating on our left, could envelop *Montfaucon*, the fulcrum of *HAGEN* in the American First Army's sector, from the east *via* Septsarges and Hill 295.[80]

Men from Penniman's C/1/313th Artillery, still parked south of the creek at the bridge site, noticed that the first German prisoners who came back in groups of twenty or thirty were escorted by "proud American infantrymen." According to Capt. Penniman:

The prisoners were all young and a large proportion wore glasses; some had intelligent faces, some very unintelligent. Many wore Red Cross brassards. Later we found machine gunners dead in their nests with these same brassards on their arms or in the act of being put on. One prisoner in passing stepped far enough out of line to pat the tube of one of our guns and say "Kamerad." All of them made comments on the camouflage paint on the American caissons,

---

[79] As cited in *1/320th Infantry*, 81-83.

[80] *2/319th Infantry*, 8.

evidently the first American material they had seen and much lighter in color than that used by the French or the Germans.[81]

As the infantry advanced, pioneers from the 305th Engineers were working with excellent skill and speed against great odds to get that bridge up. Once the component parts arrived to the bridge site, the engineers had their "Single Lock Bridge" up in no time. As the last plank was laid in position, Penniman's C/313th Artillery's first gun rolled across—the first piece of wheeled material to enter Béthincourt in four years.[82]

As the 319th Infantry advanced on the right, they received some nasty enemy enfilade M.G. fire from *Bois Forges*, which was in the Prairie Division's sector, and was forced to "refuse the line" with a company in order to continue the advance north. Remember, Bullard rightly said, "To hell with your flanks! Advance!"

According to Army Regulations, we were supposed to cover our own flanks and use the combat principles that were listed in "The Fire Attack" in order to defeat such a foe. In short, the company was supposed to use "fire and maneuver" at its own level in order to take our enemy targets.

The fire attack commences when the infantry in the firing line first opens fire and it usually ends with the charge. A charge is sometimes not necessary because the enemy withdraws from his position. The fire attack does not start until the firing line cannot advance without ruinous and demoralizing losses. It should not be over 1,200 yards from the enemy. At this time fire superiority must be gained. This may necessitate a steady, accurate fire for many hours. For this purpose the commander puts more men on the firing line than the enemy and then some more if necessary. Local supports are used if required. Having gained fire superiority, the advance by rushes commences, but each rush must leave behind or have in front of it enough rifles to maintain fire superiority. This determines the size of the rush. You cannot lose this fire superiority and advance, and once it is lost, hours may be required to regain it. The number of men in each rush will usually decrease as the enemy's position is approached. If the firing line is stopped, if fire superiority is lost and can not be regained, the firing line intrenches and holds on until darkness or until a favorable turn in the situation develops. It is suicidal to turn back. During the

---

[81] As cited in *313th Artillery*, 36.

[82] *313th Artillery*, 36.

advance, supports move up as close to the firing line as cover will permit, adopting those functions best suited to keep down losses. They may be as close as 50 yards to the firing line. They should not be as far as 500 yards in rear of it. [83]

Clearly, the Army trained us to achieve *fire superiority* before we charged a position. It's a pretty easy concept to grasp, but hard to implement. The manual states: "Having gained fire superiority, the advance by rushes commences, but each rush must leave behind or have in front of it enough rifles to maintain fire superiority." The British called this concept "advancing in clumps" so as not to invite an enemy artillery strike or M.G. cone. One can easily rehearse this while "x" squad lays down suppressive fire, "y" squad assaults, etc. But squads themselves don't have the combat power to actually break through. This is why the Army came up with the platoon combat group concept and taught us to attack in almost a machine-like manner, wave after wave, clump after clump. When one platoon, company, or battalion got chewed-up, we'd simply send in another until the objective was taken—usually at the business end of a bayonet.

On Hill 281, German M.G.s hid below ground until the attack battalion of the 319th Infantry passed over and then emerged with their M.G.s, firing into the Blue Ridgers' backs. Because of this, the support battalion (or second wave) had to be very cognizant. Not only did they have to be careful not to shoot their brethren in front, but they also had to worry about engaging a by-passed enemy who would sometimes come out of nowhere.

We would in fact argue that the support battalion had the most important (and dangerous) job of the three battalion waves. Lt. Edward Lukens of I/3/320th Infantry, who was a platoon leader in the designated support battalion of his regiment on the first day of the Meuse-Argonne Offensive, discussed how he "mopped-up" or "cleared" the over-run German trenches in the wake of the assault battalion and how he dealt with P.O.W. collection, especially when not all Germans surrendered equally:

I could not make head nor tail of where I was with reference to the companies, for I kept getting mixed up with companies from Maj. Holt's 2/320th Infantry, who I was supposed to follow, and whenever we would be delayed a little we would find ourselves crowded by Company L whom we were supposed to keep ahead of...Meanwhile, there was "mopping up" to do, although the assault companies had pretty well finished the job themselves. We were supposed to work from the left to right on our sector, but this beautiful theory didn't work in practice, for the rest of the detachment was now entirely out of my control, and

---

[83] *P.M.*, 246.

I had to trust them to take care of the ground in front of them while my platoon confined ourselves to what was in our sight...So we ran along the top of the trenches, heaving bombs into all dugouts that might contain hidden gunners or snipers, looking at scattered wounded Germans to assure ourselves that they were safely out of action, ready to kill if they showed any sight of treachery, and making the prisoners who were not badly hurt run faster to the rear. The old-fashioned way of "mopping-up" was to kill everything, and there is no possible doubt that it was necessary in the days of closer personal combat and greater danger of treachery, but in the new open style of fighting, and with the Boche's general willingness to get safely to the rear as fast as he could, it was unnecessary and almost impracticable. Furthermore, we had been ordered to take prisoners whenever possible, because the Boche will stop shooting sooner to go to the rear than when he knows he is in for sure death. One of our companies that morning had the experience of opening fire on a group of Boche coming forward to surrender, and having them return to their guns and hit several of our men before they were again subdued. But it was often hard to tell just when a Boche was safely out of action and we learned later of a case in our sector where one had slipped back to a buzzer station after being wounded, to be found and killed a few minutes later, so it is probable that if anything, we should have even rougher than we were.[84]

Lt. Lukens's above statement reinforces the point that is stated in the *I.D.R.*: "Complicated maneuvers are not likely to succeed in war. All plans and the methods adopted for carrying them into effect must be simple and direct."[85] Although we had been warned that this would be a platoon leader's war, it didn't really sink in until we fought in the Meuse-Argonne. Company and battalion commanders pretty much came up with a plan, briefed the platoon leaders, and managed what they and their platoons did, giving them as much support as they could. I know that this may sound obtuse, but one of the most important officer positions in the Army is in fact the lowest one: that of platoon leader. It's a tough job, even for the most-experienced soldier. But when assigned to the younger—although more physically fit but least experienced officers—the job is almost impossible. It is therefore up to the company and battalion commanders to constantly mentor the platoon leaders under their charge and to not simply leave it to the platoon sergeants, who have corporals and privates to mentor as well.

---

[84] As cited in *3/320th Infantry*, 61-62.

[85] *I.D.R.*, Para. 361.

In my view, the Aces-in-the-Hole of 1/318th Infantry were Maj. Sweeny and Capt. Crum, men who had had real-life combat experiences and who emphasized the basics not only to the E.M. and N.C.O.s, but to the platoon leaders and company commanders as well. In talking with others from our sister battalions after the war, most had similar "Sweenys and Crums" in their ranks. If they didn't, then they learned—really fast—the importance of keeping all things in war as simple as possible.

Beyond Hill 281, the terrain sloped away into an open meadow to *Bois Sachet* and *Village Gercourt*. While Cocheu's 319th Infantry was to attack into *Gercourt* and *Bois Juré*, adjoining with units from Prairie Division, Col. Peyton's 320th Infantry was to secure the western half of *Bois Sachet*, adjoining with the 47th Infantry from the 4th Ivy Division. In this area, *HAGEN* was in a double line, packed with M.G. nests every 50 yards! It's important to understand that unlike the American Army, which was not only organized around the rifle but also believed that the M.G. was merely "a weapon of emergency," the German Army was organized around the M.G. By 1918, pretty much every infantry platoon in the German Army was converted into a reinforced M.G. squad in which every man fired, fed, or protected a Maxim M.G. These platoons were backed by company or battalion 81mm mortars or massive 170mm (6.9-inch) or 250mm (9.8-inch) *Minenwerfers* (mine throwers) as well as pre-plotted artillery.

It's no wonder the French couldn't break through here.

Needless to say, once the assault companies of Brett's 160th Inf. Brig. hit *HAGEN* at *Gercourt* and *Bois Sachet*, they were stopped cold and literally cut to pieces. In order to get them moving forward again, supporting weapons, such as Colt-Vickers M.G.s, French-made direct-fire 37mm I.G.s, British-made 81mm Stokes Mortars, or direct-fire French-made 75mm cannon would be needed. In the mean time, responsible infantry officers would order their commands to "intrench while under fire" and wait while they sent back patrols to bring said heavy weapons forward through the bloody mess.

As patrols from the point platoons moved to the rear to escort (and help) the supporting weapons move forward, Capt. George Penniman's C/313th Artillery did everything it could do to advance in order to support said pinned infantry. According to Capt. Penniman:

[After crossing the bridge] we thought the going would be easy, but it was not. In spite of the work done ahead of us by the Engineers, and the detachment of ammunition train men who were attached to the battery for this pioneer work, the road through Béthincourt was still a series of shell holes, fallen stone walls and barbed wire entanglements, into which the horses and carriages continually slipped and fell with barbed wire twisted around the horses' legs,

tearing the flesh. To expedite matters, the infantry reserves which were now coming up pitched in to work filling holes and with their clippers cleared away the wire entanglements.[86]

Penniman's C/1/313th Artillery, led by its mounted scouts and markers, advanced to Hill 281, where it was once again forced to stop to fill in an abandoned German trench with pre-fabricated *fascines*. At this point, everyone, from Capt. Penniman down to the youngest private understood that any movement onto Hill 281 or north of it into *Gercourt* would be under constant observation from the Germans along *Côtes Meuse* near *Consenvoye*.[87] They knew that from this very exposed position, C/1/313th Artillery would be subject to intense enfilade or flanking enemy artillery or M.G. fire from the dominating *Côtes de Meuse*. In other words, if Penniman ordered his battery to stay where it was, it would be decimated—if he ordered it to advance, in order to fulfill its mission of accompanying battery of Brett's 160th Inf. Brig.—it would have to run the gauntlet of well-placed and deadly enemy artillery fire, most assuredly suffering at least 50% casualties. And if Penniman failed to get his four 75mm guns up to the attacking infantry, it would be the Doughs of the 160th Inf. Brig. who would be blown to Kingdom Come as they were stuck in the middle of it all—pinned. As Penniman pondered the fate of his unit and the mission while his cannoneers feverishly worked to fill the trench, he noticed the signs of the recent fighting all around him:

German equipment was scattered everywhere. Helmets, rifles, hand grenades, and ammunition. On one side of the road lay a German officer dying from a bayonet wound; on the other side of the road lay a German soldier nearly dead from a bayonet wound in his stomach. Near this German lay the first American dead we had seen, a sergeant in the 319th Infantry. The top of Hill 281 is spotted with a system of trenches and and dugouts."[88]

Penniman was particularly drawn to the sight of the pinned infantry lines to the northwest. They were stuck in field between *Gercourt* and *Bois Sachet* and *Juré* and were trying to break into the "skeleton-key-shaped" defensive line that elements of the 7th Prussian Reserve Division were occupying in said wood line with barbed wire, obstacles, ditches, Mauser Rifles, M.G.s, "and whotnot and whotfer" (as we would say).

To help them get moving again, Penniman sent his scouts forward to gain direct contact with the infantry. The scouts were told to signal back with semaphore flags whether the attack

---

[86] As cited in *313th Artillery*, 36.
[87] *Consenvoye* is pronounced "Cone-soan-vwa."

[88] As cited in *313th Artillery*, 37.

was progressing ("yes" or "no") and "affirmative" or "negative" whether the battery was in fact needed to move forward to deliver direct fire missions. It was therefore supposed to be a two-part message (bad move—all military communication should be short and sweet—and you'll see why).

One artillery scout found Maj. Emory, commander of 3/320th Infantry, who was in *Bois Sachet*. After a brief discussion, the scout signaled "negative" just before he was wounded in the arm by enemy M.G. fire. Unable to give the second message on whether or not to send the guns forward, Pennington assumed was that the attack was not progressing and that his battery would in fact be needed to be brought forward to offer direct fire support (always assume the worst).

As this occurred, platoons of the 319th Infantry had passed through *Gercourt* and Penniman, atop Hill 281, could see scattered groups of Germans darting from the town's northern edges and heading for *Bois Juré*. In the meantime, Lt. Col. Otto Brunzell and Majors Dunigan and Nash arrived with the balance of the 313th Artillery: 20 field guns with 20 limbers and 40 caissons. After conferring with Penniman, Brunzell decided to deploy the balance of his regiment along the reverse slope of Hill 281 with 1/313th Artillery (-) on the right of the Béthincourt-Gercourt Road and 2/313th Artillery on the left. This would place them in "flash defilade," or, according to the *A.D.R.*, "complete concealment."[89] According to Lt. Henry S. Baker of F/2/313: "The batteries of 2/313 arrived upon Hill 281 with nothing more serious to overcome than a few road jams due to the tremendous amount of traffic. German prisoners and wounded were streaming back, and ammunition, food, kitchens, and reserves going forward, with the wreckage of battle and the dead on both sides of the road, gave our first real view of the immensity of a 'big push.'"[90]

With the orders cut, Dunigan's 1/313th Artillery halted in column on the reverse slope of Hill 281, and, as specified in the *A.D.R.*, the battery commanders conducted an R.S.O.P. It was decided that the limbers were to be brought forward, that the guns were to be maneuvered into firing position at Penniman's suggestion, the caissons parked, and that battery O.P.s were to be established atop the hill, hidden in abandoned German trenches. From there, the O.P.s would be able to spot targets as far north as *Bois Dannevoux* and *Village Sivry*.[91]

---

[89] *A.D.R.*, Para. 1067.

[90] As cited in *313th Artillery*, 31. "Flash defilade" means that the enemy will not be able to spot the flame or smoke from a gun muzzle.

[91] *Sivry* is pronounced "See-vree."

As Dunigan's battalion moved into position, however, one unlucky soldier was the victim of a "German trap." In this case, the retreating Germans had wired a hand grenade to a bayonet in a trench on Hill 281. When the soldier picked it up as *prix de guerre*, the wire pulled the pin from the grenade, horribly wounding him. It was a lesson learned but one that would, unfortunately, have to be retaught many times—too many.[92]

With five batteries now on line, Maj. Dunigan ordered Capt. Penniman's C/1/313 forward to join the Doughs down below in *Gercourt* or *Bois Sachet* while the balance of the regiment fired counter-battery or interdiction missions to the east or north.[93] As Penniman prepared to move out, guns from Lt. Col. Walker's 314th Artillery also arrived, and they went into battery to the left of Dunigan's 313th Artillery, just west of Hill 281, in the open.[94]

As Walker's 314th Artillery went into battery, Dunigan told Walker about two German 77mm field guns that had almost everything intact, including stocks of ammunition, that were left abandoned on the forward slope of the hill. The only thing missing from the guns were their sights. Walker jumped at this and ordered a gun crew from Lt. Alan Means's platoon to secure the guns and fire them against German positions along the Heights of the Meuse "at maximum range."[95]

Penniman, heading down toward the infantry, meanwhile, decided to split his battery. While Lt. Edward Morgan's 1/C/313 was sent to the right to join Col. Cocheu's 319th Infantry that was fighting through *Gercourt* and on into *Bois Juré*, Lt. John Penniman's 2/C/313 (Capt. Penniman's younger brother) was sent to the left to join with the 320th Infantry that was fighting in *Bois Sachet*. Capt. Penniman accompanied his younger brother's platoon.

As ill-fortune would have it, just as the battery entered the open valley north of Hill 381, making a run for the woods and the village, a German aeroplane darted in from the north, "flying at a very low altitude." It circled above the units of Brett's 160th Inf. Brig. so closely that Capt. Penniman stated that he could clearly see the Hun pilot's face and the peculiar black German crosses on the wings. It strafed and bombed Penniman's battery, wounding two, and then swung around for a second run, firing three signal flares above *Gercourt*, directing his own

---

[92] *313th Artillery*, 34 and "*Prix de guerre*" or "Prize of war" is pronounced "Pree due gair."

[93] *Ibid*, 38-39. According to the map entitled "Meuse-Argonne" created by the American Battlefield Commission, the 80th Division did not enter *Gercourt*. This is incorrect, however, as we did. Just ask any member of the 319th Infantry or the 313th Artillery who was there that famous day.

[94] *314th Artillery*, 51.

[95] *Ibid*, 38.

artillery to open fire.[96] Lt. Morgan's platoon (two guns) followed the 319th Infantry, which had just cleared Gercourt of Germans through the use of "effective rifle grenade fire."[97]

Gercourt was the first enemy strong point captured by the Blue Ridge Division during the war-ending Meuse-Argonne Offensive.

The Germans had clearly used *Gercourt* as a *dépôt* for the now overrun trenches to the south. In the main street of *Gercourt,* for example, was located an aid station for the Prussian 7th Reserve Division, including an impressive ambulance. Capt. Charles Herr of F/2/319th Infantry remembered that the ambulance was "a royal affair with most modern equipment, leather upholstering, and a Mercedes engine. It was undamaged by shell fire and seemed to have been abandoned when its gasoline supply was exhausted."[98]

On both sides of the streets, the cellars had been converted into dugouts that were filled with mattresses, trench knives, hand grenades, dynamite, rockets, *Véry* Pistols and other signal and engineer ordnance. One concrete dugout was stuffed with medical supplies that included Red Cross bandages and rows of bottles of medicines that were noticeable particularly because most of the labels bore the name of a Chicago concern. In one corner, *les Boche* also had a cage of rabbits.[99] According to Lt. Furr of the 314th M.G. Battalion:

> *The trenches of HAGEN averaged from six to eight feet in depth and had been held by M.G.s placed at fairly regular intervals. The Hun M.G.s either shot over the parapet of through the port holes below. The whole trench being well-concealed in the underbrush at the edge of the woods, at a distance of two hundred meters to the front, it could not be detected that such a strong defensive line existed. Behind the trench, and connected with it by short communicating trenches, were deep dugouts, the plan being that while two men were in action with a machine gun, the balance of the squad or gun team could remain in the dugout in comparative safety, unless a large should make a direct hit on the dugout. These guns had caused our infantry many casualties, because they had to advance through an open field which the guns covered. In most cases the German gunners lay dead at the gun or a few paces behind it; in some cases a*

---

[96] *313th Artillery,* 38.

[97] *319th Infantry,* 24.

[98] As cited Herr, Charles Ryman. *Company F History, 319th Infantry* (N.P., 1920), 8. Hereafter cited as "*2/319th Infantry.*"

[99] *2/319th Infantry,* 8.

bayonet had done the work, but more often a hand grenade had been the weapon used by the Americans in this close work.[100]

By seizing Gercourt, HAGEN was breached and *the 80th Division was the first American division to break through the first line of the vaunted HINDENBURG STELLUNG in the Meuse-Argonne.*

Let me say that again: by seizing Gercourt, HAGEN was breached and the 80th Division was the first American division to break through the first line of the vaunted *HINDENBURG STELLUNG* in the Meuse-Argonne.

As the 319th Infantry fought its way north through *Gercourt* and into *Bois Juré*, a "lone American plane flew over. He showed great daring, though possibly poor judgment, as immediately several enemy planes toward him, and in less than ten minutes brought him down in a cornfield" between Gercourt and the woods, killing him. Earlier in the day, the men of the 160th Inf. Brig. remembered that our planes had been "thick in the air above," but as the day went on, the situation became reversed, and they also had to deal with aerial attacks along with everything else.[101]

Over on the left, with the 320th Infantry, it had advanced across the rolling, shell-torn fields between Hill 281 and *Bois Sachet*, slowed by deep and hateful craters, an occasional Hun artillery strike, rear-guard infantry actions, or pillaging. Yes, pillaging. Almost everyone did it—pillage the dead—but some of the men of the 320th Infantry, many hailing from America's "Steel City," apparently took it to another level. It was notable enough that Lt. Lukens of 3/320th Infantry openly admitted to it in his book, *A Blue Ridge Memoir* (1922):

> *One of our men's faults was their curiosity and their craze for souvenirs. I came upon a whole group of them gathered around a few prisoners, accepting presents of iron crosses and buttons which the frightened Boche offered doubtless as bribes for their lives, our men apparently forgetting that there were more enemies close at hand. By this time, I had lost all my original men, as they would be delayed at some little job and be absorbed into the companies in rear, so I broke up the souvenir party and thereby recruited a dozen or so new moppers-up. I saw a lone [Blue Ridger] lying on the ground shooting his Chauchat, so I ran over to see what the fuss was, and had no sooner dropped down beside him than he curled up with a bullet in his stomach.*[102]

---

[100] *314th M.G.*, 31.

[101] *314th M.G.*, 31.

[102] As cited in *3/320th Infantry*, 62.

With the 319th Infantry now advancing north through *Bois Juré* and the 320th attacking into *Bois Sachet*, 1/C/1/313th Artillery continued its advance as well, following Cocheu's 319th Infantry through the burned-out remains of HAGEN and across the cratered fields between *Gercourt* and *Bois Juré*.

Before long, Penniman's artillerists found the 319th Infantry and several M.G. platoons engaged in a close-up fight with *les Boche* in *Bois Juré*; the Blue Ridge Boys were advancing slowly, methodically, trying to avoid getting capped by German sniper or M.G. fire. The artillery scouts and markers from the 313th Artillery, who were now dismounted, were also fired upon and worked forward through the tall grass and undergrowth at a high crawl. They were looking for an field grade infantry officer to get instructions as to where they should deploy. They moved further up the road and entered *Bois Juré* while on all sides riflemen from the 319th infantry were rising to one knee and picking off Hun riflemen or M.G.ers. Once in the woods, the artillery scouts felt safe enough to advance a little faster, but were again driven to the ground by the sharp crack of whizzing bullets that were too close for comfort.[103]

An infantry messenger who had just left Maj. O'Bear, the commander of the 319th Infantry's attack battalion, said that he would escort the artillery scouts forward but that they must "be careful in the advance." The party eventually found Maj. O'Bear in an open stretch of ground behind a small earthen mound that was being swept by German M.G. fire from reinforced nests that were but 30 to 50 yards away. O'Bear asked the artillerists to destroy the enemy M.G. nests with indirect fire using map coordinates, thus breaching the German line and allowing his battalion to break through.[104]

At this point, the artillery had established an O.P. some 300 meters south of the target, instructed the major to pull his infantry back to them, ran telephone wire back to the guns, and determined the map coordinates and direction to the target. Once all was set, they phoned in the following commands:

"Adjust Fire, over."

"Enemy M.G. dugouts in the woods. Grid x and y."

"Length 200."

"Sheaf 45."

"Direction 15, over."

---

[103] *313th Artillery*, 40.

[104] *Ibid.*

The fire direction center (F.D.C.) near the gun line repeated the commands to ensure they were correct and determined the elevation (range) and deflection (direction) of the guns, calculating the factors of site (difference in elevation between the guns and the target) and pitch (the angle with which the guns sit). This is all done within two minutes by the battery executive officer (X.O.). Because the target was in the woods and under cover, H.E. was the round of choice. Once the lead piece of the gun section, which was back in *Gercourt*, was lined up, it fired the first round for adjustment.

"Boom!"

"Weeee."

"Ka-bloom!"

The round overshot the target by 200 meters and was too far to the right. No matter. In fact, the O.P.s were taught to overshoot their targets and adjust fire into them. To shoot short, would probably land the round on your own men.

"Direction 350."

"Drop 200, left 200, over!"

"Drop 200, left, 200, out!"

The F.D.C. would then take "Direction 350" as the point of what was meant by left or right or drop or add. With the new information, the gun would adjust its sights and fire another round.

"Boom!"

"Weeee."

"Ka-bloom!"

This round cut through the tree limbs and landed just behind the target. For 75mm artillery, this was "close enough" as the rounds had 15-meter kill radii and when several are dropped at the same time, the results are devastating. As was already explained, "length" is the length of the target and "sheaf" is the angle of the target and the guns were ordered to move their sights slightly to the right after each shot, thus firing from left to right. Gun Two then set its sights relative to Gun One and both fired at the same time five times (total of ten rounds) at a rate of fifteen R.P.M.

"Ka-bloom!"

"Ka-bloom!"

"Ka-bloom!"

"Ka-bloom!"

"Ka-bloom!"

The results were positive as "direct hits were made in the center of a nest, blowing it to pieces, those in the near-by nests scattered like scared rabbits to the four corners of the wind."[105]

With at least two M.G. nests neutralized, the bomber and assault squads of the 319th Infantry charged forward through the woods, using fire and maneuver, working their way into the enemy rear while the A.R.s and R.G.s laid down suppressive fire. The flanked Germans were shot in the back by the Blue Ridge Boys to prevent them from establishing another defensive line in the woods. I was admitted that even the officers in this particular instance switched out their auto-pistols for rifles from killed or wounded E.M. to increase the slaughter.

With the fire support from batteries of the 155th Arty. Brig. and platoons of M.G.s from the M.G. battalions, the 319th Infantry was able to press forward and establish a defensive line along the northern edge of *Bois Juré*, facing *Village Dannevoux* and *GISELHER*. In securing *Bois Juré*, as luck would have it, a platoon from 2/319th Infantry found two untapped barrels of "good German beer" in a Hun dugout and it became part of the regimental ration for at least a day.[106] At around noon, on the left of the division sector, the 320th Infantry renewed its attack against its part of *HAGEN*, which was situated in Bois Sachet. Lt. Edward Lukens of I/3/320th Infantry remembered how his platoon engaged its first enemy targets in Bois Sachet:

> *We advanced ourselves in a double skirmish line over the next hill, with apparently no sign of trouble, and the right flank of the company was approaching a small patch of woods, when a burst of M.G. fire suddenly splattered the ground about our feet, slightly wounding one man in the leg. We drooped instantly, and hugged the ground close until some men from the other end of the company, who were not in direct range, had time to work into the woods from the flank, for it is an inevitable cause of needless casualties to advance frontally on a M.G. nest if it can possibly be flanked. Then we crawled around until we could get into Bois Sachet, and a regular man-hunt developed. The woods was grown thick with laurel, penetrated by many intersecting paths, and two or three men would sneak up each fork to hunt out the prey. About eight of us, keeping on the main path, came up to a small clearing which contained two wooden shanties. Although the area had [already been swept by other companies of the regiment, one still had to be wary. As such,] we approached cautiously, watching the trees for snipers, and glancing around on all sides. We found the buildings deserted, and then saw near one of them the entrance of a dug out. I peered down, and saw something moving down in the*

---

[105] *313th Artillery*, 40.
[106] *2/319th Infantry*, 8.

darkness, so I pulled a bomb out of my pocket and struck the cap against my tin hat. At the sound of the hissing fuse, there came from the dug-out the most unholy conglomeration of yells that I ever heard from human throats—screams of terror and abject pleading. But six seconds is too short a time to negotiate a surrender; they had been kept hidden too long and could not possibly claim to be regarded as prisoners. The fuse was already going and down the hole went the bomb. I jumped back from the mouth and in an instant there was a terrific explosion and a cloud of dust and smoke came up. Why it didn't kill them all, we couldn't imagine, but no sooner had the smoke cleared than the cries started again, and we could distinguish the words "no more" in English. This time we waited and out piled eight Boche, apparently without a scratch, but as scared as men could be.[107]

In attacking north, the attack platoons of Brett's 160th Inf. Brig., as taught to them by the British in Artois and Picardy, led with the bomber squads (and sometimes the assault squads) with the platoon leader in front. Upon contact, the platoon leader would establish a firing line and lay down suppressive fire (or "establish a base of fire") with rifles and A.R.s. The R.G.s would then shoot white prosperous (W.P.) smoke rounds at the target, which was usually a Hun M.G. nest flanked by supporting trenches. These deadly W.P. rounds did two things: they laid down thick white smoke, pretty much blinding the enemy, and started fires. W.P. can actually burn through motor blocks and can cook a human being from the inside out in under a minute! As the W.P. smoke screen matured and the A.R.s gained the all-important fire superiority, M.G.s, I.G.s, and/or Penniman's 75mm field guns were brought forward to reinforce the firing line, which would be as big as a squad, platoon, or even entire company.

Unfortunately, we infantrymen found that the direct-fire I.G.s were practically useless, especially when compared to the M.G.s. But, as our mothers would too-often say, "It's better than nothing!" The Colt-Vickers M.G.s were helpful in spewing their cones of bullets, but as denoted in the *I.D.R.*, once they opened up, the Germans sent everything they had to silence them. That, plus the fact that they shot up one can of ammunition (250-rounds) rapidly, only kept them in the battle for a short time.

But, with more and more M.G. sections being brought forward, they would replace each other—leap-frogging forward—awaiting resupply to move forward again. The idea of uniting the M.G. battalions under one commander, in our case, D.M.G.O. Foley, and sending most of them forward (as opposed to perpetually attaching one M.G. battalion to each brigade) proved to be

---

[107] As cited in *3/320th Infantry*, 65.

quite effective. I don't know who came up with that idea, but I do know that most other divisions, like the 79th Division, did it, too.

Once the A.R. and R.G. squads, backed by the supporting weapons, achieved fire superiority—and that was a critical part—the platoon leader would order the bomber and assault squads to attack or charge the position. Without firing their rifles, the bombers would get to within 20 yards of the suppressed enemy position and hurl their hand grenades—sometimes three to five of them, one after the other. After that, the platoon leader, at the proper "psychological moment," would order the assault squad to charge, firing their rifles from the hip and taking the enemy position with the bayonet. The general rule was to attack in pairs: one man parried while the other man "stuck the pig." Once an objective was taken, the platoon guide or sergeant would bring the A.R. and R.G. squads and any supporting weapons forward and they would help establish a defensive line, backed by riflemen. That was the usual pattern, anyway. When one combat group or platoon got chewed up, another simply took its place in the line until the enemy target was destroyed. According to Army Regulations:

The Assault.

F.S.R. 173. If the hostile lines are held by good infantry, properly led, and supported by good artillery, fire action alone will not bring about a decision. For this purpose the assault will be necessary.

F.S.R. 174. In large forces assaults are local and not general. Combined assaults in forces larger than a division are not practicable, nor can the assaults of several divisions along an extended front be coordinated in time. Each battle unit to which has been assigned a distinctive mission must time its assault according to conditions in its own part of the field, but other units must keep the enemy in their front so occupied that he can not concentrate a heavy force to meet the assault or to make a counter-attack.

The Charge.

I.D.R. 461. fire superiority beats down the enemy's fire, destroys his resistance and morale, and enables the attacking troops to close on him, but an actual or threatened occupation of his position is needed to drive him out and defeat him. The psychological moment for the charge can not be determined far in advance. The tactical instinct of the responsible officer must decide.

I.D.R. 465. The defenders, if subjugated by the fire attack, will frequently leave before the charge begins. On the other hand, it may be necessary to carry the fire attack close to the position and follow it up with a short dash and a bayonet combat. Hence the distance over which the charge may be made will vary between wide limits. It may be from 25 to 400 yards. The charge should be made at the earliest moment that promises success: otherwise the full advantage of victory will be lost.

I.D.R. 466. The commander of the attacking line should indicate his approval, or give the order, before the charge is made. Subordinate commanders, usually battalion commanders, whose troops are ready to charge signal that fact to the commander. It may be necessary for them to wait until other battalions or other parts of the line are ready or until the necessary reserves arrive. At the signal for the charge the firing line and near-by supports and reserves rush forward.... The charge is made simultaneously, if possible, by all the units participating therein, but, once committed to the assault, battalions should be pushed with the utmost vigor and no restraint placed on the ardor of charging troops by an attempt to maintain alignment.

I.D.R. 467. Before ordering the charge the commander should see that enough troops are on hand to make it a success. Local reserves joining the firing line in time to participate in the charge give it a strong impetus. Too dense a mass should be avoided.

I.D.R. 468. The line should be strengthened by prolongation, if practicable, and remaining troops kept in formation for future use; but rather than that the attack should fail, the last formed body will be sent in, unless it is very apparent that it can do no good.

I.D.R. 469. To arrive in the hostile position with a very compact firing line and a few formed supports is sufficient for a victory, but an additional force kept well in hand for pursuit is of inestimable value.

I.D.R. 470. A premature charge by a part of the line should be avoided, but if begun, the other parts of the line should join at once if there is any prospect of success. Under exceptional conditions a part of the line may be compelled to charge without authority from the rear. The intention to do so should be signaled to the rear.

I.D.R. 471. Confidence in their ability to use the bayonet gives the assaulting troops the promise of success.

I.D.R. 472. If the enemy has left the position when the charging troops reach it, the latter should open a rapid fire upon the retreating enemy, if he is in sight. It is not advisable for the mixed and disordered units to follow him, except to advance to a favorable firing position or to cover the reorganization of others.

I.D.R. 473. The nearest formed bodies accompanying or following the charge are sent instantly in pursuit. Under cover of these troops order is restored in the charging line. If the captured position is part of a general line or is an advanced post, it should be intrenched and occupied at once. The exhaustion of officers and men must not cause the neglect of measures to meet a counter-attack.

I.D.R. 474. If the attack receives a temporary setback and it is intended to strengthen and continue it, officers will make every effort to stop the rearward movement and will reestablish the firing line in a covered position as close as possible to the enemy.

I.D.R. 475. If the attack must be abandoned, the rearward movement should continue with promptness until the troops reach a feature of the terrain that facilitates the task of checking and reorganizing them. The point selected should be so far to the rear as to prevent interference by the enemy before the troops are ready to resist. The withdrawal of the attacking troops should be covered by the artillery and by reserves, if any are available.

The Charge.[108]

There can be no rule to tell you when to charge. It may be from 25 to 400 yards. The common sense (tactical instinct) of the senior ranking officer on the firing line must tell him the psychological moment to order the charge. That moment will be when your fire has broken down the enemy's fire, broken his resistance, and destroyed his morale. The artillery increases its range. The firing line and remaining supports fix bayonets. The former increases the rate of fire, the latter rush forward under the protection of this fire, join the firing line and give it necessary impetus. Together they rush at the enemy's position. No restraint is placed upon their ardor. Confidence in their ability to use the bayonet gives the charging troops the promise of success. If the charge is successful, the nearest formed bodies are sent instantly in pursuit and under cover of them the commands are reorganized, order restored, and arrangements made to resist a counter-attack. If the charge is unsuccessful the artillery or any formed troops in rear cover the withdraw.

---

[108] *P.M.*, 247.

The biggest mistakes that too many of the companies of Brett's 160th Inf. Brig. (as well as the rest of the Army at this point) made during the "First Push" was that they either "walked ahead for the most part nonchalantly as though they were on route march" or they charged frontally against an enemy position *before* they had achieved fire superiority. In the latter case, these particular infantry platoons would simply charge pell-mell, following their platoon leader, and many of them paid for it with limb or life, becoming *hors de combat*.[109] Lt. Lukens of 3/320th Infantry remembered:

> *Our soldiers in this drive walked ahead for the most part nonchalantly as though they were on route march. Only when something was actually encountered was the atmosphere in the least intense. In fact sometimes they were too easy going, apparently too innocent to realize that sudden crises might arise [or, resigned to their fate—Joe Riddle]. They were all hungry by this time, and out came the bread and hard tack, though we did not stop.*[110]

As the day wore on, and as school was in session, the men of the rifle platoons decided to simplify the attack concept even more. Due to casualties, many platoons decided to divide themselves into but two combat groups, each with a "bomber and bayonet squad" in the lead followed by a "guns and grenades squad." The bomber and bayonet squad per each combat group would only charge once fire superiority was gained with the A.R.s and R.G.s of the guns and grenades squad. During our "Second Push" in Oct., this technique was formalized across the Army (i.e., two combat groups per platoon) and our casualty rates dropped.

One can be trained to a fine edge but it is experience in combat that really matters. All training will do is to help one survive the first engagement. If you survive, you'll know what to do, based upon your training and experience, emphasizing the basics. It takes experience to understand exactly when to charge or assault an enemy position without being butchered in the process and timing is everything. One can be either too conservative or too impetuous. As for me, I felt comfortable to order the bomber and assault squads to charge only after we had chewed up the target with A.R., M.G., I.G., mortar, or (and especially) direct 75mm artillery fire, which sometimes took ten to twenty mins. to achieve, which feels like an eternity on the battlefield. Granted, as an A.R. in a very good squad, I commanded nothing but my A.R. team. I was, however, cognizant of my surroundings and understood that it was my job to learn

---

[109] *Hors d'combat* is French for "removed from combat" and is pronounced "Oars dee coam-bat."

[110] As cited in *3/320th Infantry*, 63.

everything I could from the squad leader, platoon guide, and platoon leader, as one day, it might be me who was the only one who was left.

At around 1:00 P.M., the 314th M.G. Battalion (Mot.), was directed by the 319th Infantry to "go into action about 500 meters west of the [Gercourt-Dannevoux] Road, in a clearing extending from *Bois Sachet* to the southwestern edge of *Bois Juré*; B Company on the left and A Company on the right."[111] The M.G. sections, now acting in a defensive role, were to fire over the heads of elements of the 319th Infantry and engage Hun targets in what was later called "the Triangle." There were indications that the Germans were planning a counter-attack from *Bois Septsarges* and *Dannevoux* and were looking to re-establish HAGEN in the vicinity of *Gercourt*. Lt. Herman Furr of the 314th M.G. remembered:

No time was to be lost, for the guns were no sooner in position that a thin line of Germans was seen advancing several hundred meters out of the woods toward the American positions. All M.G.s were immediately opened on them and a number of the Germans were killed or wounded: a number temporarily fell to the ground and later ran back into the woods. Our own infantry was in a skirmish line in a slight valley about 300 meters in front. There was no time to warn them we would fire over their heads, as is usually done in a case of this kind, for the reason that a M.G. bullet has a nasty "crack" to when it is passing over one's head, even at a safe distance, and it is rather annoying to the infantry to have this happen, unless they have been warned. Again and again the Germans tried to advance, but always unsuccessfully... They located our positions and their bullets were soon striking close around us, but mostly passing over our backs, as everyone, by this time, was lying on the ground to make as small as a target as possible. The infantry seeing that the M.G.ers were fully able to stop any advance by the Germans at this point, gradually worked through the tall grass and underbrush toward the left, and finally began to enter the woods from the flank. M.G. fire was then suspended to let them finish the job at close hand, due to the danger of hitting our own infantrymen.[112]

The above passage shows how we in America's Blue Ridge Division generally solved tactical problems. Once we took ground, we'd bring up M.G.s and/or other supporting weapons as soon as possible to help hold the taken ground. The Army was correct in saying that because of its weight, the M.G. was actually a defensive weapon or a "Weapon of Emergency." But the

---

[111] *314th M.G.*, 29.

[112] As cited in *Ibid*, 30.

only way we could in fact gain the Holy Grail of fire superiority was to get as many M.G.s on the firing line as possible. This is why we assigned platoons of Doughs from the reserve battalions to help move M.G.s or I.G.s forward as soon as possible. Once the M.G.s and I.G.s were deployed with inter-locking fields of fire, the infantry, mobile little killing machines armed with grenades, rifles, bayonets, satchel charges, A.R.s, R.G.s, spoons, etc., would resume the attack, resolved to take out each and every Hun M.G. position that stood in its way.

Over on the left with Col. Parson's 320th Infantry, the biggest concern was in closing the gap between the 80th and 4th Divisions between *Gercourt* and *Cuisy*, securing the left flank of the 80th Division, and in helping the 4th Division gain a foothold in *Bois Septsarges*. Maj. Ashby Williams of 1/320th Infantry, still in regimental reserve, remembered:

> *The men were exhausted and hungry (no man had eaten breakfast that morning) and they rested in the valley in the sunlight and munched their hardtack and ate Bully Beef with relish. It was about 11:00 A.M. At length the troops in front of us passed to the left of [Bois Sachet] and went forward, and as I was not certain that any troops had passed through the woods south of the Septsarges Road, I sent for Lt. Russell, who was commanding Company D in the absence of Capt. Sabiston, and told him to comb the woods and pass on to the north edge and protect my right flank as we passed. About sixty prisoners were captured in these woods and placed under guard. In the meantime Capt. Sabiston, who had been sent out with the engineers the night before, came up from the right and I sent him with a detachment into the woods to get these prisoners. He brought them out and I sent them to the rear. I then advanced with my command to the ridge south of the road and halted them and went forward to see Maj. Holt, who had his H.Q. in a shell hole near the road. This was about noon...I talked with Maj. Holt for some time. He said that word had come that there was a wide gap between his left flank and the right flank of the 4th Division, which was in the sector to the left of us, and asked me to send him troops to fill that gap and maintain contact. I sent him part of Company A which had returned from the engineering detail and, I think, all of Company C, under the command of Capt. Miller. These troops did not return to me during the action but remained in the front line and engaged in some of the hardest fighting, suffering many casualties.*[113]

---

[113] As cited in *1/320th Infantry*, 84.

As Brett's 160th Inf. Brig. clawed, shot, bombed, and bayoneted its way to the north side of *Bois Sachet* and *Juré*, 75s from Heiner's 313th and 314th Artillery rained down fire upon Dannevoux and Sivry-sur-Meuse, the bridge and orchard at Vilosones, and Bois Septsarges and Dannevoux. During this phase of the battle, A/1/313th Artillery, which was posted behind Hill 281, took a direct hit from an enemy 77mm gun that was posted along *Côtes de Meuse*, killing or wounding an entire gun crew and putting their gun out of action. Drivers and horses were also made *hors de combat*.[114] A member of B/1/314th Artillery remembered: "The gun crews were sheltered in a deep, filthy German dug-out. Pvts. Cemillus Kennedy and John Seacrist came into contact with some enemy grenades while looking for shelter and an explosion of one of these wounded both of them. After their wounds were attended to at the battalion aid station, Pvt. Kennedy was taken to the hospital while Seacrist, not being seriously wounded, remained with the battery."[115]

By late-afternoon on the first day of the grand battle, the 319th Infantry was firmly ensconced in *Bois Juré* and the 320th Infantry was in possession of *Bois Sachet*. But the hated Hun still held *Dannevoux* and its adjoining wooded heights. To the front of the 160th Inf. Brig.'s front lay "the Triangle," which was the open area between *Bois Juré*, *Bois Sachet*, and *Dannevoux*. On the other side of the Triangle were Germans, and lots of them.

In order to resume the attack, the 313th and 314th Artillery sent scouts, signalmen, and liaison officers forward with telephone lines to establish O.P.s in the woods with the units of Brett's 160th Inf. Brig. Once positioned, any German who was spotted in or around the Triangle was blasted to Kingdom Come. As Hun infantry darted from their dugouts in the Triangle due to our artillery strikes, Doughs from the 160th Inf. Brig. took pot shots with their M1917 Enfields at "effective" or "long" ranges, which, according to the Army Regulations, was out to the ungodly range of 2 km. Many of us disagreed with opening fire at long range, however, because we saw it as a waste of ammunition. According to the *I.D.R.*, para. 402: "Beyond effective ranges important results can be expected only when the target is large and distinct and much ammunition is used. Long-range fire is permissible in pursuit on account of the moral effect of any fire under the circumstances. At other times such fire is of doubtful value."

Of course, I always thought that firing at targets with a rifle beyond 200 yards was a total waste of ammunition for the average Dough. The targets were either too small, too fast, or too masked by haze, smoke, etc., to be effectively neutralized. Anything beyond 200 yards, in my

---

[114] *Hors de combat* is the French term for "out of combat." It is pronounced "Oars day com-bat."

[115] As cited in *314th Artillery*, 51.

opinion, should be engaged by crew-served weapons like M.G.s or mortars. I also believe that M.G.s are best utilized in delivering indirect fire missions upon targets with plunging fire. At 2,000 yards, the cone or sheaf of a M.G. is deadly—even more deadly than a shrapnel round.

To protect the right flank of the 160th Inf. Brig., sections from the 314th M.G. Battalion (Mot.) were ordered to refuse the line in Bois Rond, which was the eastern half of Bois Juré (a road bisected the woods).[116] They were to at least gain visual contact with troops from the Prairie Division and prevent the enemy from mounting a counter-attack from the east, enfilading the line. It was an important mission, and one that a unit like the motorized 314th M.G. Battalion was well-suited. According to Lt. Furr of the 314th M.G.:

> *The 1st Platoon of Company A arrived in the Bois Rond early in the afternoon. While the other guns of the battalion were engaged [in the Triangle], Lt. Tom Barker had pushed his guns boldly into the woods. He engaged a very good target in the shape of enemy artillery which the Germans were making a desperate effort to save. The platoons consolidated on the ground gained, from right to left, as follows: 1st Platoon, Company A, Lt. Tom Barker, in eastern edge of Bois Rond, facing east, field of fire across the Meuse River; 2nd Platoon, A Company, Lt. Herman R. Furr [supra], in northern edge of Bois Rond, about 300 meters south of Dannevoux, facing north; 2nd Platoon, Company B, Lt. Edward Burrell, covering the Dannevoux Road; 3rd Platoon, Company A, Lt. Harvey L. Lindsay, and the 3rd Platoon of Company B, Lt. Walter Lukens, in the northern edge of Bois Jure, west of the road [in Bois Jure]; 1st Platoon, Company B, Sergeant John B. Hartman, drawn back and echeloned in depth supporting the forward guns.... Just before dusk, the German Artillery began to show some activity, throwing over some gas shells. Up to this time they had put over but a few shells in the area of "The Triangle," due to the fact that they had been forced into a hasty withdrawal by the breaking of their front line system of trenches. The first gas that came over was of the "sneezing" variety, and caused no damage, except to start several of the officers and men, who had pulled off their masks very soon after the alarm was given, to sneezing violently.*[117]

As General Brett's 160th Inf. Brig. fought its way north toward *GISELHER*, we in General Jamerson's 159th Inf. Brig. marched up the small, one-lane road from *Chattacourt* to *Mort*

---

[116] To "refuse the line" means to make an "L" to protect one's flank by establishing a perpendicular line to the main line.

[117] As cited in *314th M.G.*, 33.

Homme. The country on each side of this muddy track had been "No Man's Land" for nearly three years, and with the recent operations as well as rain, it was now almost impassable. It was a mucky, miry, bloody mess. As a consequence, the lead unit of our regiment, H.Q. Company, did not reach *Mort Homme* until mid-afternoon.

If Brett's 160th Inf. Brig. would have gotten bogged down at *HAGEN*, there was no way we in Jamerson's 159th Inf. Brig. could have come forward to help them.

During our march to *Mort Homme*, Hun aviators were very active and aggressive, so much so that the frequently reiterated assertion of Allied air supremacy seemed ridiculous to us (I always chuckled about all of the "Flyboy" movies made after the war). We ground-pounders were as vulnerable as new-born babes to them when left in the open. We watched in abject horror as adept German aviators brought down at least four Allied observation balloons ("sausages") and two American aeroplanes. Hun aircraft were usually painted red and black and a few had yellow markings. Once they gained local air-supremacy, the Huns would swoop down upon us and light us up with M.G. fire. As they made their runs against us, all we could do was to dive off the road and into the bloody muck and mire. It is amazing that we actually suffered so few casualties from the air strikes. In my company, we didn't lose a soul from this day's particular air attack.

At 5:00 P.M., we in Jamerson's 159th Inf. Brig. were ordered to advance to the area between *Cuisy* and Hill 281.[118] Lt. Craighill, Adjutant of 2/317th Infantry remembered:

The men were weary and worn out with the constant marching, taking up positions in support and being on alert at all times to fill any gap that might have occurred. The high ridge just east of Cuisy afforded splendid observation of the surrounding country, and everyone was more or less curious to see exactly what it looked like. Off to the left was a high and prominent peak; with the town of Monfaucon perched upon its crest. The slopes receding gently from about it. To the right snuggling in the valley was Dannevoux, with the heights rising in the distance on the northeast bank of the Meuse, where the Germans had masked their batteries that gave us lots of trouble... The trenches we were now occupying had been formerly manned by the Germans and the old M.G. posts were here and there were guns still mounted. There were hideous wire entanglements in abundance and the ground was literally perforated with shell holes that our barrage of 26 Sept. had made. Back behind us in the valley were dumps of various kinds springing up all around, and the roads were jammed

---

[118] *Cuisy* is pronounced "Que-see."

with supply trucks, artillery, and every kind of motor vehicle. There were gangs of engineers repairing the roads, military police directing traffic, and the whole thing seemed in such a tangle that it almost looked impossible... As evening drew on the smoke from the company kitchens curled up in long snake-like curves, wending its way heavenward, and the smell of crisp bacon, onions, and potatoes came drifting along the valley propelled by a gentle breeze. Carrying parties could be seen coming down the slope with dixies swinging by their side. They were coming back after having taken the welcome supper to the men in the trenches on the ridge. Occasionally the Boche put over a big one, searching for our ration dumps, and he was not always unsuccessful, but for the most part, little harm was done. Our batteries in turn would reply, and then things would kinder quiet down so to speak for the night.[119]

While our brothers in Brett's 160th Inf. Brig. had made rapid progress during the day, breaching *HAGEN* (the first unit to do so) at Gercourt, the 4th (Ivy) Division, on our left, was unable to make an equal advance. Their advance was critical to the overall plan as they, as well as the 30th (Buckeye) Divison were to sweep behind the German Gilbralter at *Montfaucon* while the 79th (Cross of Lorraine) Division was given the inenviable task of attacking it in front. Because the Ivy Division was to envelop Montfaucon, it was Bullard's main effort. And because the corps main effort was held up, Bullard wisely ordered a reserve regiment of an adjoining division (us), to help kick-start their advance.

Bullard ordered Cronkhite to send one infantry regiment from the 80th Division to help the 4th Division envelop *Montfaucon* from the east. Cronkhite chose the 318th Infantry, which was the closest unit to the Ivy Division. The 317th Infantry, the other regiment of Jamerson's 159th Inf. Brig., was to reinforce the 320th Infantry, which was fighting it out at the Triangle from *Bois Sachet*. Bullard's III Corps order stated:[120]

---

[119] As cited in *317th Infantry*, 60-61.

[120] As cited in Stultz, 383.

> U.S. III Corps, A.E.F.
> 1530 hrs. 26 SEPT
>
> 1. Aviation reports indicate Third Position [KRIEMHILDE] is held weakly if at all. No signs of the enemy infantry on east bank of Meuse.
>
> 2. The 3d and 1st Corps have reached [HAGEN]. 5th Corps somewhat in rear. 3d Corps will proceed at once to [GISELHER] in conjunction with 1st Corps.
>
> 3. Intervening hostile Third Position in the 4th Division zone of action will be attacked by the 4th Division, supported by available artillery required for its own progression. Corps Artillery will engage part of its guns in interdiction fire on bridge at Dun-sur-Meuse and roads leading south from this bridge and may reach junctions north of the line to be attacked.
>
> 4. Commanders of 80th Division and Corps Artillery will communicate at once by phone with the Commander, 4th Division, to arrange details. One infantry regiment, 80th Division, is attached to the 4th Division as additional reserve for this operation.
>
> 5. [GISELHER] will be reached before dark and success exploited as heretofore ordered.
>
> Bjornstad
> Chief of Staff

With this order in hand, Cronkhite directed the 319th Infantry, the first American unit to breach *HAGEN*, supported by units from Heiner's 155th Arty. Brig., to take *Dannevoux*. The thought was that it was better to attack now, while the "Third Position [*KRIEMHILDE* was] held weakly if at all." According to Lt. Furr of the 314th M.G.:

> *The Germans were only a few hundred north of us, and they also held the east bank of the Meuse, which placed them directly on our right flank as the division faced north: the 314th M.G. Battalion being on the extreme right of the division sector. The problem of the division at this hour was to make a swinging movement to the right, using the extreme right flank near Dannevoux as a pivot*

or hinge, thus clearing the west bank of the Meuse River of all the enemy in the sector of the division. This was accomplished during the next two days.[121]

The object of the 319th Infantry's attack, *Village Dannevoux*, lies in a deep valley astride *le Meuse*. It is over-looked to the east by *les Côtes de Meuse,* which, in normal times, makes a wonderful *vista*. In holding the dominating heights, however, the Hun with the Gun was able to spit deadly venom in our direction. Sometime around 5:00 P.M., just before the 319th Infantry launched its attack, the commander of the Prussian 7th Reserve Division, headquartered in *Dannevoux*, ordered the town be abandoned and its remaining supplies burned. Boy was that a sight! I mean even we could see the flames if we chose to look in that direction—and many did. Those Germans certainly had lots of stuff!

Needless to say, to order the 319th Infantry to "continue the attack" was far easier said than done, as reorganizing the 319th Infantry in and around *Bois Juré* was near impossible. What compounded the problem was that it was growing darker by the minute, it was beginning to rain again, and the enemy was starting to pound them with high-caliber artillery. Nevertheless, at 9:00 P.M., on the heels of a barrage provided by the 155th Arty. Brig., the 319th Infantry attacked north from *Bois Juré* with Capt. Eagan's 3/319th Infantry, less Company K, on the right, and Maj. Montague's 2/319th Infantry, less Company H, on the left. The 319th M.G. Company advanced in the center and Maj. O'Bear's 1/319 was in reserve. In the darkness, there was considerable confusion on the right as companies from Eagan's 3/319 lost contact with each other. This frenetic movement resulted in a German signal flare which brought down a 30-minute artillery barrage on the eastern edge of *Bois Juré* and *Bois Rond*.

Luckily for them, however, as they had advanced from the woods, few if any were hit.[122] But the same can not be said for many-a Blue Ridge M.G. crew. Lt. Furr of the 314th M.G. Battalion noted that once the infantry moved out of the woods, the M.G. sections which stayed behind, especially those from the 315th M.G. Battalion, got plastered by the noted German artillery strike:

The night was dark and the troops were very tired, having already penetrated the enemy positions to a distance of about eight km, and it was taken for granted by the M.G. officers who had taken up the defensive positions at the farthest point of advance, that the attack of the infantry would not be renewed before morning. Such was not the case, however, as word soon came from the

---

[121] As cited in *314th M.G.*, 33.

[122] *319th Infantry*, 25.

infantry that the advance would be resumed that night... At 10:00 P.M. battalions of the 319th Infantry moved up and forming in front of [our] M.G. positions [and made lots of noise]. The Germans soon got wind of what was happening and up went the S.O.S. signal to their artillery. In short order a German barrage came down into the woods, but the attacking infantry had left the woods, and, in advancing across the open, captured Dannevoux... The barrage lasted about thirty minutes.[123]

As the M.G.ers received a shellacking in the woods, Col. Cocheu's 319th Infantry attacked north across the dark fields and stormed into *Village Dannevoux*, which now consisted of burning houses, barns, and buildings turned-into-warehouses. The fire actually helped as it illuminated the darkness and kept the autumn chill away. The 319th Infantry's attack was in fact so swift that soldiers from the Prussian *Fußartillerie-Bataillon 52* were unable to remove one of their mammoth 380mm howitzers as well as four 127mm guns from *Reserve-Feldartillerie-Regiment Nr. 7* and members of the 319th Infantry secured them as *prix de guerre*.[124] This would bring the total number of captured guns for the 319th Infantry thus far to seven. Soldiers from Capt. Herr's F/2/319th Infantry also found "a wire cage or compound" that was clearly used for German soldiers (*Landsers*) for punishment.[125]

In the meantime, the 320th Infantry, on the left, resumed its attack into Bois Septsarges but was once again stopped cold only a few hundred yards in by the strong GISELHER defenses in Bois Dannevoux. Maj. Ashby Williams of 1/320th Infantry remembered:

Toward evening, it appearing that it would be impossible to advance further that night, we determined to outpost the position and wait for the morrow. I then established a line of defense along the general line of the Cuisy-Gercourt Road and put my men in such shelter as could be found in the piece of woods from which we had taken the sixty prisoners, and Majs. Holt and Emory and I established our headquarters in a dug-out in the [southern edge of Bois Sachet].[126]

---

[123] As cited in *314th M.G.*, 33.

[124] The 380mm German howitzer in question is currently on the grounds of West Point, much to the dismay of the men of the 160th Infantry Brigade as it was they, and not West Point-trained officers, who secured it (no offense to Generals Brett or Cronkhite or Col. Cocheu). To the Germans, "Foot Artillery" means "heavy artillery" and "Field Artillery" means "light artillery."

[125] *2/319th Infantry*, 9.

[126] As cited in *1/320th Infantry*, 84.

Meanwhile, the light batteries of the division, with O.P.s atop Hill 281, fired several counter-battery missions against Hun artillery positions along *Côtes de Meuse*, silencing many of them using a combination of shrapnel and H.E. A/1/313th Artillery in fact "received the personal thanks of General Brett for knocking out one of [guns] that was causing the infantry much trouble." Heiner's artillery also continued to target the bridgehead at *Vilosnes*, as well as the roads that led into it. According to Lt. Henry Baker of F/2/313, some batteries of the 155th Arty. Brig. in fact fired so many rounds that "the guns had to be drenched with water and laid off at intervals to prevent overheating." Before long, however, the artillery had to economize its firing, as ammunition re-supply by the caisson squad of each gun section was slowed by road congestion.[127]

From burned-out *Dannevoux*, patrols from the 319th Infantry were sent north into the wooded heights of *Bois Dannevoux* to probe GISELHER. Army Regulations stressed the importance of Patrolling, especially on the attack:

> *M.M.T. 959. Patrols are small bodies of infantry or cavalry, from two men up to a company or troop, sent out from a command at any time to gain information of the enemy and of the country, to drive off small hostile bodies, to prevent them from observing the command or for other stated objects, such as to blow up a bridge, destroy a railroad track, communicate or keep in touch with friendly troops, etc. Patrols are named according to their objects, reconnoitering, visiting, connecting, exploring, flanking patrols, etc. These names are of no importance, however, because the patrol's orders in each case determine its duties.*
>
> *M.M.T. 960. The size of a patrol depends upon the mission it is to accomplish; if it is to gain information only, it should be as small as possible, allowing two men for each probable message to be sent (this permits you to send messages and still have a working patrol remaining); if it is to fight, it should be strong enough to defeat the probable enemy against it. For instance, a patrol of two men might be ordered to examine some high ground a few hundred yards off the road. On the other hand, during the recent war in Manchuria a Japanese patrol of fifty mounted men, to accomplish its mission marched 1,160 miles in the enemy's country and was out for sixty-two days.*
>
> *M.M.T. 961. Patrol Leaders. (a) Patrol leaders, usually noncommissioned officers, are selected for their endurance, keen eyesight, ability to think quickly*

---

[127] *313th Artillery*, 32.

and good military judgment. They should be able to read a map, make a sketch and send messages that are easily understood. Very important patrols are sometimes lead by officers. The leader should have a map, watch, field glass, compass, message blank and pencils. (b) The ability to lead a patrol correctly without a number of detailed orders or instructions, is one of the highest and most valuable qualifications of a noncommissioned officer. Since a commander ordering out a patrol can only give general instructions as to what he desires, because he cannot possibly forsee just what situations may arise, the patrol leader will be forced to use his own judgment to decide on the proper course to pursue when something of importance suddenly occurs. He is in sole command on the spot and must make his decisions entirely on his own judgment and make them instantly. He has to bear in mind first of all his mission—what his commander wants him to do. Possibly something may occur that should cause the patrol leader to undertake an entirely new mission and he must view the new situation from the standpoint of a higher commander. (c) More battles are lost through lack of information about the enemy than from any other cause, and it is the patrols led by noncommissioned officers who must gather almost all of this information. A battalion or squadron stands a very good chance for defeating a regiment if the battalion commander knows all about the size, position and movements of the regiment and the regimental commander knows but a little about the battalion; and this will all depend on how efficiently the patrols of the two forces are led by the noncommissioned officers. 962. Patrols are usually sent out from the advance party of an advance guard, the rear party of a rear guard, the outguards of an outpost, and the flank (extreme right or left) sections, companies or troops of a force in a fight, but they may be sent out from any part of a command. The commander usually states how strong a patrol shall be.

M.M.T. 963. Orders or Instructions—(a) The orders or instructions for a patrol must state clearly whenever possible: 1. Where the enemy is or is supposed to be. 2. Where friendly patrols or detachments are apt to be seen or encountered and what the plans are for the body from which the patrol is sent out. 3. What object the patrol is sent out to accomplish; what information is desired; what features are of special importance; the general direction to be followed and how long to stay out in case the enemy is not met. 4. Where reports are to be sent. (b) It often happens that, in the hurry and excitement of a sudden encounter or other situation, there is no time or opportunity to give a patrol leader anything but the briefest instructions, such as "Take three men, corporal, and locate their (the enemy's) right flank." In such a case the patrol leader through his knowledge of the general principles of patrolling, combined with the exercise of his common sense, must determine for himself just what his commander wishes him to do.

M.M.T. 964. Inspection of a Patrol Before Departure. Whenever there is time and conditions permit, which most frequently is not the case, a patrol leader carefully inspects his men to see that they are in good physical condition; that they have the proper equipment, ammunition and ration; that their canteens are full, their horses (if mounted) are in good condition, not of a conspicuous color and not given to neighing, and that there is nothing about the equipment to rattle or glisten. The patrol leader should also see that the men have nothing with them (maps, orders, letters, newspapers, etc.) that, if captured, would give the enemy valuable information. This is a more important inspection than that regarding the condition of the equipment. Whenever possible the men for a patrol should be selected for their trustworthiness, experience and knack of finding their way in a strange country.

M.M.T. 965. Preparing a Patrol for the Start. The patrol leader having received his orders and having asked questions about anything he does not fully understand, makes his estimate of the situation (See Par. 950.) He then selects the number of men he needs, if this has been left to him, inspects them and carefully explains to them the orders he has received and how he intends to carry out these orders, making sure the men understand the mission of the patrol. He names some prominent place along the route they are going to follow where every one will hasten if the patrol should become scattered.

The Company in Scouting And Patrolling.

M.M.T. 1081. The general principles of patrolling are explained in Par. 959; so we need not repeat them here. Many of the principles of scouting are, in reality, nothing but the fundamentals of patrolling, and the main function of scouting, reconnoitering, is also the function of a certain class of patrols. So, we see that scouting and patrolling are inseparably connected, and the importance of training the members of the company in the principles of scouting is, therefore, evident.

M.M.T. 1082. Requisites of a good Scout. A man, to make a good scout, should possess the following qualifications: Have good eyesight and hearing; Be active, intelligent and resourceful; Be confident and plucky; Be healthy and strong; Be able to swim, signal, read a map, make a rough sketch, and, of course, read and write.

M.M.T. 1083. Eyesight and Hearing. To be able to use the eye and the ear quickly and accurately is one of the first principles of successful scouting. Quickness and accuracy of sight and hearing are to a great extent a matter of training and practice. The savage, for instance, almost invariably has quick eyesight and good hearing, simply from continual practice. Get into the habit of seeing, observing, things—your eyesight must never be resting, but must be continually glancing around, in every direction, and seeing different objects. As you walk along through the country get into the habit of noticing hoof-prints, wheel-ruts, etc., and observing the trees, houses, streams, animals, men, etc., that you pass. Practice looking at distant objects and discovering objects in the distance. On seeing distant signs, do not jump at a conclusion as to what they are, but watch and study them carefully first. Get into the habit of listening for sounds and of distinguishing by what different sounds are made.

M.M.T. 1084. Finding Your Way in a Strange Country. The principal means of finding one's way in a strange country are by map reading, asking the way, the points of the compass and landmarks. Map Reading. This, of course, presupposes the possession of a map. The subject of map reading is explained in Paras. 1859 to 1877. Asking the Way. In civilized countries one has no trouble in finding his way by asking, provided, of course, he speaks the language. If in a foreign country, learn as soon as you can the equivalent of such expressions as "What is the way to—?" "Where is —?" "What is the name of this place?," and a few other phrases of a similar nature. Remember, however, that the natives may sometimes deceive you in their answers. Points of the Compass. A compass is, of course, the best, quickest and simplest way of determining the directions, except in localities where there is much iron, in which case it becomes very unreliable. For determining the points of the compass by means of the North Star and the face of a watch, see Para. 1096. The points of the compass can also be ascertained by facing the sun in the morning and spreading out your arms straight from the body. Before you is east; behind you, west; to your right, south; to your left, north. The points of the compass can be determined by noting the limbs and bark of trees. The bark on the north side of trees is thicker and rougher than that on the south side, and moss is most generally found near the roots on the north side. The limbs and branches are generally longer on the south side of the trees, while the branches on the north are usually knotty, twisted and drooped. The tops of pine trees dip or trend to the north.

M.M.T. 1085. Lost. In connection with finding your way through strange country, it may be said, should you find you have lost your way, do not lose your head. Keep cool—try not to let your brains get into your feet. By this we mean don't run around and make things worse, and play yourself out. First of all, sit down and think; cool off. Then climb a tree, or hill, and endeavor to locate some familiar object you passed, so as to retrace your steps. If it gets dark and you are not in hostile territory, build a good big fire. The chances are you have been missed by your comrades and if they see the fire, they will conclude you are there and will send out for you. Also, if not in hostile territory, distress signals may be given by firing your rifle, but don't waste all your ammunition. If you find a stream, follow it; it will generally lead somewhere—where civilization exists. The tendency of people who are lost is to travel in a circle uselessly. Remember this important rule: Always notice the direction of the compass when you start out, and what changes of direction you make afterwards.

M.M.T. 1086. Landmarks. Landmarks or prominent features of any kind are a great assistance in finding one's way in a strange country. In starting out, always notice the hills, conspicuous trees, high buildings, towers, rivers, etc. For example, if starting out on a reconnaissance you see directly to the north of you a mountain, it will act as a guide without your having to refer to your compass or the sun. If you should start from near a church, the steeple will serve as a guide or landmark when you start to make your way back. When you pass a conspicuous object, like a broken gate, a strangely shaped rock, etc., try to remember it, so that should you desire to return that way, you can do so by following the chain of landmarks. On passing such landmarks always see what they look like from the other side; for, that will be the side from which you will first see them upon the return, trip. The secret of never getting lost is to note carefully the original direction in which you start, and after that to note carefully all landmarks. Get in the habit of doing this in time of peace—it will then become second nature for you to do it in time of war. It may sometimes be necessary, especially in difficult country, such as when traveling through a forest, and over broken mountains and ravines, for you to make your own landmarks for finding your way back by "blazing" (cutting pieces of bark from the trees), breaking small branches off bushes, piling up stones, making a line across a crossroad or path you did not follow, etc.

M.M.T. 1087. Concealment and Dodging. Both in scouting and patrolling it must be remembered not only that it is important you should get information, but it is also fully as important that the enemy should not know you have the information—hence, the necessity of hiding yourself. And remember, too, if you keep yourself hidden, not only will you probably be able to see twice as much of what the enemy is doing, but it may also save you from being captured, wounded or killed. Should you find the enemy has seen you, it is often advisable to pretend that you have not seen him, or that you have other men with you by signaling to imaginary comrades. As far as possible, keep under cover by traveling along hedges, banks, low ground, etc. If moving over open country, make your way as quickly as possible from one clump of trees or bushes to another; or, from rocks, hollows or such other cover as may exist, to other cover. As soon as you reach new cover, look around and examine your surroundings carefully. Do not have about you anything that glistens, and at night be careful not to wear anything that jingles or rattles. And remember that at night a lighted match can be seen as far as 900 yards and a lighted cigarette nearly 300 yards. In looking through a bush or over the top of a hill, break off a leafy branch and hold it in front of your face. In selecting a tree, tower or top of a house or other lookout place from which to observe the enemy from concealment, always plan beforehand how you would make your escape, if discovered and pursued. A place with more than one avenue of escape should be selected, so that if cut off in one direction you can escape from the other. For example, should the enemy reach the foot of a tower in which you are, you would be completely cut off, while if he reached a house on whose roof you happened to be, you would have several avenues of escape. Although trees make excellent lookout places, they must, for the same reasons as towers, be used with caution. In this connection it may be remarked unless one sees foot marks leading to a tree, men are apt not to look up in trees for the enemy—hence, be careful not to leave foot marks. When in a tree, either stand close against the trunk, or lie along a large branch, so that your body will look like a part of the trunk or branch. In using a hill as a lookout place, do not make the common mistake of showing yourself on the skyline. Reach the top of the hill slowly and gradually by crouching down and crawling, and raise your head above the crest by inches. In leaving, lower your head gradually and crawl away by degrees, as any quick or sudden movement on the skyline is likely to attract attention. And, remember, just because you don't happen to see the enemy that is no sign that he is not about. At maneuvers and in exercises soldiers continually make the mistake of exposing themselves on the skyline. At night confine yourself as much as possible to low ground, ditches, etc. This will keep you down in the dark and will enable you, in turn, to see outlined against the higher ground any enemy that may approach you. At night especially, but also during the day, the enemy will expect you along roads and paths, as it is easier to travel along roads and paths than across country and they also serve as good guides in finding your way. As a rule, it is best to use the road until it brings you near the enemy and then leave it and travel across country. You will thus be able better to avoid the outposts and patrols that will surely be watching the roads. Practice in time of peace the art of concealing yourself and observing passers-by. Conceal yourself near some frequented road and imagine the people traveling over it are enemies whose numbers you wish to count and whose conversation you wish to overhear.

The aggressive squad-sized night patrols of Col. Cocheu's 319th Infantry apparently took the Germans by total surprise. For example, some were taken prisoner while asleep in their defensive positions! Another of their dugouts was left in such a hurry that they had left their good calcium carbide light burning. The Hun prisoners in fact reported that they did not think that the Americans would renew their attack after dark and admitted to soldiers from the 319th Infantry that they had reached the west bank of the Meuse just in time to prevent reinforcement from crossing the bridge at Vilosones.[128]

---

[128] *319th Infantry*, 25.

Many soldiers of the 319th Infantry were cited for bravery for their actions on Sept. 26. Among them were Capt. Erskine Gordon, commander of Company D, for taking out several enemy M.G.s while advancing up the regiment's axis of advance. Capt. Charles Herr, commander of Company F was recognized for being slightly wounded and not leaving his command. Lt. James Hudnall of Company G was cited "for the skillful handling of his platoon and the direction of effective rifle grenade fire against a M.G. nest." Lt. George Tighlman of Company I was cited for leading his platoon even after his arm was "badly shattered by shrapnel in Bois Juré."[129]

By nightfall, the officers and men of Brett's 160th Inf. Brig., as well as those from the light artillery regiments of Heiner's 155th Arty. Brig., were pretty well spent. They had been up for over two days hours straight, had broken through one of the strongest defensive lines in history (*HAGEN*), and had advanced some seven to eight km from Béthincourt to Dannevoux. After posting sentinels, the men in the rifle companies tried to get some shut-eye in the light drizzle and waited for further orders, which were certainly going to be "attack north." Maj. Ashby Williams of 1/320th Infantry remembered:

That was not an unpleasant night we [i.e., the battalion commanders of the 320th Infantry] spent in the little dug-out on the edge of [Bois Sachet]. We talked over the events of the day and made plans for the morrow. Besides, this place in which the anxious Boche had slept the night before, was not an unpleasant place to be. There was no occasion to woo sleep; sleep was at a premium that night. It was decided that one of the battalion commanders should be on duty at all times during the night and Majors Holt and Emory and I drew turns for the two hours up. Maj. Emory drew the first, Maj. Holt the second, and I the third. I took my four hours' sleep in a little alcove on a chicken wire cot with my gas mask under my head.[130]

Those in the artillery, however, especially those assigned to the caisson squads, were pretty much up all night (again), hauling ammunition up from the corps depot that was between *Béthincourt* and *Mort Homme*. Even worse, on Hill 281 with the light batteries of the 313th and 314th Artillery, the artillerists were plagued by no less than three gas attacks. It is believed by many that the drills imposed by the British or battery gas N.C.O.s before and during the offensive is the reason why the division had suffered so few gas casualties. Invariably, however,

---

[129] As cited in *319th Infantry*, 28.

[130] As cited in *1/320th Infantry*, 85.

things did go wrong. During one such attack, for example, Driver Ejnar Kragh of F/2/313th Artillery, from Ripley, N.Y., "could not find his mask in the dark. He reached frantically for all in sight but somebody beat him each time. In desperation he ran, still holding his breath, to the picket line, found his horse, and triumphantly returned with a horse mask stretched over his face, just in time to hear Lt. Paul Crosbie of Michigan yell disgustingly: 'Remove your masks, no gas here.'"[131]

Just before midnight, Lt. Tappan Gregory of Chicago, Illinois, the Telephone Officer of the 313th Artillery and his detail got through the gas and shell fire in *Dannevoux,* bringing their usual "on the job" telephone line. These wire men had to be experts in map-reading, patrolling, night-orientation, and defense against gas and artillery attack. It was actually a very dangerous job given the 1,001 ways to die on a battlefield, including "friendly fire." According to Lt. Gregory: "The moon shone in fits and spurts as the clouds drifted across its face. The valley to the rear glistened in a cloud of mist and gas. On the front slope an occasional incendiary shell burst with huge balls of fire and red streamers."[132]

Aside from our problems, Pershing had problems, too. The first revolved around disorganization and general command confusion. Several divisions had showed signs of perplexity at all levels of command. He felt (rightly or wrongly) that too many division and brigade commanders were out of touch, that too many regimental commanders were incompetent or otherwise incapacitated, and that captains and lieutenants at the battalion and company levels did not have enough training or experience to solve the tactical problems. The only cure to all of this was experience, but at what cost?

The second and more serious problem revolved around logistics. As soon as the main attack began after dawn on Sept. 26, traffic piled up behind the lines as artillery, ambulances, supply wagons, and infantry reinforcements clogged the few available roads to the front. These traffic jams had lengthened throughout the day, making movement practically impossible. By midnight it became disturbingly apparent that the American First Army, acting in concert with the French Fourth Army to the west, would have to continue the attack without further artillery support or additional supplies of ammunition, food, or water, all of which remained stuck on the roads, and that the wounded would have to spend the next day in the open, without access to medical care except for field dressings. In other words, we front line units would have to attack with what we had, which was dwindling each hour.

---

[131] As cited in *313th Artillery,* 33.

[132] As cited in *Ibid,* 43.

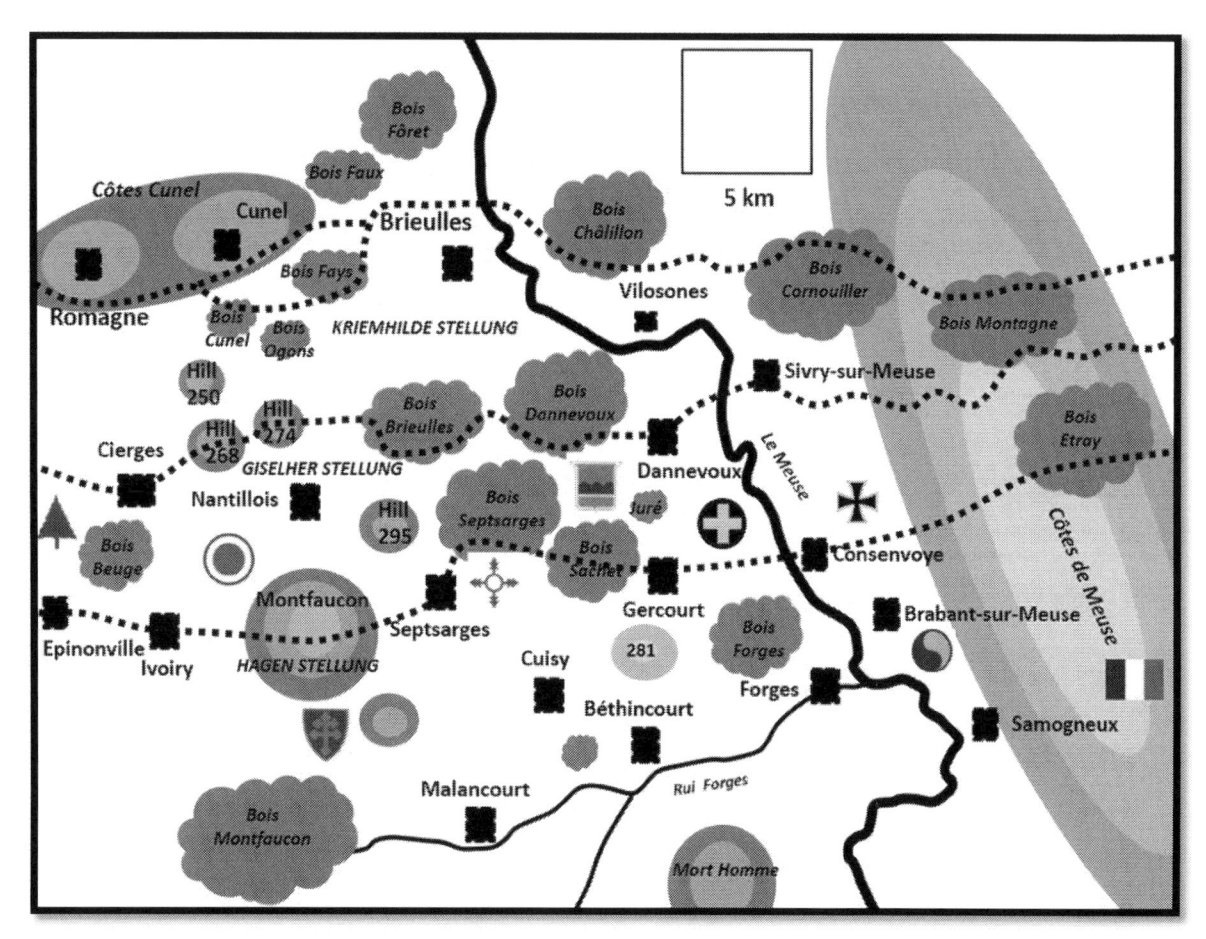

80th Inf. Div. Area of Operations, Sept. 27, 1918. While the 33d "Prairie" and "Blue Ridge" Divisions were to hold the right, the 4th "Ivy" and 37th "Buckeye" Divisions were to conduct a double-envelopment against Montfaucon on the left. The 79th "Cross of Lorraine" Division was still hung-up in front of Montfaucon, the lynch-pin of the German defenses in the area.

"Transport Congestion" at Hill 304, *Béthincourt*, Sept. 27, 1918" (L) and "Moving Forward up the Meuse-Argonne" (R).

In destroyed villes like this (L), the Hun would turn into company strong points, backed by M.G.s. "No Man's Land south of Malancourt" (R).

"Nine km in two days. This was the advance made by the 80th Div. after the jump-off in the Meuse-Argonne beginning Sept. 26. Here are seen the commanding general of the division, Maj. Gen. Adelbert Cronkhite and Col. William H. Waldron, Chief of Staff. They are examining a map of the sector on their front" (L) and Brig. Gen. George Jamerson (second from L), commander of the 159th Inf. Brig., confers with Maj. Gen. Cronkhite (second from R).

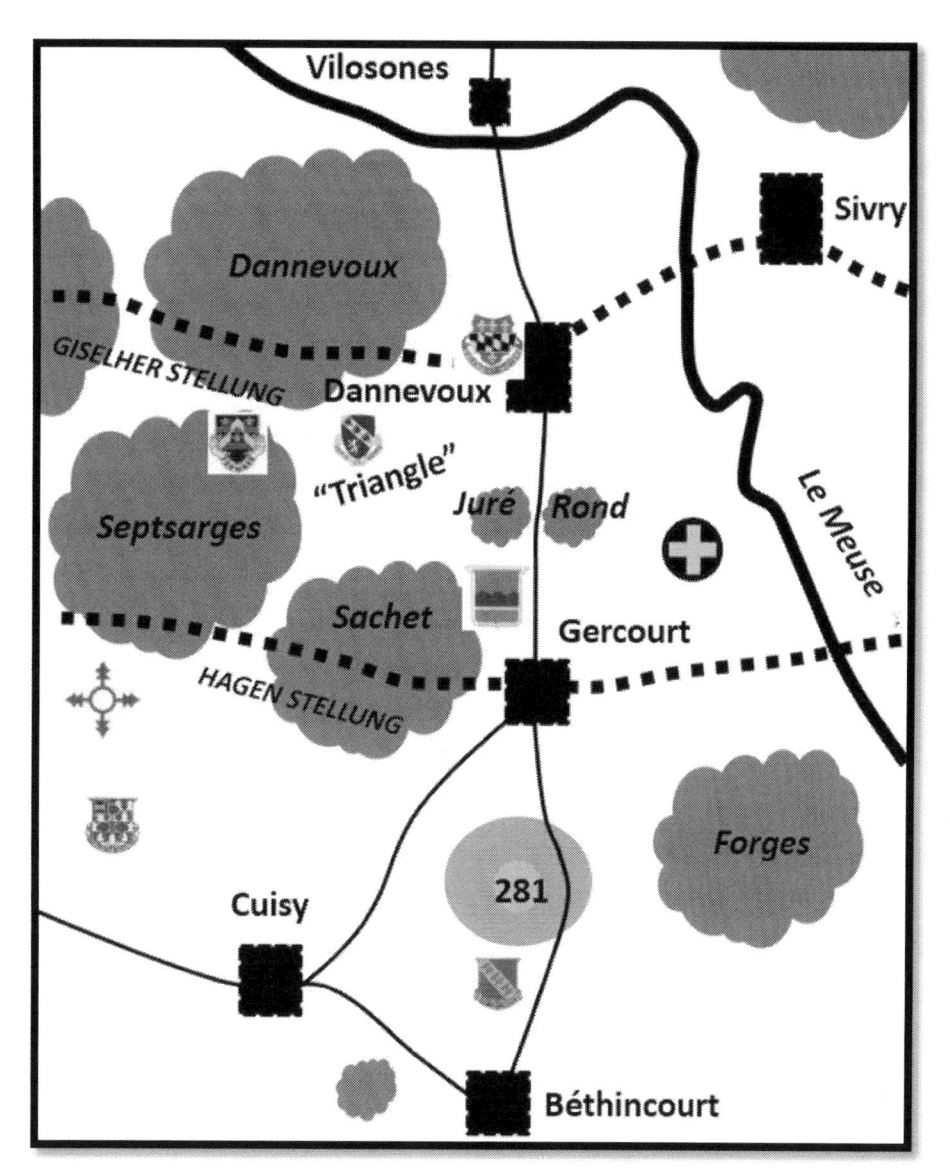

80th Inf. Div. Area of Operations, Sept. 27, 1918. While the 317th Inf. moved forward to support the 319th and 320th Inf. Regts., the 318th Inf. moved left to support the 4th "Ivy Division." The 155th Arty. Bde. was massed behind Hill 281 and between Cuisy and Béthincourt.

317th Inf. Mortar team at rest near Bois Brieulles (L) and *Generalfeldmarschall* Paul von Hindenburg, *der Kaiser*, and *General der Infantrie* (lt. gen.) Erich von Ludendorff (R).

"Camouflaged guns in the foreground at Montfaucon, Sept. 28, 1918" (L) and "French tank. Montfaucon, 9-28-18. Going into action north of Septsarges." This is a French *Schneider* medium tank (R). Of all the tanks I saw, this was my favorite design.

"American Wounded Making Way to Aid Station" by George Matthews Harding (L) and "American Plane, Gercourt. One of the first to come down in the Meuse-Argonne, 9-28-18" (R). The areoplanes were so flimsy that we called them "motorized kites."

"Ruins of Montfaucon" (L) and "Decorations of the U.S.A." *A.B.M.C.*

317th M.G. Section "Advaning in Parts" north through Bois Sachet.

Looking east across *GISELHER* into the Valley of the Meuse and the Heights of the Meuse (background). *Village Dannevoux* is off the picture to the right. This is near where 1/A/313th Arty. engaged Hun targets across the river on Sept. 27 (L) and "Looking north up the Valley of the Meuse" (R). In this vicinity, units from the 319th Inf. and the 313th Arty. engaged targets on *les Côtes de Meuse*. In this area, the Germans had a communication bridge that they destroyed on the evening of Sept. 26, 1918.

314th Arty. "Guns in Observation" (L) and German Chancellor Friedrich Ebert of the Social Democratic Party (S.P.D.) of Germany (R).

Chapter 3
The Battle for *GISELHER* (Sept. 27-30, 1918).

September 27, 1918.

Weather: Fair.

Roads: Poor.

During the early-morning hours of Sept. 27, we Blue Ridge Boys of the 318th Infantry marched north up a narrow, muddy road in column of two's expecting to find yet another traffic jam of epic proportions—this time as we slogged our way northwest into *Cuisy*. We were not disappointed and much valuable time was spent trying to snake our way "over, under, or through" the congested area (we called such circumstances a "goat rope"). At around 3:00 A.M., on a pitch black, cold, and rainy night, we finally marched into *Cuisy* where we were directed to turn off the road and to establish a "bivi" of sorts in a ravine just southeast of the blown-up village. Our regimental commander, Col. Woorilow, reported to the 4th Division's commanding general for further instructions and subsequently established his P.C. on the church steps in the town square. As for we Doughs, we checked our gear, tried to top-off our canteens, and grabbed a morsel or two from our haversacks, which were attached to our packs. At last resort, we had two cans of "E-Rats," which consisted of a can of meat or corned-beef hash, crackers, and chocolate bars. The cans of meat were usually British (or Canadian) beef that we called "Bully Beef" or "Monkey Meat" or corned-beef hash that we called "Corn Willy." The joke often was: "What's for breakfast?"

"Corn Willy, hard tack, and coffee."

"What's for lunch?"

"Hard tack, coffee, and corn willy."

"What's for supper?"

"Coffee, corn willy, and hard tack."

Sleeping under these conditions is near-impossible, although a few minutes, here and there, can be stolen. I especially remember tightening my mud-encrusted putties that dark, foreboding night in *Cuisy*. At first, I didn't like the putties—preferring our original leggings. The putties are a pain to put on and get to look right, etc. But once in combat, I realized that they were actually easier to adjust, given the fact that the buttons on the old leggings would have been extremely difficult to remove with cold fingers and cold, mud-encrusted metal buttons.

Over on the right, with the majority of the 80th Division, at 3:30 A.M., Sept. 27, after a few hours' of fitful sleep in the bloody mire, the Blue Ridge Boys in the forward lines were ordered to dig fox holes with their intenching tools, staying away from the trunks and roots of trees. Battalion commanders sent out squad or even platoon-sized patrols to connect with units on the left or right, and supply wagons were brought forward to restock the men with water, food, and ammunition. According to the *I.D.R*:

Ammunition Supply.

548. The combat train is the immediate reserve supply of the battalion, and the major is responsible for its proper use. He will take measures to insure the maintenance of the prescribed allowance at all times. In the absence of instructions, he will cause the train to march immediately in rear of his battalion, and, upon separating from it to enter an engagement, will cause the ammunition therein to be issued. When emptied, he will direct that the wagons proceed to the proper rendezvous to be refilled. Ordinarily a rendezvous is appointed for each brigade and the necessary number of wagons sent forward to it from the ammunition column.

549. When refilled, the combat wagons will rejoin their battalions, or, if the latter be engaged, will join or establish communication with the regimental reserve.

550. Company commanders are responsible that the belts of the men in their companies are kept filled at all times, except when the ammunition is being expended in action. In the firing line the ammunition of the dead and wounded should be secured whenever practicable.

551. Ammunition in the bandoleers will ordinarily be expended first. Thirty rounds in the right pocket section of the belt will be held as a reserve, to be expended only when ordered by an officer.

552. When necessary to resupply the firing line, ammunition will be sent forward with reenforcements, generally from the regimental reserve. Men will never be sent back from the firing line for ammunition. Men sent forward with ammunition remain with the firing line.

553. As soon as possible after an engagement the belts of the men and the combat wagons are resupplied to their normal capacities. Ammunition which can not be reloaded on combat wagons will be piled up in a convenient place and left under guard.

During the frenzied fighting of the previous day, too many men of Brett's 160th Inf. Brig., against Army Regulations, apparently ditched most of their gear except their weapons and ammunition. Although this allowed them to pursue the Hun more easily, the loss of canteen, slicker, blanket, etc., began to be felt. There was no water to be found except that found in shell holes, which was usually tainted with mustard gas. Those who had kept their canteens and packs shared with those who had not. Luckily for the men, canned tomatoes somehow arrived ahead of the water carts and they were promptly punctured the contents quickly slurped down. Lt. Lukens of 3/320th Infantry, in Bois Sachet, remembered:

> *The ground was damp, a chilly night had followed a day of profuse sweating and we had not carried our blankets, as a man cannot fight with a heavy pack. Lt. France and I had been lucky enough to find a "Jerry" blanket in one of those shanties, and a few of the others did the same, but even with them our teeth chattered all night, and it must have been a good deal worse for those who were less lucky.*[133]

The decision to carry all of one's gear into battle or not is actually a difficult one. For an infantryman "Up the Line," especially on the attack, his life-expectancy is short—life is cheap. What's better? "Stripping down for the fight" but then freezing at night, being bereft of blanket, slicker, or shelter half, or carrying everything, slowing one's advance and increasing his chances of getting killed or horribly wounded but "sleeping" in tolerable comfort during the night? Because life was cheap, and living into the next day was a thought that a Dough dare not embrace, most chose to ditch their gear and suffer through the night if they in fact survived the day's fighting. "It's better to come down with pneumonia than be cut down by a bullet" many would reason. Besides, pneumonia would get one "off the line" once his temperature topped 104°. For me, I think it's best to compromise because most of us, in fact, did make it to the next day and the next and the next. Coming down with pneumonia wouldn't have helped anybody—not the the soldier, the unit, the Army, nor the nation. Granted, moving through the tore-up woods, which looked more like a tornado blow-down than a glen in which Little Red Riding Hood strode, was tough—almost impossible. And always moving forward with a pack strapped to one's back didn't make it any easier. During those times—getting through a difficult obstacle—take the pack off. Have a partner hold it for you, put it back on, and then continue the advance. Did we need two blankets, a slicker, and a shelter-half while we advanced? No. Would it have been good to at least have the slicker and shelter half on hand? Yes, and that's what many of us did. That's what I did. In fact, Getz and I agreed to carry different pieces of gear so we

---

[133] As cited in *3/320th Infantry*, 66.

would not go without. For example, I carried a blanket and Getz carried a shelter half and a slicker.

As for using captured enemy gear, like Lt. Lukens of I/3/320th Infantry noted when he took possession of a Hun blanket, one does take a chance with "cooties." But again, it comes down to: "What would you rather have? Pneumonia or cooties?" The lieutenant wisely chose "cooties" because he knew that he'd probably get them anyway and, when all was said and done, lice can be cleared up fairly easily compared to other maladies, like pneumonia. These choices, although foreign to a person living in civilization, were very important ones for we Doughs who had to survive "Up the Line" in the Animal Kingdom.

As was already stated, nighttime is a bevy of activity for the artillery, especially for the drivers of the caisson squads who rolled back to the corps ammunition point to re-supply their batteries under the cover of darkness and they weren't the only ones on the road. Capt. Peck of the 319th Infantry remembered that "the roads in rear were cut-up badly but were repaired as quickly as possible. But, notwithstanding the rapidity with which they were made passable, the congestion of traffic rendered it impossible for the necessary transport to keep up with the infantry."[134] While the artillery caissons wove their way to the rear, the men of the gun squads generally hunkered down and shot an occasional fire mission. Several men from Capt. Clarence Brown's E/2/314th Artillery noted that they had scooped up abandoned German uniform items, such as low-quarter boots, and wore them instead of their worn-out Army brogans. Like many Doughs with Brett's 160th Inf. Brig., many-a Blue Ridge Artillerist also rolled up in discarded German blankets, which, to their great dismay, were also laced with "cooties." In fact, lice bites became just another threat to the health of a Doughboy operating in France.[135]

"How many ways are there to die here?" I'd sarcastically ask Getz.

"Well it depends, Rid."

"It depends on what?"

"Well there are about a thousand ways to die here. For example, let's say you're brushing your teeth with that nasty brush but forget to wash it off. And suppose that brush got coated with some Chlorine gas. And suppose you stuck that brush in your mouth when..."

"...When a Heinie aeroplane came a-swoopin' in and..."

"...Dropped a can of Monkey meat on your head..."

---

[134] As cited in *319th Infantry*, 27.

[135] *3/320th Infantry*, 64.

At 4:30 A.M., the 80th Division was ordered our corps commander "Eugene" Bullard (that's what Getz and I called him, and I don't know why) to renew its attack against *GISELHER* in the vicinity of Dannevoux and to head for Brieulles and *KRIEMHILDE*.

Ha! Fat chance.

In compliance with the order, at 6:30 A.M. the 317th and 320th Infantry, in the center of the division line (the 318th Infantry was on the left and the 319th Infantry was on the right), attacked *Bois Dannevoux* from *Bois Septsarges* and *Sachet*. The 319th Infantry, which had already taken most of *Dannevoux*, supported the attack on the right. In attacking north through *Bois Septsarges* with elements of the 4th (Ivy) Division, the 320th Infantry was once again tasked with taking out M.G. positions that were arrayed in inter-locking fields of fire and protected by wire entanglements. Lt. Lukens remembered how his unit took out one of these positions, pretty much matching what became our S.O.P. for this important but dangerous task:

> *Attempts were being made to bow out a M.G. nest at the head of the path with R.G.s. The platoon along the trail was lying flat, a heavy stream of bullets cutting the twigs just above them, though an advance of a few more yards would have brought them over a little cleft in the slope where the bullets were just skimming the ground. Lt. Schultz of Company K came up the path as coolly as though it had been a village street, and learned that several rifle grenades had missed their aim, so taking a rifle from one of the men he advanced up the path with Sergeant Barnhart, to try another shot. A burst from the M.G.s was heard, and an instant later we saw the sergeant running up the path, carrying Lt. Schultz limp in his arms, a perfect hail of bullets playing about them. How he got down to the safety of the swale, running at full height, seemed a miracle. He could have crawled down, dragging the wounded officer with him, in comparative safety, but his one idea was to get him to a place where his wound could be instantly attended to. The lieutenant was already beyond medical help, with a clean hole through the abdomen, against which the utmost promptness and skill would have been useless, and there in the woods he died, too stunned to suffer, in less than five minutes. He was the first of our battalion to die, and a braver one had never lived among us. Sergeant Barnhart was awarded the Distinguished Service Cross for his gallant effort to save him.*[136]

---

[136] As cited in *Ibid*, 68-69.

According *I.D.R.*, the basics of "Military Leadership" are prescribed this way:

358. The art of leadership consists of applying sound tactical principles to concrete cases on the battle field. Self-reliance, initiative, aggressiveness, and a conception of teamwork are the fundamental characteristics of successful leadership.

359. A correct grasp of the situation and a definite plan of action form the soundest basis for a successful combat. A good plan once adopted and put into execution should not be abandoned unless it becomes clear that it can not succeed. Afterthoughts are dangerous, except as they aid in the execution of details in the original plan.

360. Combats that do not promise success or some real advantage to the general issue should be avoided; they cause unnecessary losses, impair the morale of one's own troops, and raise that of the enemy.

361. Complicated maneuvers are not likely to succeed in war. All plans and the methods adopted for carrying them into effect must be simple and direct.

362. Order and cohesion must be maintained within the units if success is to be expected.

363. Officers must show themselves to be true leaders. They must act in accordance with the spirit of their orders and must require of their troops the strictest discipline on the field of battle.

364. The best results are obtained when leaders know the capacity and traits of those whom they command; hence in making detachments units should not be broken up, and a deployment that would cause an intermingling of the larger units in the firing line should be avoided.

365. Leading is difficult when troops are deployed. A high degree of training and discipline and the use of close order formations to the fullest extent possible are therefore required.

366. In order to lighten the severe physical strain inseparable from infantry service in campaign, constant efforts must be made to spare the troops unnecessary hardship and fatigue; but when necessity arises, the limit of endurance must be exacted.

367. When officers or men belonging to fighting troops leave their proper places to carry back, or to care for, wounded during the progress of the action, they are guilty of skulking. This offense must be repressed with the utmost vigor.

370. The latitude allowed to officers is in direct proportion to the size of their commands. Each should see to the general execution of his task, leaving to the proper subordinates the supervision of details, and interfering only when mistakes are made that threaten to seriously prejudice the general plan.

Teamwork.

371. The comparatively wide fronts of deployed units increase the difficulties of control. Subordinates must therefore be given great latitude in the execution of their tasks. The success of the whole depends largely upon how well each subordinate coordinates his work with the general plan. A great responsibility is necessarily thrown upon subordinates, but responsibility stimulates the right kind of an officer.

372. In a given situation it is far better to do any intelligent thing consistent with the aggressive execution of the general plan, than to search hesitatingly for the ideal. This is the true rule of conduct for subordinates who are required to act upon their own initiative. A subordinate who is reasonably sure that his intended action is such as would be ordered by the commander, were the latter present and in possession of the facts, has enough encouragement to go ahead confidently. He must possess the loyalty to carry out the plans of his superior and the keenness to recognize and to seize opportunities to further the general plan.

373. Independence must not become license. Regardless of the number of subordinates who are apparently supreme in their own restricted spheres, there is but one battle and but one supreme will to which all must conform. Every subordinate must therefore work for the general result. He does all in his power to insure cooperation between the subdivisions under his command. He transmits important information to adjoining units or to superiors in rear and, with the assistance of information received, keeps himself and his subordinates duly posted as to the situation.

374. When circumstances render it impracticable to consult the authority issuing an order, officers should not hesitate to vary from such order when it is clearly based upon an incorrect view of the situation, is impossible of execution, or has been rendered impracticable on account of changes which have occurred since its promulgation. In the application of this rule the responsibility for mistakes rests upon the subordinate, but unwillingness to assume responsibility on proper occasions is indicative of weakness. Superiors should be careful not to censure an apparent disobedience where the act was done in the proper spirit and to advance the general plan.

375. When the men of two or more units intermingle in the firing line, all officers and men submit at once to the senior. Officers and platoon guides seek to fill vacancies caused by casualties. Each seizes any opportunity to exercise the functions consistent with his grade, and all assist in the maintenance of order and control. Every lull in the action should be utilized for as complete restoration of order in the firing line as the ground or other conditions permit.

376. Any officer or noncommissioned officer who becomes separated from his proper unit and can not rejoin must at once place himself and his command at the disposal of the nearest higher commander. Anyone having completed an assigned task must seek to rejoin his proper command. Failing in this, he should join the nearest troops engaged with the enemy.

377. Soldiers are taught the necessity of remaining with their companies, but those who become detached must join the nearest company and serve with it until the battle is over or reorganization is ordered.

Due to the density of the woods and the strength of the enemy defenses, the 317th and 320th Infantry Regiments were unable to breach *GISELHER* and were pretty much *hors de combat* for the rest of the day.[137] Companies from different battalions were mixed, platoons from different companies were mixed, etc. Lt. Lukens of I/3/320th Infantry remembered trying to claw his way north with an odd-collection of units from regiment: "Parts of C, I, K Companies were there, totaling perhaps 350 men—we were off our sector, to the left and front of our regiment and completely cut-off from communication with our battalion commander, and with nothing to prevent *les Boche* from cutting off our rear."[138] Over on the right, with the 319th Infantry, things fared no better. Because of the strong defenses in *Bois Dannevoux*, (they met "sturdy opposition from the high ground in *Bois Dannevoux* to which *les Boche* had retired and fortified himself with many M.G.s"), General Brett called off the attack until far-more supporting arms could be pushed forward. [139] As such, the 160th Inf. Brig. (+) established a

---

[137] *Hors de combat* is a legal term for "taken out of combat." It is pronounced "Oars day com-bat."

[138] As cited in *3/320th Infantry*, 70.

[139] As cited in *1/320th Infantry*, 87.

defense in depth (two lines) in the vicinity of the Triangle. On the right, around *Village Dannevoux*, Capt. Josiah Peck of H.Q./319th Infantry remembered:

> *Early on the morning of 27 Sept., enemy planes flew over the positon, locating the line, and shortly afterwards, hostile artillery located in commanding positions on the heights east of the Meuse put down a heavy fire along the whole of the regiment's line and over the area in the rear. To part of the line, the fire was enfilading, rendering the position barely tenable and the communication to and from the rear extremely hazardous.*[140]

As the day progressed, information was culled from a German prisoner that the infamous Prussian 28th (Flying Shock) Division was going to launch a counter-attack through Bois Dannevoux in order to reestablish *HAGEN* at *Gercourt* We knew that elements of the 5th Bavarian Reserve Division were now in the area, but the arrival of the "Flying Shock Division" surprised us. The Prussian 28th (Flying Shock) Division (*Das Fliegender Sturm Division*) consisted of the 55th Inf. Brig. (*Infanterie-Brigade 55*) with the 40th Fusilier Regiment "Prince Karl-Anton von Hohenzollern" (*Füsilier-Regiment 40, Fürst Karl-Anton von Hohenzollern*), the 109th Badenese Life Grenadier Regiment (*Badisches Leib-Grenadier-Regiment 109*), the 110th Badenese Grenadier Regiment "Kaiser Wilhelm I" (*Badisches Grenadier-Regiment 110, Kaiser Wilhelm I*), the 37th Machine Gun Sharpshooter Detachment (*Machiengewehr-Scharfschützen-Abteilung 37*), the 2nd Squadron, 5th Light Horse Regiment (*Eskadron 2/Jäger-Regiment zu Pferde 5*), the 28th Artillery Command (*Artillerie-Kommando 28*) with the 14th Baden Field Artillery Regiment "Grand Duke" (*Feldartillerie-Regiment Großherzog, 14*), and the 55th Heavy Artillery Battalion (*Fußartillerie-Bataillon 55*), two companies of Badenese Engineers, the 28th T.M. Company (*Minenwerfer*), and the 28th Division Signal Command.

According to Capt. Charles R. Herr, commander of F/2/319th Infantry, the "attack of the so-called Hun Shock Division worried no one at the time."[141] As Capt. Herr and other Blue Ridge officers from western Pennsylvania saw it, the Germans were in fact retreating because they had just blown up their last bridge over the Meuse at *Vilsones*. Herr's battalion commander, Maj. James Montague of 2/319, didn't want to take any chances, however, and he ordered his men to "Stand To" and coordinated with the artillery, telling it to be prepared to deliver what was then called "counter-attack fire."[142]

---

[140] As cited in *319th Infantry*, 26.

[141] As cited in the *2/319th Infantry*, 9.

[142] "Stand-To" is everyone up, or 100% security; "Tat-To" is almost everyone down.

At around 4:00 P.M., Capt. Joseph Peppard's A/313th Artillery, the designated accompanying battery for Brett's 160th Inf. Brig., was ordered to establish a position in an orchard between *Bois Sachet* and *Juré*, providing direct or indirect fire support for Brett's brigade just in case the Flying Shock Division did in fact attack. During the movement to the orchard, one gun from Peppard's battery flipped while passing over a mine crater in the road that split *Bois Juré*. Upon arriving to the orchard, the 3,400-pound field guns were hurriedly placed in the scant cover of the orchard with the limbers making wide turns into battery, the gun squads unhitching the gun carriages from the limbers, and the limber drivers moving the horse teams into *Bois Sachet* with the caissons. The gunners then dug trail holes while the instrument sergeant laid the pieces with his specialized gear. [143]

While Peppard's guns were being positioned, enemy shells were dropped into the area in a sort of a "wherever it goes" fashion—but nothing close. Because Peppard's artillerists had trouble with the telephone wire (again), a relay team of runners was formed to communicate between the O.P. up with the infantry and the guns in the orchard. This time, the officer in charge of the O.P. wrote the commands down, usually designating one target and shifting from it for new missions. The artillery calls this a "shift from a known point" fire mission. The officer or N.C.O. would command: "Shift from Target 1, left 500, add 500, enemy M.G." What the infantry really needed silenced, however, were the German 77mm "Whiz-bangs" that were firing down from the north. German 77mm guns were high velocity pieces that fired rounds that travelled faster than the speed of sound. They were so fast, in fact, that you could only hear them at the last second. Thus the term, "Whiz-bang." These guns and its "Whiz-bang" sound scared us the most. To this day (1938), if I hear anything like it, I freeze. Hun *Minenwerfers* (mine-throwers) shot huge, whooshing rounds. They were in fact so large that they looked like big black garbage cans sailing through the air (and you could actually see them, as in combat, everything slows down due to the heightened awareness) and sounded like a train passing by, thus the "whoosh." We called them "G.I. Cans." When these monsters hit, they churned up what seemed to be a half-acre of dirt. That's right, when they hit, it was like an agitated giant dumping a half-acre of juicy earth upon you. In King Vidor's 1925 silent film "The Big Parade," starring John Gilbert, Renée Adorée, and Hobart Bosworth, a movie that I saw three times at the local bijou in Richmond after the war, it shows exactly what ground explosions look like. In fact, of all of the movies made after the war, including Carl Laemmle's 1930 talkie "All Quiet on the Western Front," I thought that "The Big Parade" came the closest in showing show what it was like for the

---

[143] *313th Artillery*, 42.

average Doughboy in France, except for the lack of blood and gore.[144] Other movies that came out about the war revolved around the "Flyboys": *viz.*, "Wings" (1927), starring Buddy Rogers and Richard Arlen (one of the last silent movies made), "Hell's Angels" (1930) starring Ben Lyon and Jean Harlow, and "Dawn Patrol" (1930), starring Douglas Fairbanks, Jr. They weren't bad, but as a Dough, I chuckled to myself how great those motorized kites looked on the big screen.

During this particular bombardment, "a large Boche shell" hit within two yards of Gun 3 of B/1/314th Artillery, killing Pvt. William Tittle and severely wounding Pvts. Fritz, Chappin, and Reynolds. "Pvt. Tittle's death was the first of the 314th Artillery and he was buried in the nearby woods, Lt. Ober conducting the ceremony."[145]

Eventually, the Germans stopped firing their Whiz-bangs against the 319th Infantry and Capt. Peppard sent the following message to Lt. Col. Otto Brunzell, commander of the 313th Artillery, who was still back on Hill 281:[146]

```
BRUNZELL:
We have silenced the enemy artillery but believe that they are moving
back to take up other positions. Still suggest keep regiment on west
side of Bois Jure as this point too easily swept with enemy artillery
and only 2,000 meters from front line, which lies on this side of the
river and makes it nearly absolutely necessary to put artillery on
crest of hill without defilade in order to hit enemy. A position
further back will give much range and protection. See sketch on other
side.
                                                              PEPPARD.
```

At this point, the biggest threat for the men of Brett's 160th Inf. Brig. (reinforced by the 317th Infantry as well as most of the divisional M.G. battalions) and Heiner's 155th Arty. Brig. was in fact not an attack by the Flying Shock Division, but artillery strikes that delivered H.E., shrapnel, or mustard gas. The thing about gas attacks is that they are more annoying than anything else, especially when one is in the defense, because it requires a soldier to wear his mask for long periods of time. All they really did was make us angrier. For example, when we

---

[144] Laemmle also directed the great horror flicks *Dracula* (1931), *Frankenstein* (1931), *The Mummy* (1932), *The Old Dark House* (1932), *The Invisible Man* (1933), and *Bride of Frankenstein* (1935).

[145] *314th Artillery*, 51.

[146] As cited in *313th Artillery*, 43.

rolled-up their our German prisoners during the first hours of the Sept. 26 attack, we actually felt sorry for them. The prisoners were seen as fellow human beings who were locked in an event beyond their control—just like us. But after being shelled and gassed by their brethren, time and time again, we grew very cold—almost dead on the inside. Using poison gas in war is stupid as it serves no real purpose. Gas really doesn't kill that many people once the masks are on. It would have been better, in my opinion, to fire H.E. or shrapnel because they actually killed people or destroyed equipment.

To better protect the brigade's flanks, Brett deployed platoons from the division M.G. battalions, the 313th M.G. on the left with the 320th Infantry, and the mobile 314th M.G. on the right, with the 319th Infantry. Later, the mobile guns of the 314th M.G. were replaced by Jack Ass Artillery from the 315th M.G. Battalion and the motorized 314th M.G. was ordered to fall back to the east side of Hill 281 to better defend and assist the guns of Heiner's 155th Arty. Brig. According to Lt. Furr of the 314th M.G.:

> *The Germans having been cleared away on the north by the night attack, the battalion faced east to confront the enemy on the east bank of the Meuse River. Orders from the D.M.G.O. were to take position on the extreme right flank of the division, for the purpose of protecting that flank from the enfilade fire from Sivry, across the Meuse River. Reconnaissance revealed the fact that there was a gap of about one km between the right of the 80th Division and the left of the 33rd Division. The only troops in this gap were companies of the 314th M.G. Battalion.*[147]

For us in the 318th Infantry, in the 4th Division's sector, we were still hunkered down in a ravine outside of *Cuisy*, trying to not be killed by the occasional Hun artillery strike or strafing from a Heinie motorized kite armed with M.G.s. In fact, the thing we learned in that particular ditch was to respect and fear enemy aeroplanes, which pretty much flew over us at leisure (where was our flying corps?). It wasn't so much their strafing or bombing, it was their smoke trails or signal flares. When an enemy aeroplane circled overhead and spotted us, it sent a white puff of smoke out its tail, communicating our position to a Hun artillery H.Q. Not three minutes later, as sure as a sunrise, we'd get hit by artillery. Sometimes German artillery would miss its target, but most times not, especially since the whole area was inundated with targets. In fact, it was almost like shooting fish in a barrel!

---

[147] Ac cited in *314th M.G.*, 34-35.

While the morning passed without incident for us, all of a sudden, two H.E. shells exploded about 100 yards away from us. It was a direct hit on where A/1/318th Infantry was hidden in an abandoned German trench. Five soldiers were hit and we could heard their cries for help. Private Cary F. Jarratt was one of the wounded. He was hit by shrapnel in his knee, thigh, and forearm. He had been preparing lunch with other A/1/318th Infantry members, including his hometown friend, Pvt. Walter Finney. Jarratt and Finney had grown up together, mustered into the Army together, took the same train to Camp Lee, and were both assigned to A/1/318. But war is cruel and can separate friends, at any time, without notice. Finney wrote about Jarratt's injuries:

I knew his wounds were pretty bad but we all thought he would get along all right. He was treated by first aid men just as soon as he was hurt. And friends carried him to the first aid station in just a few minutes after he was wounded and in that respect he was more fortunate than a lot of the boys that were wounded in the days that followed. I lost sight of him after he was taken to the aid station and there was no way for me to get in touch with him anymore.[148]

Private Jarratt later died of his wounds in an Army hospital.

A little after noon, the commander of the 8th Inf. Brig., 4th Division, ordered one company from the 318th Infantry to be sent forward on outpost duty to the west of *Cuisy* in order to better protect the left flank of the 4th Division, to attempt to link up with the 79th (Cross of Lorraine) Division, which was still bogged down before *Montfaucon*, and to guard against enemy infiltrators (our lines were not solid). Our commander, Col. Worrilow, chose C/1/318th Infantry, and off it went. We wondered out loud why we were attached to the 4th Division, especially since we had been pretty much sitting on our *Kiesters* in the mud while our brothers in Brett's 160th Inf. Brig., 80th Division, continued to engage the Hun with the Gun in *Bois Dannevoux*.

At dusk, Sept. 27, we of the 318th Infantry marched north into *Village Septsarges* where the American 8th Inf. Brig., 4th Division, was operating.[149] Our regiment, with attached sections from the 313th M.G. Battalion, were to reinforce the 8th Inf. Brig. in order to breach GISELHER

---

[148] "Private Walter Finney Letter to Jarratt Family, March 5, 1919." Private Finney did not learn until months later that Private Jarratt had been evacuated to U.S. Army Base Hospital # 48 hundreds of miles away from the front lines. Despite surgery, the shrapnel that shredded through Private Jarratt's mud-caked, dirty uniform had allowed filth, bacteria and germs to enter into his body. Infection eventually set in and he died six weeks later of septicemia (blood poisoning). While war is bloody, illness and disease were also major causes of death.

[149] *Septsarges* is pronounced "Sept-sarge."

in Bois Brieulles. We took up our positions in the dark of an unusually wet and black night, without the advantage of a preliminary reconnaissance, and were consequently moved the next morning. Because the 4th Division's 8th Inf. Brig. and the 58th Infantry already had their P.C.s in Septsarges, our regimental P.C. was established in the only available shelter left, the school building which, being practically intact, offered a most attractive target for the Germans.

September 28, 1918.
Weather: Fair
Roads: Poor
The early-morning hours of Sept. 28 found Brett's 160th Inf. Brig. (+) holding positions south of *Bois Dannevoux* in front of *GISELHER* while other units of Pershing's American First Army were just now breaking through *HAGEN* in their assigned sectors to the left of Cronkhite's 80th Division. Lt. Lukens of 3/320th Infantry in Bois Septsarges remembered:

> *It was shortly after 1:00 A.M. that I woke up, stiff and shivering, to find Capt. Miller talking to me. He wanted me to patrol through the woods to the east, and get in contact with the other companies, or that failing, at least to see if there were any Boche in that direction and pick a better defensive position to which the men could be moved before dawn. The men were sleeping all around in the dark, and it took some time to find the right men to come with me. I had to walk the along line, waking men up at random, and letting them go back to sleep if they did not happen to be men whom I knew and trusted. I finally came across Sergeant Gontz and two privates with whom I was satisfied, and we set out. I will never forget that expedition; it was not particularly dangerous, for we were small enough group to keep out of trouble and our mission did not require fighting unless cornered; but the loneliness of it and the fear of getting lost in the woods gave us a sort of "spooky" feeling that it was hard to shake off.*[150]

Maj. Ashby Williams of 1/320th Infantry similarly remembered:

> *Throughout the night [rations were sent up] and they were brought to the south edge of [Bois Septsarges] across the ridge from us... [On the morning of Sept. 28], not having received satisfactory information from the front, I went forward to see Maj. Holt. He had changed his H.Q. and was now located in a little house built by the Germans. The Boche was now shelling the woods. I*

---

[150] As cited in *3/320th Infantry*, 71.

asked him if I could be of any assistance. He told me to send him such assistance as I could. I went back and sent him the remainder of Company D and, I think, the remainder of Company A... I remember the Boche was shelling us with alternating gas and H.E. shells. I remember how I played hide-and-seek with them, but not like the game I used to play as a boy. I found Maj. Holt munching a bit of hard bread and eating out of a can, no doubt of beans. It appeared that the Boche had withdrawn to a sheltered ridge on Lemont Hill and fortified it with a great number of M.G.s and attempts were made to take the place.[151]

Just after day-break, the Bavarian 5th Reserve Division, recently arrived from Brieulles, launched what seemed to be a battalion-sized counter-attack into the muzzles of the 320th Infantry and elements of the 313th M.G. Battalion, who were in a defense along the northern edge of Bois Septsarges. In the subsequent ten-minute fight, the Blue Ridgers gained a lot of confidence, as they eviscerated the beer-swilling Bavarians. On the heels of this engagement, later that morning, Brett's 160th Inf. Brig. (+) was once again ordered to storm *GISELHER* with the 319th Infantry on the right, the 317th Infantry in the center, and the 320th Infantry on the left. But as the men of the 320th Infantry learned earlier in the morning, it was far easier to defend than to attack, and the reinforced brigade was stopped cold in its tracks. The well-placed and dug-in German M.G. positions, coupled with the noted peculiarities of the woods, would not allow the Blue Ridgers to pass. Lt. Lukens of 3/320th Infantry remembered: "As on the previous day, we had a hard struggle through the underbrush, but this time the company commanders were determined to keep in touch, even at the expense of less-open deployment.... As luck would have it...our organizations [again] became badly broken up in the thick tangle of forest...with men of every company of the regiment hopelessly intermingled."[152]

During this phase of the battle, Lt. William B. Arrants, a medical officer serving with the 317th Infantry in Bois Dannevoux, earned the Distinguished Service Cross for conspicuous gallantry. His citation reads:

For repeated acts of extraordinary heroism in action in Bois Dannevoux, France, 28 Sept., 1918. Lt. Arrants with his battalion aid unit accompanied his battalion into action in Bois Dannevoux and promptly opened an aid station within 100 yards of the front line, where he worked all night under continuous fire, giving aid to the wounded. When there was a shortage of stretcher bearers,

---

[151] As cited in *1/320th Infantry*, 88.

[152] As cited in *3/320th Infantry*, 72.

he assisted in bringing in the wounded. Under intense fire he undertook to locate the ambulance dressing station and personally directed the evacuation of wounded to it.[153]

The Distinquished Service Cross (D.S.C.) and the Distinquished Service Medal (D.S.M.) were new decorations that were authorized by the President in January 1918. While the D.S.M. was awarded to "any person who, while serving in any capacity with the Army of the United States shall distinquish himself or herself in specially meritorious service to the government in a position of great responsibility," the D.S.C. was created to reward "extraordinary acts of heroism in connection with military operations against an armed enemy, not warrenting the Medal of Honor." While the latter can only be earned in actual combat, the former is be awarded for "specially meritorious service to the government in a position of great responsibility in connection with military operations against an armed enemy." The D.S.C. can only be awarded within three years of the performance of the act of which it is given, except if an individual was recommended for the Medal of Honor and failed to qualify, or if an individual was cited in orders for his heroism. A Silver Star is also issued for gallant action; a Purple Heart is issued for wounds suffered in action.[154]

Nobody wanted a Purple Heart.

As Brett's 160th Inf. Brig. tried to reorganize for yet another attack, German artillery and *Minenwerfer* fire poured in from the north and the east—from the direction of *KRIEMHILDE* and along *Côtes de Meuse*—placing the Blue Ridgers in a deadly cross-fire. Due to the desperate situation, Brett reluctantly ordered his brigade back into *Bois Juré* and *Sachet*.[155] All knew that this ran contrary to Pershing's directive that plainly stated, "Don't Give Up Ground Already Taken," but Brett also utilized the doctrinally-sound principle of "Live to Fight Another Day." During the "retrograde repositioning," as our officers liked to call it, 80th Division artillerists posted along Hill 281 misheard that the 160th Inf. Brig. (+) was in fact retreating in the face of a strong German counter-attack (Joe Latrinsky apparently told them that the Flying Shock Division had broken through). As such, the gunners of the division "prepared to defend the guns

---

[153] *317th Infantry*, 90. The citation reads: "*Bois de la Gote Lemont,*" which is a section of Dannevoux Woods.

[154] Harbord, 197 and *American Armies and Battlefields in Europe: A History, Guide, and Reference Book* (Washington, D.C.: Government Printing Office, American Battle Monuments Commission, 1938), 510-12. Hereafter cited as "*A.B.M.C.*"

[155] *313th Artillery*, 45.

to the last," and the 314th Artillery, posted just west of the hill, facing *Bois Septsarges* to the north, even went so far as to refuse some of their guns to the left "in the event of a rupture."[156]

For the rest of the day, the biggest threats America's Blue Ridge Division continued to be well-directed German artillery or *Minenwerfer* strikes (we hated *Minenwerfers*) delivered mostly from *les Côtes de Meuse*. Lt. Lukens of 3/320th Infantry correctly noted that, "It is useless to try to describe a barrage. We crouched down in the meager protection of a ditch and waited, wondering where each one was going to strike, and whether the Boche infantry would come over. It was not heavy stuff, but there was plenty of it, and even three-inch shells can rip things up when they come like M.G. bullets."[157] It was felt by many in Brett's 160th Inf. Brig. that the French XVII Corps, American First Army, which included the American 29th (Blue and Grey) Division and fighting its way north across *les Côtes de Meuse*, had to clear those heights of enemy artillery before Bullard's American III Corps—the American 33rd, 80th, and 4th Divisions—even had a prayer in breaking *GISELHER* in the vicinity of Dannevoux. Cameron's V Corps, to the Ivy Division's left, also had to get closer to *GISELHER* before it could be seriously breached and exploited.

To help defeat the Kraut artillery, elements of Col. Frank Cocheu's 319th Infantry and Brig. Gen. George Heiner's 155th Arty. Brig. spent the rest of the day attempting to silence pesky batteries of German "Whiz-bangs" on the heights. They knew that one such battery was somewhere down in the valley near *Vilosones* but couldn't find it. Much like the cagey West Virginia gunners of the 155th Arty. Brig., the German artillerists were also adept at the art of camouflage. Lt. Henry Baker of F/2/313 went so far as to state: "Like the gas non-coms, the camouflage non-coms rendered excellent service and saved the regiment many casualties by their hard and persistent work. Whatever had to be done was well done by these mountaineers and miners, and the officers of this regiment believe that no better soldiers can be found anywhere than in the mountains of West Virginia."[158]

Maj. James L. Montague of 2/319 sent the following to Lt. Shelton Ackerman, the platoon leader of 1/A/313:[159]

---

[156] As cited in *314th Artillery*, 38-39.

[157] As cited in *3/320th Infantry*, 74.

[158] As cited in *313th Artillery*, 33.

[159] *Ibid*, 44.

> ```
> Put whizz-bangs out of commission. Infantry can take care of enemy in
> bottom land if you clean out the whizz-bangs. You have my authority to
> move your guns farther to rear when your present position is
> disclosed. Keep your O.P. on this hill.
>                                                             MONTAGUE
> ```

At about 11:00 A.M., Lt. Ackerman towed one of his M1897 75s, using chains hooked to the wheel hubs and pulled "by prolong," to the ridge overlooking *Vilosones*. While Lt. Donald Fullerton of A/1/313th Artillery reported to Maj. Montague of the 319th Infantry as the observer, Lt. Ackerman sat in the gunner's seat and Capt. Peppard, the battery commander, acted as his spotter. Thus situated, they went "Hun gun huntin'" with Ackerman's gun, supported by some infantry. Poking the piece just over the ridge with the carriage in defilade, Ackerman fired.

"Boom!"

"Clink."

"Thump."

"Tink."

"Clink."

"Up!"

After each shot, Ackerman popped up from his seat, squinted over the gun's firing shield, and shouted to Peppard: "Did-ja see that one, Pep!?"

"No. Fire again! Go right!"

After a few more shots, Ackerman fired into a long low building across the river, in Vilosones.

"Ba-boom!"

"Well, that's different!" yelled Peppard.

What was different about it was that the targeted building was filled with Heinie ammunition. More importantly, the round finally elicited a response from a German gun crew that was situated in a woodlot just east of Vilosones.

"Gotcha!"

"Whiz-bang!"

A Hun "whiz bang" round zipped past the gun to the left, hitting the ridge.

"Crruppp!"

The round was close enough to scatter dirt upon the crew and clip off a three-inch pole from the camouflage netting near the muzzle of Ackerman's gun, but not close enough to cause any casualties. According to Capt. Peppard: "Luckily the gun stood in a small depression, a sort of saucer, forty to fifty meters wide." Ackerman's crew next fired several rounds into the wooded lot across the river.[160]

Meanwhile, over on the left with my beloved 318th Infantry Regiment, which was attached to the Ivy Division, my battalion, Maj. Charles Sweeny's 1/318, received orders to take up position alongside the 59th "Let 'Em Have It" Infantry, 4th Division, atop Hill 295, which was just northwest of what was left of *Village Septsarges* (mostly a pile of broken up brick, stones, or timber).[161] The codename for the 59th Infantry was ("Dixon"). We in 1/318 were designated as the attack battalion of the regiment and as such, had soldiers from the 305th Engineers, several sections from the 318th M.G. Company and the 313th M.G. Battalion, two I.G.s, and four 81mm mortars attached to us. 2/318, as the support battalion, was ordered to refuse the left of the 59th Infantry Regiment to help protect its flank, which was "in the air," as the right-most units of the shot-up 79th Division were just now moving toward *Nantillois* (it remarkably took the German citadel of Montfaucon, but at great cost). Behind 2/318 was 3/318, which was designated as the regiment's reserve battalion. Our mission was to support the 4th Division breach *GISELHER* in Bois Brieulles while Brett's 160th Inf. Brig. (+), on the right in Bois Dannevoux, did the same.

As we moved into position, we were thoroughly drenched by a cold and heavy rain, forcing us to slog through deep mud and a virtual slaughter pen of mangled, unburied bodies. The sight of cut-up men, with body parts here and there, to-and-fro, will never, ever leave me. Neither will the smell. Dead bodies, to me at least, smell like a hundred pounds of congealed hamburger and pork that had been baked in the sun like road-kill. I think that this was the time when I was the most afraid. I also think this is the point when I quietly said goodbye to the old Joseph Riddle, and hello to the new killer, "Automatic Rifleman Joe Riddle of B/318th Infantry Regiment, 80th Division." The transformation happened that quickly.

That night, we slumped down in the mud and tried to catch an hour or so of sleep. Of course, no fires were allowed and nobody dared wander off too far from their unit lest they get lost or even shot by a nervous sentry as the Germans would send raiding parties through the fissures in our lines to try to snag some prisoners or locate some of our artillery. We of course did the same to the Hun. Lt. Lukens of I/3/320th Infantry, still stuck in *Bois Septsarges*, remembered:

---

[160] *313th Artillery*, 45.

[161] The U.S. 59th "Let 'Em Have It" Infantry Regiment was formed in 1917 from personnel from the Regular and National Armies. As of this writing (1938), it is in the Inactive Reserves.

It was a mean night. No one was allowed to sleep because of the danger of, and there was no place to sleep anyhow, for the bottom and sides of the ditch were three inches in mud. Our muscles and nerves were worn out by the strain of the past three days, and we were still living on the hoarded remnants of our original two days' emergency rations. The cold drizzling rain that added to our discomfort was for once welcome, for we could catch a little water in our mess tins and lick the wet leaves of the bushes to take the worst edge off our thirst.... Our training had always been to "defend in depth," but the woods were so thick that in this situation the front line alone could take part in the defense, and someone in authority way back in the rear was so afraid of an infantry counterattack that he forgot to consider that a crowded front line invites casualties from shell fire.[162]

<u>September 29, 1918.</u>

Weather: Rain

Roads: Heavy

With the Army stalled in front of *GISELHER*, Pershing decided to replace Brett's 160th Inf. Brig. of the 80th Division with the 65th Inf. Brig. of the 33rd (Prairie) Division. Upon relief, Brett's brigade, and eventually the entire division, would be sent farther to the left to help breach *GISELHER* and *KRIEMHILDE* in the vicinity of *Village Cunel*.[163] Once relieved by the 65th Inf. Brig., the 160th Brigade (minus the 317th Infantry) was to march south to *Bois Montfaucon* and conduct what we called "recovery operations." Meanwhile, the 317th Infantry, which had been attached to the 160th Inf. Brig., was to return to Jamerson's 159th Inf. Brig. that was operating in the 4th Division's zone by marching west and assembling behind us in the 318th Infantry. The divisional M.G. battalions were also to join Jamerson's 159th Inf. Brig. (remember, every gun up), and Heiner's 155th Arty. Brig. was ordered to stay between *Béthincourt* and *Forges* to provide the same fire support to the 33rd Division as it had for the 80th Division.[164] Maj. Ashby Williams of 1/320th Infantry remembered:

We were relieved by the 30th Division, composed of Illinois troops. I remember as we passed back through Bois Septsarges the nauseating odor of shell gas

---

[162] As cited in *3/320th Infantry*, 73.

[163] *Cunel* is pronounced, "Que-nel."

[164] *317th Infantry*, 58.

added to the sight of dead and mangled bodies would have made one sick under ordinary conditions. As we passed out of the woods we passed through an area that had been saturated with gas from Boche shells not long before and many of us got a whiff or two too much. I remember also as we came down the slope we passed a dead Boche lying on his back on the ground with his hands stretched over his head. He had died on his face and had been turned over after he was stiff. The terror on his face was horrible to look at. Someone had derisively placed a helmet on his head. I remember the soldiers kicked him and cursed him as they passed. Such are the horrors of war... I assembled my battalion on a field near the dugout which had been used by Majors Holt, Emory, and myself the first night, and which had been adopted by regimental H.Q., and I got my orders for moving out. I was directed to proceed at once along the Gercourt-Cuisy-Malancourt Road and, passing through the latter town, halt in Bois Montfaucon. I moved out, I dare say, about 10:00 A.M. I remember the men were tired and hungry and wet and all that sort of thing, but the change was to their liking and there was no mistaking the fact that they were glad to be going away from the hell that they been in for the past three days. The road to Cuisy was lined with artillery with their muzzles over the roadway and in many places we had to go into the fields to pass around them to keep from being blown to pieces by our own guns.[165]

As Brett's brigade waited to be relieved, we in the 318th Infantry, fighting with the 4th Division, was to attack north and help breach *GISELHER* in Bois Brieulles. At around 2 A.M., we in the 318th Infantry received the following attack order from the 8th Inf. Brig., 4th Division, extracts from which follow:[166]

---

[165] As cited in *1/320th Infantry*, 88-89.

[166] *318th Infantry*, 62-64. *Bois Septsarges* is pronounced "Bwa Sep-sarg" and *Bois Brieulles* is pronounced "Bwa Brew-lay."

> 8th INFANTRY BRIGADE.
> 4th DIVISION.
>
> 28 Sept. 1918
>
> 1. This brigade, reinforced by the 318th Infantry and two batteries of the 16th Artillery, will pass through the 7th Infantry Brigade tomorrow morning and continue the advance to the Army's objective. Upon arrival on this line, the position will be immediately prepared for defense.
>
> 2. The 59th Infantry, with one battalion 318th Infantry, one company of the 12th M.G. Battalion and one battery 16th Artillery, will pass through the sector held by the 47th Infantry. It will place two battalions in the front line, one battalion in support, and the remainder of the regiment in the regimental reserve.
>
> 3. The 318th Infantry, less one battalion, and the 12th M.G. Battalion, less two companies, will constitute the Brigade reserve. One battalion of the 318th Infantry, and the regimental M.G. Company, will follow the 58th Infantry at a distance of one kilometer along the left border of the division sector, prepared to resist hostile attacks from the northwest and west. One battalion, 318th Infantry, will follow approximately one kilometer in rear of the center of the Brigade.

At 5:30 A.M., Sept. 29, our attack began, making little progress because of the deadly German artillery and M.G. fire we encountered. As stated in the order, while we in 1/318th Infantry were to support the attack of the 59th Infantry, 2/318 and 3/318 were to support the attack of the 58th Infantry, which was to our left. In this way, the 59th Infantry actually had four battalions and the 58th Infantry had five. To our right was the 160th Inf. Brig. from the 80th Division (soon-to-be-relieved by the 65th Inf. Brig. of the 33rd Division). Most of the enemy artillery fire that was hurled at us that day still came from *Côtes de Meuse*, no doubt called in by artillery spotters posted along Côtes de Cunel. Like us, the enemy would usually telephone their H.Q. to "fire, target-x," which was pre-plotted, and let us have it. The key to surviving an artillery strike is to either dig-in or to *keep moving forward*. If that proved impossible, then a movement somewhere else was critical because if you simply stayed where the massive shells were landing, the law of averages were against you. But then again, the higher you are during an artillery strike, the greater the change you'll get clipped by a red hot piece of twisted metal.

We in 1/318th Infantry were ordered to fill the gap between the battalions of the "Let 'Em Have It Regiment" that were attacking abreast north through *Bois Septsarges* and into *Bois Brieulles* and *GISELHER*. According to our regiment's official history, which is entitled, *History of the 318th Infantry Regiment of the 80th Division, 1917-1919*, it states: "Due to the failure of these two battalions [of the Ivy Division] to make the progress anticipated (the sector was wooded and heavily defended), we in 1/318th found ourselves pushed well to the front, forming the apex of a triangle. Our position was an extremely perilous one, from which the splendid judgment, great coolness, and personal bravery of Maj. Sweeny, the battalion commander, finally successfully eradicated them after they suffered heavy casualties."[167]

I'd like to expand upon this narrative with my own recollection, and yes, we did suffer "heavy casualties." That morning, in the mud and cold, our platoon was assembled to move north. We were in the center of the bombed-out town of *Septsarges*, and enemy artillery fire was raining down upon us, killing horses, mules, and, from time-to-time, Doughs. I remember being soaked to the bone. It was probably 45° and we were tired, wet, cold, and hungry. Everyone was scared. Before long, we were ordered to advance "Indian File" up the muddy road, following Company A. We marched between Hill 295 and *Bois Septsarges* and saw the ghastly remains of battle—both dead and mangled Doughs and Huns.

Once we passed into the western edge of Bois Septsarges, we could hear the cacophony of fire to our front in Bois Brieulles. The Hun and the 4th Division boys were really going at it with M.G. and rifle fire, as well as grenades. The intrepid Maj. Sweeny, who was always in the thick of the fight, was in front, in the middle of the battalion. He deployed us from column into line and from left to right it was Companies A and C with D with B in support (it was doctrine for our battalions to fight two companies up and two in back).

In my first real engagement of the war, the breach of *GISELHER* in *Bois Brieulles*, my A.R. Squad was commanded by Cpl. Oliver Ward and my A.R. Team consisted of myself as gunner, Albert Getz as assistant gunner and Boss Adkins and Wort Wise as the ammunition bearers/riflemen. While most of the squad carried M1917 Enfield Rifles, the A.R.men, people like myself, carried an "Automatic Rifle, Model 1915 (Chauchat)." Our platoon leader was Lt. Harry Myers, our company commander was Capt. James S. Douglas, our battalion commander

---

[167] *318th Infantry*, 64.

was Maj. Charles Sweeny, and our regimental commander was Col. Ulysses Worrilow. They were all good, brave men, thrown into an impossible situation.

As our battalion advanced further into *Bois Brieulles* with myself, in the A.R. squad of our platoon behind the assault squad, the battle became far-more pitched. Again, we saw dead and wounded Doughs and Huns scattered across the wooded floor. There were still leaves on the trees, but they had turned color and were falling, just like some of us were about to. I remember advancing through elements of the 59th Infantry of the 4th Division. Our heads were down as if we were in a heavy rainstorm. Then it happened. M.G. fire ripped through my platoon's ranks. M.G. fire from a Maxim is frightening—especially when you are on the receiving end. It zings and it rattles and when fired, it sounds like rhythmic "rat-a-tat-tat-rat-a-tat-tat." It may not be that accurate, but it was accurate enough to make us eat the wet leaves and the moist dark earth.[168]

After I "dove into the dirt," my helmet was lodged down over my eyes and my respirator bag was digging into my ribs. In order to see, I had to flip my respirator bag to my left side (where it stayed for the rest of the war), adjusted my helmet, put my Sho-sho to my right shoulder in the prone position, like how we were trained at Camp Lee, and "scanned my lane for targets." I saw nothing—*nada, nichts*. I heard a lot though! I heard M.G. bullets zipping over my head, screams, and other noises that I could not quite discern.

At this point, the bombers advanced on their bellies, followed by the assault squad. Corporal Ward led us to the right, where he ordered us to fire into the embrasures of what looked like a Hun M.G. nest to our right-front. Behind us came the R.G. squad, which started to shoot W.P. smoke grenades at the same embrasures. Once I got situated, I pulled the trigger on my "Sho-sho" and let the enemy have it.

"Bump, bump, bump."

"Bump, bump, bump."

The German M.G.ers, firing their criss-crossed cones of fire against us, simply redoubled their efforts.

"Rat-a-tat-tat-rat-a-tat-tat."

---

[168] *Das Machinen Gewehr 08* was the German Imperial Army's standard M.G. during the war and is an up-grade of Sir Hiram Stevens Maxim's British M1884 M.G. It shoots 500 7.92 x 57-mm rpm from a 250-round fabric belt (or 1 belt every 30 seconds—8 rounds a second). To alleviate over-heating of the barrel (and thus bending) due to the high-rate of fire, Sir Hiram wrapped the barrel with a hollow metal tube that contained one gallon of water (called a "water jacket"). In 1914-15, the M.G. 08 was mounted on a heavy and cumbersome (but sturdy) "sled mount" or "quad-prod" that is called a *Schlittenlafette* and it took four men to carry it (which is why they organized their infantry squads around the M.G.). In 1915, the Germans made another adaptation to the gun, adding a wooden pistol grip and mounting it on a bi-pod. This version is called the M.G. 08/15. In the Meuse-Argonne, we engaged both configurations, the 08 being called a "Heavy M.G." and the 08/15 a "Light M.G." even though both fired the same bullet at the same rpm.

"Zing, zing, zing."

"Rat-a-tat-tat-rat-a-tat-tat."

"Zing, zing, zing."

To get a better shot, I crawled even further through the wet, mud-smeared leaves, inching forward with the "Sho-sho" cradled in my arms. Before I knew it, my two hand grenades, which I carried in a canvas bag, also started to dig into the ground under my belly (we carry way too much gear!) I was afraid that one of the pins would be pulled and that I'd be blown to smithereens by my own grenades, my guts decorating the forest. So I rolled over onto my back and slung the satchel over to my right side.

Finally, Albert Getz and I started to hone-in on one of the embrasures of a Hun M.G. nest. Another barked to our left, "Rat-a-tat-tat-rat-a-tat-tat!" The nests were dug-in with packed earth and logs and camoflagued with branches placed on the roof. On the near side, we could see two German riflemen with painted helmets (green and brown) taking aimed shots.

"Pop! Pop!"

"Rat-a-tat-tat-rat-a-tat-tat."

"Rat-a-tat-tat-rat-a-tat-tat."

At this point, the thick white smoke from the R.G.ers' W.P. rounds was really starting to billow and the bombers were able to crawl even closer to the nest on the left. After five or so more minutes, two M1915 Colt-Vickers M.G.s reinforced our firing line and we really let them have it!

"Bump-bump-bump."

"Rat-a-tat-tat."

"Rat-a-tat-tat."

"Bump-bump-bump."

Sensing that fire superiority had in fact been achieved (Maj. Sweeny emphasized this point to his officers), Lt. Myers ordered the bomber and assault squads to attack with himself in the lead. As rehearsed, the bombers took a knee and hurled their hand grenades.

Boom!

Boom!

Boom!

As they did so, however, they took several casualties from Hun M.G. and rifle fire. The Germans then reciprocated and threw their "Potato Masher" or "Stick Grenades" right back at the bombers.

Boom!

Boom!

Boom!

German stick grenades (called *Stielhandgrenaten*) had a little more range than average "baseball" hand grenades as the stick, acting as a lever, enabled the thrower to whip it as far as thirty or so yards. Both sides had the baseball hand grenades but only the Germans and the Austrians had *Stielhandgrenaten*. [169]

The Hun M.G. nest in question was sending its cone of bullets to the right, in a crisscross, interlocking with another one on the right, which was firing its cone to the left. While our platoon was taking on the nest to the left, the second platoon was taking on the one to the right. This was the war for us: one Hun M.G. nest at a time.

Although deadly, it was plain and simple.

With grazing fire coming in from the right, covering the front of the targeted nest, our assault squad charged through the bombers, taking several hits from the M.G. firing on the right and Hun riflemen firing to the front. The nest had about five riflemen covering each flank of the M.G. from a trench. The assault squad, charging through the woods, got hung up on a final line of protective wire that protected the M.G. nest, however, and the bombers, coming up from behind, actually took the attack "home." At this point, Sergeant Brown, our platoon guide, ushered the A.R.s and R.G.s forward to hold the position.

I remember getting up with my "Sho-sho" and darting through the woods with Getz and the rest of my team to meet up with what was left of the assault and bomber squads. In getting there, a piece of barbwire jumped up and bit me, tearing my wool putties and causing a minor scratch. It was sheer pandemonium around the captured Hun M.G. nest. Because we captured ours first, taking out the "interlocking field of fire," the second platoon suffered less casualties in taking theirs. With two Hun M.G. positions now in our possession, we had created what we called a "hole in the line" a "breach," or a "salient." Through this breach, our company and battalion commanders sent the rest of their commands through it, like milk from a straw. From this salient point, they would either roll up the Huns' flanks or attack deeper into their lines.

The 80th Division Always Moves Forward.

One must understand that rational thought in combat are usually replaced by instinctive or animalistic ones. Charging a M.G. position, for example, is not a rational action. A rational person would run away and keep on going until he reached his living room. But in combat, it's not only a soldier's mission and duty to take out an enemy M.G. nest, it's also his animalistic

---

[169] *"Stielhandgrenaten"* is pronounced, "Shteel-hand-gren-aa-ten."

desire to kill the foe who is trying to kill him or his brothers. To me, it felt like I was having a tug of war inside. But when the firing started, the animal side won out almost every time. If it didn't, then I simply froze with fear (which happened once). Before the war, even in training, I didn't know that the "animal" part of me even existed. After our first hammering here in the woods, however, it came in full force and was well-fed over the next three weeks. It has remained with me ever since (believe it or not). The Reverend James R. Laughton, a pastor (or "Holy Joe") from western Virginia serving with the 80th Division remembered:

We ceased to be human—we became beasts lusting for blood and flesh. We were no longer normal, but abnormal. Indeed the abnormal was the normal. It was a hard life. We lived hard. We fought hard. We dealt in hard terms. Men called one another names that, in civilian life, would have been insults. Soldiers swore going over the top, though they had New Testaments in their pockets and read them. Many died with curses on their lips... Men swore who never swore before, men who taught Sunday School classes back home. There was much to make them swear. The atmosphere was charged with profanity.

In breaching *GISELHER*, our company suffered several casualties—mostly wounded. We killed eight Hun and captured two very scared Bavarians, an older man named Heinrich and a younger one named Peter (the other Krauts got away). They both pleaded for their lives, thinking that we were going to shoot them. Lt. Myers, who was worn out and still upset that he got tangled up in that damned barbed wire, spoke some German and was able to somehow assure them that we would not kill them if they cooperated.

As part of the consolidation, my A.R. squad was sent forward into the woods about twenty yards to establish a defensive position while Capt. Douglas reorganized the company. Soon after we set up, however, we got hit by an artillery strike—probably German. It was shell and it blew the tops off trees.

Deciding not to stay put for the next artillery salvo to cut us into bloody strips, Lt. Myers, who was slightly wounded in the attack, moved us a hundred yards north, hoping that the Hated Hun wouldn't hit us again. There we dug-in for the night, assuming a defensive posture, as our officers oversaw the reconsolidation of our units, our resupply, the evacuation of the wounded, the dead, and the prisoners, and determined what to do next. As a front line man, I didn't know what went on in the rear, but imagined that the lone dirt road back to *Septsarges* was choked with trucks and horses—that chaos reigned.

As our company adjusted its lines in the woods, we survivors at the platoon level decided to advance the next time in a skirmish lines in "clumps" of five. We also agreed that if we encountered a sniper (which was likely in these woods), some of us would have to act as the bait and that the better shots like Boss Adkins would have serve as counter-snipers. To simply lay there would mean sure death.

In Maj. Wise's 2/318's zone, they advanced along the left of the 4th Division's sector in support of the 58th Infantry. Progressing a km, 2/318th Infantry was stopped cold between Nantillois and Hill 295 due to intense enemy artillery fire. For the next several days, 2/318 would hold Hill 295, in the open, exposed to frontal and enfilade fire from Hun artillery and M.G. fire. Many casualties were suffered, among them the popular commander of F/2/318th Infantry, Capt. John Crum, a man who really shaped our training at Camp Lee.

His time was up.

Deployment For Defense.

I.D.R. 495. The density of the whole deployment depends upon the expected severity of the action, the character of the enemy, the condition of the flanks, the field of fire, the terrain, and the available artificial or natural protection for the troops.

I.D.R. 496. If exposed, the firing line should be as dense in defense as in attack. If the firing line is well intrenched and has a good field of fire, it may be made thinner. Weaker supports are permissible. For the same number of troops the front occupied on the defensive may therefore be longer than on the offensive, the battalions placing more companies in the firing line.

I.D.R. 497. If it is intended only to delay the enemy, a fairly strong deployment is sufficient, but if decisive results are desired, a change to the offensive must be contemplated and the corresponding strength in rear provided. This strength is in the reserve, which should be as large as the demands of the firing line and supports permit. Even in a passive defense the reserve should be as strong as in the attack, unless the flanks are protected by other means.

Maj. Henry Burdick's 3/318th Infantry, which had been ordered to follow one km in the rear of 1/318 and 2/318, moved into the northern edge of *Bois Septsarges* and came under heavy Hun artillery fire that inflicted a number of casualties. The end of the day therefore found the 318th Infantry strung out in a battle line from Hill 295 on the left and *Bois Brieulles* on the right. I was in *Bois Brieulles* with my battalion.

Throughout the night, we improved our defenses and sent out reconnaissance patrols north through the rest of *Bois Brieulles*. I don't know who actually had it worse: us, in the cold woods between *GISELHER* and *KRIEMHILDE*, or 2/318, which was stuck atop that exposed hill for all to see. For me, I'm glad that I was in the woods and not out on that damned hill. According to the *History of the 318th Infantry Regiment of the 80th Division, 1917-19*:

> [The] patrols gathered much valuable information for the commanding general of the 8th Brigade, of which he was generous enough to make official mention to the commanding officer of this regiment. While during this period [Sept. 29-Oct. 2], only the 1st Battalion had actual clashes with the Hun, the shelling was so constant and casualties so numerous as to make it a very trying period for the men and the officers, without the relief of action and with little opportunity for rest. The transport personnel during this time distinguished themselves by their devotion to duty, and, by bringing the trains up to the troops (in the case of the 1st Battalion right up to the front line) made it possible for the men to get hot meals.[170]

<u>September 30, 1918.</u>

Weather: Rain.

Roads: Heavy.

On Sept. 30, 1918, the 80th Division was still divided. While Jamerson's 159th Inf. Brig. was operating in the vicinity of *GISELHER* with the Ivy Division, Brett's 160th Inf. Brig. was headed south to *Bois Montfaucon*, and Heiner's 155th Arty. Brig. was still providing fire support for the 33rd (Prairie) Division, which held the right of the corps line. In general, artillery units stayed in zone, keeping up constant fires, while infantry units were rotated in and out. Later that day, Bullard issued the following order to his corps:[171]

```
                        III Corps, A.E.F.
30 Sept., 1918.
The 4th Division stands fast; reorganizes itself for another advance
and attends to its traffic. 80th Division will get itself into its new
place and prepare to support the 4th, either in advance or in defense.
It will pay special attention to its supply of ammunition and also
look out for its traffic and get things in good shape.
                                                         BULLARD
                                              Lt. Gen., Commanding
```

---

[170] As cited in *318th Infantry*, 65-66.

[171] As cited in Stultz, 404.

Two officers from the 314th Artillery were cited for exceptional bravery on this day while conducting operations with the 33rd Division in Bois Dannevoux: Lts. Kenneth Blue and Landreth L. Layton:

> *On Sept. 30, 1918, Lt. Blue was adjusting fire of the batteries of his battalion from a German observation tower on Dannevoux Ridge. The tower was under direct observation of the enemy, who opened fire on it before the adjustment was completed. Lt. Blue continued to fire his batteries until severely wounded in both legs by shell fragments. Although suffering great pain, Lt. Blue would not permit the officers of his battalion to leave their posts on his account and gave no thought to his own condition, but only to the successful completion of the fire.*
>
> *On Sept. 30, 1918, Lt. Layton at Dannevoux Ridge, after having been severely wounded in the left leg and while still under enemy shell fire, assisted in moving several wounded comrades to a place of safety, and ignoring his own safety, continued the adjustment of his battery to its completion.* [172]

Although artillery can fire both a direct and indirect missions, I always regarded it as a direct fire system because O.P.s, like the lieutenants above, were always directing the fire. Were they actually pulling the lanyards on the pieces? No. Where they shooting at targets? Yes. After the war, the Army correctly labeled the artillery the "King of Battle" and the infantry the "Queen of Battle" in part to match the moves of said Chess pieces. But make no mistake about it—the infantry can not move forward without timely and accurate artillery support and artillery can not take ground. The only thing that wins a battle is a proper mixing of the combined arms—infantry, artillery, cavalry, engineers—and ensuring that they all work together.

At our level, we were never ever able to get artillery exactly when and where we wanted it. We simply followed a prescribed barrage pattern. Why? Because the communication technology of the time would not allow it. There was no way for us to communicate directly with the guns if we were too far forward or were in woods, which we usually were. As of this writing, however (1938), the Army seems to have solved this problem and in the next war, if there is one (hope not!), the artillery will become even more deadly (if that's possible) because a single well-trained F.O., with a working radio, can call in hell fire from *battalions* of artillery onto a small spot.

Later that evening, General Cronkhite congratulated the men of America's Blue Ridge Division by sending out the following circular. It was one of his best:

---

[172] As cited in *314th Artillery*, 44.

P.C. 80th DIVISION, A.E.F.

30 Sept., 1918

To: The Officers and Enlisted Men of the 80th Division:

I wish to express to you my deep appreciation of the great work accomplished by you, in your first active operation.

Your work has received the highest communication from our Corps Commander, and his confidence in your military prowess is evidenced by the demands he has made upon your services.

You will soon be called upon for another push.

Remember that you made the Army Objective your first call.

Remember that the 80th Division never stops short of the Army Objective, wherever it may be placed.

The enemy is faltering; his allies are deserting him. His infantry will not stand before your onrush.

Continue to smother his machine gunners by skillful maneuvering: hit his line hard and push through.

GET HIM ON THE RUN, AND WE SHALL EAT OUR THANKSGIVING DINNER IN PEACE.

A. Cronkhite

Major-General, Commanding.

Battery of heavy American artillery servicing targets.

Blue Ridgers moving through Montfaucon (L) and "Moving Up" (R).

Moving "Up the Line." A motor ambulance is in the background (L) and "Overhead View of Nantillois," looking east (R).

Poor *Nantillois* (L) and Light arty. moving north (R).

Waiting in a ditch for the next attack (L) and advancing up our axis of advance in the Meuse-Argonne (R).

Platoon from the 318th Inf. advancing under the cover of smoke in the Meuse-Argonne.

Overhead view of Nantillois, looking east.

"The Hun." The average Prussian or Bavarian soldier we fought in the Meuse-Argonne looked like this. He was armed with a 7mm K98, several stick grenades and ammunition bandolier around his neck.

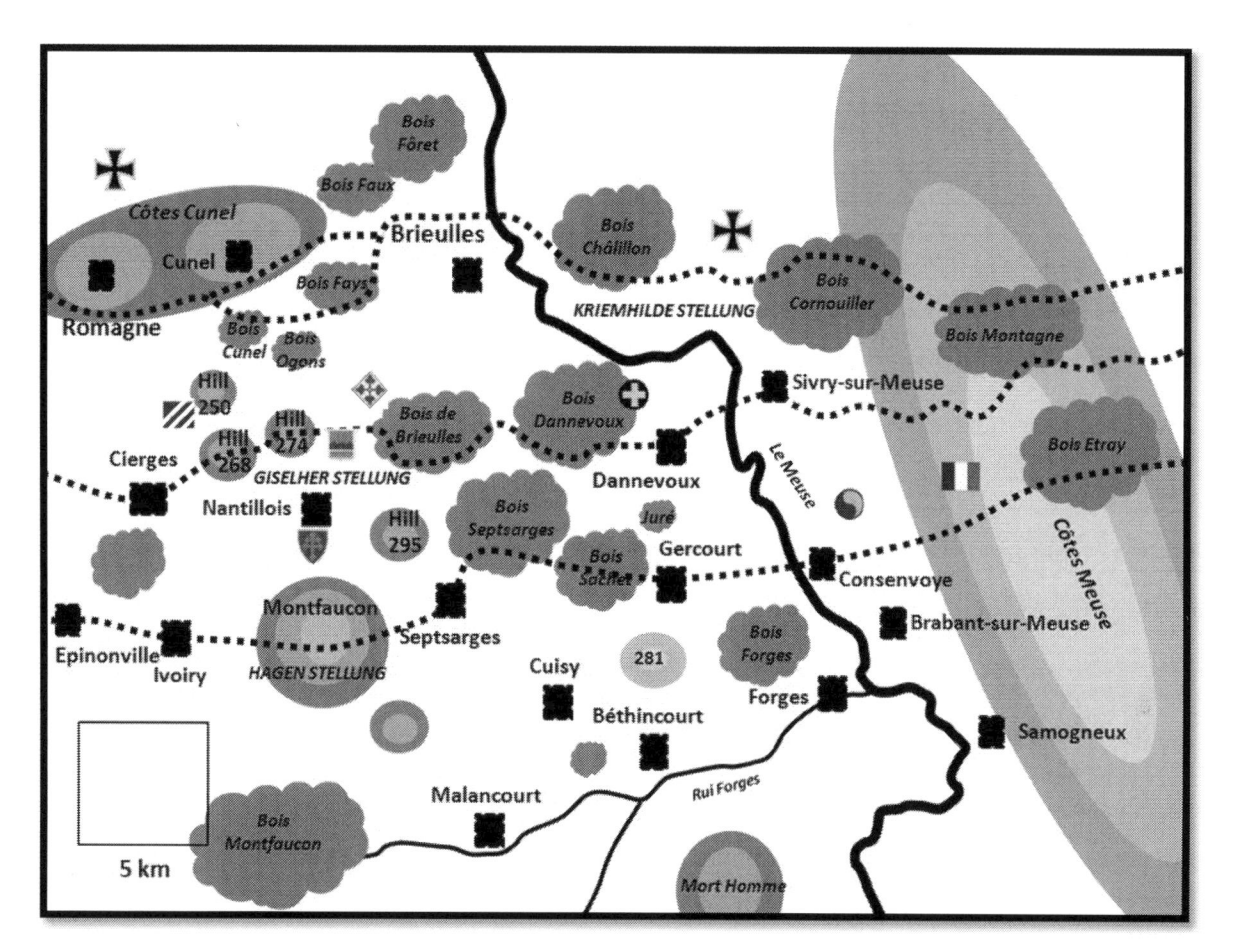

80th Division area of operations Oct. 2-3, 1918.

Chapter 4
Combat in *Bois Brieulles* (Oct. 1-3, 1918).

October 1, 1918.

Weather: Rain.

Roads: Heavy.

By Oct. 1, Pershing's American First Army had made limited gains and suffered horrendous losses in the Meuse-Argonne. The Allied commander-in-chief, Ferdinand Foch, was reportedly so alarmed that he considered calling off the attack in the Meuse-Argonne, especially considering the great advances the British were making in Flanders. But Pershing assured Foch that his Doughboys would in fact break through *FREYA* and take Sedan from the south, even if it meant the death of every one of us. The conversation was relayed to us by "Joe Latrinsky" in this way:

"But we cannot afford such losses, *mon ami*," Foch reportedly said to Pershing.

"You're right General, and I don't intend to take any more than I need to. But rest assured, the American Army will take Sedan!"

"Well General , if you need any more support, you will let me know, no?"

"Yes sir. I need the French corps on my flanks to push farther and faster. The guns on the Heights of the Meuse are tearing my men to pieces!"

"*Oui*, General, we must get them moving."

"Thank you, sir." With that, Pershing returned to his H.Q. to meet with his corps commanders Bullard, Liggett, and Cameron, "Gentlemen," he said, according to Joe Latrinsky who used a Mark Twain accent as Pershing was from Missouri, "I am under extreme pressure to keep the attack moving forward. The British are driving the Germans back at Arras and we have an opportunity to snag hundreds of thousands of the enemy if we take Sedan within the next few days. I know the men are tired, I know we have a lot of inexperienced officers. Corps commanders, I need you to lay the wood. Replace anyone you want. There are no bad soldiers, only bad officers. Be relentless. Get up to the front and put fire into these people and make them realize that we have a chance to end the war right now, in just a few weeks. If we don't, the Germans will simply pull back in an orderly fashion, reestablish their lines, and this war may last until 1920. Do you understand?"

"Yes, sir," they answered in a choral response. And of course Bullard had to pitch in (using a thick Mississippi accent that bothered even we Tidewater, Virginia-types): "Sir, we will break through even if it takes every single one of my men, including me and my staff."

"That's what I want to hear, Bull, now get moving!"

Clearly none of us were there during this exchange, but "Joe" was and that was our understanding of the "low-down." Writing after the war, Lt. Lukens of the 320th Infantry noted pretty much what we all were thinking while we were the Meuse-Argonne:

Things were not moving as rapidly up front as they had at the first jump-off. As our own first drive had shown us, the thick woods which checkerboard the hills [of the sector], and which had not been fought over since the Huns originally took them, made far-more difficult going than the bald, shell-pocked hills around Verdun. The nature of the country lent itself wonderfully to the defensive plans of the Boche; the proportion of forest to clearing was just about enough so that all the clearings were covered by the field of fire from unseen guns in the woods, while the woods were filled with snipers and accurately ranged for artillery. The job was done by brute force, a division going in on a narrow sector and advancing in spite of everything until its momentum was lost, then another one relieving it and doing the same thing.[173]

For the rest of the day of Oct. 1, the infantry regiments of the 80th Division either maintained their positions or continued to move into their new positions while batteries from the 155th Arty. Brig. provided fire support for Brett's departing 160th Inf. Brig. and the Prairie Division in the vicinity of the Triangle. In so doing, Heiner's artillery brigade suffered a few casualties and five soldiers from the 314th Artillery were cited for exceptional gallantry during the day's operations: 1Sgt. Harold Marshall of Battery A, Sergeant Charles R. Shelton of Battery A, Pvt. Glenn D. Hughes of Battery A, Pvt. Roy E. Burroughs of Battery B, and Pvt. Walter L. Paynes of Battery B:

On Oct. 1, 1918, 1Sgt. Marshal was in charge of a detail to load and unload ammunition. The ammunition trucks to which this detail was assigned became jammed on Cuisy Ridge. The road on which the truck was halted was under heavy enemy shell fire. Sergeant Marshall, by his own coolness and courage, succeeded in extricating the trucks from the jam and bringing the ammunition safely to the battery positions.

On Oct. 1, 1918, Sergeant Shelton was in charge of a detail of men from A/314 at the ammunition dump near Cuisy. Although the dump was subjected to heavy

---

[173] As cited in *3/320th Infantry*, 77-78.

shell fire Sergeant Shelton continued to move ammunition from the dump until all of the ammunition had been removed to safety.

On Oct. 1, 1918, Pvt. Hughes was acting as a telephone operator at the battalion O.P. on Dannevoux Ridge. Pvt. Hughes was wounded by a shell fragment while at his post but he nevertheless continued to operate the telephone and refused to leave until ordered to do so by his battery commander.

On the afternoon of Oct. 1, 1918, on Hill 262, the Number 1 Gun of B/314 received a direct hit from a German shell, most of the gun crew either being killed or wounded. Pvt. Burroughs carried to safety 3 members of this gun crew. This work was done under continued heavy shelling of the battery positions.

For us in 1/318th Infantry, Oct. 1 was spent clawing our way further north through *Bois Brieulles* between *GISELHER* and *KRIEMHILDE* with units from the 4th Division. Although we suffered some casualties, it was actually a pretty light day, considering that it was between two of the Germans' main defensive lines. Our patrols reported some enemy activity beyond *GISELHER* but we all knew, "for certain sure," that the ridge to our front, upon which *Village Cunel* and *KRIEMHILDE* were located, was infested with Hun, thick as fleas on a mangy dog from Norfolk. And in front of it was a huge open field with outstanding fields of fire. In fact, the Hun were probably licking their chops waiting for us to attack.

Get out the shovels boys!

It was the waiting for the inevitable that I think was the worst part.

To the south, in Bois Montfaucon with Brett's 160th Inf. Brig., their recovery operations were going as well as expected, although the men were still paying the price for the decision to leave the majority of their packs behind. Lt. Lukens of I/3/320th Infantry remembered:

We went on back, knowing that our job was done for the time being, stopping when chance offered to pick up a loaf of bread or a can of tomatoes from a pile of rations, or to fill our stomachs and canteens at a spring, or to "bum" a smoke, and in this way we drifted back until we came upon our kitchens, where we found a meal of hot canned beef and coffee waiting, our first real honest meal since four days or more.... The comforts of our new position were not expensive, as half of our blankets had been lost, and there was no further weather protection for the men than the "bivvies" they could construct.[174]

---

[174] As cited in *3/320th Infantry*, 75.

Due to his abilities and time in grade, Col. James Cocheu, commander of the 319th Infantry, was tapped for promotion and sent to the General Staff School in Langres to eventually serve as the operations officer for the III Corps. He was replaced by Col. James Love, the 318th Infantry's one-time X.O. Maj. Hugh O'Bear, the commander of 1/319, was also tapped for promotion and was also transferred out of the division. All other major leadership positions stayed in place, until our second drive, which would take a real toll on the Blue Ridge Division.[175]

October 2, 1918.
Weather: Rain.
Roads: Heavy.

On Oct. 2, as Pershing and his corps commanders adjusted their lines to punch through *KRIEMHILDE*—the main German defensive line—General Cronkhite was ordered to concentrate the entire 80th Division just south of *Bois des Ogons* (or *Bois d'Ogons*), between Hill 274 and *Bois Brieulles*, with Jamerson's 159th Inf. Brig. designated as the attack brigade and Brett's 160th Inf. Brig. as the reserve brigade. The object would be to breach *KRIEMHILDE* in the vicinity of *Village Cunel*. While two battalions of the 318th Infantry would be arrayed to lead the attack into *Bois d'Ogons*, my battalion, 1/318, was to remain in *Bois Brieulles* until relieved by a unit from the Ivy Division.[176]

This was to be the big fat fight for the 80th Division, our *sine qua non*.[177]

For the up-and-coming fight, it was decided to breach *KRIEMHILDE* with Col. Woorilow's 318th Infantry (-) on the left, adjoining with elements of the 3rd (Rock of the Marne) Division near Hill 268 and and Col. Howard R. Perry's 317th Infantry on the right, adjoining with with 1/318 in Bois Brieulles.[178] Brett's 160th Inf. Brig., the reserve brigade, would be concentrated near Septsarges, and Heiner's 155th Arty. Brig., currently providing artillery support for the Prairie Division, would be brought over to support the infantry brigades of the 80th Division south of Nantillois.

With receipt of the order to deploy south of Nantillois, Welsh, as the artillery brigade operations officer, sent his battalion and battery commanders, and his scouts and markers out to the area between Septsarges and Nantillois to conduct an R.S.O.P. While conducting said

---

[175] *319th Infantry*, 29.

[176] *Bois d'Ogons* is pronounced "Bwa Doe-gawn."

[177] *Sine qua non* is Latin for "reason of existence."

[178] *Nantillois* is pronounced "Nawn-till-lou-wah."

reconnaissance, Capt. Shelton Piney of 1/313th Artillery was wounded in the foot and Capt. Penniman took command of the battalion with Lt. Morgan taking command of C/1/313th Artillery. With the R.S.O.P. complete, it was decided to place the 314th Artillery between *Septsarges* and Hill 295. While C/1/314th Artillery would be the accompanying battery for Worrilow's 318th Infantry (-), a battery from the 313th Artillery was assigned to be the accompanying battery for the 317th Infantry.[179]

In preparation for the new offensive, Brett's 160th Inf. Brig. moved northeast from Bois Montfaucon and took up positions around Cuisy. Maj. Ashby Williams of 1/320th remembered:

> *As we were going down the hill into Cuisy. I remember a Boche plane came over. flying very low and firing his A.R. as he came. My men opened fire on him but he got away, apparently unhurt. He was evidently looking for the French artillery which was camouflaged along the road and I remember how the French gunners beat a hasty retreat to their cover to prevent having their pictures taken. We then proceeded down through the town of Cuisy and up the ridge to the south of it. Here the brigade adjutant came up and said that it was the general's plan that the brigade should occupy the trench systems along the parallel ridges, one in front of Cuisy, one in back of it, and the other in back of that, the 320th on the right and the 319th on the left. I hastily drew up a plan in accordance with this direction and sent it to the other battalions of this regiment and the other regiment. Ultimately, however, the ridge in front of Cuisy was under such constant and heavy shell fire that the battalions located there had to move back to the ridge back of Cuisy...From the ridge where my troops were located the country round about spread out in panoramic view. Indeed, the terrain thereabout presented some aspects of unusual interest, both from tactical and historical points of view. To the northwest, about a mile-and-a-half distant, standing in its majestic desolation on a bold summit, was the historic town of Montfaucon, which had been such a formidable stumbling block in the way of the 79th Division a few days before. It was from a high tower in this town that the German Crown Prince is said to have watched, with the aid of powerful glasses, the great battle of Verdun. A few miles to the southeast was Bethincourt and the famous Dead Man's Hill, where we had jumped off a few days before in the sector to our right. Just in front of us in the valley, not more than a few hundred yards away, were the walls of the little town of Cuisy, battered to*

---

[179] *314th Artillery*, 39; *317th Infantry*, 63.

pieces by the German guns searching for the French artillery that lined the slope just beyond the town. Indeed, the Germans never ceased to shell the town and the area thereabout while we were there... The terrain around Cuisy, and as far as the eye could see for that matter, was a series of parallel ridges absolutely devoid of trees or habitations of man. The whole country presented the aspect of having been especially fashioned by some devilish hand for the special purpose of fighting man against man, and the appearance was heightened by the fact that every ridge was furrowed and seamed on its crest and forward slope by a network of trenches and the valleys and slopes were massed with wire entanglements that had been battered to pieces in the fighting that had taken place a few days before. Indeed, one was impelled to admire the splendid valor of the troops of the 4th Division who took the area. The toll of dead and wounded must have been terrific, although there was no way we could tell, because the battlefield had been policed up before we reached the place.[180]

As we in the 159th Inf. Brig. waited for the final attack order, we were subjected to relentless artillery and gas attacks throughout the day and during the night. According to Lt. Craighill of 2/317th Infantry: "Gas sentries necessarily had to be on all night, and several times the alarm was given and our needed rest disturbed."[181] Lingering gas was always a problem, and arsenic poisoning of water in the bottom of shell holes was known to occur. Mustard gas, which could eat flesh like lye, particularly in damp and moist areas like the Meuse-Argonne, would often destroy the testicles of those who took shelter in the craters where the gas lingered. I would also like to note that a mustard gas injury often had long-term effects. Some Doughs returned home disfigured from it. For example, during the 1920s, several American municipalities possessed the temerity to make it illegal for a disfigured veteran to even walk down a public street without wearing a mask. The law was called "Being Ugly in Public." Can you believe that!?

Rocked and blasted for almost a week straight, some of us began to crack (myself included), but the higher-ups refused to change their plans. No matter what, they insisted, the Blue Ridge Boys would breach *KRIEMHILDE* even if it meant the death of every last one of us (don't worry, as there was another division somewhere out there to replace us). As for me, I thought that my life was worth more, but if Germany had won the war, retaining Belgium and Luxemburg, much of the East like most of present-day Poland, Ukraine, and the Baltic States,

---

[180] As cited in *1/320th Infantry*, 89-90.

[181] *317th Infantry*, 61.

and gaining several Belgian and French colonies, then Great Britain would probably be next. And after them, would no doubt come us. Besides, if Britain and France lost, they'd no doubt renege on repaying their war loans to U.S. banks, collapsing our already-fragile economy. That was what Joe Latrinsky told us, anyway.

Some readers may wonder why I have foot-noted other authors when discussing division operations. The answer is easy. During the war, I only really understood what was going on in my squad or platoon—sometimes company. In the Army, one is little interested with what does not directly concern him, and while I found after the war that we all had similar experiences, I do not want to deliver a "Joe Latrinsky" to the reader. Again, what we remember, we write, and what we don't or won't, we don't. Much of this, for us lowly Doughs at least, is at best a fuzzy memory, clouded by the trauma of war.

As the men of America's Blue Ridge Division awaited the up-and-coming assault against *KRIEMHILDE*, we were occasionally awed/entertained/horrified by what went on above us, in the air. Every day, sometimes twice a day, we'd get raided by Hun aircraft flying in from the north. My platoon called them "J.E.B. Stuart's" after the famous Confederate cavalry Maj. Gen. "Jeb" Stuart from Virginia who was known for his lightning raids during our failed War for Southern Independence. Maj. Ashby Williams of 1/320th Infantry, in his trench near Cuisy, remembered one particular air battle that occurred above him:

> *[My particular area] was lined with six-inch howitzers that never ceased to fire day and night. The fire of these guns was observed and directed by an observer in a balloon suspended high in the air to the right of the guns. The Boche planes were constantly trying to destroy the balloon and thus put out the eyes of the big guns. His first two trials were a failure, although the shots were well-enough directed to compel the observer to take to his parachute and jump to the ground, a distance of perhaps two hundred meters. The third time the Boche came after the balloon, the plane dived out of a cloud that hung rather low that day and heading with his nose straight to the balloon, fired with his M.G., using incendiary bullets, the blue traces of which could be plainly seen going into the gas bag of the balloon. The observer jumped with his parachute and the balloon had gone up in smoke before he reached the ground. It was a beautiful and a thrilling sight. It was a drama and a tragedy in real life with 10,000 spectators looking on. Of course our M.G.s and our riflemen, too, for that matter, opened fire on the Boche plane, sending thousands of shots in his direction, but he got away apparently unharmed and no doubt rejoicing at his quarry. I admired*

that Boche extravagantly and so did many others who saw that heroic act, and I believe that if he had fallen into our hands we would have treated him as a real hero. Such is the sporting instinct of an American soldier.[182]

October 3, 1918.

Weather: Fair.

Roads: Heavy.

"The morning of Oct. 3 burst forth beautifully clear with a faint mist hanging in the valleys," remembered Lt. Craighill of the 317th Infantry. "But for the occasional burst of a shell you would hardly believe that a war was in progress."[183] I remember waking up that morning wrapped in our dirty shelter half while Getz manned the "Sho-sho." I remember being tired, cold, stiff, and hungry. In fact, that's what I remember the most from the war—the feeling of total discomfort marked by extreme periods of fear, hate, and action. Getz probably said to me when I woke up:

"Good morning sunshine! Did you have a good night's rest!?"

"Uh, no."

"Well there there, now, what can Papa Getz do to make you feel better?"

"How about a cold glass of beer, a warm bed, and a hot woman?"

"No can do, brother, because I already got 'em! You missed it all while you were sleeping!"

"I'll bet that they were as ugly as you!"

"Maybe so, but beggars can't be choosy. How about some Corn Willy and coffee?"

"How about a steak?"

"Sure, as long as it looks like Corn Willy!"

At 8:00 A.M., orders were received from division, whose P.C. was in a ravine between Béthincourt and Cuisy, along the Béthincourt-Cuisy Road. Exerpts from the order are as follows:

---

[182] As cited in *1/320th Infantry*, 91.

[183] *317th Infantry*, 61.

80th Infantry Division.
A.E.F.

F.O. 17
Oct. 3, 1918
MAP: DUN SUR MEUSE: 1/20,000

3. 159th Infantry Brigade
(a) the 159th Brigade will lead the attack in the 80th Div. Zone.
(b) The initial disposition for the attack will be with Regiments side by side, the 317th on the right, the 318th Inf. (less 1 bn.) on the left; each regiment in column of battalions. The rear battalion, 317th Inf. will constitute the Brigade reserve at the disposal of the Brigade Commander.
(c) The zone of action and objectives as indicated on maps furnished.
(d) One Co. 313th M. G. Bn. is assigned to the 317th Inf. and one Co. to the 318th Inf. They will report at the time and places to be designated by the regimental commanders.
(e) During the night of D-1 day units will occupy positions as indicated verbally by the Brigade Commander. All units will be in position by 4:30 a.m. on D day....
(g) One Btry., 313th F. A., will be placed at the disposal of each regiment of Infantry, as accompanying artillery. One Btry. will be held at the disposal of the Brigade Commander. Batteries assigned to regiments of infantry will report at the time and places to be designated by regimental commanders.
(h) Brigade Reserve consisting of 1 bn., 317th Inf., 2 Cos. 313th M. G. Bn., 1 Btry. 313th F. A., and 1 Co. 305th Regt. of Engrs., will occupy the following positions: Bn. 317th Inf. 500 M. east of Fayel Fme. ravine N. of Montfaucon-Cuisy road; M. G. Cos., vicinity of Trench des Fainaentes 1 km. E. of Montfaucon; Art. Btry. point to be designated later; Co. Engrs. in Trench running E. from Malancourt-Montfaucon road 200 Ms. S. of and parallel to Montfaucon-Cuisy road.

By order of the Commander.
WALDRON, Chief of Staff.

Field Order 17 called for the battalions of the 159th Inf. Brig., minus 1/318, which remained in its forward position in Bois Brieulles, to assemble between Nantillois and Bois Brieulles. At 1:30 P.M., General Jamerson, the commander of the 159th Inf. Brig., met with all of his regimental and battalion commanders in blown-up Nantillois. He delivered a verbal order that outlined the army's plan of attack for the next day, Oct. 4, 1918. The commanders were told that the decimated 79th (Cross of Lorraine) Division had been replaced by the veteran 3rd (Rock of the Marne) Division, recently-arrived from *Saint-Mihiel*, and that Jamerson's 159th Inf. Brig. would lead the attack in the 80th Division's zone by maneuvering north up the right side of the Nantillois-Cunel Road, blow past Hill 274, attack through *Bois d'Ogons* and *Ferme Madeleine*, and storm KRIEMHILDE at *Cunel* (the objective).[184] In the bigger picture, the 3rd Division was to attack *Cunel* from the west, the 4th Division was to attack it from the east, and the 80th (Blue Ridge) Division was to attack it "hey diddle, diddle, right up the middle" (i.e., a double-envelopment with the 80th Division holding the middle).

Enveloping Attack

Cover the front of the enemy with sufficient force to hold his attention and, with the rest of your command, strike a flank more or less obliquely. Since your line is now longer than his, and you have more rifles in action, your fire is converging while that of your enemy's is diverging. Never attempt the envelopment of both flanks unless you greatly outnumber your enemy. Cooperation between the frontal and enveloping attack is essential to success. The fraction of the command that envelops the enemy is generally larger than that part in his front. A wide turning movement is not an enveloping movement. It is dangerous because your troops are separated and can be defeated in detail. In an enveloping movement your line will usually be continuous; it simply overlaps and envelops the enemy. An enveloping attack will nearly always result locally in a frontal attack, for it will meet the enemy's reserve. Let us repeat: do not attempt a wide turning movement. Your forces will be separated, they may not be able to assist each other, and can be defeated in detail. The tendency of a beginner is to attempt a wide turning movement. The error of dispersion is then committed.[185]

As stated in the above directive, "never attempt the envelopment of both flanks unless you greatly outnumber your enemy. Cooperation between the frontal and enveloping attack is

---

[184] *Ferme Madeleine* or "Farm Madeleine" is pronounced "Fairm-ah Mad-awl-ayn."

[185] *P.M.*, 243-44.

essential to success. The fraction of the command that envelops the enemy is generally larger than that part in his front." It was essential, then, that the flanks of the attack, i.e., the 3rd and 4th Divisions, be "larger that that part in front," which was us. Once our officers learned of the plan, they started to quote, by memory, Alfred Lord Tennyson's famous stanza from "The Charge of the Light Brigade":

"Forward, the Light Brigade! Charge for the guns!" he said:
Into the Valley of Death rode the 600.
"Forward, the Light Brigade!"
Was there a man dismay'd?
Not tho' the soldier knew
Someone had blunder'd:
Theirs not to make reply,
Theirs not to reason why,
Theirs but to do and die.

Up to this point, from Sept. 26-Oct. 3, America's Blue Ridge Division had captured 35 Hun officers, 815 men, 21 pieces of artillery, 23 trench mortars, 92 M.G.s, lots of ammunition and stores, including over five million rounds of small arms ammunition, and over 5,000 boxes of hand grenades. The German stores at Dannevoux alone valued at more than $10 million. In our first major action, Brett's 160th Inf. Brig. had attacked along a two km front which widened to five, had advanced nine km and reached its assigned objective (*GISELHER*) by midnight of the first day of the battle.

The only other division to reach the Army objective during the First Push was the 33rd (Prairie) Division, which was to our right. To be fair, the Prairie Division in fact had a couple km less distance to travel than we did in the 80th Division and the German Second Position (*GISELHER*) did not extend across its sector, like it did in ours, it had only one woods to conquer instead of a half-dozen, and it had no strongly held heights barring its way. But they certainly did suffer lots of casualties from artillery that was fired from the Heights of the Meuse!

The truth is that German tenacity increased generally in proportion to the distance west of the Meuse. For example, the Prairie Division suffered 296 casualties on Sept. 26 and its total for Sept. 26-Oct. 7 was 1,370, with 197 K.I.A., including one regiment's loss of 588 wounded to 53 dead. During this period the Prairie Division put all four of its infantry regiments into line along the river when it took over the 80th Division's front as well as its own. Since it staged no attacks after Sept. 26 until Oct. 8, its casualty list demonstrates the effectiveness of German artillery firing from the Heights of the Meuse.

In contrast, the Blue Ridge Division's casualties from Sept. 26-Oct. 3 were 1,100, with 252 K.I.A. This figure includes the 150 casualties suffered by the 318th Infantry while with the 4th Division. Of the 252 K.I.A., 166 were from infantry regiments (66%). In comparison, the 4th Division suffered 2,627 casualties, with 564 K.I.A. in its infantry regiments. The 79th (Cross of Lorraine) Division, which was assigned the horrible job of attacking Montfaucon frontally, suffered a whopping 3,529 casualties, including 740 K.I.A. in its infantry regiments.

Several factors kept the 80th Division's casualties relatively low. We believe that the most important was that in Cronkhite there was no desire to make any personal "reputation" at a needless cost in life. He had nothing more to prove to the Army, as he had already "been there/done that." Was he resolute that the subordinate units of the division took the assigned objectives? Yes. But not to merely enhance his prestige within the Army bureaucracy. Cronkhite simply wanted it taken on time. Another advantage that we had is that most of our field grade officers were solid performers and we were generally spared from bungling. If they were were not inspired "military geniuses" like Alexander, Caesar, Frederick the Great, Napoleon, or Robert E. Lee, the very least that could be said about them was that they were able, conscientious men who knew their business, avoided costly errors, and accomplished their missions.

As for our junior officers, who, almost to the man, were as new to the Army as we selectees were, they either learned fast or were killed fast. They gained invaluable experience in almost impossible terrain during the First Push. Our engineers also distinguished themselves and our Red Legs had shown they could move over, under, or through obstacles as well as shoot. Full use had also been made of our M.G. sections and supporting weapons, as command had insisted. Our S.O.S. was apparently better than in some other divisions. Most importantly, our infantry proved resolute and reliable—they not only possessed doggedness, but also fighting spirit.

True, the Germans in front of us were fighting merely a delaying action, but they were also skilled soldiers who, if they lacked enough infantry for serious counterattacks because they'd been caught napping with their supports on the wrong side of the river, they still fought with efficiency and steadfastness. Every one of their numerous M.G.s, light and heavy, had to be eliminated—at the cost of somebody's life. Through the rain and fog and darkness-drenched woods, out into the open spaces to face the interlocking M.G. fire, with no dry spot on which to rest, we men of the Blue Ridge Division *Always Moved Forward*. If sleep were possible, it was by lying in the rain to wake with fingers so numbed they could not move.

Although our spirit was always good, I think that it was never better than it was at this point in the campaign. For example, cooks insisted that their companies should have hot food, and once done, many asked if they could go out on patrol. Drivers kept their trucks and teams going in spite of shells and mud, still undecided which one was worse. Determination to "help the other fellow," to back him up and to pull one's full weight, was in evidence everywhere.

For the big attack slated for Oct. 4, the division's "Second Push," Cronkhite directed Jamerson's 159th Inf. Brig. (minus 1/318) to attack into *Bois d'Ogons* with the 318th Infantry (-) on the left and the 317th on the right, in column of battalions (with two companies in front, two in support). Brett's 160th Inf. Brig. was ordered to follow Heiner's 159th Arty. Brig. and be ready to deliver *le coup de grâce*.[186] We in Sweeny's 1/318th Infantry, on the right meanwhile, were instructed to prepare to hand over our hard-won positions in *Bois Brieulles* to a battalion from the 4th Division in order to eventually join our Blue Ridge brothers who would soon be attacking in the vicinity of *Bois d'Ogons,* which was to our left front.

Maj. Wise's 2/318th Infantry was to lead the epic attack into *Bois d'Ogons* up the left flank of the division's axis of advance, followed by 3/318. Lt. Cabell's G/2/318 was on the left, adjoining with members of the 3rd Division and Lt. Lakin's F/2/318 was on the right, connecting with a company from Col. Perry's 317th Infantry Regiment, 80th Division. Companies E and H, commanded by Lt. Neubauer and Capt. Moore, respectively, were in support. Like the other battalions, Companies G and F were in front, followed by E and H in support (in combat, we numbered the companies 1, 2, 3, 4 by their position in the line—1 and 2 in the front, with 1 being on the left). Col. Worrilow's P.C. was established in Nantillois itself, about 300 yards behind 2/318. Lt. Craighill of the 317th Infantry remembered:

> *The colonel, the three majors, and several other officers filed into our trench and we could see by the serious look on all their faces that there was a big job ahead. A rather long discussion ensued, and there was much talk about the time being too short for proper preparation. This talk was useless though, because it had to be done and we were soon told that the regiment was to go over the top the next morning. There was no time to lose—the men had to be gotten ready, orders had to be issued, and many, many details had to be attended to. There was no time for reconnaissance of the ground and without exception the terrain was entirely unfamiliar to all concerned.*[187]

---

[186] *Le coup de grâce* is French for "the final blow" and is pronounced "Lay Coo day Grah."

[187] *317th Infantry*, 61-62.

The division M.G. battalions were assigned either barrage or direct support duties. While one M.G. company each was sent to support the assault infantry battalions, the rest were ordered to establish barrage positions atop Hill 295.[188] The division's artillery brigade was ordered to support the infantry attack no later than dawn, Nov. 4. At dusk, Nov. 3 therefore, the brigade, led by Lt. Col. Brunzell's 313th Artillery, departed its firing positions around Hill 281 and headed for Septsarges *via* Gercourt. Preceded by artillery reconnaissance officers, scouts, and markers, Capt. Frank Crandall's E/2/313th Artillery led the brigade move to Nantillois. When the battery moved into an open vale to the north of Hill 281, however, it was immediately struck by a Hun artillery strike from the Heights of the Meuse. One round exploded under the carriage of a gun, badly damaged it, mortally wounded its section chief, and wounded several horses. Battery E then let out at a trot across country toward Septsarges, paralleling Bois Sachet, still under fire and with the wounded horses bleeding badly. Understanding the insanity of moving farther, Capt. Crandall informed Maj. Nash of 2/313th Artillery to turn back and find another route.[189]

With this information in hand, Nash decided to weave his batteries, which stretched out to about a km in length, south through the ruins of *Béthincourt* and then north through *Cuisy* and into *Septsarges* where he met with the regimental reconnaissance officers, scouts, and markers who directed the entire regiment to go into battery between *Bois Septsarges* and Hill 295. According to Lt. Thomas Crowell, the telephone officer of the 313th Artillery:

> *This was the first and only time that the whole regiment fought from the same position. All the batteries were together, almost in line. 1/313 was echeloned in the western edge of the woods, B and C side by side and A shooting over them. There was excellent cover in the woods and excellent defilade, but the field of fire was limited. 2/313 was located in a little strip of the woods just west of A Battery. They had fine cover and good defilade and a large field of fire. The men had cover in fox-holes near the guns and in parts of an old trench system in Bois Septsarges. Access was good in both positions from roads in rear and excellent echelons were established in Bois Septsarges.*[190]

The 313th Artillery was soon joined by its brethren from Walker's 314th and Goodfellow's 315th Artillery, Whitaker's 305th Ammunition Train, and H.Q./155th Arty. Brig. While in this position near Septsarges, the batteries of the brigade were shelled throughout the night of Oct.

---

[188] *317th Infantry*, 63.

[189] *313th Artillery*, 49.

[190] As cited in *Ibid*, 49-50.

3-4 with a hateful mix of gas and H.E. Because of this, the fire direction officers (those who actually calculated the gun solutions) had to plot their up-and-coming barrages while wearing gas masks and the men positioned the guns, dug the trail holes, etc., similarly handicapped. Nobody in the division had had a good night's rest for ten days and nearly all had marched several km under very fatiguing conditions. Most of us had been under direct enemy fire for a about week, which seriously worked on our nerves.

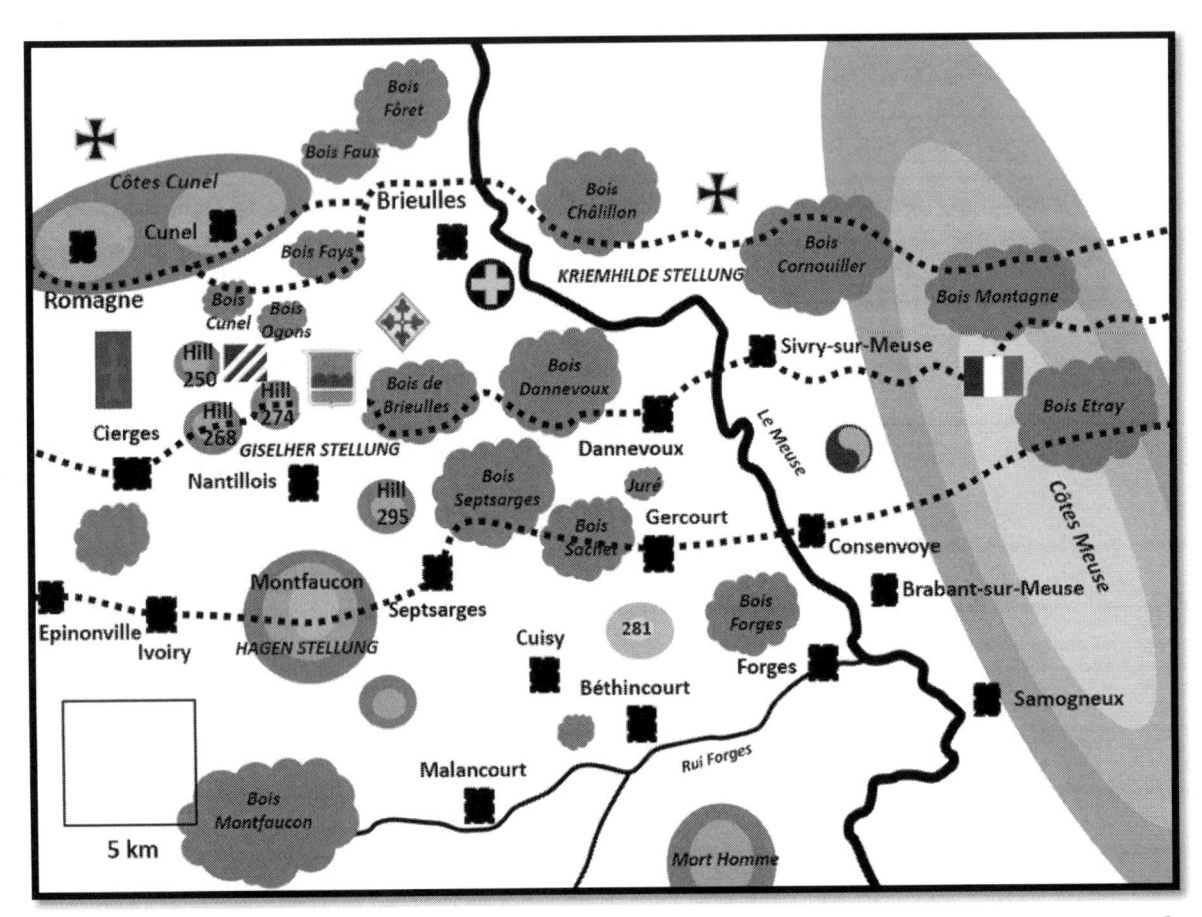

80th Division Area of Operations, Oct. 4, 1918. While the Blue Ridge Division was supposed to attack Bois d'Ogons "Hey-Diddle-Diddle-Right-Up-the-Middle," the 3rd and 4th Divisions were to conduct a double envelopment around its flanks, taking the Heights of Cunel.

The American 3rd, 4th, and 80th Divisions were up against the 5th Bavarian Reserve Division, the 7th Prussian Reserve Division, the 28th Prussian Division, and the 236th Prussian Division.

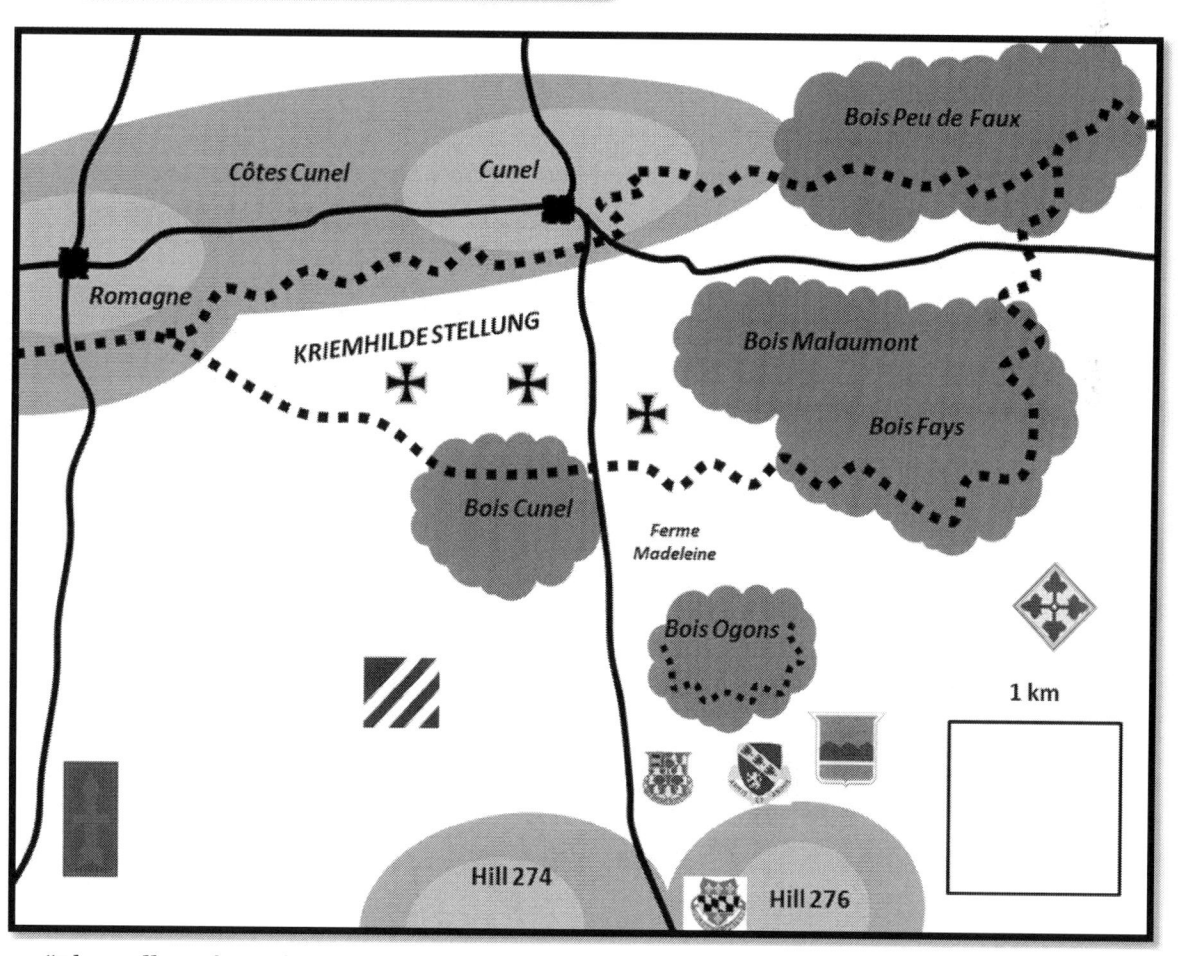

"The Valley of Death" at Ferme Madeleine, Oct. 4, 1918. The 159th Inf. Bde. Was on the attack with the 318th Inf. on the right and the 317th Inf. on the left. The 319th Inf. was in reserve on Hill 276.

Cunel-Nantillois Road looking north (L) and Our attack axis into *Bois d' Ogons* (background) (R). This picture was taken during the winter of 1918-19.

"Bois d'Ogons and slopes to the south."

(L) Cunel-Nantillois Road on right and *Côtes Cunel* in the background. While the 317th Inf. attacked up the right side of the road, the 3rd Inf. Div. up the right. Bois d'Ogons is in the right background of the picture. Ferme Madelaine looking north (R). In the background is Bois Cunel. This place was the bane of our existence.

Hun outpost line being assaulted by Doughs (L) and Pvt. Atherton Clark, L/3/317th Inf., 80th Div. His respirator box is "At the Ready."

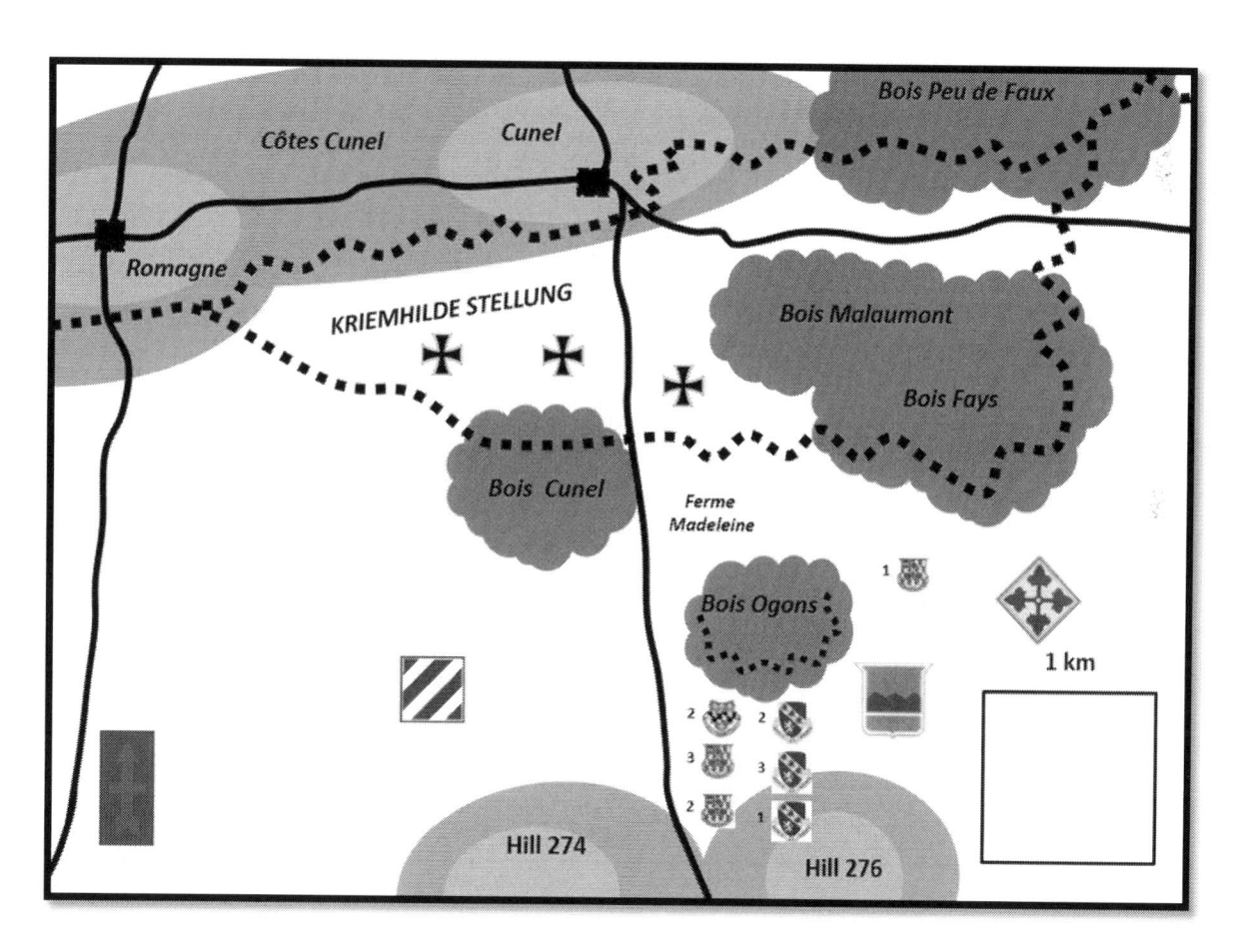

Straight into the belly of the beast, Oct. 5, 1918, A.M. Typical brigade attack with assault, support, and reserve battalions.

La Ferme Madeleine, right in the heart of the "Valley of Death." Bois Cunel is in the background.

"Sunday Morning at Cunel" (L). This captures what it was like for us in Bois d'Ogons and the Valley of Death. "Typical scene in Bois Malaumont" (R). We felt like we were with Bobby Lee in the Wilderness, 1864.

"The French 75" (L) was renown for its rapid firing, "Let's Go!" (C), and "Mosquito Tank in the Ditch" (R). This is what we mostly saw of our tanks.

French Renault "Mosquito" tanks advancing through a bombed-out French ville.

"Tank Attack" by Harvey Dunn.

"No Man's Land, 11-1-18." A soldier from the 319th Inf. stands besides a knocked out French Renault tank, objects which we Doughs derisively called "Clank-ity-clanks."

"German Anti-Tank Gun in Firing Position, Oct., 1918" (L) and "German plan forced down near *Cierges*, Oct. 4, 1918" (R).

Chapter 5
The Hell of *Bois d'Ogons* and *KRIEMHILDE* (October 4-6)

<u>October 4, 1918</u>.

Weather: Rainy.

Roads: Fair.

During the early-morning hours of Oct. 4, Lt. Craighill of the 317th Infantry remembered:

> *The sky was clear but the stars were dimmed as a slight mist hung closely to the ground. The whir of a big bombing machine could be heard far off on its way leaving a wake of utter desolation and destruction. Occasionally the burst of a large shell illuminated the surroundings, and the flash from our guns made one think of a far-off thunder storm with its intermittent flashes of lightning. On and on trudged the long column, struggling over huge heaps of earth thrown up by terrific explosions. Time was creeping on and the leading battalion had not yet reached the designated forming up place.*[191]

On its way north to its assigned attack position, the 317th Infantry got lost.

You heard me right—lost.

This may sound incredible but given the very difficult circumstances, I'm shocked that it didn't occur more often.

Lt. Craighill remembered that the regiment "closed up on the *Montfaucon-Septsarges* Road, just west of *Septsarges*, and passed through several batteries of French 75s" until it reached the vicinity of Hill 295, which was held by a battalion from the 318th Infantry, the appointed brigade concentration area. "The going was hard—there were numerous thick horny hedges to go through and the grade at this particular juncture was very steep. The fog had gotten pretty thick, making it almost an impossibility to arrive at a true sense of direction." Here the men "cut their blanket rolls loose from the packs, leaving them with only reserve rations and a few necessary toilet articles, and one blanket adjusted in a circular shape, tied around the haversack." Gas masks were put in the "alert position" and the "companies formed in platoon columns." Before long, the lead battalion, 2/317, reached the top of the western edge of the hill in the Egyptian darkness and started down the forward slope. At this point, it was decided that they were bearing too far to the left, which was true. The regimental commander, Col. Howard R. Perry, therefore decided to steer more to the right or east. Even then, however, he never made

---

[191] As cited in *317th Infantry*, 63.

it to the correct concentration area before H-Hour, appreciably under-minding the up-and-coming attack.[192]

The day's objective was the small, blown-up *Village Cunel*, which stood atop a low-lying ridge north of *Bois d'Ogons*. This doesn't sound like much, but we were, in fact, supposed to break the strongest defensive line of the vaunted HINDENBURG STELLUNG: KRIEMHILDE. Each infantry platoon was to advance using as much cover and concealment as possible. Individual soldier initiative and fitness to move forward with his rifle, bayonet, and grenades, was essential. Once a platoon was knocked out due to casualties or sheer exhaustion, a following platoon would take its place. As many M.G. sections as possible would be pressed forward. We were told that the area in question was held by the Prussian 236th Infantry Division.

They have 236 divisions!?

At 5:35 A.M., a rolling barrage delivered by the division's 155th Art. Brig. kicked off the attack, targeting *KRIEMHILDE* between *Bois d'Ogons* and *Cunel*. About fifteen minutes later, the Hun answered with a counter-barrage, which, for once, made ours seem like that of a small boy. It was bad. Scores of Blue Ridgers were either blown to bits or buried beneath the vomiting earth.

At 6:00 A.M., 2/318 crossed the L.D. north of Nantillois and advanced two kms up the axis of advance—guiding on the right or east side of the Cunel-Nantillois Road—and pushed into Bois d'Ogons by 7:30 A.M., following the barrage line. Company F was on the right and Company G was on the left, using the road as a guide, with E and H in support. Behind them was 3/318.[193]

Perry's 317th Infantry, which was supposed to attack in conjunction with the 318th Infantry, was nowhere to be found, as it was still making its way over from the left, and some of the divisional M.G. sections were still coming up from the south.[194] Because of this, the right flank of the 318th Infantry was exposed, although we in 1/318 were holding the left flank of Bois Brieulles.

It was hoped that Bois d'Ogons would simply be out-posted—that the "rough stuff" would start only once we began to cross the open fields of *Ferme Madeleine* and frontally assault *KRIEMHILDE* between Bois Cunel and Fay. That's where command thought we'd suffer 50% or more casualties and they were already calling it the "Valley of Death," hearkening back to the

---

[192] *317th Infantry*, 63.

[193] *318th Infantry*, 172.

[194] *317th Infantry*, 65.

accursed area between Little Round Top and Devil's Den at the Battle of Gettysburg. There, it was thought, we'd hand the battle over to Lt. Col. James Love's 319th Infantry of Brett's 160th Inf. Brig. and they would deliver *le côup de grace*, breach the line, and seize the heights.

That was the plan, anyway.

The hopes of the men of 2/318 were soon dashed, however, when it learned that *Bois d'Ogons* was in fact strongly held by the Hun with the Gun and those woods became *the absolute bane of our existence*—the defining days of our many months in France. One can plainly see how our first attack failed by reading the message traffic. At 7:35 A.M., Maj. Wise, commander of 2/318 (HATFIELD) sent the following message to Col. Worrilow, commander of 318th Infantry (HAMMOND): "HAMMOND, this is HATFIELD: No signs of HARPER [317th Infantry]. I am enfiladed three ways by machine guns." At 7:50 A.M.: "HAMMOND, this is HATFIELD: Held up by machine guns in Ogons Woods, rear slope, under observation and heavy shelling. You must turn wood from right or left."[195]

With Perry's 317th Infantry still coming up from the left, Col. Worrilow moved 3/318 from reserve and deployed it to the right of 2/318. But still, the 318th Infantry could not advance, the German line being too strong and the thick woods of Bois d'Ogons impeding the effective use of A.R.s, R.G.s, I.G.s, M.G.s, or mortars, let alone artillery. At 8:15 A.M., B/1/314th Artillery, the 317th Infantry's accompanying battery, could only get as far north as the back side of Hill 274, where it went into position on the right side of the road and established an O.P. on top of the hill. According to one soldier from the 314th Artillery: "The infantry had not met with the hoped-for success nor were they anywhere near Cunel…Capt. Graves was told that the infantry had no mission for him and his battery was returned to 1/314 in the afternoon."[196] We all later believed that the first attack through Bois d'Ogons failed for the following reasons:

1. The 317th Infantry (HARPER) was unsuccessful in crossing the line of departure (L.D.) at the same time as the 318th Infantry (HAMMOND), thus leaving 2/318 (HATFIELD's) right flank "in the air."

2. The Rock of the Marne Division also failed to advance as expected, leaving HATFIELD's left flank "in the air."

3. The exposure of both of 2/318's flanks made it necessary to throw out strong flank guard detachments from 3/318 (HANSCOM) and involved them in the attack much earlier than should have been necessary.

---

[195] As cited in *318th Infantry*,

[196] As cited in *314th Artillery*, 39.

4. The failure of flanking units to advance resulted in Companies F and G of 2/318 being ripped to pieces by German M.G. fire not only from front, but also from both flanks.

5. Being at the apex of a triangle, Hun artillery delivered massive artillery against 2/318, which had its neck stuck far-out in Bois d'Ogons.

The inevitable result was that Maj. Wise's 2/318th Infantry suffered very heavy casualties, including the major himself, and its battered remnants fell back to the L.D., which was held by H.Q./318. This first attack into Bois d'Ogons cost 2/318 all of its company commanders and 60% of its remaining officers were made *hors de combat*. Everyone blamed Col. Perry, the commander of the 317th Infantry.

Fair? Probably not, but that's just the way it is.

During this day's battle, Pvt. Eddie Baum of M/3/318th Infantry earned the D.S.C. His citation reads:

> *For extraordinary heroism in action in the BOIS OGONS, France, 4 October, 1918. Private Baum was acting as a stretcher bearer with another soldier who was shot by a sniper. Going out under fire from the sniper, he captured the latter with the aid of another man. While taking his prisoner to the rear, Private Baum found a wounded man whom he carried to the aid station under heavy fire, while his companion went on with the prisoner. Upon returning from the aid station he continued his work of rescuing the wounded.* [197]

To make matters even worse for us, believe it or not, Hun artillery attacks launched from *les Côtes de Meuse* (yes, still!) continued throughout the day. These types of attacks are especially trying to troop morale, especially when they come from one's right flank or right rear as it gives troops the feeling that they are being fired upon by their own artillery. Soon after noon, 2/318 sent the following message: "HAMMOND to HAROLD [159th Inf. Brig.]: Request counter-battery work on batteries east of the Meuse."[198]

I say again: *the battle for Bois d'Ogons Oct. 4-6, 1917, was the most challenging of all of our fights—it was hell on earth—the Devil's Cauldron*. The 159th Inf. Brig. had already suffered some 40% casualties since it crossed the L.D. on Sept. 26 and how we were actually going to punch through that witch-bitch *KRIEMHILDE* near Cunel we did not know. In fact, we all thought we were going to die and then a follow-on division would move in and take all the glory.

---

[197] As cited in *318th Infantry*, 69.

[198] *Ibid*, 172.

With the attack stalled at *Bois d'Ogons*, Cronkhite (HAMILTON) ordered the one battalion from Brett's 160th Inf. Brig. to be sent forward to support the attack of Jamerson's 159th Inf. Brig. The selected battalion was Maj. James Montague's 2/319th Infantry (white circles on their helmets and code-named "HALIBUT"), which was stationed atop Hill 295 with the regiment's supporting weapons. HALIBUT was attached to the 318th Infantry to take the place of we in 1/318, which was still operating in *Bois Brieulles* with the Ivy Division. At 3:45 P.M., Cronkhite sent the following message to 3/319: "HALIBUT, this is HAMILTON: Move into HAROLD sector. Two companies in first wave, two in second. Pass through HATFIELD and HANSCOM and attack Bois Ogons following barrage, which will start at 4:30 P.M."[199]

In moving forward, Montague's 2/319 was strafed by a German aeroplane near Hill 295. As the plane looped around for a second run, however, it was brought down by some "Archies" and crash-landed into a camouflaged battery of the 314th Artillery, which suffered no casualties. Shortly after, another Hun aeroplane was brought down in a similar fashion, but this one completely collapsed and caught fire before it hit the ground.[200] Lt. Furr of the 314th M.G. remembered:

> *Both the Allied and German air fleets showed great activity that morning—four German planes were brought down within an hour. German plans swept low, machine-gunning the railroad cut and the hill on which the battalion was located and incidentally stirring up everyone in the vicinity to take a shot back at them—"Archies," M.G.s and the "Doughboy" with his rifle.*[201]

The second attack against *Bois d'Ogons* was launched soon after 4:30 P.M. with 1/317 on the right and 2/319 on the left. In 2/319, Capt. Herr's Company F was on the right and Capt. Keezel's Company H was on the left as the attack companies. 3/318 was in support of 2/319 and the now-decimated 2/318 was in reserve. For the 317th Infantry, 2/317 was support and 3/317 was reserve.

This second attack also failed to break the German line, although 2/319 did make some advances through the dark and accursed wood, which was still defended by scores of Hun M.G. teams—and very adept snipers. Lt. Craighill of 2/317th Infantry reported:

---

[199] *318th Infantry*, 173.

[200] *2/319th Infantry*, 10.

[201] *314th M.G.*, 40.

The first wave was met by very heavy M.G. and artillery fire from the north, northeast, and east and part of this fire enfiladed our lines and only a few of our troops succeeded in reaching the edge of the Bois de Ogons. No further advance could be made beyond this position during the day. In addition to the H.E. and shrapnel used by the enemy, he also threw over a great many gas shells in the vicinity of Nantillois and the ravines around the town.[202]

The key to advancing against dug-in *Boche* M.G. positions was to find holes or fissures in their line, through the woods and under the brush. While the R.G. and A.R. squad, reinforced by M.G.s, I.G.s, or even direct fire light artillery pieces, held the German M.G. positions in front, gaining *fire superiority*, the bomber and assault squad would maneuver closer to the left or right and try to find a point to assault through. I cannot emphasize the concept of *gaining fire superiority before you maneuver onto an objective* enough. Starting with your A.R.s and R.G.s and culminating with your M.G.s, blanket the target with converging fire—dominate it like a fire fighter puts out a raging blaze with a high-powered hose. Only then, under the cover of smoke, should you send your assault units forward. If you can't see the target, then keep on firing until you do. If you run out of ammunition, command will simply send up another unit to take your place while you get replenished. Also understand this, due to the terrain and other factors, companies and battalions could not advance as one—only platoons could. As such, the threat of so-called "friendly fire" was great in *Bois d'Ogons*. Every time a Hun darted through the brush, for example, an attacking Dough thought that he might be a fellow from another company. Hence a challenge was usually made before firing.

This saved the life of many-a-Hun.

To break the stalemate, Jamerson's 159th Inf. Brig. would have to somehow get a light battery from Heiner's 155th Arty. Brig., with support from Spalding's 305th Engineers, into *Bois d'Ogons* in order to blast the Hun M.G. positions with direct fire. As of yet, Capt. Robert Perkins of B/313th Artillery, which was the accompanying battery for Perry's 317th Infantry and Capt. Lester Graves's C/314th Artillery, which was the accompanying battery Worrilow's 318th Infantry, believed that the terrain alone would not enable them to get their guns up there. And if they tried, they'd be sitting ducks and would be quickly destroyed by artillery fire from the Heights of the Meuse. This meant that more M.G.s (or "Jackass Artillery") would somehow have to get into the accursed woods. With that in mind, at 8:00 P.M., Maj. Robert Cox's 314th M.G. Battalion (Mot.) received orders from General Jamerson stating that it was to join the 319th Infantry and other M.G. sections that were taking up defensive positions south of *Nantillois*. Once Cox

---

[202] *317th Infantry*, 65.

arrived to the position, he learned that because the attack had been stalled and that the 318th Infantry had been punched in the face, more units of the 319th Infantry would be sent north to support them and that the 314th M.G. Battalion would be part of this particular operation.[203]

October 5, 1918.
Weather: Clear.
Roads: Fair.

Due to the mix-ups, which directly led to the 80th Division's failure to take *Bois d'Ogons* on Oct. 4, Col. Perry of the 317th Infantry was relieved of command by General Cronkhite and replaced by Lt. Col. Charles Keller, the regimental X.O. (executive officer). At about 4:00 A.M. Oct. 5, in the cold, wet, inky-black darkness, we in 1/318 (Red Squares) finally reached the 159th Inf. Brig.'s sector southeast of *Bois d'Ogons* and prepared to support our brigade's attack into it by advancing through *Bois Fays* in conjunction with units from the 4th Division.[204] With this move, battalions from Worrilow's 318th Infantry would now be positioned on both flanks of the 159th Inf. Brig., the 80th Division. At 5:30 A.M. Maj. Montague of 2/319 reported to Col. Worrilow: "Battalion in woods with elements of 317th and 318th. Unable to mop up M.G.s. Have no support left."[205]

Even though the infantry regiments of the 80th Division were now below 50% strength, Bullard, our corps commander, ordered us to renew our attack against *KRIEMHILDE* anyway. He apparently did not care (or was ordered not to care) about the condition of his troops and insisted that we fixed bayonets and attacked the enemy no matter what. Jamerson's 159th Inf. Brig. would therefore once again attack up the right side of the Cunel-Nantillois Road and into *Bois d'Ogons*. To its right was the 4th Division and to its left was the 3rd Division. We in the 80th Division were supposed to pin or hold the Germans in front while the 3rd and 4th Divisions conducted a double-envelopment against the heights. Just as General Lee told his corps commanders at Gettysburg on July 3, 1863—"The general plan of the attack remains unchanged"—the same held true for us. Behind us were the infantry and M.G. companies of the 160th Inf. Brig. and the firing batteries of our artillery brigade.

Before dawn, Cronkhite, with Bullard breathing down his neck, sent the following message to Jamerson, commander of the 159th Inf. Brig.: "The reputation of the division is at

---

[203] *314th M.G.*, 40.

[204] *Bois Fays* is pronounced "Bwa Fay."

[205] As cited Stultz, 439.

stake. Ogons Wood must be taken!" We later learned that Bullard said to Cronkhite, and I quote: "Give up the attack and you are a goner—you'll lose your command in 24 hours!" Generals apparently like to yell at each other, as that's apparently how they communicate.

Shortly after dawn, Jamerson, backed by artillery from Heiner's brigade, ordered the attack battalions of his brigade to renew their advance north through *Bois d'Ogons* and *Fays* with the ultimate objective of breaching KRIEMHILDE at what was left of the tiny *Cunel*. Once the 3rd, 80th, and 4th Divisions broke through KRIEMHILDE at Cunel, it was hoped, the American First Army would only have one more line to breach and then, after that, we would finally pass into the "Open Warfare" phase that would more than likely force the German government to capitulate. As usual, the attack started with an artillery barrage. According to Lt. Thomas Crowell, the Telephone Officer of the 313th Artillery: "Preparation fire was delivered from about 5:00 to 6:00 A.M. and a rolling barrage from 6:00 to 8:00 A.M. with 50 meter jumps at three minute intervals."[206]

During this particular attack, the third against *Bois d'Ogons* in two days, we in 1/318th Infantry were to seize the western boundary of *Bois Fays* and continue the attack into *Bois Malaumont*. 1/318 was on the right, 2/317 was in the center, and 2/319 was on the left, using the Cunel-Nantillois Road as its left guide. Behind 2/319, 3/318 was in support with 2/318 in reserve. Behind them were the remaining infantry battalions of the 319th and 320th Infantry of Brett's 160th Inf. Brig., as well as several divisional M.G. sections, namely from Cox's 314th M.G. Battalion (Mot.).[207] During the artillery preparation, Col. Welsh, the Operations Officer for the 155th Arty. Brig., directed Lt. Col. Walker of the 314th Artillery "to transmit orders for cooperation to a French battalion of 75s which were in position near 2/314." The French commander informed Walker that he could "take no orders coming through such channels," however, and the attack was deprived of an entire battalion of field guns.[208]

Speaking of French support, the attack of Maj. Montague's 2/319 on the division's left was supposed to be supported by three French Renault "Mosquito" Tanks that were armed with Hotchkiss air-cooled heavy M.G.s. The tanks were to advance straight up the Cunel-Nantillois Road between Hill 274 and *Bois d'Ogons* and seize *Ferme Madelaine*. The Mosquito Tanks were quickly taken out by massed Hun artillery, however, and their crews bolted to the rear. This is one reason why we called tanks "Clink-it-ty-Clanks" (the main reason was because of the sound

---

[206] As cited in *313th Artillery*, 51.

[207] *314th M.G.*, 40.

[208] *314th Artillery*, 39.

their caterpillar tracks made when moving). Lt. Higgins of 3/318th Infantry, in the leading company of the support battalion, remembered seeing the French tank crews streaming back to the rear down the road. Thinking that they were in fact Germans who had slipped through the lines, he hurled a hand grenade at them "which completely deranged what little morale the crews retained."[209] Before long, he realized who the men really were, and off they disappeared through the thick smoke and fog to the south.

We believe that the main reason why the Hun artillery was so accurate in the sector, aside from the fact they had lived here for years and had every square meter plotted out (!), was that several parallel lines of telegraph poles ran over Hill 274, enabling the Hun to adjust their fire upon the reverse slopes with great accuracy. Hun aeroplanes also continued to fly about at will, directing fire and, from low altitudes, sweeping the rear slope clear of our boys with their M.G.s. One of these "motored kites" even dropped propaganda leaflets upon us, which explained to us "How to Stop the War" by surrendering to the Kaiser. I don't know how effective the leaflets were and I don't know of anybody who actually crossed over to German lines.

Unable to maintain communication between battalion and regimental H.Q., due to constant cutting of the field telephone wire and runner casualties from enemy M.G.s, the 2/318's P.C. was moved back to a pit at the rear base of Hill 274 where the enemy had maintained a M.G. nest. But even here it was difficult to maintain command and control. The large number of wounded who sought cover in the pit and other traffic soon attracted the attention of the hostile planes which twice fired directly into the P.C. Several of the wounded there were killed by shrapnel.

At 10:00 A.M., we in 1/318th Infantry began our attack into *Bois Fays*. After advancing some 500 yards further into the dark, wet woods, we discovered abandoned German barracks that were arranged like little gnome villages. I for one was awestruck by the boardwalks running through the woods from one building to another and the carefully tended gardens that were planted among them. The surreal peace of "Gnome City" didn't last long, however, as concealed German Maxim M.G.s and snipers opened fire on us, slicing up several officers and men. Huge *Minenwerfer* H.E. rounds ("G.I. Cans") followed the M.G. bullets.

"Shew, crrupp!"

"Rat-a-tat-a-tat!"

"Rat-a-tat-a-tat!"

"Rat-a-tat-a-tat!"

"Shew, crrupp!"

---

[209] *318th Infantry*, 68.

"Rat-a-tat-a-tat!"

We were once again getting plastered and took cover in a nearby dip in the woods. We fixed bayonets and waited for a Hun counter-attack that never came.

"Shew, crrupp!"

"Rat-a-tat-a-tat!"

"Rat-a-tat-a-tat!"

"Rat-a-tat-a-tat!"

Scream.

Faced with this nasty attack, we pulled back in order to get more men. During this action, Sergeant William T. Johnson, A/1/318th Infantry, was later awarded the D.S.C. for "extraordinary heroism." His citation read:

> *For extraordinary heroism in action in the BOIS DE FAYS, France, 5 October, 1918. While leading a patrol Sergeant Johnson encountered terrific machine gun fire, which forced him to order his patrol to cover. He then advanced alone, working his way to the nest which he destroyed, and allowed for the continuance of the patrol. Later the same day he braved the perils of an extremely heavy barrage to bring to safety a wounded comrade who was lying 300 yards in advance of the lines.*[210]

At about noon, an Archie and a gas and flame section from the American III Corps, placed at the disposal of General Jamerson, arrived to Hill 274. Like the French tanks, their arrival brought down a terrific fire from the German artillery.

Jamerson therefore ordered them out.

With their withdrawal, the fire abated somewhat, though the enemy continued to "crash" the position periodically with several "battery one's" (the artillery battery fires one round per gun), including a heavy battery from the right rear beyond the Meuse. To the observers of these Hun batteries the rear crest of Hill 274 was apparently plainly visible. With our attack stalled, at around 2:30 P.M., our own artillery shellacked the strong German positions north of *Bois d'Ogons* and *Fays* with H.E. and shrapnel so that Jamerson's 159th Inf. Brig. could once again claw its way forward, eliminating Hun M.G. nests one-by-one in the all-too-familiar, bloody fashion.

During these "lulls" or "operational pauses," we Doughs were generally assigned to help evacuate the wounded, bring up ammunition or other supplies, etc. Those of us not so engaged,

---

[210] As cited in *318th Infantry*, 70.

would usually smoke or chew tobacco or ate canned (or corned) beef and crackers to help sooth our nerves and to occupy our minds. Sometimes, we'd even read old letters—anything to take our minds off the terror that was unfolding around us. But despite all of these "diversions," we were still 100% wired to tell when the next round or the next bullet was going sail into our position, making minced meat of any of us.

On the far-left, near the road, Capt. Herr's F/2/319 of Maj. Montague's infantry battalion suffered a direct hit by an enemy artillery strike "wounding several men and causing some of those near to temporarily lose their sense of direction and consequently were separated from the company and were taken prisoner."[211] These Doughs were held by the Germans for three months as prisoners of war (P.O.W.s), after the Armistice was signed in mid-November. (See Appendix 2 on their P.O.W. experience.) Montague's battalion surgeon, Lt. James R. St. Clair, who had followed F/2/319 into the fight, also became separated after the devastating strike. He actually made his way out of the woods with Company F's Bugler, Pvt. Michael A. Cerra, but was soon driven into a water-filled shell hole by Hun M.G. fire from Hill 250. Every time St. Clair and Cerra tried to exit the hole, the Heinies opened up on them from the hill. These two men were pinned for eighteen hours until a patrol from the Rock of the Marne Division stumbled upon them on Oct. 6.[212]

With this attack thrown back, what was left of 2/319th Infantry assembled along the reverse slope of Hill 276, which was the regiment's L.D. There they dug-in with their intrenching tools, tried to eat and sleep, and posted sentries, all under constant enemy M.G. and artillery fire. It was "one bloody hell of a mess," for sure.

Being pinned, for any amount of time, makes a person feel helpless and worthless and when it occurred, we begged God for relief.

"To get the attack moving again," Bullard stormed in the H.Q.s of his divisions, including that of the 80th Division, and demanded a resumption of the attack. After his one-sided meeting with Cronkhite, Bullard issued the following directive:

---

[211] As cited in *2/319th Infantry*, 11.

[212] *2/319th Infantry*, 11.

> 1. Give orders for Jamerson to reorganize at once for another effort.
> 2. Give him a barrage and let him follow it closely and make another attack this afternoon, at an hour to be fixed by you.
> 3. Organize a good barrage for him.
> 4. The best information obtainable from the 3d Division, its right located in the woods containing Hill 250, southwest of BOIS DES OGONS. Report efforts being made to clean up this wood. They may have small detachment in vicinity of CUNEL-BOIS CUNEL. Not cleaned up on our right flank. 4th Division holding west side BOIS FAYS and BOIS FAUX on the north, line about 200 yards south of CUNEL-BRIEULLES ROAD. Eastern side of BOIS DE FAYS and BOIS DE FAUX thickly wooded and may not be penetrated by men.
> —BULLARD

Generally, it is bad form (and practice) to tell a subordinate commander "how" to do a job. It's best to simply tell him what to do and resource his "how." If, however, you lack confidence in your subordinate, then it is appropriate, due to time-constraints, to tell him not only what to do, but how to do it. If this situation occurs—that you feel the need to tell a subordinate commander how to do it—then said subordinate commander should be replaced at the earliest possible moment. If, however, you feel the need to exhibit tight control, you'll be considered being a "micro-manager" or a "martinet," or a "puppet master," all of which hold negative connotations. During the Meuse-Argonne Offensive, Pershing did become a martinet of sorts, as did Bullard. At times, Bullard would issues orders to brigades or even battalions without going through the chain of command (e.g., through Cronkhite). This is a mistake because once this is done, then the subordinate commander, in this case, a division commander, has just lost control of his unit in battle. Is it appropriate to tell a division commander: "Take Hill 546"? Yes. But not, "Order 1/319th Infantry to swing to the left, 2/320th Infantry to the right, etc." That's a division and/or brigade commander's job. Anyway, Cronkhite's subsequent directions to Jamerson were as follows:

> Starting from X ravine south of BOIS DES OGONS, under cover of barrage to be arranged by you with Welsh at earliest possible hour move forward as directed and make every effort possible to establish and hold a line in the northern part of BOIS DES OGONS. Urge upon regimental and battalion commanders the importance of this effort which must be successful if it is possible to make it so, and proceed with the reorganization of battalions in the rear. Every possible use should be made of tanks at your disposal. Use the gas company that reported to you last night. The line established by you must be reorganized in depth to the special view to protecting both your flanks. 4th Division was subjected to a heavy counter-attack this morning, which may be repeated. The 4th Division is receiving fire from the northeast, probably from the TRANCHEE DE TETON as well as from BRIEULLES.
>
> —CRONKHITE

The difficulties confronted by General Jamerson and his staff at this time were increased by incorrect information supplied by Bullard's Chief of Staff, Brig. Gen. Alfred W. Bjornstad. In his eagerness to move the corps forward, disregarding standard procedure (i.e., using the chain of command by contacting the 80th Division's chief of staff), the corps chief telephoned the brigade commanders directly, insisting that their units were "lagging." Convinced by careful reconnaissances that the 3rd and 4th Divisions were not where Bjornstad had told him where they were, Jamerson contacted the commander of the 7th Inf. Brig., 4th Division himself. The latter informed him that units of the 7th Inf. Brig., 4th Division, were in fact farther south than what the American III Corps believed or hoped. Informed of this by Jamerson, Cronkhite determined to end this non-regulation practice right then and there. Accordingly, he insisted henceforth that all orders, instructions, and/or information for the 80th Division be transmitted directly to division H.Q. and never again to his brigades. The protest of General Cronkhite and his chief of staff, Col. Waldron, naturally did not make them popular at corps H.Q., but they didn't care, as they were "Rough and Regular" and comfortable in their skins.

Once the doctrinally incorrect practice of micro-management was fixed, the next attack was set for 6:00 P.M. By the time battalion commanders, summoned about 4:30 P.M., had received their instructions at regimental headquarters and returned to their commands, however, they only had about thirty minutes to prepare for the push which would be made across the entire divisional front. This time, battalions from the French 228th Artillery Regiment would join in the barrage.

At 6:00 P.M., the division's fourth attack in two days into *Bois d'Ogons* commenced behind another rolling barrage. We in 1/318th Infantry led out on the right, attaining the southwest corner of *Bois Fays* while 2/317th Infantry attacked into *Bois d'Ogons* in the center and the 2/319th Infantry attacked into the accursed woods on the left. Of all the battalions, Montague's 2/319, had the hardest time of it and suffered far more casualties than we did on the right in *Bois Fays*. Montague attacked with Capt. Herr's shot-up Company F on the right, Capt. Keezell's Company H on the left, and Companies E and G in support. Behind them was 2/318, followed by 3/318. Col. Worrilow expressly directed that Hill 274 was not to be uncovered until Maj. Montague had made good his hold upon the wood. In 2/318, Lts. Lakin, Ulrich, and Atkinson commanded the first wave, and Lts. Davidson and Crocker commanded the second wave, composed of only about 100 men.

What really hurt Montague's battalion was that soon after the attack was launched, a friendly barrage fell upon his lead companies, followed by enemy barrage. Nevertheless, Maj. Montague was able to get his battalion across the swale and into the wood before enemy M.G.s really started cutting meat. Luckily for the men of Montague's 2/319, the Huns had withdrawn from the damned woods and pulled back to *Côtes Cunel* and KRIEMHILDE, leaving but a small rear-guard. At 7:15 P.M., Maj. Montague sent the following message to Col. Worrilow: "HALIBUT [2/319] entered woods in good order, following barrage."[213] Capt. Charles R. Herr of F/2/319 remembered:

> *We hugged the barrage, making use of all available cover against the M.G. fire. For a space of three hundred yards we moved down a hill, coming across a small stream and up the other slope facing the fire of the enemy over perfectly open ground. Thanks to the shell holes our casualties were few. We followed the barrage through the woods until our objective was reached where we started to dig in at once.*[214]

By 8:30 P.M., well after dark, Montague's 2/319th Infantry finally reached the northern edge of *Bois d'Ogons*. There they peered through the darkness across the open fields to barely discern *Ferme Madelaine* and *Côtes Cunel* in the moonlight. Montague ordered F and H/2/319th

---

[213] As cited Stultz, 442.

[214] As cited in *2/319th Infantry*, 11.

Infantry to advance to the bombed-out farmstead. Capt. Keesell's H/2/319th Infantry became misdirected in the dark woods, however, (no surprise!) and did not advance as far as Capt. Herr's F/2/319. One of Keesell's platoons was in fact "lost" for several hours. To hear Capt. Herr of Pittsburgh tell it: "Company F was pressing on when M.G. fire burst upon it and, failing to find friendly troops on the left, changed direction in order to get back to the rest of the battalion. As the men were doing this, a grenade burst among them, scattering them. Since it was impossible to reorganize under the intense fire in the dark, the order was given to follow in file across the road, into Bois Cunel, which was still enemy-held, in the 3rd Division's area."[215] It was 10:00 A.M. next day before the survivors—three officers and thirty men—got back across the road, returning to the battalion. Montague's 2/319 suffered almost 50% casualties in *Bois d'Ogons*, pretty much making it *hors de combat* for the rest of the battle.

Faced with these stunning losses, Montague ordered his remaining companies, E and G/2/319, to consolidate their position 200 yards back from the northern wood line of Bois d'Ogons, to evade intense enemy M.G. and artillery fire delivered from *KRIEMHILDE*. Once situated, Montague gave the command "defend." According to the *I.D.R.*:

> *Defense.*
>
> *498. Supports are posted as close to the firing line as practicable and reinforce the latter according to the principles explained in the attack. When natural cover is not sufficient for the purpose, communicating and cover trenches are constructed. If time does not permit their construction, it is better to begin the action with a very dense firing line and no immediate supports than to have supports greatly exposed in rear.*
>
> *499. The reserve should be posted so as to be entirely free to act as a whole, according to the developments. The distance from firing line to reserve is generally greater than in the attack. By reason of such a location the reserve is best able to meet a hostile enveloping attack; it has a better position from which to make a counter attack—it is in a better position to cover a withdrawal and permit an orderly retreat. The distance from firing line to reserve increases with the size of the reserve.*
>
> *500. When the situation is no longer in doubt, the reserve should be held in rear of the flank which is most in danger or offers the best opportunity for counterattack. Usually the same flank best suits both purposes.*

---

[215] As cited in *2/319th Infantry*, 11.

501. In exceptional cases, on broad fronts, it may be necessary to detach a part of the reserve to protect the opposite flank. This detachment should be the smallest consistent with its purely protective mission.

502. The commander assigns to subordinates the front to be occupied by them. These, in turn, subdivide the front among their next lower units in the firing line.

503. An extended position is so divided into sections that each has, if practicable, a field of fire naturally made distinct by the terrain. Unfavorable and unimportant ground will ordinarily cause gaps to exist in the line.

504. The size of the unit occupying each section depends upon the latter's natural strength, front, and importance. If practicable, battalions should be kept intact and assigned as units to sections or parts of sections.

505. Where important dead space lies in front of one section, an adjoining section should be instructed to cover it with fire when necessary, or machine guns should be concealed for the like purpose.

507. Unless the difficulty of moving the troops into the position be great, most of the troops of the firing line are held in rear of it until the infantry attack begins. The position itself is occupied by a small garrison only, with the necessary out guards or patrols in front.

508. Fire alone can not be depended upon to stop the attack. The troops must be determined to resort to the bayonet, if necessary.

509. If a night attack or close approach by the enemy is expected, troops in a prepared position should strengthen the out guards and firing line and construct as numerous and effective obstacles as possible. Supports and local reserves should move close to the firing line and should, with the firing line, keep bayonets fixed. If practicable, the front should be illuminated, preferably from the flanks of the section.

510. Only short range fire is of any value in resisting night attacks. The bayonet is the chief reliance. (See Night Operations.)

Theory of the Defensive.[216]

The defense is divided into the purely passive defense and the active defense. The passive defense seeks merely to delay the enemy. The results can never be other than negative. It is usually for the purpose of gaining time and most frequently used by a rear guard. Since the idea of taking up the offensive is absent, no strong reserves are held out for a counter-attack—the firing line is as strong as possible from the first; every advantage is taken of obstacles, natural or artificial. The flanks must be made secure. The active defense seeks to attack the other side at some stage of the engagement. It seeks to win and only the offensive wins. It is often necessary for a commander to assume the defensive (active) either voluntarily, in order to gain time, or to secure some advantage over the enemy; or involuntarily, as in a meeting engagement where the enemy gets a start in deployment for action or where the enemy's attack is impetuous and without sufficient preparation. In either case the defensive force contents itself with parrying the blows of the enemy, while gathering and arranging its strength, looking and waiting for the right place and time to deliver a decisive blow which is called the counter-attack. Hence, a counter-attack is the offensive movement of an active defense. Its success greatly depends on being delivered with vigor and at the proper time. It may be delivered in two ways: 1st, straight to the front against a weak point in the attacking line, or 2d, by launching reserves against the enemy's flank after he is fully committed to the attack. The latter method offers the greatest chances for success and the most effective results.

Advantages and Disadvantages of The Defensive.[217]

The defense has the following advantages over the attack:

1. Troops attacking afford a better target than the troops of the defensive.

2. A larger amount of ammunition is usually available.

3. The men shoot better because they are not fatigued by advancing.

4. Losses will be less if good cover is secured.

The defense has the following disadvantages over the attack:

---

[216] *P.M.*, 248.

[217] *Ibid*, 249.

1. The defender surrenders the advantage of the initiative as the attacker can elect the point of attack and the defender must be prepared at all points.

2. The defender must fight amidst his dead and wounded, which is depressing.

3. The defender, seeing the enemy continually advancing, becomes conscious of his inability to stop him. This is depressing to the defender and is injurious to his morale.

The Passive Defense.

F.S.R. 184. A force may at times fully accomplish its mission by retaining its position for a specified time with or without combat. Here the object is to avoid giving the enemy the decision, either by avoiding combat altogether or, if he attacks, by preventing him from carrying the position held by the defensive troops. The position taken up is selected, as far as the mission will permit, with reference to its natural defensive features. Since the idea of offensive combat is absent, every advantage is taken of obstacles, natural or artificial, that hinder or altogether prevent the advance of the enemy. Negative rather than positive measures are relied upon to prevent the enemy from seizing the position. In this form of defense, the firing line is made as strong as possible from the first. If the flanks are not secured by other means, reserves strong enough for that purpose must be provided, but no reserves need be held for a decisive counter-attack. Supports and local reserves need be only strong enough to replace losses, to strengthen or reinforce the firing line where the enemy's attack is most threatening, and to repair breaches in the line.

F.S.R. 185. The purely passive defense is justified where the sole object of events is to gain time, or to hold certain positions pending the issue of events in other parts of the field. Its results, when it accomplishes its mission, can never be other than negative.

The Active Defense.

F.S.R. 186. The active defense or, the defense seeking a favorable decision, is the only form of defense that can secure positive results. A force whose intentions are offensive may at times be forced to assume the defensive either voluntarily in order to gain time or to secure some advantage over the enemy, or involuntarily, as where, in recontre, the enemy gets a start in deployment for action, or where the enemy's attack is impetuous and without sufficient preparation. In either case the defensive force contents itself from parrying the blows of the enemy, while gathering its strength and looking for the opening to strike a decisive blow.

F.S.R. 187. The crisis of this form of the defensive to the counter-attack, which marks the change from the defensive to the offensive. Upon the superior leader falls the responsibility of perceiving the right moment at which this change should be made and of having at hand the means necessary to effect it. The general reserve affords him the weapon necessary for his purpose. In this class of the defensive, therefore, strong supports and reserves are essential. The firing line is made as short as possible at first, in order to permit of the holding out of local supports and reserves strong enough to meet all movements of the enemy and to hold the line throughout up to the time of the decisive COUNTER-attack, and the retention until that time of a reserve strong enough to make a counter-attack a success. An open field of fire for effective and close ranges is essential. Obstacles immediately in front of the position that might impede the counter-attack are objectionable.

Defensive Positions and Intrenchments.

I.D.R. 489. The first requirement of a good position is a clear field of fire and view to the front and exposed flanks to a distance of 600 to 800 yards or more. The length of front should be suitable to the size of the command and the FLANKS should be secure. The position should have lateral communication and cover for supports and reserves. It should be one which the enemy can not avoid, but must attack or give up his mission. A position having all these advantages will rarely, if ever, be found. The one should be taken which conforms closest to the description.

I.D.R. 490. The natural cover of the position should be fully utilized. In addition, it should be strengthened by fieldworks and obstacles. The best protection is afforded by deep, narrow, inconspicuous trenches. If little time is available, as much as practicable must be done. That the fieldworks may not be needed should not cause their construction to be omitted, and the fact that they have been constructed should not influence the action of a commander, if conditions are found to be other than expected.

I.D.R. 491. When time and troops are available the preparations include the necessary communicating and cover trenches, head cover, bombproofs, etc. The fire trenches should be well supplied with ammunition. The supports are placed close at hand in cover trenches when natural cover is not available.

I.D.R. 492. dummy trenches frequently cause the hostile artillery to waste time and ammunition and to divert its fire.

Deployment for Defense.

I.D.R. 495. The density of the whole deployment depends upon the expected severity of the action, the character of the enemy, the condition of the flanks, the field of fire, the terrain, and the available artificial or natural protection for the troops.

I.D.R. 496. If exposed, the firing line should be as dense in defense as in attack. If the firing line is well intrenched and has a good field of fire, it may be made thinner. Weaker supports are permissible. For the same number of troops the front occupied on the defensive may therefore be longer than on the offensive, the battalions placing more companies in the firing line.

I.D.R. 497. If it is intended only to delay the enemy, a fairly strong deployment is sufficient, but if decisive results are desired, a change to the offensive must be contemplated and the corresponding strength in rear provided. This strength is in the reserve, which should be as large as the demands of the firing line and supports permit. Even in a passive defense the reserve should be as strong as in the attack, unless the flanks are protected by other means.

Use of Ground.

I.D.R. 406. The position of firers must afford a suitable field of fire. The ground should permit constant observation of the enemy, and yet enable the men to secure some cover when not actually firing. Troops whose target is for the moment hidden by unfavorable ground, either move forward to better ground or seek to execute cross fire on another target.

I.D.R. 407. The likelihood of a target being hit depends to a great extent upon its visibility. By skillful use of ground, a firing line may reduce its visibility without loss of fire power. Sky lines are particularly to be avoided.

Requisites of a Good Defensive Position.[218]

If you were looking for a good defensive position, what points would you have in mind and of these points, which would be the most important? The requisites to be sought in a good defensive position are:

1. A clear field of fire up to the effective range of the artillery.

2. flanks that are naturally secure or that can be made so by the use of the reserves.

3. Extent of ground suitable to the strength of the force to occupy it.

4. Effective cover and concealment for the troops, especially reserves.

5. Good communications throughout the position.

6. Good lines of retreat.

All of these advantages will seldom if ever be found in the position selected. The one should be taken which conforms closest to the description, but you should bear in mind that a good field of fire and effective cover, in the order named, are the most important requisites. In tracing the lines for the trenches, avoid salient (a hill, spur, woods, etc., that juts out from the general line in the direction of the enemy). Avoid placing the fire trench on the skyline. Locate it on or below the military crest (the crest from which you can see all of the ground in the front and are not silhouetted against the horizon).

Preparing a Defensive Position.[219]

Now let us suppose ourselves as part of a battalion that is to occupy a defensive position. What would probably be done? How and in what order would it be done? What would the major do? He would decide upon the kind of defense (active or passive) to offer, and then find a suitable defensive position in harmony with his plans. He would determine exactly where the firing and other trenches are to be dug. He would then call up the company commanders and issue his defense order in which the task of each company would be made clear. Those to occupy the firing line would be assigned a sector of ground to the front to defend and a corresponding section of the fire trench to construct. The supports would construct their trenches and the communicating trenches. He would, if necessary, issue the necessary orders to protect the front and flanks by sending out patrols. He would indicate how the position is to be strengthened

---

[218] *P.M.*, 250.

[219] *Ibid*, 251.

and make arrangements for distributing the extra ammunition. If time is a serious consideration, the major would direct the work to be done in the order of its importance, which is ordinarily as follows:

> *1. Clearing of foreground to improve the field of fire and construction of fire trench.*
>
> *2. Head or overhead cover concealment.*
>
> *3. Placing obstacles and recording images.*
>
> *4. Cover trenches for supports and local reserves.*
>
> *5. Communicating trenches.*
>
> *6. Widening and deepening of trench; interior conveniences.*

Now having cleared the foreground, dug the trenches, recorded ranges to the important objects in each sector, etc., the position can be occupied. The citizen ordinarily pictures the firing trench full of soldiers when he is told the trenches are occupied. Not so. Patrols will be operating well to the front to give timely warning to one or two sentinels in each company fire trench of the approach of the enemy. These sentinels would in turn inform the company which would probably be resting in the trenches to the rear.

Clearly, this particular defense in *Bois d'Ogons* was a "passive" one: "*F.S.R.* 185. The purely passive defense is justified where the sole object of events is to gain time, or to hold certain positions pending the issue of events in other parts of the field. Its results, when it accomplishes its mission, can never be other than negative." The other tenets of defense though, such as depth, or fields of fire, etc., cannot always be exploited simply because of your position in the line. Sometimes your unit will be assigned a position that is just a bad place to defend. But don't worry, as it's probably a bad place to attack, too! For us, we put as many supporting weapons up front, guarded our flanks with patrols, and kept a substantial reserve, no less than a platoon. Army Regulations warned us about deploying our reserves in "driblets." In fact, maintaining a reserve in the defense is far more important than holding a strong front line. As a rule of thumb, one-third of your command should be held in reserve. If the enemy breaks through, then commit the entire reserve—throw back the enemy—and return said unit back to mobile reserve status.

The other thing to remember about defending at night is not to fire the supporting weapons like M.G.s or A.R.s first (if at all). Instead, throw a hand grenade, as it won't give away your position. Also, as stated in Army Regulations and proven in battle by our experience, be prepared to use the bayonet during periods of limited visibility.

For M.G.s in the defense, particular attention must be paid to the necessity for sweeping all ravines and valleys with enfilading fire. A.R.s like Chauchats, Lewis Guns, or, later, Browning Automatic Rifles (B.A.R.s) should cover areas not covered by the M.G.s. It is also expected that each pointer or gun commander calculates the necessary firing data, provides limiting stakes and flash arresters (if available—to conceal bursts at night), creates a range card (a terrain sketch with traverse and elevation coordinates), and familiarizes himself with the routes of approach to all other M.G. positions, front or rear, which it may become necessary for his crew to occupy. He should also know the locations and the fields of fire of his own and neighboring M.G.s. Furthermore, all pointers are expected to turn over to relieving units all available data which will be necessary for the proper functioning of the crew.

At 8:45 P.M., Maj. Montague reported to Col. Worrilow: "HALIBUT has reached objective and is digging in." We in the 1/318 (Red Squares) obtained similar results as we were able to reach the northwestern edge of *Bois de Fays* once we took out several Hun M.G. positions along our axis of advance in the same fashion, losing a few men per each Hun gun taken. I don't remember who we lost during this phase. I do remember, however, that once we reached the tree line that fronted the Madeleine Farm, looking west, we too were driven further back into the woods by concentrated German artillery and M.G. fire that was being directed from *KRIEMHILDE*.

By the close of Oct. 5 therefore, the 80th Division had finally secured Bois d'Ogons after suffering some 2,000 casualties. And for the rest of that hellish night in *Bois d'Ogons* and *Fays*, we once again suffered frequent artillery and gas attacks, forcing us to wear our hated masks almost all the time, even as we attempted to sleep. It was either that or die. For his actions on Oct. 4-5, Lt. Col. Charles Keller, the new commanding officer of the 317th Infantry, was awarded the D.S.M. His citation reads:

> *He took command of a regiment at a critical moment, after two unsuccessful assaults had been made by the brigade. He reorganized the regiment under fire and made possible the taking and holding of Bois d'Ogons, displaying the highest order of leadership and exhibiting the masterful qualities of a commander.* [220]

Two other soldiers from the 317th Infantry were also cited for heroism while operating in *Bois d'Ogons* during this period. They are representative of the thousands of gallant actions that

---

[220] As cited in *317th Infantry*, 89.

were performed that memorable day. The noted soldiers are: Sergeant Manley Bradley of Company D and Sergeant James T. Jenkins of Company G. Their citations read:

> *Sergeant Bradley was wounded in the head while leading his platoon across a valley swept by machine gun fire but he continued to lead his men to their objective, refusing to report to the dressing station until he was ordered to do so.*
>
> *Patrolling himself in front of the line, Sergeant Jenkins came upon a M.G. emplacement manned by a German officer and three men. He wounded the officer and one soldier by rifle fire, captured the other two men and took them with the M.G. to the rear.* [221]

October 6, 1918.

Weather: Clear.

Roads: Fair.

Sometime around 2:00 A.M., Sunday, Oct. 6, 1918, we in 1/318th Infantry were relieved by a battalion from the Ivy Division and were ordered to a march to *Dannevoux* and await further orders. For the rest of the day, the bulk of Jamerson's 159th Inf. Brig. remained in defensive positions in *Bois d'Ogons*, with sections from the 313th M.G. Battalion providing primary defensive fires. At around noon, 2/319 and 2/317 moved about 400 yards back through the woods to enable the "big guns" of Goodfellow's 315th Artillery to reduce enemy positions just north of *Ferme Madeleine*. This artillery fire was timed to support an attack by the 3rd Division on our left. After completion of the barrage, which ended at about 3:00 P.M., 2/319 and 2/317 returned to their tree-line defensive positions. During the day's operations, Lt. Charles K. Dillingham, M/3/318 Infantry, the regiment's designated support battalion, was later awarded the Army's Distinguished Service Cross. His citation reads:

> *For extraordinary heroism in action near NANTILLOIS, France, 6 October, 1918. Lieutenant Dillingham, on duty as battalion intelligence officer, twice volunteered and led a patrol through woods known to be occupied by hostile machine guns. Working his way through artillery and machine gun fire, he succeeded in ascertaining the position of units on the right and left of his own. Throughout the action around NANTILLOIS and the BOIS DE OGONS this*

---

[221] *317th Infantry*, 90.

officer was a constant inspiration to his men by his devotion to duty and disregard for personal safety. [222]

Throughout the rest of the day, batteries from Heiner's artillery brigade fired several harassing, raking, or zone searching missions along *KRIEMHILDE*. It also suffered some casualties. For example, Gun 3 of B/1/313th Artillery burst and acting Cpl. Thomas S. Riley from Weston, West Virginia, was killed near *Bois Brieulles*. He was the first man in 313th Artillery to be killed outright. Several others were horribly wounded and were carried on stretchers along the road that led back to *Septsarges* until an ambulance was found. According to Lt. Crowell of the 313th Artillery: "The trip was made under gas and shell fire, the men at times having to wear their masks."[223] Lt. John B. Wise of the 314th Artillery was wounded by "bursting shell" and was also evacuated to the aid station.

As Jamerson's shot-up 159th Inf. Brig. held its positions in *Bois d'Ogons*, Cronkhite ordered Brett's 160th Inf. Brig. to relieve it in place, no later than dawn, Oct. 8, minus the divisional M.G. battalions, which were to stay in place, anchoring the defensive line. Maj. Ashby Williams of 1/320th Infantry remembered his moving into the front lines around Nantillois during the early-morning hours of Oct. 7:

I started out with my company commanders and my orderly, toward Nantillois. We followed for the most part the little trench railway that wound around the barren ridges until we reached the Nantillois-Septsarges Road at a pint about 500 yards from Nantillois. There were many evidences that a great struggle had taken place over this ground in the battle of a few days before. Equipment and broken wagons and dead horses were everywhere. There were no dead men scattered over the fields, as they had been picked up and laid in a long row on the bank beside the road leading to Nantillois. There were perhaps a hundred of them. It was indeed a pathetic sight. They were Boche and Americans, lying side-by-side, calm and peaceful and unhating in death waiting for that final act of the crude hands of the living to shove them into the waiting grave, back into the bosom of the mother from which they sprang, to be known and seen no more upon the face of the earth... [I met with Col. Love, commander of the 319th Infantry, in an abandoned German bunker.] We went over the entire situation together, he explaining to me for the first time that my battalion would likely

---

[222] As cited in *318th Infantry*, 69.

[223] As cited in *313th Artillery*, 52.

take over a sector in the front line, running through Bois d'Ogons. Col. Love was frankly not optimistic about the situation at the front and did not hesitate to picture to me the great difficulties I might be expected to encounter. He was undoubtedly impressed with the fact that former attempts to advance beyond the place had been attended with such sanguinary results.[224]

Lt. Edward Lukens of 3/320th Infantry similarly remembered:

Maj. Emory led the way, for which I admired him, for this was not to be a fight, but an ordinary digging job that he might easily have delegated to a junior officer had he been less conscientious. After a hard struggle through the mud across and open field, we came to a road near Nantillois, and it was on the brow of the hill in front of the road that the trenches had been taped out by the engineers. For over three hours the men dug, in darkness, rain and constant apprehension of shelling, until the early-morning hours the job was declared done, tools turned in, and we started back to where our packs were piled.[225]

Jamerson's 159th Inf. Brig. had had a rough time of it and was persistently dogged by ill-fortune—primarily due to the situation it was emplaced. In attacking *Bois d'Ogons* as it did, defended by a very adept enemy, it did not have the benefit of hours of corps and army artillery shellacking, of fresh troops, or of adequate accurate information. Yet we had pushed forward 2 km on a 2-km front. Up to this point, Keller's 317th Infantry had lost 92 K.I.A. and 433 W.I.A., a total of 525, including the casualties while serving with Brett's 160th Inf. Brig. My very own 318th Infantry had suffered 941 casualties, including 107 K.I.A., 832 W.I.A., and 2 M.I.A. Of these, 34 were killed and 153 were wounded while serving with the 4th Division. All told, our losses were about a third of our strength. In 2/318, whose casualties were highest in the division, four officers and 46 E.M. lost their lives and the wounded totaled nine officers and 291 E.M. These figures do not include the rather severe casualties of Maj. Montague's 2/319 or Maj. Huidekopper's 313th M.G. Battalion.

Many recommendations were made for the D.S.C. for actions performed in *Bois d'Ogons*. But "because of the lack of definite knowledge of how to property submit these recommendations, very few of them were approved."[226] We never did buy this line, but that was Worrilow's explanation to us. There is no doubt that it does matter who the commanding officer

---

[224] As cited in *1/320th Infantry*, 107.

[225] As cited in *3/320th Infantry*, 80.

[226] *318th Infantry*, 69.

is. Some simply think that an infantryman's job is to be brave and that "above and beyond" is to be truly super human. Others, however, saw "above and beyond" as compared to someone at home, working on a farm or in a factory. In truth, somewhere in the middle is probably the best place for a commander to be when it comes to awards. The other factor to consider is that once an "extraordinarily heroic act" is performed, it must be witnessed, those witnesses need to have survived to report it, and they had to actually like or respect the recipient. That, plus the officers had to recover from the shock they themselves suffered to even write them up. Nevertheless, the 318th Infantry Regiment takes just pride that several soldiers actually received said decoration.

```
       318th Infantry Regiment, 80th (Blue Ridge) Division Casualties.
                         Sept. 26-Oct. 6. 1918.
                     K.I.A.              W.I.A.              M.I.A
Unit       Officers     Men      Officers     Men      Officers     Men
H.Q.          0          5          0          49          0          0
M.G.          0          3          2          40          0          0
Supply        0          0          0          3           0          0
Medical       0          2          3          8           0          0
1/318         3          30         8          242         0          2
2/318         4          46         7          291         0          0
3/318         0          15         5          174         0          0
Total         7          101        25         807         0          0
```

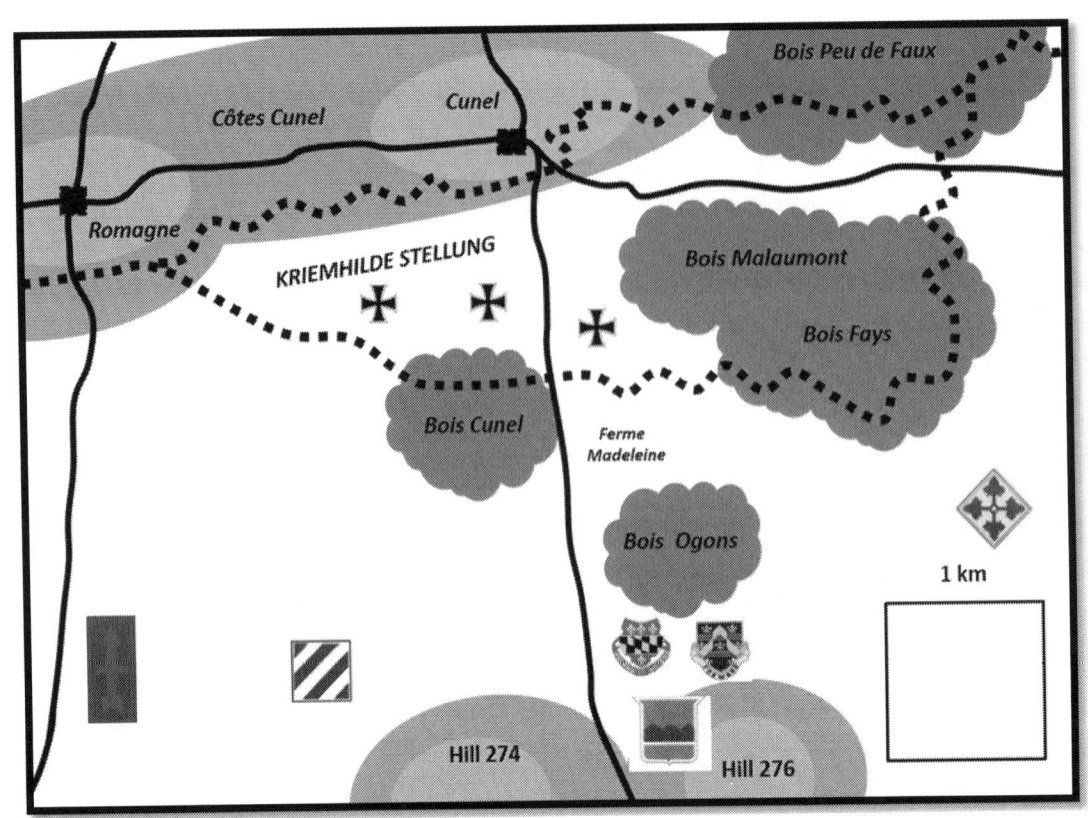

160th Inf. Brig., 80th Division Area of Operations, Oct. 7-8, 1918. The 320th Inf. is on the right and the 319th Inf. is on the left. The mission: demonstrate in the vicinity of *Ferme Madeleine* while the 3rd and 4th Infantry Divisions conducted a double-envelopment, breaching *KRIEMHILDE* and taking Cunel.

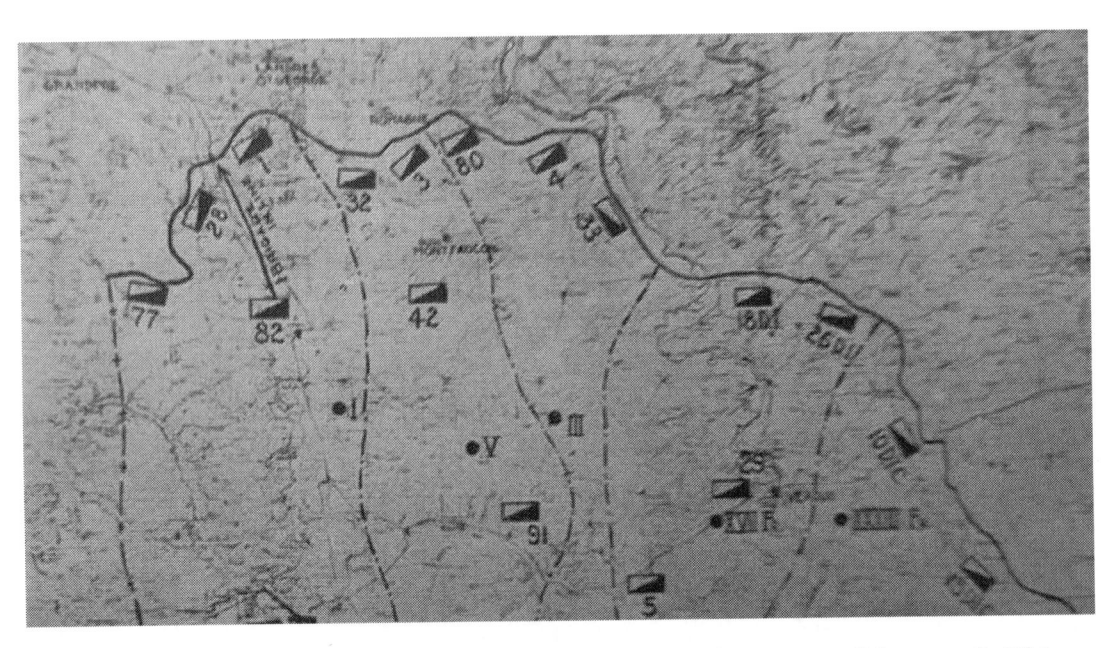

"The Argonne Operation, Oct. 7." The 80th Div. is in the center of the attack. This is a period map.

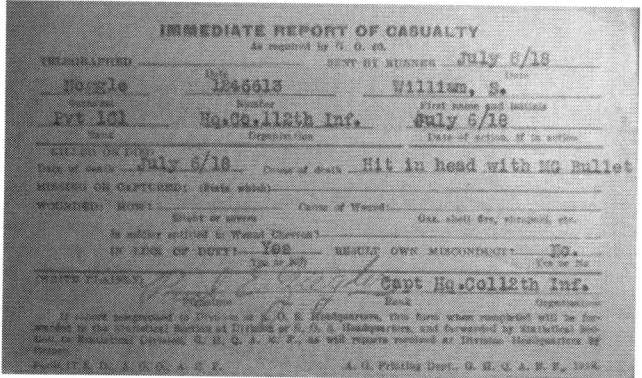

One of our supply camions being used as an ambulance (L) and a copy of "Immediate report of Casualty" (R). This states that Pvt. Wm. S. Noggle, Service No. 1246613 of H.Q./112th Inf. was K.I.A. "Hit in head with MG Bullet" on July 8, 1918.

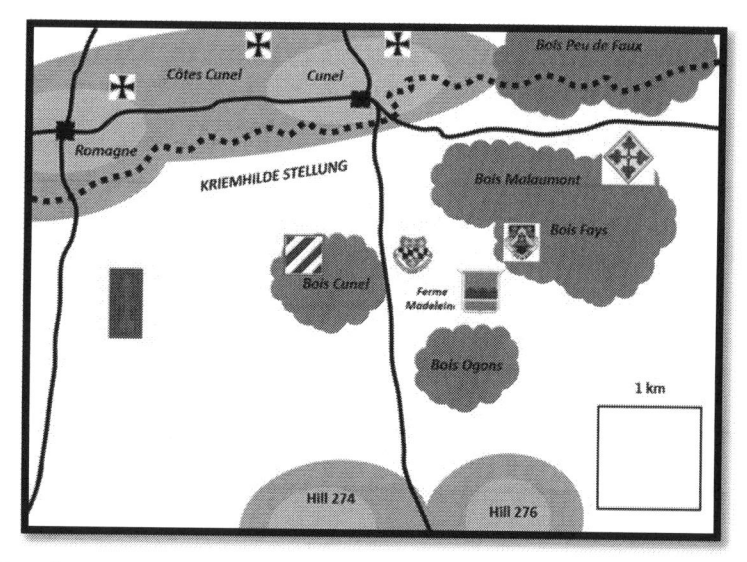

160th Inf. Brig., 80th Division Area of Operations, Oct. 9-11, 1918. The Hun fought ferociously to maintain *KRIEMHILDE*.

Scene on the left captures the combat around *Ferme Madeleine* and a typical Hun M.G. position along the Heights of Cunel, facing south (R). We had to push through their blasted beaten zones (middle of pic.) and get into their defilade to have any chance of moving forward. And the 80th Division Always Moves Forward!

We can't make it any more clear than this: the *largest American cemetery in France* was built between Cunel and Romagne. This was the area that the 3rd, 4th, and 80th Divisions fought, scraped, clawed, and bled. R.I.P.

"Supply Train Passing Through Cuisy, Oct. 11, 1918" (L) and Y.M.C.A. Hut at Les Islettes Petites (R).

A real shower and new uniform thanks to the Q.M. Corps! It helped clean "the animal" off us at *Les Islettes Petites*.

The inventor John Browning's son, Lt. Val Browning, with the M1917 Browning Auto Rifle (B.A.R.) (L) and "Soldier with a Browning M1917 Automatic Rifle, 30.06." (R). We actually had Lt. Browning demonstrate his wares to us. We so loved the B.A.R. that we thought that every Dough should have one!

Lt. Val Browning himself demonstrated the new M1917 M.G. to M.G.ers of the Blue Ridge Division. It fed better and faster than the older M1915.

The popular Maj. Gen. Joseph Dickman (L), commander of the 3rd Inf. Div., the I Corps, and the Third U.S. Army in France. The 80th Division was attached to Dickman's I Corps for our Third and Final Push up the Meuse-Argonne. Generals John Pershing and Charles Summerall (R). Summerall, on the right, commanded the the V Corps upon the relief of General Cameron.

The Kaiser's last Army Chief of Staff, Wilhelm Groener with his wife (L) and Crown Prince Max von Baden (R), the man who helped facilitate the armistice. The prince is mourning the death of the Second German Empire with his black arm band.

"At home in a shell hole, 10-24-18" with the 319th Inf. in the Argonne Forest (L) and "*Fôret d'Argonne*. The Germans were turned back at this point" (R).

The intrepid Maj. Sweeney, 1/318th Inf. at the battalion P.C. in the Argonne Forest (L) and a French *camion* (motor truck) driven by French Indo-Chinese (R).

Chapter 6
The Battle for *Ferme Madeleine* and Recovery (Oct. 7-31, 1918).

October 7, 1918.

Weather: Fair.

Roads: Good.

During the morning of Oct. 7, Brett's 160th Inf. Brig. completed its relief of Jamerson's shot-up 159th Brigade in *Bois d'Ogons*. We later learned that Jamerson's brigade had been up against "the best in the German Army," which was desperate to stop our advance through Bois d'Ogons, *viz.*, elements from the 5th Bavarian Reserve Division, the Prussian 28th (Flying Shock) Division, and the Prussian 115th and 236th Infantry Divisions, as well as several *Sturm* or *Stoss* battalions.[227] Maj. Ashby Williams, leading his 1/320 into the new position, proceeded north through Nantillois in an effort to obtain more guides than the two sent by Col. Love. With him went the battalion surgeon, adjutant, intelligence men and runners. He wrote:

> *I raised a great deal of fuss and even went so far as to cuss a little, as I considered that I should have one guide for each company at least, even one for each platoon. My troops were going in the darkness into an area which neither I nor my officers had reconnoitered in daylight...We were grateful for the darkness that gave a sense of security from the whining shells that searched the area, and the noise of many guns with their flashes lighting the sky stimulated and exhilarated the body and mind beyond all powers of description. I remember how fatigued in mind and body we were after the four-kilometer hike and how relieved we were when we finally, about 1:00 o'clock of the morning of October 8, reached Col. Love's headquarters and went inside to place of safety. When we went through the front room of the vault I had to literally walk over the top of the men who were lying on the floor, so crowded were they, and the atmosphere was so tense that it could have been cut with a knife... I remember as we got into the colonel's room a circumstance which under different environment might have been laughable, but betrayed the state of mind of the men in that room. The vault was closed up tight with heavy iron blinds, and the candles were burning all around the room. My doctor had rolled a cigarette and he struck a match to light it. Col. Love turned on him in an instant and said: "For God's sake, man, put out that light. Do you want us all killed in here?" [We*

---

[227] *317th Infantry*, 67 and *319th Infantry*, 31.

then continued our advance north]. The march of my troops up the hill [into Bois d'Ogons] that night was all Col. Love told me it would be. It was hell. The night was dark and the way was difficult and the Boche were sweeping the place from across the Meuse with light and heavy shells and with those most dreaded demons of all weapons, the Austrian 88s, or the "Whizbangs" as they are called. He was also putting over gas in great quantities. Indeed, it is hard to understand how any living creature could have passed up that hill that night without injury, and it seems almost incredible that we should have suffered only fourteen casualties...My P. C. was on a ridge about 600 meters north of Nantillois...It was a little oblong affair, perhaps four feet high in the front, about five feet wide and ten feet long, built up about a foot above the surface of the ground and covered with timber and earth. It resembled, indeed, a sunken log cabin, with...its dirt walls, and dirt floor, and shelter-half before the entrance to keep the candle light from shining out toward the Boche, as he had built the place and the opening was, of course, in his direction.[228]

Brig. Gen. George H. Jamerson, commander of the 159th Inf. Brig., 80th Division.

Brig. Gen. Lloyd M. Brett, commander of the 160th Inf. Brig., 80th Division.

---

[228] As cited in *1/320*, 110.

In his "Post Operation Report" about our hellish time in Bois d'Ogons, Brig. Gen. Jamerson wrote a scathing review.[229] It reads, in part:

> 1. Orders for Corps attack on 4 October 1918 were not issued in time to permit proper reconnaissance or instruction of subordinate commanders.
> 2. Our casualties from flanking M.G. fire and violent artillery fire from the front and right flank were severe.
> 3. It was demonstrated during the action of 3-6 October that a position defended by belts of flanking machine gun fire can only be successfully attacked when absolutely coordinated and effective liaison with neighboring troops is maintained at all times.
> 4. The fact that incorrect information was received as to the positions reached by neighboring troops was responsible for much misunderstanding and heavy losses from flanking M.G. fire from points which were reported to be in our hands.
> 5. The scarcity of maps available during these operations was a decided handicap.
> 6. On 4 October, north of Nantillois, an Infantry contact plane called for our front line. At that time our front line was under flanking M.G. fire and in such a position that to have displayed panels as desired by the plane would have involved heavy casualties. In addition there were low-flying enemy planes about and a display of panels would have disclosed our exact line to the enemy, with the probability that our front would have suffered still more heavily from the enemy's fire.

We found that too many officers above the rank of captain (i.e., field and general grades) too often got too touchy when it came to constructive criticism from subordinates. On the one hand, we were expected to follow orders without question. On the other, as explained by Baron

---

[229] As cited in Stultz, 446.

von Steuben, American soldiers also expect to be told "why" and not to be treated like simple automations. We were also taught to tell the truth—to "tell it how it is." Sometimes, if a field or general grade officer sensed "disloyalty" or "lack of enthusaiam" or "quibbling" from a subordinate officer, however, too many them removed said officer and said officer ended up in a dead-end position. In war, I'm not so sure that this is the best policy, but it's the way our Army operated. I guess my only suggestion to an officer who needs to constructively criticize an operation is to "make it about the plan and not the man." Don't personalize things. Say things like, "we need to do a better job at..." In war, when nerves are fried and life is cheap, this is very hard to do. But do it! Get another officer to help you write it. Ask the other officer to "filter" what you say and to "focus on the plan and not the man." Cronkhite, in his operations report, backed Jamerson's assertions, which fell squarely on the lap of the corps commander, General Bullard:

> *The entire operation of the 159th Brigade was seriously hampered by misinformation coming from the flanking divisions. As an example of this, at 9 o'clock on the morning of the 4th, the 3rd Division on our left reported that it had reached the Trench 9245 and the 4th Division on our right reported that it had reached well within the Bois de Fays. This information was communicated to the III Corps and by them given to this division. Acting on this information, repeated attempts were made to outflank the strongly held Bois des Ogons. However, in every case heavy machine gun fire was encountered, and it was later learned that neither of the flanking divisions had advanced their line as far as our own.*[230]

By mid-day, the 319th Infantry was on the left and the 320th Infantry was on the right, with two companies up and two in back. They were told that they were going to attack across the *Ferme Madeleine* and straight into the concrete-reinforced German M.G. nests atop *Côtes Cunel* and *KRIEMHILDE*. Capt. Charles R. Herr of F/2/319th Infantry remembers:

> *Throughout the day the Boche shelled us heavily; his aeroplanes were constantly overhead correcting the fire of his artillery. Out-posts were established and every effort made to make the position capable of defense. The snipers came up from the rear with orders to ascertain the strength of the enemy. They had no sooner gotten beyond our line than the enemy cut loose with M.G. and artillery fire.*[231]

---

[230] As cited in Stultz, 447.

[231] As cited in *2/319th Infantry*, 11.

The batteries of the 313th and 314th Artillery also suffered intermittent German artillery fire throughout the day with "considerable amounts of gas being used." 2/314th Artillery, for example, lost Maj. Granville Fortesue, Capt. Dwight Beebe, Capt. Samuel B. Ridge (the battalion surgeon), Lt. Frank Heacock, and five E.M. to gas attacks. A Hun artillery observation balloon from the Heights of the Meuse looked down upon our batteries around Hill 295 and directed several counter-battery fire missions against them. *Les Boche* even hurled massive 210mm *Minenwerfer* bombs into *Bois Septsarges*, killing several S.O.S. men from the 80th and 4th Divisions. The other problem was that scores of German aircraft, who seemingly owned the skies, continued to swarm the line, spraying it with M.G. fire. They would also spot our artillery, run circles around them, and pop flares, alerting their own artillery crews.[232]

This artillery fire kept the signalmen busy, as telephone lines, which were insulated with cloth, constantly went down. Telephone lines from the O.P.s to the gun line, lines from the batteries to the battalions, lines from the battalions back to brigade were constantly cut. Personnel from Whitaker's 305th Ammunition Battalion were also kept quite busy trying to keep the hungry guns fed. Every night, like clockwork, they had to drive their caissons back to the corps ammunition dumps in *Cuisy*, which was a "hot and happenin' place." The roads there were under constant enemy shellfire. The decrease of horse power among the artillery battalions was only getting worse, especially once influenza started to take hold and the horses were forced to work beyond their limits, like the men.[233] According to Capt. Peck of the 319th Infantry:

---

[232] *314th Artillery*, 40.

[233] *313th Artillery*, 53.

Throughout the night of Oct. 7-8, the shellfire was particularly heavy over the area, a continuous fire of H.E. and gas being directed at the crossroads in Nantillois and the batteries located in close-proximity to it. A number of casualties were suffered in the village during the night and runners from the H.Q. and the medical detachment being constantly exposed to the fire. The regimental aid station was located in the cellar of a ruined building near the water point miraculously escaped that night, but was hit later, two or three men—one medical officer—being killed and others wounded.[234]

Maj. Ashby Williams of 1/320th Infantry similarly remembered:
It was hell. The night was dark and the way difficult and the Boche was sweeping the place from across the Meuse with light and heavy shells and with those most dreaded demons of all weapons, the Austrian 88s, or the whiz-bangs, as they were called. Indeed, it is hard to understand how any living creature could have [survived in the position we held that night].[235]

Following its relief by Love's 319th Infantry, Worrilow's 318th Infantry reached the designated concentration area southeast of *Cuisy* mentally and physically exhausted, and, due to numerous casualties among its officers and N.C.O.s, rather badly organized. From Sept. 26-Oct. 6, one must remember that we had been under constant enemy fire and had suffered numerous casualties on an hourly basis. The other infantry regiments of the division shared a similar, if not even worse, fate. Lt. Edward Lukens of the 320th Infantry put it succinctly when he wrote: "There were more divisions used and more companies and battalions used up, in the neighborhood of the little village of *Cunel*, than any other place that I know of on the American front, and the [80th Division], many another good outfit, had its turn on these hills, gained a little ground, and went back for replacements."[236] Let it be remembered that the main American military cemetery in France is built atop the Heights of Cunel. That, in and of itself, speaks volumes.

As Jamerson's 160th Inf. Brig. assumed their new positions Up the Line, Bullard issued orders for the next corps attack. Here they are, truncated for clarity, as well as the converted operational memo cut by division H.Q.:[237]

---

[234] As cited in *319th Infantry*, 31.

[235] As cited in *1/320th Infantry*, 109.

[236] As cited in *3/320th Infantry*, 78.

[237] As cited in Stultz, 457-59.

1-2

From: Chief of Staff.
To: Commanding General, 160th Infantry Brigade.
Subject: Operations.

1. I am enclosing herewith copies of field order No. 24, 3rd Corps.
2. The Commanding General directs that you hold your entire brigade (less Montague's battalion 319th Infantry) in readiness to execute the provisions of this order and especially to carry out the last sentence of paragraph 3 (b), (c) of it. Authority will be obtained by these headquarters for the use of the 320th Infantry now bivouacked south of the Cuisy-Montfaucon Road. Should necessity arise for the use of these troops in the execution of Field Order 24 prior to the receipt of the authority referred to above, you will be authorized to use them upon application to these headquarters.
3. Artillery: The Commanding General, 155th Artillery Brigade will see you and Colonel Welsh, at which conference you will arrange:
(a) The line on which the barrage will be put down.
(b) How long it will remain stationary.
(c) The rate at which it will roll, which will be not faster than 100 meters in 8 minutes unless ordered by higher authority.
(d) The distance to the front that the barrage will advance.
(e) The plans for bombarding with the 155s of the fringes of the woods in the Divisional Sector.
(f) The plans for the use of smoke barrages.
(g) Plans for the utilization of the Gas and Flame Company under your command. This organization is equipped with 4" Stokes Mortars, and have a range of 1100 yds. and fire thermite projectiles.

2-2

4. Infantry: Special measures will be taken for the advance of the infantry:

(a) To insure their starting at the proper time and following the barrage closely.

(b) To employ thin lines of scouts to work around machine gun nests and attack them from the flanks and rear.

(c) To mop up the ground passed over.

(d) To employ the least vulnerable formations and take the fullest advantage of any available cover in passing over the ground lying between Nantillois and the south edge of the Bois des Ogons which is exposed to artillery fire from the N.E.

(e) To echelon the battalions in depth during the attack and prevent troops from crowding into the forward line.

(f) To provide for the protection of the left flank of the attacking line against M.G. fire from the Bois de Cunel.

5. Liaison: Special precautions will be taken to maintain liaison throughout the command and with these headquarters. Troops of the forward line will be especially instructed to stake out their line with the panels when called for by aeroplane.

6. All men will carry two extra bandoliers of ammunition and an effort will be made to provide a supply of phosphorus hand grenades. C-1 will take up this matter with the least practicable delay.

7. All of the details for this operation to be made with the least practicable delay so that it can be launched on receipt of orders to do so. Liaison with the troops of the 4th Division on the right and the 3rd Division on the left will be maintained so that the closest cooperation may be secured with them.

By command of Major General Cronkhite:

J. B. Barnes,
Lieut. Colonel, General Staff,
For the Chief of Staff.

P. C. III Army Corps, A.E.F.
7 October 1918.
17:30 o'clock.

SECRET.

Field Order No. 24.
Maps: Same as Field Order No. 23.

1. No change in the hostile situation. The 1st American Army will seize and hold the COTES de MEUSE east of CONSENVOYE on October 8, 1918, and on the following day the heights west of ROMAGNE-sous-MONTFAUCON.

2. The Third Corps will protect the flanks of the attack of the V Corps and XVIII Corps.

3. (b) The 4th Division and 80th Division will accurately establish their own and enemy front lines and prepare complete rolling barrage tables for their front. They will prepare complete plans for bombarding with 155s the fringes of woods in their sectors as far as the Combined Army First Phase Line. Plans will also be prepared for the use of smoke screens to the extent possible with the means at their disposal. They will be prepared to attack and seize the heights in their immediate front upon orders from the Corps Commander....
(d) The 5th Division will be prepared to march on two hours' notice.
(e) ARTILLERY: The Corps and Divisional artillery will assist the attack of the V and XVII Corps by counter battery and interdiction fire as opportunities offer; also be prepared to support the prospective attack of the III Corps.
(f) The Air Service will carry out its mission in accordance with Field Order No. 23 and be prepared for an attack by this Corps....
(g) DIVISION COMMANDERS WILL TAKE SPECIAL MEASURES TO INSURE THE INFANTRY FOLLOWING CLOSELY THE BARRAGE.

4. Administrative details: No change.

5. P. C.s and Axes of Liaison: No change.

By command of Major Brig. Gen. BULLARD:
A. W. BJORNSTAD,
Brigadier Brig. Gen., G. S.,
Chief of Staff.

A simple perusal of the above orders/instructions will show how we became more and more reliant upon smoke and bombs. The comment: "To employ thin lines of scouts to work around M.G. nests and attack them from the flanks and rear" was inferred from the regulations and drawn from our post-operation reports. Although it's not a bad idea to publish "tactical recommendations" for subordinate units to follow, to enshrine them in an order to expect them to be followed at all times is somewhat whimsical if not impractical and wrong, in my opinion. But this is what higher command gives us: as much support as it can, coordination, and a view of the "bigger picture." Other than that, it's pretty much up to the company commanders, platoon leaders, top sergeants, platoon guides, squad leaders, and the men themselves to accomplish the mission.

Scary but true.

Typical "bivi" while on the move in France. Getz and I as well as all of the other Doughs were just trying to survive into the next day. On the right is an example how we used "pig tail" barb wire posts to help construct our bivis. This is one part of Army life we will not miss.

October 8, 1918.

Weather: Fair.

Roads: Good.

During the early-morning hours of Oct. 8, as units from Brett's 160th Inf. Brig. prepared for the up-and-coming *Götterdämmerung* against KRIEMHILDE at *Ferme Madeleine*, its men had to endure "severe gas shelling with a liberal mix of H.E," forcing them to wear their nose-pinching masks most of the night.[238] Capt. Peck of the 319th Infantry remembered:

> *The line remained at a standstill, the enemy maintaining an uninterrupted fire. During the night, the area was subjected to severe gas shelling with a liberal mixture of H.E. The concentration was so heavy in the valleys as to necessitate the wearing of masks most of the night. The personnel at regimental H.Q. wore their masks the greater part of the night, the runners and signalmen who were obliged to go and come in the darkness suffering fearfully. The runners were oftentimes the only means of communication, the buzzer line being put out of commission, many times daily, by shell fire.*[239]

Our own 155th Arty. Brig. of course answered in kind and the 313th Artillery gassed Hun positions in *Village Brieulles*, which was ablaze at this point. Lt. Crowell, the Telephone Officer of the 313th Artillery wrote:

> *Brieulles enfiladed our infantry positions. The 4th Division had found it impracticable to take the town by storm as it would be gradually surrounded with the breaking of the Kriemhilde Stellung to the west. Our fire upon Brieulles was at a rate of three mustard shells and one H.E. after five minutes of preliminary lethal. Reports from the infantry indicated that this fire was very effective.*[240]

Maj. Ashby Williams, the commander of 1/320th Infantry, remembered the absolute devastation of the area—the real effects of modern warfare on the land and the people:

> *After daylight I received word from Col. Love that I would be held responsible for the safety of the forward zone. I determined, therefore, to go over the positions of the entire sector. [Bois d'Ogons], which is situated upon a crest, was*

---

[238] *Götterdämmerung* is pronounced "Got-ter-dame-air-unk"; it is the mythological last battle of the gods—the end of the earth.

[239] *319th Infantry*, 32.

[240] As cited in *313th Artillery*, 52.

literally torn to pieces with shells, great trees broken off and torn up by the roots, and the whole place saturated with the nauseating odor of phosgene gas. Capt. Sabiston, my orderly, and I started out, therefore, on the morning of Oct. 8 on our tour of inspection. By the light of day we could see what havoc had been wrought on the Americans in the attempts that had been made to advance beyond the Bois d'Ogons. Due to the continued heavy fire, details had not been able to police up the battle field, and dead men were scattered everywhere; some of them were my men who had been lost the night before, but most of them belonged to the battalions that had experienced such sanguinary results in their attempts to take the place. It was, indeed, a pathetic sight. We passed by Company D in the third echelon and on to Companies B and C that were in the trenches newly-constructed before the Bois d'Ogons in anticipation of a great drive, and thence on to the Bois d'Ogons. I stopped and talked with Capt. Hooper of the 319th Infantry, the fighting parson of Culpeper, Virginia, whose regiment occupied a sector on my left. After smoking a few of his cigarettes I went up the road further into the woods and came up to Capt. Ted Davant, whose M.G. company had been attached to my command for the operation. I passed along the wood road leading eastward to Company A and to the outpost line of that company along the north and northeast edge of the Bois d'Ogons. From the positions of the outpost lines I could see the Bois de Fays and the terrain to the front. I have often wondered why we were not shot to pieces as we were in plain view and range of the M.G.s we afterwards encountered. With the changes I made I considered the place will-nigh impregnable against any attack the Boche might put over.[241]

Soon after dawn, Brett's 160th Inf. brig. attacked north. As the day progressed, reconnaissance patrols from the 319th and 320th Infantry located several strong Hun M.G. positions in *Bois Malaumont* and *Cunel* and they were turned into targets for Heiner's 155th Arty. Brig.[242] While the big guns of the 315th Artillery were usually focused on counter-battery missions well-behind the front lines, they were also, according to doctrine and practice, assigned to suppress or destroy priority or hard-to-kill targets with high-angle fire. Our M.G.s were used to focus on smaller but critical targets or areas about the size of a small house and blast it with a cone of either direct or indirect fire.

---

[241] As cited in *1/320*, 110.

[242] *Malaumont* is pronounced "Mal-ah-moan."

We were finally making some headway against *KRIEMHILDE*.

Revived by a few hours of uninterrupted sleep and a hot meal, Oct. 8 found us in the 159th Inf. Brig. in better spirits and we steeled ourselves for any eventuality. "Army Hard" or "As tough as a British cracker," we called it. Others would simply repeat: "You're in the Army now, you're not behind a plow, you'll never get rich, you son-of-a-bitch, you're in the Army now."

While we were behind the lines conducting recovery operations near Cuisy and the 160th Inf. Brig. was preparing to breach *KRIEMHILDE* in the vicinity of Cunel, French and British armies, farther north, were making similar gains in Champagne, Picardy, and Flanders. "Just one more push" it was hoped, and we'll be pissing in the Rhine by Christmas! Joe Latrinsky was also telling us that Germany was in a state of rebellion due to starvation and heavy losses. Of course, this was only Joe talking, but we all liked Joe and, more importantly, felt it first hand at the front as we heard it from the German captives. When we overran their positions, we noticed that their tan canvas haversacks, which they usually wore on the back of their belts, were empty of provision. Hun troops at the front were in fact starving and if they were, it is "fer sure" that the homefront was, too, especially considering the general make-up of the German Imperial system.

During our *Interregnum* from the front lines, Cronkhite and Jamerson issued the following citations to the officers and E.M. of their respective commands:

```
              HEADQUARTERS EIGHTIETH DIVISION, A.E.F.
                                            7 October, 1918.
To the Officers and Men of the 159th Brigade:
The Division Commander wishes to express his great appreciation of the
highly important successes gained by Brig. Gen. Jamerson's 159th
Brigade and Major Montague's attached battalion of the 319th Infantry.
Continually under effective artillery fire on your flank, as well as
machine gun fire from your front and flanks, you nevertheless returned
again and again to the attack until your objective was gained and
held.
Your success has earned the repeated congratulations of your Corps
Commander as well as the thanks of your Country.
                                            ADELBERT CRONKHITE.
                                         Major General, Commanding.
```

> HEADQUARTERS 159th INFANTRY BRIGADE, A.E.F.
> 8 October, 1918.
> The Brigade Commander desires to add to the above his expression of appreciation of the work accomplished by the Brigade and by major Montague's Battalion, 319th Infantry, during the three days' fight for the BOIS DE OGONS, and his pride in the command of an organization possessed of that iron will and determination which alone could win success in the face of such odds.
>
> G.H. JAMERSON.
> Brigadier-General, Commanding.

Later in the day, the 159th Inf. Brig. was moved three miles southwest into *Bois Montfaucon*, the same location that the 160th Inf. Brig. had refitted the week before, *via* the bombed-out town of *Malancourt*. Along this route, we passed through several artillery and M.G. units as well as ammunition and supply trains that were tirelessly bringing much-needed *matériel* to the front. This march was made without interruption and by early afternoon the men of the regiment had our "bivies" up among the shattered trees and fallen timber. Luckily for me, ole Albert Getz was still above ground and we again shared a shelter tent.

Once established, we were instructed to continue recovery operations, which also included the assimilation of scores of new infantry lieutenants, fresh from the O.T.C. (Officer Training Camp) at Langres, and to be ready to move at a moment's notice. Just before we settled in for the night, however, we were informed that the entire upper echelon of the 159th Inf. Brig. had been sacked—that "the house was cleaned out." We understood why Col. Howard Perry was relieved—right or wrong, good or bad—but did not quite understand why our very own Col. Ulysses Grant Worrilow, the popular commander of the 318th Infantry, was relieved. Our brigade commander, Brig. Gen. George H. Jamerson, who had commanded our brigade since April 1918, had broken his foot just south of *Bois d'Ogons,* and was sent to the rear to recover. Assuming that Jamerson's absence would be short, Cronkhite chose to directly command the 159th Inf. Brig., acting through the brigade adjutant, Lt. Col. Edmund A. Buchanan, who simply passed Cronkhite's orders along to the regimental commanders. Col. Worrilow was replaced by Lt. Col. Charles L. Mitchell and Col. Perry of the 317th Infantry was replaced by Lt. Col. Charles Keller. They were the ones who got us across the final line.

October 9, 1918.
Weather: Misty.
Roads: Muddy.

On Oct. 9, General Pershing ordered his corps commanders (Liggett, Bullard, and Cameron) to renew their attacks against *KRIEMHILDE*. Being in the center, we in the 3rd, 4th, and 80th Divisions were designated as the American First Army's main effort and as such, received Pershing's reinforcing artillery. As before, the 80th Division, this time, Brett's 160th Inf. Brig., was to attack "hey-diddle-diddle-right-up-the-middle" through *Ferme Madeleine* and the Valley of Death while the 3rd and 4th Divisions enveloped *Cunel*, the army's main objective, from the east and west.

Right or wrong, Pershing pretty much terrorized his corps commanders to keep pushing north toward Sedan no matter the cost, who, in turn, terrorized their division commanders to do the same. Although we never heard these strong words *per se* (e.g., "no matter the cost"), we certainly felt the pressure, esp. those in the infantry regiments. But then again, what was Pershing supposed to do? He understood the big picture and we didn't. He was the one getting the reports from signal scouts in the air about what was in front of us. We in the infantry really only moved at night and when we attacked during the day, we could only see things in a 500 x 500 yard box—if that.

On Oct. 9, Liggett's American I Corps, now including the famous 1st Division, backed by an infantry brigade from the 91st (Wild West) Division, was to attack Côtes Romagne from the west. To Liggett's right was Bullard's American III Corps, which had the 3rd Division on the left, the 80th Division in the center, and the 4th Division on the right, with the 5th (Red Diamond) Division in reserve. In the Rock of the Marne Division's sector, the 38th Infantry was to attack on the left and the 30th Infantry was to attack on the right. On the 3rd Division's right was the 80th Division's 319th Infantry (3/319 as the attack battalion, 1/319 as the support battalion, and 2/319 as the reserve battalion). To the 319th Infantry's right was the 320th Infantry with 1/320 as attack, 3/320 as support, and 2/320 as reserve ("attack in depth" and "defend in depth" were our mantras). We were to attack *en echelon* from the left: The 3rd Division was to attack first, then the 80th Division, and then the 4th Division.

Under this scheme, the 160th Inf. Brig.'s attack time (H-Hour) was contingent upon the progress of the 3rd Division, just as the 4th Division's attack time was dependent upon the 80th Division. Reportedly, the forward units of the 3rd Division were a km ahead of the 319th Infantry on the left, holding *Bois Cunel,* and the 4th Division was a kilometer ahead of us on the right, occupying *Bois de Fays* up to the Cunel-Nantillois Road. It will be remembered that the western part of *Bois Fays* originally had been in the 80th Division's sector and had been seized by we in Maj. Sweeney's 1/318 on Oct. 5.

From the map, then, Brett's 160th Inf. Brig. would be protected on both flanks for at least a km, between *Bois Cunel* and *Fays*. The open ground between the two woods was bad enough—we called it "the Valley of Death"—especially around *Ferme Madelaine*. At 3:00 P.M., H-Hour for the 160th Inf. Brig. was announced for 3:30 P.M. At 3:15 P.M. there was to be a fifteen-minute artillery barrage on an east-west line just north of *Ferme Madeleine* and then a rolling barrage was to cover the advance.

At 3:30 P.M. with the 320th Infantry on the right and the 319th Infantry on the left, hugging the Cunel-Nantillois Road, the 160th Inf. Brig. left the cover of *Bois d'Ogons* and attacked into the "Valley of Death." Capt. Gerald Egan's 3/319th Infantry was the designated attack battalion in the western sector with I/3/319 on the right and Company L/3/319 on the left, Companies M and K in support. It was followed by 1/319 and then 2/319.[243] Maj. Williams's 1/320th Infantry was the attack battalion in the eastern sector with B/1/320 on the right and A/1/320 on the left followed by Companies D and C, respectively, in support.[244] Behind them, stacked up by battalions, were Maj. Emory's 3/320, followed by Maj. Holt's 2/320. Lt. Lukens's platoon from I/3/320, being part of the support battalion, was assigned as one of the regiment's "combat liaison groups" or flank guards. Its primary mission was to connect with the right of the 319th Infantry and to take care of any enemy infiltrators who might squeeze through.

During this attack, Brett's 160th Inf. Brig. reached *Ferme Madeleine* in the "face of heavy fire."[245] Like us two days before, they fought through the familiar pattern of taking down well-supported M.G. positions and rifle trenches, climbing over, under, or through barbed wire or other entanglements, and endured multiple enemy artillery strikes, which vomited up earth and split men in two. Maj. Ashby Williams, the commander of the attack battalion (1/320) in the center of the corps axis of advance, remembered the intense Hun artillery and *Minenwerfer* barrages and the capture of scores of German prisoners:

> *It was a beautiful afternoon and it seemed a pity to spoil it with so much din of war and bloodshed...I passed by the post of Company D, over the ridge and through the wire, thence by Companies C and B. The latter company was just forming the battle line...In the meantime the standing barrage had come down*

---

[243] *319th Infantry*, 33.

[244] *1/320th Infantry*, 112.

[245] As cited in *319th Infantry*, 33.

and the shells from our artillery were going over our heads by the thousand...a music that was rudely marred by the discordant sound of the demoralizing whiz-bangs (the Austrian 88s), and the insistent trench mortar shells that the Boche was putting over...As I waited at the edge of the Bois des Ogons and saw my brave boys in battle line coming up the hill to meet whatever fate might have in store for them, calmly, stoically, and indeed, sadly, I looked on them in wonder and admiration, and my heart went out to them in pity and in sorrow. In such a time as this one knows, indeed, that "War is Hell." In a few minutes the remainder of the headquarters came up and...we moved from shell hole to shell hole to the southern slope of the ridge running east from the wood. Here I could perceive that my right flank companies had been held up just in front of me and I established headquarters which, for the time being, included myself and my adjutant, in a fresh shell hole and waited for further developments. I immediately sent out a messenger to Capt. Little, who was in command of Company B, in the right front, asking him for information of his situation, and in a short time received word that he was being held up by enemy machine gun fire in the edge of the Bois de Fays in our right front. I sent him word at once to take a patrol through the woods through the right and take the enemy guns from the flank, as I knew the general situation of the guns from the map and from the reports of the patrols of the day before... Immediately after sending this message I ordered the trench mortars and the one-pounders to come up to take care of the Boche guns if they could not otherwise be reached. I remember Lt. Zouck as he came up with his trench mortars; he was full of eagerness to do what he was ordered to do, a smile playing always on his youthful face. It was good for him, poor fellow, that he did not know that he had only one more day to live. I sent him and the officer in charge of the one-pounders to the edge of the woods at the crest of the ridge to be ready to give such fire as might be found necessary. In the meantime, I waited for action on the right flank... After about thirty minutes hold-up, [the enemy] opened on the ridge on which my troops and I were located with his trench mortars, those little six-inch monsters that shoot around thrity shots a minute, and with the demoralizing whiz-bangs, traversing from right to left and from left to right along the slope of the hill crest. The [Minenwerfer] shells, coming in rapid succession, were digging holes on each side of me the size of the one that I was in, and the merciless whiz-bangs were going over the parabola of the hill. The noise was so intense—noise of bursting shells, of the hideous crying of particles of flying steel - that I had to speak at the top of my voice to make myself heard by Lt. Preston, who was in the shell hole with me...A Boche prisoner who was sent by Lt. Pownall on the supposition that I might get some information from him was trembling from head to foot and could hardly speak. I saw at a glance that I could not get any information that was worth having from a man in his condition. I pointed to the rear... We never sent fighting men back with prisoners as we could not spare fighting men for this duty, unless there was a great body of prisoners.[246]

Lt. Edward Lukens of Maj. Emory's 3/320, positioned in support behind Williams's 1/320 with his platoon, remembered:

We advanced at a steady walk, while the Boche planes circled over our heads, and the shells tore holes in the earth around us. Our advance over this shell-torn field was a witness to the value of our open formation, and to our experience in quick dropping. Time after time a big one would come tearing through the air, a dozen men nearest it would drop, a cloud of earth and smoke would appear and one would wonder whether any of them had escaped. In an instant one would get up, and then another, and often the whole crowd would jump into their places again, but sometimes one or two would lie still, or would rise slowly and start painfully toward the rear...Had we been in close masses, or had the men failed to drop flat when one landed in a small group, the battalion would have been blown sky-high. On the edge of the woods we saw a fearful spectacle. Phosphorus shells were breaking in air, throwing down blazing streamers of yellowish gray smoke in fantastic shapes, like weird monsters of death.[247]

By 6:00 P.M., the attack of the 160th Inf. Brig. brought it to a line about 500 yards north of *Ferme Madeleine* along a German Army-built narrow-gauge railroad supply line, where they consolidated their position before they resumed their final (and epic) attack against *KRIEMHILDE*. Although "pauses" or "rests" in battle are not only needed but are also inevitable, ensure not to make them too long as the men will lose the "fire in their bellies" that is required to charge across an open field with bayonets fixed! In the railroad cut, company combat carts and water buffalos surprisingly came forward to replenish ammo and water (ammo wasn't

---

[246] As cited in *1/320th Infantry*, 121.

[247] As cited in *3/320th Infantry*, 82.

much of an issue, as the men hadn't fired much—yet). Sanitary teams dealt with the wounded. Squad leaders and platoon guides reminded the men how to set their sights for 1,000 yards (set the leave sights at "10"), artillery liason officers started plotting targets, and battalion and company commanders positioned the supporting weapons.

When all was set, just before dusk, the battalion commanders blew their attack whistles, followed by the company commanders, followed by the platoon leaders and off the combat groups of the 160th Inf. Brig. went—charging up the low and clear ridge that was *KRIEMHILDE*. According to Capt. Peck of the F/2/319th Infantry, this attack "marked the beginning of the 'wildest night' in the history of the regiment." In order to try to flank the well-fortified and positioned Hun M.G.s of *KRIEMHILDE*, each company of the brigade apparently went its own way, crisscrossing the others' zones, some even moving into Bois Cunel, which was in the 3rd Division's area of operations. In so doing, a highly-trained, very-experienced German *Stoss* battalion, attacking east from *Bois Cunel*, infiltrated among the units of the 319th Infantry and "all hell broke loose" just north of the farm. Although the support and reserve battalions of 319th Infantry held their positions, it was, according to all who were there, a near thing.[248] Lt. Edward Lukens of I/3/320th Infantry remembered: "The situation was mixed up, and no one knew just where any other outfit was. Several companies of the 319th Infantry had apparently advanced some distance ahead of us by 'sliding through,' that is, going past M.G. nests in the dark without clearing them out."[249] Maj. Williams, in command of the 320th Infantry's Attack Battalion, on the division right, experienced similar confusion. He writes:

> *In going over the map and by the use of the compass I could easily see that, in the darkness and confusion of battle and what not, my companies had to some extent lost their sense of direction and we were not heading with sufficient accuracy in the right direction for progress in the sector that had been assigned to us, and I determined upon a complete readjustment of positions before attempting further progress. Moreover, I was convinced that, unprecedented as it was, the peculiar situation here gave a fine opportunity for combing the Bois de Fays and Bois de Malaumont in my sector at night and clearing up my front to the Cunel-Brieulles road. Some of my company commanders were doubtful whether such a mission could be accomplished at night, but I believed it could, fully appreciating the difficulties of keeping contact in the woods at night,*

---

[248] As cited in *319th Infantry*, 33.

[249] As cited in *3/320th Infantry*, 84.

especially where men must fight for the most part hand to hand with the enemy. I therefore ordered Companies B and D to reform in the same order in which the attack was begun and to fall back about 300 yards to where a little trench railroad ran out of the Bois de Fays and to comb the latter woods to the ravine between the Bois de Fays and the Bois de Malaumont and to report to me when that mission was accomplished. This movement began at 9:30 P.M. Company C and one platoon of A Company I directed to await further orders. In the meantime I waited for developments... During the process of combing the Bois de Fays some of my men had captured a German corporal and they sent him to me. He had been in the war four years and was glad to get out of it. I asked him how many men were in the Bois de Fays and in the Bois de Malaumont. From what I afterwards ascertained it appeared that the information he gave me was correct. I also asked him the strength of the enemy along the ridge north of the Cunel-Brieulles Road, which I knew to be a strongly held enemy position. He said they were a thousand strong and a relief had taken place the night before, bringing in fresh troops. This was interesting if not cheerful news, although I could not afford to place too much credence in any statement he might make. I sent him happily on his way back toward Nantillois and suppose he reached there safely. At length, the mission given to Companies B and D of combing the Bois de Fays to the ravine having been accomplished in due time and many prisoners and guns having been taken, the company commanders reported to me.[250]

Confusion or not, Capt. Egan ordered his 3/319th Infantry to continue the attack. Always Move Forward! "Confusion is built into the plan!" we'd often joke. "It's part of the deception plan! If we don't know what we're doing, then neither will the enemy! It's in the *I.D.R.*!" We'd also say things like "Chaos is our friend!" or "Poor bastards! We've got them exactly where we want them—totally confused!" After several well-placed R.G. shots, one of Capt. Egan's platoons was actually able to break through *KRIEMHILDE* and Egan quickly funneled what was left of his battalion through the breach point like milk through a straw, charged up the road, and entered Cunel, capturing some two hundred Germans, including two Hun battalion H.Q.s!

The 319th Infantry Regiment of the 80th Division was the first American unit to breach *KRIEMHILDE*.

---

[250] As cited in *1/320th Infantry*, 128.

Let me say that again: *The 319th Infantry Regiment of the 80th Division was the first American unit to breach KRIEMHILDE.*

To reiterate, the 319th Infantry of the 80th Division was the first American unit to not only breach *HAGEN*, but also *KRIEMHILDE*, which was the prize.

Capt. Egan instructed his men to stuff the Hun prisoners into the church of the tiny, bombed-out town (which no longer exists), and ordered them to comb the entire area for the enemy while he waited (hoped) for the rest of Col. Love's 319th Infantry Regiment to arrive to help hold the place.

And then it happened.

American artillery, fired mostly from our very own 155th Arty. Brig., roared down upon the officers and men of 3/319th Infantry.[251]

Of course, those in Capt. Egan's battalion didn't know for sure whose artillery it was—they simply knew that they were taking several casualties and that they were all alone in Cunel. With that, Egan ordered a retreat back to the farm, bringing his casualties with him. For all intents and purposes, 3/319th Infantry was considered *hors de combat* for the rest of the fight, and as such, became the regiment's reserve battalion.

Nevertheless, *KRIEMHILDE* had been breached, if only for an hour. And we in Cronkhite's 80th Division had done it, just like we had done it with *HAGEN*. And both times, it was Brett's 160th Inf. Brig. that had pulled it off. Maj. Ashby Williams, commanding the assault battalion of the 320th Infantry during the day's fight, summed up the battle in this manner:

> *We were fighting our way through the Kriemhilde-Stellung line, which was the third German main line of defense, which was made up of strongly defended and heavily manned positions which were supplied by a trench railway coming from back of the German lines, and we all knew that the Boche would hold this line to the last ditch, if possible... It was upon this line of defense that the Boche endeavored to hold up the advance of the great American Army through the Argonne Forest. A strong line of defense as this was, is a series of mutually-supporting positions. We had plowed our way through several of these mutually-supporting positions and were now face-to-face in our immediate front on the ridge east of Cunel with three heavily-manned and strongly-defended mutually-supporting positions.*[252]

---

[251] *313th Artillery*, 52-53 and *314th Artillery*, 40.

[252] As cited in *1/320th Infantry*, 122-23.

The "mutually-supporting positions" that Maj. Williams denoted primarily emanated from the right in Bois Melaumont and Bois Fays. They shot enfilade fire from east to west into the 320th Infantry, which was moving north from *Ferme Madeleine*. The 320th Infantry, tasked with eliminating these strong points, had a hell of a time clearing *Bois Fays* let alone storming *Bois Melaumont*. On top of this, the Hun had O.P.s atop *Côtes Cunel* and had every square meter honed in for artillery strikes. We understood that the 80th Division was supposed to simply launch demonstrating frontal attacks—holding the Germans by the nose—while the 3rd and 4th Divisions, on our flanks, were actually to breach the line and conduct a double-envelopment. The problem was, however, that the 3rd and 4th Divisions couldn't break through, either.

October 10, 1918.
Weather: Misty.
Roads: Muddy.
On Oct. 10, Bullard's corps renewed its attack against *KRIEMHILDE* in the vicinity of *Cunel*, supported by guns from Heiner's 155th Arty. Brig., 80th Division. Although Brett's 160th Inf. Brig. held *Ferme Madeleine* and parts of *Bois Cunel* and *Fays*, "the Hun with the Gun" still held *Bois Malaumont* and *Côtes de Cunel*, the corps objective. Because of the terrain and enemy activity, no light batteries could be brought forward to act as accompanying artillery, offering direct fire support against the strong German positions. They did move farther north, however, establishing firing positions just south of *Bois d'Ogons*. During our post-war reunions, the Blue Ridge artillerymen reminded me that firing batteries had to be very careful as to how close they got to a tree line, as it affects the angle of a gun, thus curtailing its range. Too close, for example, and the guns have to be angled higher, thus targets of only "x-range" can only be serviced. Remember, the primary job of the artillery is to suppress or destroy enemy targets in support the Infantry. As such, the guns had to be positioned in order to actually hit those targets. Cover and concealment, although important, were thus secondary.

Once the 160th Inf. Brig. was set, Brett ordered it to attack *KRIEMHILDE* once again, heading for *Cunel*, in conjunction with the 3rd and 4th Divisions. Many of the educated men in the brigade likened the previous attack to A.P. Hill's dusk attack against Cemetery Ridge at Gettysburg on July 2, 1863, when the Confederates held the center of the Federal position, if only for a short time. This next attack, it was thought, would be "Pickett's Charge," and most of us knew how that turned out. While Maj. Wilfred Blunt's 1/319th Infantry would attack on the left soon after 10:00 A.M., Maj. Williams's 1/320th Infantry would attack on the right, each with two companies abreast and with attached supporting weapons (i.e., M.G.s, I.G.s, and mortars, which were always in the thick of the fight). 2/320th Infantry was assigned to support the attack of 1/319th Infantry and as such, the 320th Infantry attacked without a reserve.

As usual, the Germans were ready to meet them, and the attacking units were thrown back with heavy loss, especially from Hun "whiz-bangs." Maj. Ashby Williams of 1/320th Infantry remembered:

> [I had] Capt. Barringer place his mortars in an open space in a ravine in Bois Fays, which was the only available location (he said) for the weapons with a view to bringing fire on the triangular Bois Malaumont...Whether by accident or whether they had information, I do not know, but almost on the instant that our barrage was laid down the Boche opened a counter-barrage which was the most intense bombardment I ever heard or experienced. His H.E. shells poured down on us like a monster hail storm, putting the candles out in my P.C. and shaking the place to its very foundation. I shall never forget that memorable morning. As I stood at the foot of the steps I remember the storm of bursting shells was so terrific I waited a few minutes hoping that the storm would break, but there was no let-up. [After the devastating barrage], I stepped out of my P.C. and literally walked over the top of dead men and a hundred feet from the place at the edge of the woods where I turned to the right towards the ravine. Dead men were lying everywhere. I remember particularly a group of 3 that had been killed by the concussion of one shell... The Boche artillery had indeed wrought terrible execution upon the American boys.[253]

Lt. Edward Lukens of I/3/320th Infantry similarly remembered:

> Oct. 10 was a day full of mixed-up situations, moving back and forth and sideways with little accomplished, and shelling everywhere. Many a time that morning I cursed my job, and wished I was a "buck private" so that I could attach myself to any outfit I happened to meet instead of having to continue wandering around trying to learn the situation and find my own outfit... At one point I found myself in with the 4th Division [!], and thought of going forward with them to fight as a private, but reminded myself that I could do as a single extra man would not compensate for what might happen if a gap were

---

[253] As cited in *1/320th Infantry*, 128.

left between the 319th and 320th Infantry Regiments, so I kept on combing the northern slope of Bois d'Ogons until I finally ran into our battalion and found that most of my men had landed there already, though some never did find it and were used during the rest of the drive as stretcher bearers or ammunition carriers by the reserve companies that handled those jobs.[254]

To speak to Lt. Lukens's revelations about the difficulty of being a company-grade infantry officer in the U.S. Army during a war, it's a tough job—probably the toughest job in the world. Tougher, I would argue, than that of a field or general grade officer simply because of the time-in-grade (not much) and great responsibility involved. It must also be remembered, however, that those who choose to take on this responsibility, chose it. The Army never, ever, forced them to take a commission. Most of us privates, however, especially those from the "National Army" divisions, were forced into the Army by government decree. If you aren't up to the job, lieutenant or captain or major or whatever, then you owe it to the Army and those in your charge to return to the ranks. Conversely, it's not that easy being a private soldier, either. His pay is low, especially compared to that of a company grade officer's, his living conditions are always the worst the Army has to provide, and his life expectancy is low (although not as low as infantry lieutenants). Go no farther than check out a casualty roster: "Private, Private, Corporal, Private, Sergeant, Private, Private, Lieutenant, Private, Private, etc." Granted, there are for more privates in the army than lieutenants (about one to forty), and I know that by percentage Infantry lieutenants suffer far more casualties, but remember, nobody forced said lieutenant to take a commission.

Once again stopped cold by the strong German defenses along the Heights of Cunel, Brett's 160th Inf. Brig. fell back to the farm, with the H.Q. elements operating from *Bois d'Ogons.*[255] Maj. Williams remembered:

A strong line of defense, as this was, is a series of mutually supporting positions. We had plowed our way through several of these mutually supporting positions and were now face to face in our immediate front on the ridge east of Cunel with three heavily-manned and strongly defended mutually supporting positions. Upon the map they are designated as follows:

(a) A small triangular piece of woods located about 300 meters north of Cunel-Brieulles road, which triangle was heavily manned with machine guns

---

[254] As cited in *3/320th Infantry*, 85-86.

[255] *319th Infantry*, 34.

and with small artillery and flanked by small ridges on either side; (b) A system of enemy trenches about 300 meters north of the Cunel-Brieulles road and about 300 meters east of (a), which position was strongly held by machine gunners and riflemen, and (c) A strongly-held system of trenches on the ridge and in the edge of the Bois de Foret, about 300 meters north of (b). Those three positions, in addition to being strongly defended in themselves, mutually supported each other, and in addition were mutually supported also by a heavy volume of machine gun fire from the piece of woods over the rise to the west of our sector (d), by machine guns in the town of Cunel, and by a heavy volume of machine gun fire from the southeast edge of the [Bois Faux]. The three latter positions which mutually supported the enemy positions in my front were located in the sector of the 319th Infantry on my left. In addition to this flank fire from my left, there was also enemy flank fire from the south edge of the Bois de Foret in the sector of the 4th Division on my right. On the morning of October 10, therefore, I was attempting an advance upon information that my left flank was protected, but in reality it was completely exposed to fire from (d), from Cunel and from [Bois Faux], and with knowledge that my right flank was exposed. The latter situation was taken care of by my own dispositions. When my advance began, therefore, my left flank companies had not gone 200 yards north of the Cunel-Brieulles road before, coming over the edge of the slope, they were exposed to a murderous machine gun fire from the (d) position and from Cunel and [Bois Faux], all of which positions were on my left flank in the 319th Infantry sector. Moreover, those flanking enemy positions were able to hold up my left flank companies until the barrage had passed over the triangular position (a) in my front, and permitted the machine guns in that position to open on my troops from the front. It is needless to say that in the face of this murderous cross-fire it was suicide to advance further in that flank, and it therefore became necessary for my left flanking companies to withdraw into the woods just south of the Cunel-Brieulles road. I cannot speak too highly of the calmness and courage of my officers and men in the face of this difficult situation. The lines were reformed and company commanders directed to await further orders.[256]

---

[256] As cited in *1/320th Infantry*, 122-23.

In mid-afternoon, Cronkhite received the following message from Bullard's III Corps H.Q., announcing Pershing's "great dissatisfaction with the progress of the attacking divisions." It reads, in part:

> At 2:40 P.M. today the Army commander expressed to the corps commander his great dissatisfaction with the progress of the attacking divisions, taking into consideration the fact that the enemy is not now holding his front with sufficient strength to counterattack and is, therefore, very evidently holding it merely with successive machine gun positions. He directs, through the corps commander, that division commanders require brigade and regimental commanders to get in personal touch with front line conditions and see to it that energetic measures are adopted at once to reduce these machine gun nests. The Army commander is convinced that the enemy holds principally with M.G. groups, with little support in the rear, and that these groups can be reduced by aggressive action on the part of officers. The Army Commander also directs that ground once gained shall not be yielded, but on the contrary troops on the flanks will be pushed forward in support and also troops from the rear when necessary. The Army commander demands that the Brieulles-Cunel position be penetrated and captured.
>
> BJORNSTAD

If we would have seen this message during the fight, we may have marched right on up to Pershing, who we understood knew what combat was like, and said, "Then you do it!" Cronkhite was really good at shielding us from this nonsense, as was his job. Is it appropriate for one general officer to speak to another in the third person about "disappointment?" Yes, I guess (I'm not a general, nor ever will be one). Is this an appropriate communication from one general to another? Sure. Why not. We don't know whence Pershing got his information, but if his units were taking high casualties, then the enemy was clearly in strength. I'd understand his frustration if we were reporting 1% casualties—but we weren't. According to Lt. Lukens from I/3/320: "One high-ranking officer who was in the line told me the Corps Staff was a bigger obstacle in his way than the Boche."[257]

That night, as the men from the 160th Inf. Brig. licked their wounds, Heiner's artillery continued to pound away at the enemy. Pvt. Allen S. Hartman of H.Q. Company/314th Artillery was cited for bravery during this time:

> *On the night of Oct. 10, 1918, in the vicinity of Nantillois and during the particularly heavy concentration of enemy shell fire, Pvt. Hartman though already wounded, went to the assistance of a severely wounded infantryman, assisted in placing him on a stretcher and carried him to the first aide station. While carrying the stretcher Pvt. Hartman was again struck by a shell fragment.*[258]

October 11, 1918.
Weather: Cloudy.
Roads: Good.

Soon after dawn on Oct. 11, 1918, the 80th Division launched its forth attack (!) against *KRIEMHILDE* in conjunction with enveloping attacks from the American 3rd and 4th Divisions. Although this attack also failed to take *Cunel* ("the Army mission") the Blue Ridge Boys were able to finally secure *Bois Malaumont*. As before, the 319th Infantry, on the division left, attacked *Côtes Cunel* pretty much head-on and got slaughtered. The 320th Infantry, attacking on the division right through *Bois Fays*, however, was able to finally secure *Bois Malaumont* and push as far north as *Bois Faux* in conjunction with units from the Ivy Division.[259] Maj. Williams, still in charge of the attack battalion of the the 320th Infantry, was so low on men that he had to consolidate his four companies into two. He writes:

> *My companies had been much depleted by casualties, and in order to be ready for the new attack when H-Hour should be announced, I reformed my battalion, putting Companies A and C into one company and drawing Company L from the support battalion, which latter company was placed in support behind*

---

[257] As cited in *3/320th Infantry*, 86.

[258] As cited in *314th Artillery*, 45.

[259] *Faux* is pronounced "Foe."

Company D, so that the dispositions for the attack were as follows: Front line, Company B on left; Company D on right. In support, Company A (with Company C) on left; Company L on right... I had rations and water taken to the men, and men and officers alike took such shelter as they could find from the high explosive shells that never ceased to fall in our area. Late in the afternoon our own artillery was putting shells on my troops, no doubt by a misjudgment of the range and by a lack of observation, and I had to phone back and ask to have the firing stopped. During the afternoon a detachment was sent out toward the left front, and by infiltration took a machine gun that was established in a foxhole along the open ridge called St. Christophe and which had been giving us much trouble.[260]

Lt. Lukens of I/3/320th Infantry, coming up behind 1/320, similarly remembered: *At last the order came for a fresh advance, and in the morning we formed in the field in front of the farm and started up the hill, but had to wait again for a few minutes in shell holes while our artillery repeated the now-familiar process of shelling the wrong place. This lack of liaison with the artillery was our greatest handicap throughout the Cunel drive, as further events of that morning showed. We resumed the advance, and soon came in sight of the church tower of Cunel, only a km or so away, but between it and us were patches of woodland filled with M.G.s and field pieces as thick as pumpkins in a corn field. We had crossed over a protecting ridge in the field and were approaching one of these little woods, when the M.G.s opened up on us. We dropped flat, and started at once to advance "by rushes," or "filtering," a few men at a time jumping and running a few yards, then diving behind any slight swale they could find, like a baseball player sliding for a base, and so getting under cover before a gun could be sighted on them.*[261]

In combat, we from B/1/318th Infantry acted similarly to Lt. Lukens's platoon from I/3/320th Infantry. I'm sure it was like this across the division, if not the entire A.E.F. What I mean by this is that we moved as a platoon "combat group" and each weapon-specific squad maneuvered forward by short rushes. Generally we'd say things like "I'm up, I'm seen, I'm down" to control how long we stayed up under fire. Other men would say things like, "Yankee

---

[260] As cited in *1/320th Infantry,*

[261] As cited in *3/320th Infantry,* 87-88.

Doodle Dandy." All of this was spelled out in the *I.D.R.* that we learned even while at Camp Lee. Our experiences with the British in Artois and Picardy and later, here, in the Meuse-Argonne, solidified the practice. The key is to get up to "the last 100 yards" as soon as possible with as many men as possible. After that, it becomes a platoon-level fight—at fifty yards, a squad-level fight, and after that, a buddy team fight. Never, ever train to expect to get any help from higher, as you'll simply get frustrated and upset. When help does arrive from higher—and it might if you're deemed to be important—then see it as a combination of Christmas and Halloween. We Doughs of the 80th Division, in fact of the entire A.E.F., cannot emphasize enough the importance of platoon-level training, as the platoon will be your war. Learn to attack, defend, move, recover, and utilize supporting weapons at that level. The company commander is, in fact, merely an expert platoon leader. He'll show up every now and then to provide some extra firepower or advice to the platoon leader, but remember, he has three other platoons to command with a battalion commander breathing down his neck, and not always in a good way. The same holds true for the battalion commander—consider him as an expert platoon leader with some nifty supporting weapons at his disposal. In short, once we crossed the L.D., our platoon, for all intents and purposes, was "alone and unafraid." That was the message the Army and General Pershing were trying to get across to us Doughs all along. The field grade officers, as agents of the Army, would provide the plan, the training, the guidance, the weapons, the food, the equipment, etc., but it was up to us at the company and platoon levels to actually win the battle and as Frederick the Great famously said: "Battles win wars."

As the violent contest progressed, the 320th Infantry linked up with elements of the 4th Division in Bois Faux. It was from Bois Faux where the high command hoped to finally breach *KRIEMHILDE* as the clear fields of fire of Côtes Cunel were just too deadly. The 319th Infantry and other units could attest to that fact. Lt. Lukens of I/3/320th Infantry, still assigned as the support battalion of the regiment remembered:

We emerged from Bois Malaumont at the northern edge without difficulty, for the woods had been already cleared except for a few snipers by the companies on our right, and we dropped into the ditch of the Cunel-Brieulles Road which ran traverse in front of the woods. Maj. Emory came up and ordered Lt. Dunmire's 1st Platoon to recon the patch of woods to our left-front... [We soon thereafter followed and advanced into Bois Malaumont], small though it was, and [lost contact with the 319th Infantry]. This gap was my concern, and the major sent me back to find its extent, and to see that no harm resulted from it. A whole platoon could no longer be spared from I/3/320th Infantry, so I took with me only a small patrol, consisting of Sergeant Sugden, Corp. Shay, and two or three privates. As we were going back, keeping just inside the cover of the woods, we ran into a streak of the strongest gas we have ever experienced. I do not know what kind it was, for it had none of the typical odors, but was rather anesthetic in effect, choking you like ether, and had we not instantly put on our masks we would have been quickly knocked out.[262]

But like the 319th Infantry, on the left, the 320th Infantry, on the right, could advance no farther. Cronkhite reluctantly reported this fact to Bullard, our corps commander. Cronkhite stated that the Blue Ridge Division was spent and that it could no longer be expected to breach *KRIEMHILDE*, especially given the fact that the Germans had stacked *Côtes Cunel* with some of their best units. Bullard surprisingly concurred and ordered the fresh 5th (Red Diamond) Division to replace the 80th Division in order to renew the attack (so much for "the enemy is not now holding his front with sufficient strength to counterattack and is, therefore, very evidently holding it merely with successive machine gun positions"). But the men of the 160th Inf. Brig. weren't out of the woods yet (no pun intended) and they had several more hours to endure real combat. Lt. Edward Lukens of I/3/320th Infantry remembered:

Our job now was not only to protect the gap [between the 319th and 320th Infantry Regiments], but at the same time to locate all the nearby companies so that we would be certain just how great the gap was and could judge how best to place our men. The 5th Division was to relieve us about midnight, so we knew that if we could keep the Boche from filtering back, for five or six hours more, our job would be done and we could shift our burden to the fresh troops with no apologies. We were near to the limit of our physical strength, and but for this knowledge of the coming relief, we would have felt almost hopeless...As it was now quite dark, we decided to go around the edge of the woods in the open field; instead of attempting to use the trails through, and as we reached the southwestern edge of [Bois Faux], near the scene of our morning's skirmish, we could distinguish the figures of men lying in almost shell hole. I wondered what platoon this could be that, unknown to us, had come to help us fill our gap, and I went up to one group of them and asked in a whisper who they were. None answered, and thinking they might have fallen asleep at their posts, I shook one of them by the shoulder. Only then did I realize that I was speaking to a dead

---

[262] As cited in *3/320th Infantry*, 90.

man, and every one of those men, who lay in their holes so naturally, facing the enemy as though still intent on defending their ground, had already finished their fight, and had been relieved ahead of us...[I eventually found the rest of my battalion in the woods and] there were still several hours to wait until our relief should come, and we lay still, watching and waiting with what patience we could muster. As our good luck would have it, nothing happened...other than Boche artillery was in action, and here again our luck was with us. An "Austrian 88," apparently not more than half-a-mile away, kept firing point-blank into the woods all night. Enough shells landed in the middle of that woods, at intervals of about 2 minutes, to have killed every man who lay in the fields north and west of the woods, and not a man there was hit by them. For hours we spent listening to them, and fervently praying that they would go on battering the empty woods and not change range or deflection... At last relief came. About 2:00 o'clock in the morning the companies of the 5th Division began coming in single file around the corners of the woods, guided by our runners. In silence we got up out of our shell holes and they dropped into them, and we filed out, away from out never-to-be-forgotten ["Valley of Death" and back to Ferme Madeleine].[263]

To better protect the shot-up 160th Inf. Brig. during its relief-in-place, Cronkhite wisely ordered the 314th M.G. Battalion (Mot.) to move a company onto Hill 274. The 314th M.G. sent its Company A with its six Ford "Specials" that carried the men, ammunition, guns, and equipment to the southern slope of the hill where it established indirect fire positions to target the roads that led into Cunel.[264] Lt. Furr of the 314th M.G. Battalion remembered:

It was decided to place the twelve M.G.s of Company A in echelon on Hill 274, south of the woods, within easy reach of the infantry commander [319th Infantry Regiment] when needed. There was no doubting the seriousness of the fire, as the wounded were being carried back toward Nantillois on stretchers in a constant stream. The M.G. squads were placed in "fox holes" for protection against the artillery fire. In these positions one of the guns of the 3/A/314th M.G. was destroyed by a direct hit, but the marvel of it was that Corporal L.B. Smith and two men lying in the same hole with the gun, were uninjured. A battery of

---

[263] As cited in *3/320th Infantry*, 96.

[264] *319th Infantry*, 34; *314th M.G.*, 42-43. The American 5th (Red Diamond) Division consisted of the 6th, 11th, 60th, and 61st Infantry Regiments and the 19th, 20th, and 21st Artillery Regiments.

German artillery seemed to have a particular spite against the one hundred meters of ground occupied by this platoon, as it had no more than taken up the position when shells began falling here, and continued throughout the whole day to hit in approximately the same area. After the gun was blown up the platoon was moved a few hundred yards to the east and remained there without further mishap. As usual, toward dusk, the artillery increased in activity and the hills south of Bois des Ogons were given a general shelling, firing continuing until early morning, but the men were well dug in and were more fortunate than the artillery several hundred meters in the rear of the company, which had several casualties during the night.[265]

Meanwhile, back in *Bois Montfaucon* with the 159th Inf. Brig., we continued to try to recover from the physical and psychological trauma of the previous battle as well as assimilate replacements, including my new platoon leader, Lt. Harry Ashby (Lt. Myers was wounded in *Bois d'Ogons*—like most other platoon leaders). Individually we were in almost as bad shape as we were by companies and battalions. It is a mistake to think that because a man is not wounded he is not affected physically and mentally by what he has undergone during combat. Fortunately, young men of sound constitutions have wonderful recuperative powers, and after a week or so more of sound sleep and hot food, they are usually "good to go." However, the long-term effects are telling as the war negatively affected the health of many of us, in varying degrees. For example, some of us became alcoholics, being forever haunted by the war. Some had lung problems from being gassed. Others suffered from rheumatism, the piles, etc. It must be remembered that when an Infantry outfit comes out of the line, it comes out hollowed-eyed, half-starved, and half-crazed. Most of us also had severe diarrhea because of the stress and bad diet. In other words, we were "all in."

At 4:00 P.M., orders were received for Jamerson's 159th Inf. Brig. to march to *Fôret Hesse*, a distance of some eight km to the south, back across Rui Forges, keeping off the road as much as possible.[266] My regiment was under way at 5:00 P.M. and in camp at 10:30 P.M. after having made a very strenuous hike across country—this area being a devastated "No Man's Land" of a continuous series of shell holes, destroyed trenches, and hidden wire. Here we were told that the entire 80th Division, minus its artillery brigade, would be consolodated for future

---

[265] As cited in *314th M.G.*, 43-44.

[266] *Fôret Hesse* or "The Forest of Hessia" is pronounced "Four-et Hess."

action. The forest had numerous old French dug-outs from the battle of Verdun days, and that's where many of us chose to "cocoon up."

October 12, 1918.
Weather: Misty.
Roads: Muddy.

During the fight for *KRIEMHILDE*, "that evil witch-bitch" as we came to call it, from Oct. 5-11, the 80th Division suffered horrendous casualties. The number stood at 139 officers and 3,412 E.M., or about 18% of our assigned strength. The vast majority of the casualties, of course, were inflicted upon the infantry regiments and their casualty figures numbered closer to 50%.[267] Lt. Edward Lukens of I/3/320th Infantry later noted:

> *The fighting around this region was apparently not handled as well from above as was the initial stage of the drive. No such great barrage was prepared our way as was laid down on Sept. 26. Frequent changes of orders and uncertainty to just what we were supposed to do, incorrect artillery firing, and almost total absence of aviation, were annoying features. Lack of good "liaison" perhaps includes the others. Instead of preparing a coordinated attack, as on Sept. 26, and on Nov. 1, the staff apparently allowed each outfit to work out its own salvation, depending on the original impetus which had in fact been totally expended long ago. Some mistakes were made by line officers, but the greatest bungles were made higher up. In spite of everything, we gained ground, and in the course of time other divisions carried on until the Hun's death grip was loosened, but we took our turn in Hell to do it.*[268]

During the night of Oct. 11-12, 1918, Brett's 160th Inf. Brig. was transported south to *Fôret Hesse* to rest, refit, and reorganize alongside their brothers from Jamerson's 159th Inf. Brig. after it was relieved by the 10th Inf. Brig., 5th Division, in the Valley of Death. Maj. Ashby Williams of 1/320th Infantry remembered:

> *I had not slept, except for a minute or two now and then from sheer exhaustion, and I had not shaved for over a week and must have looked as bad as I felt. But I am frank to confess that there was a spring in my step and, in some fashion, a*

---

[267] *317th Infantry*, 68.

[268] As cited in *3/320th Infantry*, 78.

sense of joy in my heart, and I noticed this in the step and voice of my companions, as we passed the Bois d'Ogons and out of that shell-swept area with its ever-present, nauseating odor of shell-gas and the horrible specter of dead and dying men, joy perhaps that I had not suffered their fate.[269]

As was S.O.P. (standard operationg procedure), the artillery regiments of the division remained in place, providing fire support for the newly rotated infantry units coming into their zones. Remember, according to Army doctrine: "the artillery is never held in reserve." For reasons that weren't totally communicated to us, on Oct. 12, Brig. Gen. George Heiner, the commander of the 155th Arty. Brig., was replaced by Col. Robert S. Welsh, his able operations officer. "Joe Latrinsky" told us that Heiner could not handle the stress of battle and that he was leaning too heavily upon Welsh, late of the 314th Artillery. Welsh was therefore officially given command of the brigade.[270]

To show you how things usually go, soon after the 9th Inf. Brig., 5th (Red Diamond) Division took over the zone in the Valley of Death at around 1:00 A.M., Walker's 314th Artillery Regiment received "a hysterical report" from the *dilettante* Red Diamonds (this was their first real "Up the Line" experience—too bad for them!) that it was being attacked by Hun tanks coming down from the Heights of Cunel! In response, Walker ordered Lt. Raymond Shean's platoon from F/314th Artillery to move forward and destroy the tanks with direct fire while the O.P. called in a grid for indirect fire from the big guns of Col. Goodfellow's 315th Artillery.

Shean drove his guns as far north as the horses could go. Undaunted, he ordered the guns unhitched from their limbers in *Bois d'Ogons* and they advanced north through the dark, cut up woods by hand or "by prolong" (i.e., using ropes tied to the hubs with one horse). The problem with this method is that it's slow and, more importantly, one can only carry a few rounds of H.E. with them, the limbers and caissons being left to the rear. By the time the guns actually arrived to *Ferme Madeleine* (they had to be wheeled over or around scores of downed trees), it was daybreak and the Blue Ridge artillerists discovered that the so-called German tanks were actually painted canvas shapes on frames mounted on farm wagons, objects which we called "Red Monkeys."

Needless to say, Shean's 2/F/314th Artillery stayed in place in case any real tanks arrived and prepared for the next push against *KRIEMHILDE*. During subsequent night's action, three

---

[269] As cited in *1/320th Infantry*, 137.

[270] Stultz, 497.

soldiers from Walker's 314th Artillery were cited for bravery, Sergeant Charles G. Kleeh of Battery E and Privates George Spotts of Battery F, and William F. Garland of H.Q. Battery:[271]

> *On the night of Oct. 12, 1918, Sergeant Kleeh, under severe enemy shell fire, directed the moving of ammunition to the gun emplacements west of Nantillois. Sergeant Kleeh remained at his work encouraging the men under him until wounded.*

> *On the night of Oct. 12, 1918, Pvt. Spotts, after carrying a message to the infantry front lines, voluntarily made 2 more trips over the Cunel-Nantillois Road, which was subjected to continuous enemy shellfire.*

> *On the night of Oct. 12, 1918, Pvt. Garland was ordered to carry an urgent message from the regimental P.C. near Monfaucon to the battalion P.C.'s one km north of Nantillois. Pvt. Garland was severely wounded in the shoulder near Montfaucon, but refused to go to the hospital and delivered both messages before seeking surgical treatment.*

October 13, 1918.
Weather: Cloudy.
Roads: Muddy.

The morning of Oct. 13 found those of us in 2/B/1/318th Infantry in fairly good spirits (all things considered). We'd had at least two nights of relatively uninterrupted sleep, hot chow, the sounds of battle were distant, and life in *Fôret de Hesse* wasn't all that bad. It did take several days before most of us got rid of a chronic tired feeling, however. Within an hour after breakfast, for example, we would feel as though we had done a full day's work, and to walk a mile or two was still a burden. It also took several more nights before we could actually sleep soundly for a few hours straight without being awoken by the sound of incoming Artillery. At this point, an electrical fear had been ingrained into us that our bodies actually took years to recover, believe it or not (and some never did).

While in Fôret de Hesse, N.C.O.s continued to train the new E.M. and the squads, filled with replacements, slowly learned to act as a team. We were, in fact, almost an entirely new infantry company (if not battalion and brigade). Naturally, we did not start any very strenuous

---

[271] As cited in *314th Artillery*, 45.

training right away, but gradually worked into it as our "pep" slowly came back. The irony is that the least experienced of us had the most energy while the most experienced had the least.

I guess it all evens out.

Our new platoon leader, Lt. Ashby, played it right. He mostly watched and listened. He learned who the key players of the platoon were and got to know our platoon guide, Sergeant Brown. I have to thank Capt. Douglas in large part for this, as he took an active interest, unlike other company commanders, in developing our platoon leaders. He did not simply push them off on the platoon guides. He understood that while the officers commanded the unit, the N.C.O.s commanded and looked after the men. As the *M.M.T.* said: "The officer is the owner and the N.C.O. is the foreman." For us that meant that the company commander was the owner, the platoon leader was the owner's son, the platoon guide was the foreman, and the squad leaders were his muscle.

We also understood that company-level officers didn't have to know everything (but a lot) and they didn't have to be the strongest, the fittest, the fastest, or even the smartest. But they had to represent the Army and at least attempt to model its high standards. They were the Army to us, like it or not. We expected our officers to know Army Regulations backwards and forwards. For us, that meant that they not only had to know what was written in the *I.D.R.* and the *F.S.R.*, but also how to properly *teach and apply* their principles. They had to lead, setting the example as articulated in the *I.D.R.*, all of the time. Whether they liked it or not, officers were "the book" to us and they were always being watched and evaluated by the N.C.O.s and E.M. They had to know how to take the soldiers that the Army entrusted to them and form them into an unbreakable team. Not the fastest? Fine, then be fast enough find who is and train that soldier to do those jobs that require speed. Not the smartest? Then be smart enough to find out who is and train that soldier to accomplish those tasks. I don't mean to trust everyone, either. There will always be somebody, especially in the N.C.O. corps, who will try to bring an officer down, even at the expense of the unit or the mission.

Company-grade officers, especially those in the infantry, cavalry, or artillery branches, have to be brave. Again, it doesn't mean that they have to earn a D.S.C. during every mission, every day, or at all, but they have to be there—they have to learn to control their fears and be in charge of the unit/situation or else somebody else will be. And once somebody else takes over, that officer is no longer in charge. Once this occurs, it will be very hard for said officer to regain the respect of his subordinates again, especially if engaged in combat, which is the *sine qua non* of the Army. Granted, I was just a lowly A.R.-man during the war, but I watched and I learned from the best. After the war, in 1926, I chose to became an Army Reserve infantry lieutenant and am currently (1938) an assistant regimental operations officer with the 317th Infantry, which is based in Richmond (more on that later), with the rank of major. According to the Army, the following is mentioned about "Leadership":

> *I.D.R. 358. The art of leadership consists of applying sound tactical principles to concrete cases on the battle field. Self-reliance, initiative, aggressiveness, and a conception of teamwork are the fundamental characteristics of successful leadership.*
>
> *I.D.R. 359. A correct grasp of the situation and a definite plan of action form the soundest basis for a successful combat. A good plan once adopted and put into execution should not be abandoned unless it becomes clear that it can not succeed. After thoughts are dangerous, except as they aid in the execution of details in the original plan.*
>
> *I.D.R. 360. Combats that do not promise success or some real advantage to the general issue should be avoided—they cause unnecessary losses, impair the morale of one's own troops, and raise that of the enemy.*
>
> *I.D.R. 361. Complicated maneuvers are not likely to succeed in war. All plans and the methods adopted for carrying them into effect must be simple and direct.*
>
> *I.D.R. 362. Order and cohesion must be maintained within the units if success is to be expected.*
>
> *I.D.R. 363. Officers must show themselves to be true leaders. They must act in accordance with the spirit of their orders and must require of their troops the strictest discipline on the field of battle.*
>
> *I.D.R. 364. The best results are obtained when leaders know the capacity and traits of those whom they command—hence in making detachments units should not be broken up, and a deployment that would cause an intermingling of the larger units in the firing line should be avoided.*
>
> *I.D.R. 365. Leading is difficult when troops are deployed. A high degree of training and discipline and the use of close order formations to the fullest extent possible are therefore required.*

I.D.R. 366. In order to lighten the severe physical strain inseparable from infantry service in campaign, constant efforts must be made to spare the troops unnecessary hardship and fatigue—but when necessity arises, the limit of endurance must be exacted.

I.D.R. 367. When officers or men belonging to fighting troops leave their proper places to carry back, or to care for, wounded during the progress of the action, they are guilty of skulking. This offense must be repressed with the utmost vigor.

I.D.R. 369. The post of the commander must be such as will enable him to observe the progress of events and to communicate his orders. Subordinate commanders, in addition, must be in position to transmit the orders of superiors. Before entering an action the commander should be as far to the front as possible in order that he personally may see the situation, order the deployment, and begin the action strictly in accordance with his own wishes. During the action, he must, as a rule, leave to the local leaders the detailed conduct of the firing line, posting himself either with his own reserve or in such a position that he is in constant, direct, and easy communication with it. A commander takes full and direct charge of his firing line only when the line has absorbed his whole command. When their troops are victorious, all commanders should press forward in order to clinch the advantage gained and to use their reserves to the best advantage.

I.D.R. 370. The latitude allowed to officers is in direct proportion to the size of their commands. Each should see to the general execution of his task, leaving to the proper subordinates the supervision of details, and interfering only when mistakes are made that threaten to seriously prejudice the general plan.

A.D.R. 1499. The greater part of any field artillery command goes into action and remains under the immediate control of responsible officers. However, in reconnaissance work, in the ammunition supply service, and even in the batteries when communications fail; or emergencies suddenly occur, subordinates will be thrown upon their own responsibilities. Subordinates must therefore be given great latitude in the execution of their tasks. The success of the whole depends largely upon how well each subordinate coordinates his work with the general plan.

A.D.R. 1500. In a given situation it is far better to do any intelligent thing consistent with forceful the execution of the general plan than to search hesitantingly for the ideal. This is the true rule of conduct for subordinates who are required to act upon their own initiative. A subordinate who is reasonably sure that his intended action is such as would be ordered by the commander, were the latter present and in possession of the facts, has enough encouragement to go ahead confidently. He must possess the loyalty to carry out the plans of his superior and the keenness to recognize and seize opportunities to further the general plan.

A.D.R. 1501. Initiative must not become license. Regardless of the number of subordinates who are apparently supreme in their own restricted spheres, there is but one battle and but one supreme will to which all must conform. Every subordinate must therefore work for the general result. He does all in his power to insure cooperation between the subdivisions under his command. He transmits important information to adjoining units or to superiors, and, with the assistance of information received, keeps himself and his subordinates duly posted as to the situation.

A.D.R. 1502. When circumstances render it impracticable to consult the authority issuing an order, officers should not hesitate to vary from such order when it is clearly based upon an incorrect view of the situation, is impossible of execution, or has been rendered impracticable on account of changes which have occurred since its promulgation. In the application of this rule the responsibility for mistakes rests upon the subordinate, but unwillingness to assume responsibility on proper occasions is indicative of weakness. Superiors should be careful not to censure an apparent disobedience where the act was done in the proper spirit and to advance the general plan.

As we concluded our recovery operations in *Forêt de Hesse*, the artillery of America's Blue Ridge Division continued its support of the Red Diamond Division, which was slugging it out against *KRIEMHILDE* at *Cunel* and repelling a strong German counter-attack in the Valley of Death (welcome to the war, "Fightin' Fifth!"). 1/313th Artillery reported: "Positions heavily shelled in early morning. Repulsed counter-attack at 16.00h. Reported our barrage very effective in breaking up the counter-attack and catching the Germans when attempting to return to their own lines."[272] During the day's fight, the 314th Artillery suffered five casualties, including Lt. Robert Ober of B/314, who was K.I.A.[273] For their actions during the savage enemy barrages, Lt. Ober and Pvt. Royal W. Wynings of A/1/314 were cited for conspicuous gallantry:[274]

> *On the afternoon of Oct. 13, 1918, Lt. Robert Ober was directing the barrage of B/314 Artillery, at the battery positions north of Nantillois. In the course of the barrage the battery was spotted by a German aeroplane and the fire opened by the German battery with which the aeroplane was working. The first enemy shell which fell made the accuracy of the German adjustment obvious to all at the battery position. In spite of this fact, Lt. Ober continued to direct and encourage his gun crews. The example of his bravery and coolness inspired his men to forgetfulness of their own danger and a better performance of their duties.*
>
> *Pvt. Wynings, telephone lineman, maintained telephone communication the entire night of Oct. 13, 1918, between his battery position and the battalion P.C. near Nantillois. Although the field between the two P.C.s was under terrific enemy shell fire and the telephone lines were almost completely destroyed several times. Pvt. Wynings did not allow communications to be interrupted for more than a few minutes.*

October 14, 1918.
Weather: Rain.
Roads: Poor

Oct. 14 meant two things to the 80th Division: the great news that the American First Army had finally broken *KRIEMHILDE* at Cunel *via* Bois Melaumont and *Village Romagne* and the Blue Ridge Division's movement south to *Pretz-en-Argonne*, where we received new equipment, namely, brand-new Browning M1918 Automatic Rifles (B.A.R.).[275] According to the "War Diary" of the 314th Artillery: "After an elaborate artillery preparation, the infantry attack [of the 5th

---

[272] As cited in *313th Artillery*, 158.

[273] *314th Artillery*, 40.

[274] As cited in *314th Artillery*, 44.

[275] *Pretz-en-Argonne* is pronounced "Prey awn Are-gone."

Division] was launched at 8:30 A.M. We assisted the 313th Artillery in delivering accompanying fire which rolled north across Cunel."[276] During the attack, the 313th Artillery suffered ten casualties when a gun from Battery A was hit by a Hun H.E. round. During the momentous attack, the 32nd (Red Arrow) Division breached *KRIEMHILDE* at *Romagne* on the left and the 4th and 5th Divisions breached *KRIEMHILDE* on the right, plowing into *Cunel* from the east (the breach at *Romagne* earned the 32nd Division the moniker, "Breakthrough"). With that, the American First Army did the impossible: it breached *KRIEMHILDE*, one of the strongest defensive systems the world had ever seen! After this, there was only one formal German line left, *FREYA*, which was up near Barricourt and Buzancy.[277] And after that, it would be "Open Warfare" that Pershing often talked about (and emphasized), and we'd then be performing what is called "Pursuit Operations."

The momentous day started for us in the 318th Infantry at 5:30 A.M. when we were ordered to march south from *Fôret Hesse* through *Esnes* to *Montzéville*. There we were trucked south through *Béthelainville* and *Sivry-La-Perche* to *Pretz-en-Argonne* where we were to continue recovery operations (we loved recovery operations) in the adjoining villages of *Vaubecourt, Sommaisne,* and *Beuzee*. While billeted in barns and houses of *Pretz-en-Argonne*, we received a new issue of clothing, including brand-spanking-new wool overcoats! It was like Christmas times five, as it was the first time in many months that I felt this clean! Every stitch of clothing, from my socks and underwear to my tunic, trousers, putties, and field cap were brand new!

We A.R.-men also received new "Browning Automatic Rifles" (B.A.R.s). Unlike the "Sho-sho," which is made of stamped metal, the B.A.R. is solid. It weighs around sixteen pounds, has a twenty-round box magazine that fires, just like our M1917 Enfields and American Chauchats, 30.06 caliber rounds (but this time, well). It has an effective range as far as one could see out to 2,000 yards (in battle, we could only really see out to two or three hundred yards). We were taught to fire three-to-five-round bursts while walking forward ("moving fire") and when the magazine ran out of rounds, to take a knee, reload with the help of an assistant, and then continue the attack. The assistant would hand the gunner a new magazine while the gunner gave him the empty one. We loved the B.A.R. so much that we thought that *every other* Dough should be armed with one!

---

[276] *314th Artillery*, 40.

[277] *Freya*, Wotan's wife, is pronounced "Fray-yah," *Barricourt* is pronounced "Bar-ree-core," and *Buzancy* is pronounced "Booze-awn-see."

The American First Army's strength was so reduced by mid-October that General Pershing ordered that the rifle companies be reorganized on the basis of four platoons and eight half-platoons or "combat groups." Recent experience had demonstrated that the platoon-sized combat groups used in the previous drives (i.e., four task-specific squads) did not possess enough flexibility for the attack. The new formation called for a platoon of sixty soldiers, one commissioned officer and fifty-nine N.C.O.s or E.M., that was divided into two combat groups or "half-platoons" of three squads each (one A.R./R.G squad, one bomber squad, and one assault squad). While each squad was to be commanded by a corporal, each combat group was to be commanded by a sergeant. This was new because before, the platoon was our "combat group" and it had four squads performing separate but complementary tasks, all under the *aegis* of the platoon leader. Now we would have two co-equal combat groups per platoon, each led by a sergeant, which had three squads of mixed weapons and capabilities. With the new organization, each A.E.F. infantry company had around 250 Doughs, each infantry battalion around 1,000, each infantry regiment around 3,000, and each infantry brigade around 6,000. This, of course, did not include attachments from the sanitary, quartermaster, ordnance, artillery, or signal corps.

My platoon, 2/B/1/318th Infantry, was commanded by Lt. Harry Ashby, a newly-minted "90-Day Wonder from Langres" who was once an N.C.O. from the 317th Infantry. Our platoon guide was still Sergeant Brown, who would help Lt. Ashby lead the platoon and steady the men. My combat group was commanded by newly-promoted Sgt. "Fightin' Bill" Murray, and it had three squads. My squad, the 3rd Squad, one of the A.R. and R.G. Squads of the platoon, was led by Cpl. John Zubal, a man who I would follow into hell itself (and had!), and who was armed with an M1917 Enfield Rifle. The squad itself had two teams. Team One consisted of Private First Class (P.F.C.) Joe Riddle (me), who was the designated B.A.R.-gunner, P.F.C. Albert Getz, who was my assistant gunner (A.G.) and general "partner in crime," and P.F.C. James Stewart, who was the B.A.R. ammo carrier (bandoliers and a canvas satchel filled with B.A.R. magazines). Pvts. Earl Andrews and Wort Wise were our important R.G.ers and Jim Bruce and Boss Atkins were their ammo carriers/designated marksmen. Team Two consisted of P.F.C. Ben Schuyler who was the B.A.R.-man, P.F.C. Richard Grubbs, who was the A.G., Thornton Ridinger who was the B.A.R. ammo carrier, John Spratt and William Dunlap who were the R.G.s, and Harry Harmon and Larry Parker who were the R.G. ammo carriers.

Each B.A.R. gunner and his A.G. carried at least two B.A.R. magazine bandoliers that were crisscrossed over their shoulders, looking much like Pancho Villa. Each bandolier carried ten magazines and each magazine weighed about three pounds. The B.A.R. ammo carrier also sported bandoliers as well as a canvas satchel that was filled with another ten or so box magazines. That means that each B.A.R. team carried at least 1,500 rounds of 30.06 ammunition to suppress or destroy enemy targets while on the move, which means that each A.R. squad/battle group had at least 3,000 rounds while on the move! And that ammo really weighed down the ammo carriers.

Our 1st Squad, one of the bomber squads of the platoon, was commanded by Cpl. Thomas Merritt. It consisted of two teams of seven or eight men each, armed with M1917 Rifles and hand grenades. As before, they were to get within twenty yards of a designated target, usually a concrete and camouflaged Hun pillbox, throw their hand grenades from the prone or kneeling positions. Once they hurled their grenades, the 2nd Squad, one of the assault squads of our platoon, was to charge through the bombers and take the objective with rifle and bayonet. This squad was the type of squad that suffered the most casualties in the A.E.F. The men carried most of their rifle ammunition in M1903 Bandoleers and their grenades in satchels or sand bags. They were to re-load their rifles from their bandoleers first.

Ammunition Supply.

I.D.R. 550. Company commanders are responsible that the belts of the men in their companies are kept filled at all times, except when the ammunition is being expended in action. In the firing line the ammunition of the dead and wounded should be secured whenever practicable.

I.D.R. 551. Ammunition in the bandoleers will ordinarily be expended first. Thirty rounds in the right pocket section of the belt will be held as a reserve, to be expended only when ordered by an officer.

I.D.R. 552. When necessary to resupply the firing line, ammunition will be sent forward with reenforcements, generally from the regimental reserve. Men will never be sent back from the firing line for ammunition. Men sent forward with ammunition remain with the firing line.

I.D.R. 553. As soon as possible after an engagement the belts of the men and the combat wagons are resupplied to their normal capacities. Ammunition which can not be reloaded on combat wagons will be piled up in a convenient place and left under guard.

To help fill our T.O., the infantry regiments of the 80th Division received replacements from the 76th (Liberty Bell) Division, men from New England. It was "bad enough" that we had Pennsylvania "Yankees" with us, but now we had New England, Clam Chowder-slurping actual Yankees among us! Needless to say, we treated them coldly. Not necessarily because they were from New England (which didn't help) but because they were "fresh fish" who knew nothing of war (and this was coming from a crew that only served a couple of weeks in battle). Even worse, they were replacing our friends from Camp Lee who had been blown to pieces and these new replacements made us feel like our friends were nobodies—that they were easily replaced—that we were all expendable—just like a canvass pistol belt, a canteen, or other issue item.

But once the Liberty-Bell-turned-Blue-Ridgers survived their first engagement, they were "in like Flynn" and true-blue Blue Ridgers. The 314th M.G. Battalion (Mot.), arguably one of the more-important units of the division, received twenty replacements from the 40th (Sunshine) Division, men drawn mostly from California.[278]

During our time in the Meuse-Argonne, Pershing's American First Army apparently issued several "Combat Instructions" to the chain of command. At our level, of course, we never heard about them directly but were indirectly affected by them as the instructions were included in our operations. When I read them after the war, during the 1930s, I actually found them a little insulting. I was inspired to read them when I read Pershing's *Experiences in the World War* (1931) and when I read some of the nonsense that came out of the "Instructions," my esteem for him dropped a little—not much—but a little. He'd often blame our "lack of forward movement" on "fear" or "lack of vigor."

Look, I was never a general. In fact, during the war, I was simply a lowly A.R.-man so I don't know what motivates general officers. But what I do know is that E.M. seek resources to do the job that includes leadership, guidance, and instruction. That's it. Officers: don't be a Degoutte or a Bullard—be a Cronkhite. Some of Pershing's instructions, for example, once again pressed "the primacy of the rifle" and argued that our supporting weapons—A.R.s, R.G.s, M.G.s, I.G.s, mortars, etc.—were "merely adjuncts."

At our level, at least in Maj. Sweny's 1/318 Infantry, we never heard this tripe. We in fact learned early on, starting with our time with the British in Artois, of the importance of "supporting" or "auxillary" arms. Does this mean that infantrymen should not be trained to be as proficient as they can be with the rifle and bayonet? Certainly not—on the contrary. But infantrymen also need to be trained how to operate and integrate supporting arms at all times. If not, they'll go pell-mell into hell with only a rifle, bayonet, hand grenade, and fork to simply be mowed down by deadly modern-day weapons.

Above all, infantrymen need to be taught to "Always Move Forward" with every means available as the modern battlefield is festooned with poison gas, shell holes, barbed wire—sometimes one hundred yards deep—H.E., shrapnel, bullets, and even aeroplanes dropping

---

[278] *314th M.G.*, 44.

much of the same. To stay in place, especially in the open, will mean sure death. You can bet your life on that.

October 15-30, 1918

On Oct. 15, the Ottoman Empire, a member of the Central Powers, asked for an armistice (cease fire) because most of its possessions in the Levant and Mesopotamia had been over-run by British or French forces and it was engulfed in an internal insurrection that was led by Mustafa Kemal (Ataturk), a member of the Ottoman General Staff. For us in the infantry units of the Blue Ridge Division, however, this meant little as we continued to prepare ourselves in *Pretz-en-Argonne* for the up-and-coming attack north against *FREYA* (the Third Push). But again, it was a good sign. Keep on pushing and it will soon be over!

Welsh's 155th Arty. Brig. continued to support the Red Diamond Division that was operating in the area of north of Cunel until Oct. 22, when it was replaced by the 90th (Tough Hombres) Division. Welsh's brigade thereafter conducted hundreds of fire missions for the Tough Hombres, which, like the Red Diamonds, did not have an assigned artillery brigade. This attachment lasted until until Nov. 1, when the 155th Arty. Brig. was returned to the 80th Division south of Buzancy. On Oct. 15, 1918, P.F.C. Oscar Riggs of H.Q./314th Artillery was cited for conspicuous gallantry for helping to maintain communications among his battalion:

> *On the night of Oct. 15, 1918, being on duty at 1/314 O.P. near Cunel, P.F.C. Riggs volunteered to go out under intense enemy shell fire and heavy gas concentration to repair breaks in the telephone lines. In spite of the greatest difficulty he maintained communication throughout the night between the O.P. and the regimental central at Madeleine Farm.* [279]

On Oct. 17, just a few days after Ottoman Turks dropped out, Pershing informed his new Army Group (American First and Second Armies, commanded by Lt. Gens. Hunter Liggett and Robert Bullard, respectively) that the Central Powers, conscious that they were losing (the Germans having shot their bolt with *Friedensturm*), were now begging for a cease fire. This meant that we had to continue to press the offensive vigorously in order that, under the plea for an armistice, the enemy may not gain time to restore order among their forces in order to

---

[279] *314th Artillery*, 45.

recuperate. Pershing said: "There can be no conclusion to this war until Germany is brought to her knees."[280]

As far back as Aug. 8, when Hindenburg informed the Hun Emperor that "the war is lost," the Germans have been asking for an end to the war based on Wilson's Fourteen Points. The problem was that the Allies, meaning France, Britain, and Italy, wanted Germany, and especially its nobility, to pay. In exchange for peace, the Kaiser and Germany's entire noble coterie was to abdicate, Germany was to become a republic, the German Army was to abandon its artillery and retreat to the east bank of the Rhine, its fleet was to be turned over to the British, Alsace and Lorraine were to be returned to France, and the independent "Republic of Poland" was to be carved out of Old Prussia and the newly-conquered territories. This, the Germans were not quite willing to do (yet), and the war would go on (this is why it lasted until Nov. 11, 1918). According to *Reichsfeldmarshal Wilhelm Groener*, who replaced Hindenburg as the General-in-Chief of the German Army (*Erster Generalquartiermeister*) on Oct. 29, 1918:

The withdrawal of the front to the line "Antwerp-west of Brussels-Charleroi-Meuse River" had become necessary...But the decision had to be taken in clear recognition of the inevitable consequences, because our first duty is and remains that of avoiding under all circumstances a decisive defeat of the army. When once the enemy breaks through, the danger of such a defeat is there, since the Supreme Command no longer disposes of reserves of the necessary fighting quality.[281]

Maximilian, the Crown Prince of Baden (Max von Baden), who became the German Imperial Chancellor (*Deutsches Reichskanzler*) or Prime Minister on Oct. 1, 1918 remembered:

As the result of this falling back of the northern sections of the army to the given line, [the army] would only hold out the prospect of avoiding serious engagement for perhaps a fortnight, and thus giving the exhausted troops a little rest. But since the new line was not finished building, the military situation as a whole would not be improved... But one thing more must not be allowed to happen: the American Army, or any considerable portion of it—must be

---

[280] As cited in Harbord, 449.

[281] *Ibid.*, 462. The ranks of general officers in the German Army, 1914-18, were: *Generalmajor* (brig. gen.), *Generalleutnant* (maj. gen.), *General der Infantrie*, or *Artillerie, Cavalrie*, etc., (or "of the branch"—lt. gen.), *Generaloberst* (Brig. Gen.), *Generalfeldmarschall* (the U.S. Army does not have equitable rank but it would be equal to an "Army Group Commander" like Pershing was during the last month of the war. Of the field grades, *Major* (maj.), *Oberstleutnant* (lt. col.), and *Oberst* (col.); of the company grades, *Leutnant* (2lt.), *Oberleutnant* (1lt.), and *Hauptman* (capt.).

prevented from advancing north of Verdun; the moment the fresh troops, who were far superior to our completely exhausted troops, advanced, it would be impossible to hold the position for long.[282]

On Oct. 22, the M1915 Colt-Vickers M.G.s of America's Blue Ridge Division were turned-in and replaced by brand-spanking-new M1917 Browning M.G.s, which were improved models of the Colt-Vickers. According to one M.G. officer, they "immediately became a favorite with the men."[283] I'd like to echo that comment. Like the Colt-Vickers, the M1917 Browning M.G. is a crew served, belt-fed, water-cooled M.G. that fired 30.06 bullets at around 500 R.P.M. (or two belts of ammunition per minute). The M1917 M.G. had a range of about 4,000 yards in the indirect fire mode. Remarkably, Lt. Val Browning, the inventor's son, was sent by the Army to help train our M.G. platoons and to monitor the newly-fielded weapon "in action." Why we in the 80th Division were honored with the combat field-testing, I know not. We assumed that it was because Pershing had confidence in us and that we would put the new weapon to good use, as not all divisions received the water-cooled Browning M.G.[284] The reason why we had M1917 Enfiled Rifles and Colts-Vickers M.G.s, and not M1903 Springfield Rifles and Hotchkiss M.G.s is simply because we came to France in the second wave. Those divisions in the first wave, the ones that were built around Regular Army or National Guard formations, were generally armed with Springfield Rifles and Hotchkiss M.G.s.

I'm glad we came in the second wave.

On Oct. 23, B/1/314th Artillery, providing fire support for the Tough Hombres, again received the command to move forward and take up a new position, under threat of a Hun infantry counter-attack. According to Capt. Beebe:

Our battery led the battalion and upon reaching Romagne it was reported from the front that the Germans had broken through the Infantry lines about four hundred meters off the road. So the battery pulled to one side and prepared for action, awaiting the command to fire point-blank at the supposedly on-rushing hordes of Huns. M.G.ers were called forward and placed in position and the gun crews were ordered to load their side arms. Later reports brought us the good

---

[282] As cited in Harbord, 463.

[283] As cited in *314th M.G.*, 44.

[284] *317th Infantry*, 71.

news that the first report was either a false one or that the enemy changed his mind and the fact is they were definitely checked by the infantry.[285]

On Oct. 24, 1918, Jamerson's 159th Inf. Brig. was loaded aboard scores of French *camions* and departed *Pretz-en-Argonne* for *Islettes Petites* in the Argonne Forest where the 77th (Metropolitan) Division had fought its way north while we were busy fighting our way up through *Bois Septsarges* and *Brieulles* a few days before.[286] Hitching a ride with a French motor transport unit is an experience in and of itself. Let's just say that speed in loading was not one of their priorities. This particular *camion* unit was commanded by French officers and N.C.O.s but was operated by four to five-feet-tall Vietnamese from French Indo-China who wore strange hats and goat skin coats. This truly was a world war! The sight and sound of these French-speaking southern (Indo) Chinamen threw us for a loop. Each rifle company was lined up along the road and ordered to count-off by sixteen. With that, the chosen sixteen were directed by a French-speaking Indo-Chinaman to load up aboard his *camion*. Our chain-of-command had nothing to do or say with the loading. After a few hours aboard *les camions*, catching as much sleep as we could, we arrived at *Islettes les Petites* at around 11:00 A.M. and were ordered to establish company bivi sites. Once again, my good friend and A.G., Albert Getz, was my tent mate.

We knew that we were to get ready for the next push and for the next week or so, the air was electric with anticipation of the coming attack, which all expected to be even more successful than the previous ones. The Associated Powers had been hammering *les Boche* for a month now without cessation and the whole battle line from the Meuse to the North Sea was on fire. While pessimists still existed who foresaw the war lasting into 1920, many, like me, were willing to bet (and hoped!) that the Hun would capitulate before the year was out.

On Oct. 27, five soldiers from the 314th Artillery, Corporal Clarence R. Sandy of H.Q. Battery, P.F.C. John Babbit of H.Q. Battery, Private Albert L. Tomblin of Battery A, Private Williard H. Groff of Battery C, and Private Chester Sprouse of the regimental supply company, were cited for conspicuous gallantry while conducting operations in the vicinity of Cunel-Romagne:

On Oct. 27, 1918, Private Groff, at ROMAGNE, while under exceptionally heavy shell fire from the enemy, carried messages between his battery and the battalion P.C. until severely wounded.

---

[285] *314th Artillery*, 52.

[286] *Islettes Petites* or "Small Islands of the Tiny" is pronounced "Ees-lets Pet-eat-ays."

On Oct. 27, 1918, Wagoner Sprouse was driving a wagon with rations to be delivered at the battery positions near ROMAGNE. The cart was hit by a shell and Wagoner Sprouse was wounded. In spite of the fact that the road remained under constant shell fire he continued his way, delivered his rations, and returned.

On the night of Oct. 27, 1918, at the P.C. of 1/314 north of ROMAGNE, where all communication had been destroyed by enemy shell fire concentrated on the battalion telephone central. Telephone Corporal Sandy was ordered to have communication established at once. Rather than send out his men under the intense fire, he went himself, restored communication, and with the assistance of one man maintained it until the bombardment ceased. There were sixteen circuits leading into the central, all of which was cut at least three times during the bombardment.

On the night of Oct. 27, 1918, at 1/314 P.C. north of ROMAGNE, where all communication had been destroyed by enemy shell fire, P.F.C. Babbitt, of his own accord, left the dugout and repaired all of the lines. This was especially difficult in view of the fact that the area in which the breaks occurred was subjugated to a constant interdiction fire and many wires were broken again immediately after they had been repaired.

On the night of Oct. 27, 1918, Pvt. Tromblin was lead driver of a caisson team which was hauling ammunition to the battery positions at ROMAGNE. A shell exploded on the road in front of his team, wounding Pvt. Tomblin and one of the other drivers. In spite of this fact, Private Tomblin continued with his team until a place of safety was reached. [287]

---

[287] As cited in *314th Artillery*, 44-45.

American 75mm artillery wailing away at a Hun target. Note the spend shell casings of the fixed ammunition. Blam! Blam! Blam!

On Oct. 28, Corporal Thomas H. White of H.Q./314th Artillery was cited for gallantry in maintaining effective communications, allowing his unit to maintain effective fires:

On Oct. 28-29, 1918, Corporal White (then P.F.C.), a member of 2/314th telephone detail, was on duty as a lineman at the battalion O.P., which was located a short distance west of BOIS-DE-RAPPES. Corporal White was the only lineman on duty on a line about three kilometers long and without aid maintained communications by extraordinary efforts on his part. Corporal White was repairing the line continually from 9:30 P.M. until 4:30 A.M. and was in the midst of heavy shell fire from the enemy during this whole period. [288]

On Oct. 29, 1918, Col. Harry C. Jones superseded Lt. Col. Charles Mitchell as commander of the 318th Infantry, Mitchell being returned to being regimental X.O. A number of other officers also reported to the regiment, almost filling our T.O. This, coupled with the fact that we had some real veterans in our ranks, our company, battalion, regiment, brigade, and division was as ready for action as it never had been before.

M.M.T. 926. Fear. The emotion of fear acts more powerfully upon the feelings of the individual soldier than any other emotion, and it is also probably the most infectious. Fear in a mild form is present in every human being. Nature wisely put it there, and society could not very well get along without it. For example, we stop and look up and down a crowded street before starting to cross, for fear

---

[288] As cited in *314th Artillery*, 45.

of being run over—in going out in the cold we put on our overcoats, for fear of catching cold. In fact, we hardly do anything in life without taking a precaution of some kind. These are all examples of reasonable fear, which, within bounds is a perfectly legitimate attribute of a soldier in common with other human beings. For example, we teach the men to take advantage of cover when attacking, and we dig trenches when on the defense, in both cases for fear of being shot by the enemy. It is the unreasoning type of fear that plays havoc in war, and the most deadly and common form of it is a vague, indefinite, nameless dread of the enemy. If the average man was to analyze his feelings in war and was to ask himself if he were actually afraid of being killed, he would probably find that he was not. The ordinary soldier is prepared to take his chance, with a comfortable feeling inside him, that, although no doubt a number of people will be killed and wounded, he will escape. If, then, a man is not unreasonably afraid of being killed or wounded, is it not possible by proper training and instruction to overcome this vague fear of the enemy? Experience shows that it is. If a soldier is suffering from this vague fear of the enemy, it will at least be a consolation to him to know that a great many other soldiers, including those belonging to the enemy, are suffering in a similar manner, and that they are simply experiencing one of the ordinary characteristics of the human mind. If the soldier in battle will only realize that the enemy is just as much afraid of him as he is of the enemy, reason is likely to assert itself and to a great extent overcome the unpleasant feelings inside him. General Grant, in his Memoirs, relates a story to the effect that in one of his early campaigns he was seized with an unreasonable fear of his enemy, and was very much worried as to what the enemy was doing, when, all at once, it dawned upon him that his enemy was probably worrying equally as much about what he, Grant, was doing, and was probably as afraid as he was, if not even more so, and the realization of this promptly dispelled all of his, Grant's, fear. Confidence in one's ability to fight well will also do much to neutralize fear, and if a soldier knows that he can shoot better, march better, and attack better, than his opponent, the confidence of success that he will, as a result, feel will do much to dispel physical fear. By sound and careful training and instruction make your men efficient and this efficiency will give them confidence in themselves, confidence in their rifles, confidence in their bayonets, confidence in their comrades and confidence in their officers...It is a well-known saying that a man in battle frequently regains his lost courage by repeatedly firing off his rifle, which simply means that his thoughts are diverted by physical movements. This is no doubt one of the reasons why the attack is so much more successful in war than the defense, because in the attack the men are generally moving forward and having their minds diverted by physical motion from this vague dread of the enemy.

As was already stated, Lt. Gen. Hunter Liggett, the commander of the American I Corps, replaced Pershing to become the American First Army commander, which was operating in the Meuse-Argonne. Lt. Gen. Robert Lee Bullard, the commander of the American III Corps, became the new American Second Army commander, which was still operating in Saint-Mihiel. Pershing, as commander-in-chief of the A.E.F., now acted as the American "Army Group Commander." By war's end, the American Third Army would also be formed. That night, we finally received our operations order to breach *FREYA* in the vicinity of Buzancy.

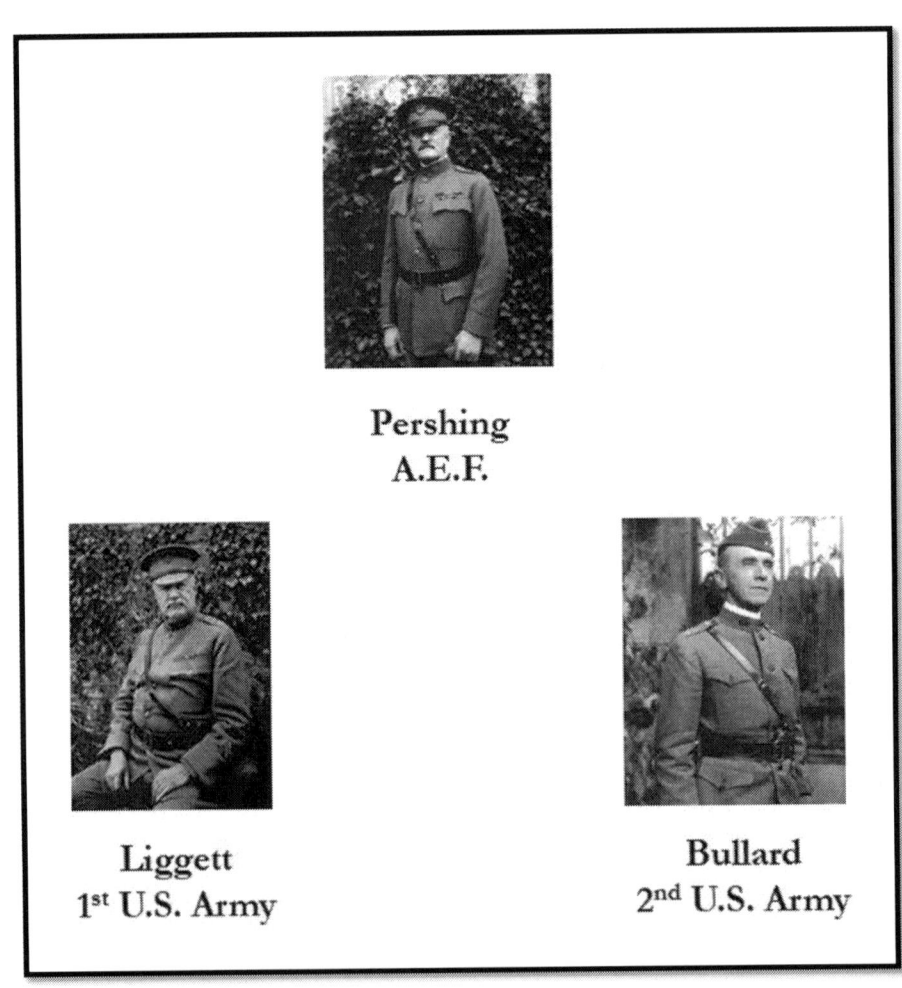

Pershing
A.E.F.

Liggett
1st U.S. Army

Bullard
2nd U.S. Army

1-3
P. C. HAMILTON.
A. E. F.

29 October, 1918.
15 hours.

SECRET.

FIELD ORDER NO. 27.
MAPS: (BUZANCY - VOUZIERES 1/20,000).
(BUZANCY 1/50,000).
(VERDUN - MEZIERES 1/80,000).

I. (a) The First American Army, while continuing its operation east of the MEUSE, will attack on its front west of the MEUSE in the near future. The I Army Corps will attack on its present front, with 3 divisions in line. The attack will be an enveloping one from the right. The high ground south of VERPEL will be carried on D day, with the object of driving to BOULT-AUX-BOIS upon further orders.
(b) CORPS BOUNDARIES: East: - VAUQUOIS (inclusive) CHEPPY (exclusive), CHARPENTRY (inclusive), BAULNY (inclusive), EXERMONT (exclusive, FLEVILLE (inclusive), SOMMERANCE (exclusive), ST. GEORGES (exclusive), thence along 300th meridian to ridge just north of IMMECOURT, thence northeast along ridge between BAYONVILLE and SIVRY lez BUZANCY, FOSSE (exclusive), VAUX en DIEULET (inclusive). West: - No change.
(c) The 2d Division (V Army Corps) will attack on the right of, and the 77th Division will attack on the left of, the 80th Division.
(d) Troops attached to the 80th Division:
157th Field Artillery Brigade.
2 Batteries 65th C.A.C.
6 Batteries 247th R.A.C.P.(Fr.).(From H plus 2 hours, D Day to O hour, D plus 1 day).
219 R. A. C. P. (Fr.)
1st Aero Squadron
2d Balloon Company (also with 77th Division)
2 Companies 53rd Pioneer Infantry
Co. E, 1st Gas Regiment

2-3

II. GENERAL PLAN:

(a) Mission and Zone of action of the 80th Division:
The 80th Division will cover the left of V Corps. It will seize the high ground to the north of SIVRY LEZ BUZANCY on the first day.
Right (east) limit: - Same as limit of the Corps.
Left (west) limit: - APREMONT (inclusive), CHATEL CHEHERY (exclusive), CORNAY (exclusive), meridian 298 from the AIRE River to the western edge of BUZANCY, thence north to ST. PIERREMONT (exclusive).

(b) The objectives are those portions of the Corps Objective lying within the zone of action of the 80th Division, as follows:
1st Objective: IMMECOURT (exclusive)-ALLIEPONT (inclusive)
2d Objective: MALMY - SIVRY LEZ BUZANCY (inclusive-298.0-291.2
Corps Objective: FME. DES PARADES-COTE 278-299.0-293.0
Subsequent Objective: Ridge west of FOSSE-BUZANCY-HARRICOURT.

(c) Initial disposition for the attack will be with attacking Brigade with regiments side by side, each regiment in column of battalions.

(d) General direction of the attack: True north, (compass bearing 13 degrees east of north), to the 2d Objective.

(e) Upon reaching the Corps Objective patrols will be pushed well to the front preparatory to a further advance on the second day. The Corps Objective will be gained before dark D day.

III. DETAILED INSTRUCTIONS FOR UNITS:
(a) 1. The 160th Brigade will be the attacking Brigade.
Attached troops:
1 battalion Field Artillery.
1 company 305th Engineers.
Co. E 1st Gas Regiment.
2 Boundaries: Its zone of action and objective are those of the division.

(b) Division Reserve:
159th Brigade.
314th Machine Gun Bn.
1 company 305th Engineers
3. At H plus 3 hours the line (also 77th Division) advances from the First Objective.

3-3

4. At H plus 6 hours and 30 minutes the line advances from the Second Objective.

(a) The 313th and 314th Machine Gun Battalions will, under direction of the Division Machine Gun Officer, execute long range overhead and indirect fire from H minus 1 hour to the time limit of safety of the infantry advance. After the execution of this fire these battalions will not move forward but will revert to the Division Reserve.

(b) Combat troops will be in position at D day at H minus 4 hours. The attack will be pushed with the utmost vigor.

IV. LIAISON:

(a) The Commanding General, 160th Brigade, will provide a combat liaison detachment of one company of infantry and one machine gun platoon to connect with a similar detachment of the left division of the 5th Corps (2nd Division). The command of this combined detachment will be designated by the Commanding Brig. Gen. of the 2d Division.

(b) Details of combat liaison with the 77th Division on the left will be indicated later.

(c) Axis of Liaison: - CHEHERY - FLEVILLE - ST. JUVIN - ALLIEPONT - SIVRY lez BUZANCY - BUZANCY - FOSSE.

V. COMMAND POSTS:
80th Division: CHEHERY
2d Division: CHARPENTRY
77th Division: CHEHERY
160th Brigade: SOMMERANCE
159th Brigade: POINT 04.08
Div. Artillery: CHEHERY

A. CRONKHITE
Major General, Commanding.

The reader will note that for this particular operation ("FIELD ORDER NO. 27"), "the 313th and 314th M.G. Battalions will, under direction of the division machine gun officer, execute long range overhead and indirect fire from H minus 1 hour to the time limit of safety of the infantry advance. After the execution of this fire these battalions will not move forward but will revert to the division reserve." By this time in the war, we had become convinced of the utility of M.G. barrages and accepted the fact that M.G.s took lots of time and effort to get to the front line of troops. In the mean time, why not shoot out several belts of 30.06 in a barrage!? On Oct. 30, P.F.C. Howard L. Ashcroft of D/2/314th Artillery was cited for bravery while serving at an O.P. with an infantry outfit of the 5th (Red Diamond) Division: "On the night of Oct. 30, 1918, near Romagne, P.F.C. Ashcroft, being stationed at the battalion O.P. as telephone operator, repaired several breaks in the line during the night under heavy enemy shell fire."[289]

October 31, 1918.

Weather: Fair.

Roads: Good.

On Oct. 31, 1918 (Halloween), the 80th Division, minus its artillery brigade, was attached to Maj. Gen. Joseph T. Dickman's American I Corps, which was advancing up the left of the Meuse-Argonne Sector. As such, America's Blue Ridge Division was ordered to move to a concentration area south of *Cornay*, a distance of some 25 km *via* the attack axes of the 77th (Metropolitan) and 28th (Red Keystone) Divisions during the first week of the great offensive.[290] Brett's 160th Inf. Brig. was to lead, followed by Cronkite's 159th Inf. Brig. Division assets were spread throughout. According to the Army, an infantry brigade took up about 5 km of road space. Dickman was an old cavalry officer from the Regular Army who had fought in the Apache Wars, the War with Spain, and in the Boxer Rebellion. Before this particular war, he was serving with the Army's General Staff. In the A.E.F., Dickman had successfully commanded the 3rd (Rock of the Marne) Division at Chateau-Thierry and the IV Corps at Saint-Mihiel. Clearly, he was a "heavy."

This particular column of our division reminded me of a gypsy caravan. In my battalion alone, there were twenty-one horse or mule-drawn vehicles, including four company rolling

---

[289] As cited in *314th Artillery*, 45.

[290] *Cornay* is pronounced "Core-nay."

kitchens, clumsy-looking things with their blackened chimneys sticking way up, ten combat carts, three general service wagons, and two water buffaloes. These vehicles, especially the rolling kitchens, were especially-prized items and we took great care in protecting them from enemy fire. As such, the men assigned to them, usually the older men or those who were still injured, etc., were never, ever looked down upon by we veterans in the rifle platoons "Back in B.C." ("Before Combat") we Doughs did in fact look down upon them—that's for sure. But "A.C." or "After Combat," nothing doing. Without these vehicles, cooks, mechanics, ammunition handlers, etc., an infantrymen wouldn't last forty-eight hours in modern combat. We learned that every soldier has a purpose—don't judge them by their job or their looks—judge them by how well they do their job. If the Army did not believe that a particular task was important to the "Big Green Machine," then it wouldn't have assigned a soldier to fill it in the first place. Not everyone can, nor should, be in the infantry. I should not have been in the infantry, that's for sure! But I was (and still am).

We marched north up through *Forêt d'Argonne*, up the 77th Division's old attack axis, through cut-up trees, blown-up German M.G. nests, piles of abandoned *Boche* gear, combined with some scattered Metropolitan Division equipment.[291] If I would have made this trek on Sept. 26, 1918, I would have been unnerved. But now, after taking out several Hun M.G. positions in *Bois Septsarges, Brieulles,* and *Fays* myself, I was pretty numb to it all. But to the average casual observer, the scene would have been horrific: human corpses, horse carcasses, shattered trees, abandoned, blood-encrusted gear, etc.

We even marched through the now-blasted hollow where Maj. Charles Whittlesey's 1/308th Infantry (reinforced by K/3/307th Infantry and C and D 306th M.G. Battalion) was cut off or "lost" from Oct. 2-8, 1918, while we were fighting it out in *Bois d'Ogons*. This area is just a few km southwest of *Village Apremont*. We then marched just west of *le Chene Tondu* (which was a hill in which severe fighting took place between the Germans and the 28th Division), through *Châtel Chéhéry*, which was destroyed, and into a wooded glen just south of Cornay.[292]

This march was the toughest (but not the longest) march of my life. It took some thirteen hours to maneuver north through the Argonne Forest. It wasn't until 9:00 P.M. that we made camp—in the open—between *Cornay* and *Châtel Chéhéry*, which was held by the 82nd (All-American) Division. Like the National Guard's 42nd "Rainbow Division," the 82nd Division, a National Army division, consisted of recruits from throughout the U.S. We were told that the

---

[291] *Forêt d'Argonne* is pronounced "Fore-et Dar-gone."

[292] *Apremont* is pronounced "Ap-pray-mon," *le Chene Tondu* is pronounced "Luh Chawn Ton-due," and *Châtel Chéhéry* is pronounced "Shat-tel Chay-er-ee."

area in which we were encamped was near the place where then-Corporal Alvin York of G/2/328th Infantry, on Oct. 8, 1918, had single-handedly taken out 32 Hun M.G.s (!), killed 28 Germans, and captured another 132, later earning him the Medal of Honor. "Why York, you've captured the entire German Army!"

The infantry, artillery, and M.G. battalions of America's Blue Ridge Division spent the rest of the night of Oct. 31 in shallow foxholes, trying to get some sleep. The shellfire was intermittent, at times becoming heavy. The men of Brett's 160th Inf. Brig., which was in front of Cronkhite's 159th Inf. Brig., noticed that the All-American Division's artillery was positioned practically hub-to-hub in the vicinity of Cornay.

The next big push would be soon.

Maj. Chas. Whittlesey, commander of the 77th Division's famous "Lost Battalion," 1/308th Inf. (L), the wooded gully where Whittlesey made his stand (C), and Corporal Alvin York of G/2/328th Inf., 82nd Division (R). "Why York, you've captured the entire German Army!"

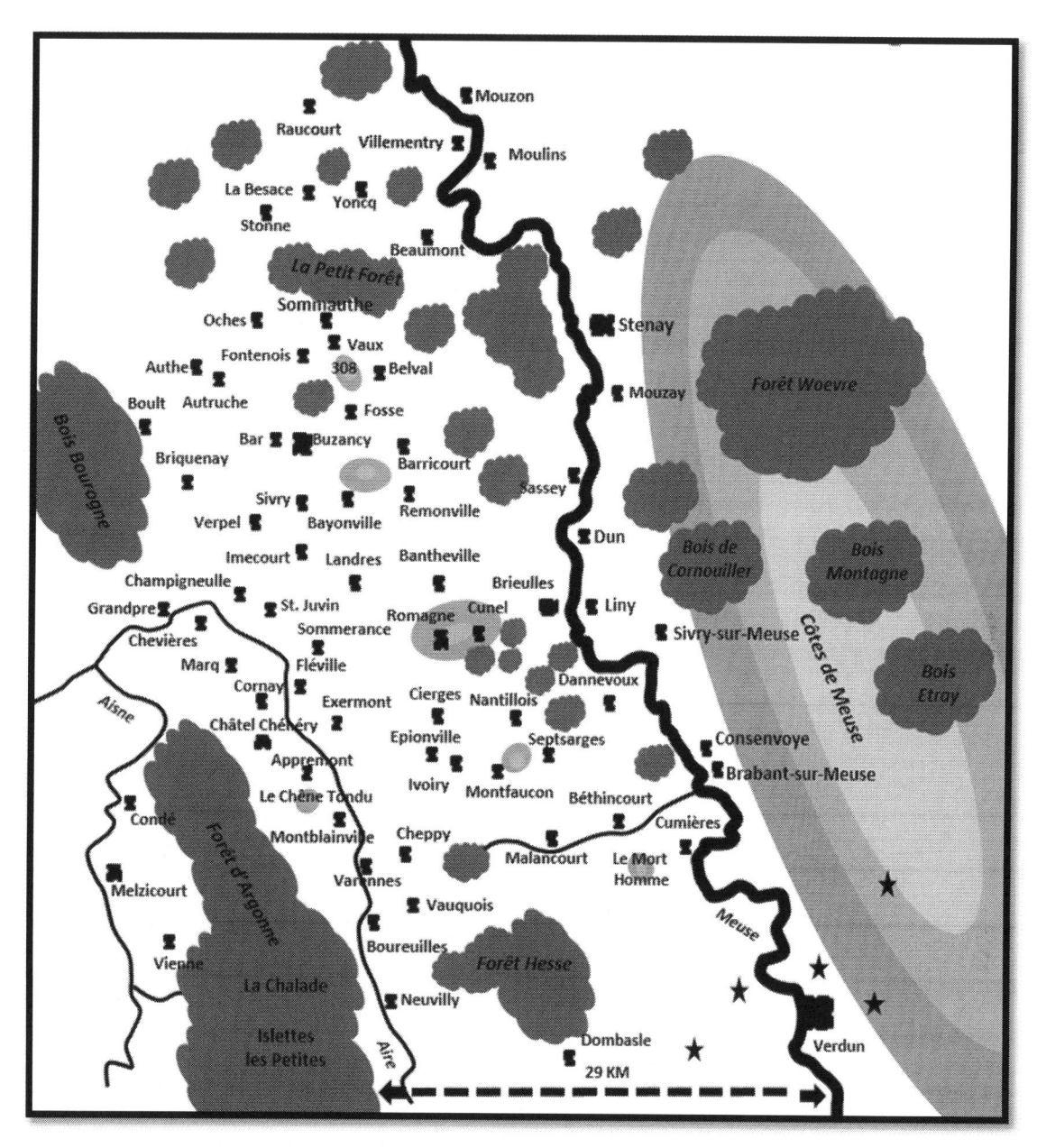

80th Inf. Div. Area of Operations, Sept.-Nov., 1918.

A.E.F. pontoon bridge across the Aire at Varennes (L) and "A Brig. Gen. view of the German dugouts on a hillside at Varennes," looking south (R).

"German dug-out in the Argonne Forest" (L) and "The western edge of the Meuse-Argonne Sector" (R).

Appremont and the Chene Tondu, looking north. Heavy fighting here with the 28th "Keystone" Division (L). We marched past this height on our way to Buzancy and old 77th "Metropolitan" Division trenches in the Argonne Forest near Le Chene Tondu (R).

Crossing the Aire River near Varennes.

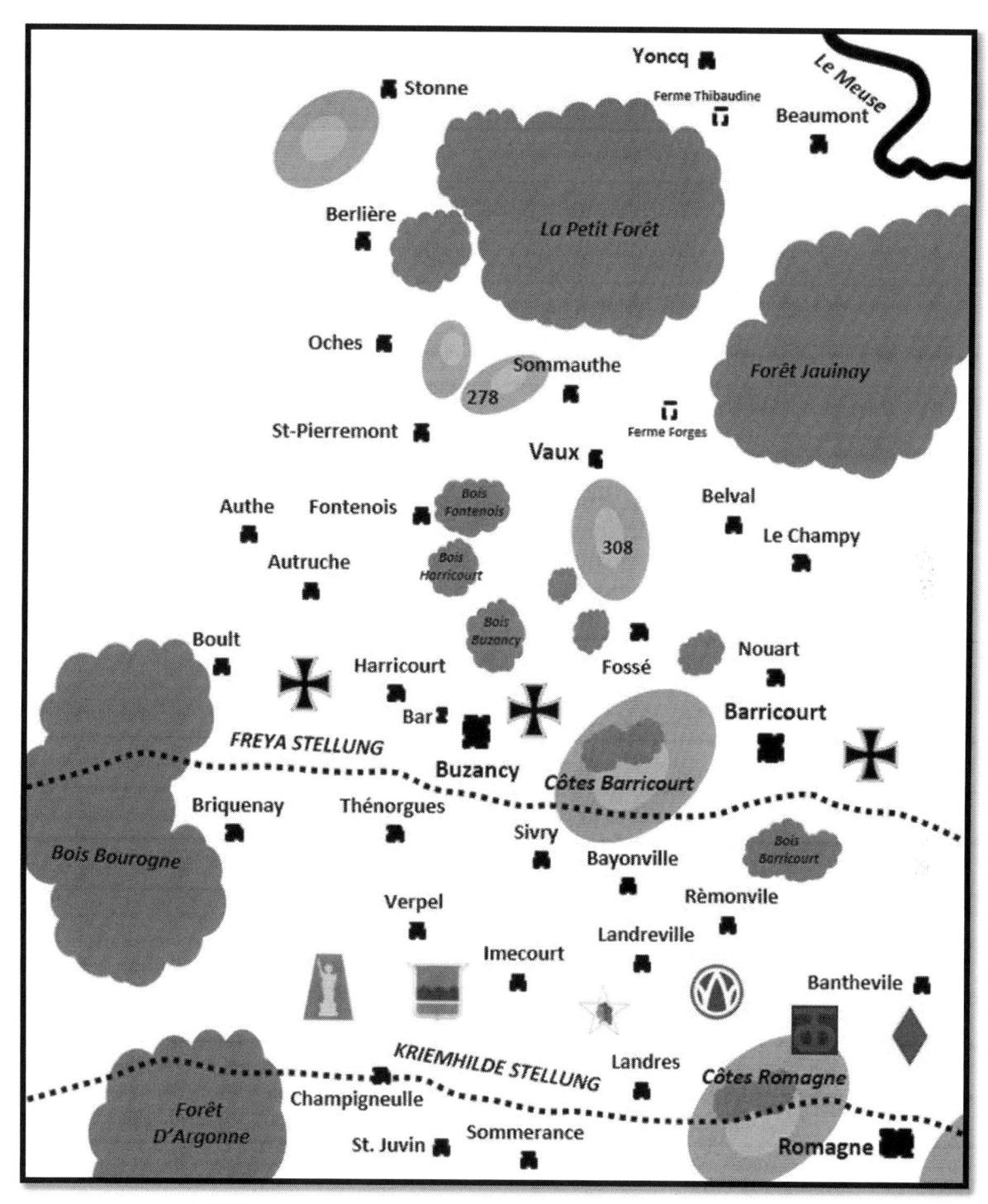

Approach to *FREYA* and Buzancy. From left to right: 77th Division, 80th Division, 2nd Division, 89th Division, 90th Division, and 5th Division. Once the American First Army broke through FREYA, the last of the strong German defensive lines, maneuver would once again be restored to the battle, achieving decisive results.

Maj. German Emory, commander, 3/320th Inf., K.I.A. in *Vallée De Rui Saint-Georges* between Champigneulle and Verpel (L). A military map that we used during our attack against FREYA. Each grid square is 1 km x 1km. We attacked up the "80" grid square corridor past Verpel and into Buzancy (R).

"Under Shellfire at St. Georges, 11-1-18" with the 319th Inf.

155mm howitzer firing from behind a destroyed building in the Meuse-Argonne.

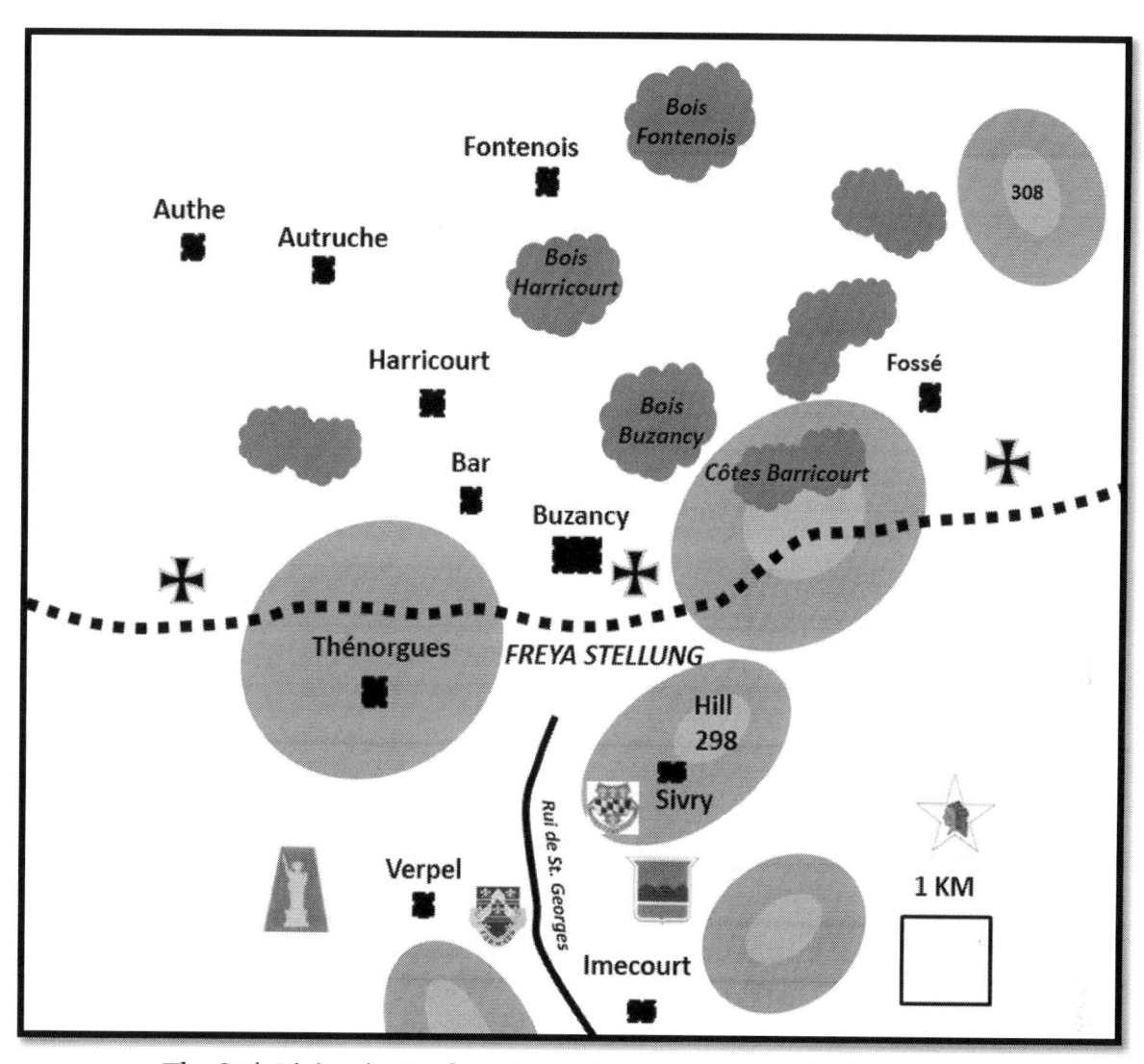

The 80th Divison's attack up Saint-Georges and into *FREYA*, Nov. 1, 1918. The 319th Inf. is on the right and the 320th Inf. is on the left. On the division's flanks are the 77th and 2nd Infantry Divisions.

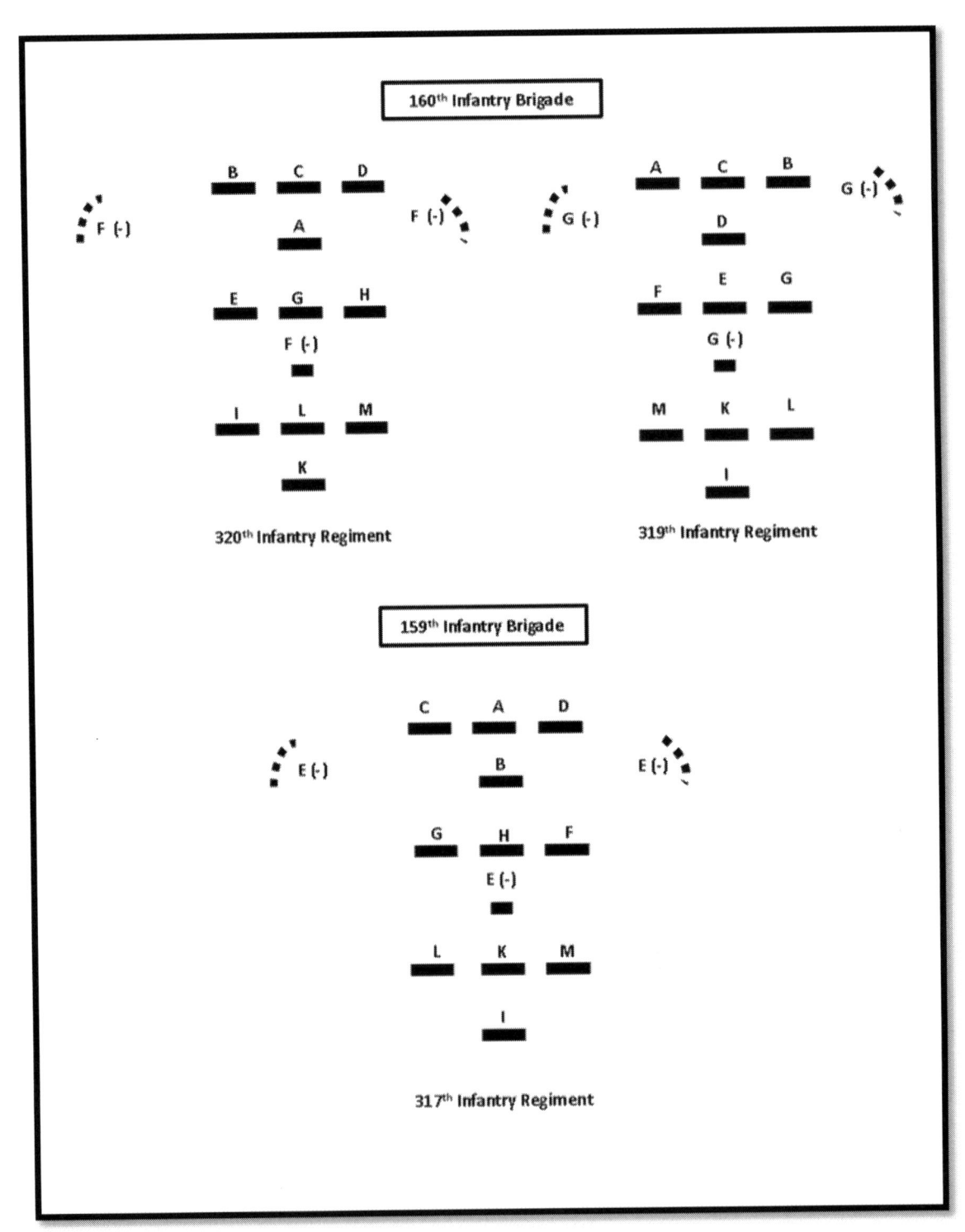

Combat Formation, Nov. 1, 1918. Company lettering is notional. Generally, we numbered our companies in the attack 1-4 per battalion. Each regiment is arrayed with an assault battalion, support battalion, and reserve battalion.

B/318 INF (240)

C.O.

P.L.　　　　　　　P.L.　　　　　　　P.L.

SGT　SGT　　　SGT　SGT　　　SGT　SGT

P.G.　　　　　　　P.G.　　　　　　　P.G.

P.L.

SGT　SGT

⌒⌒⌒ Either Assault, Bomber, or A.R. and R.G. Squads

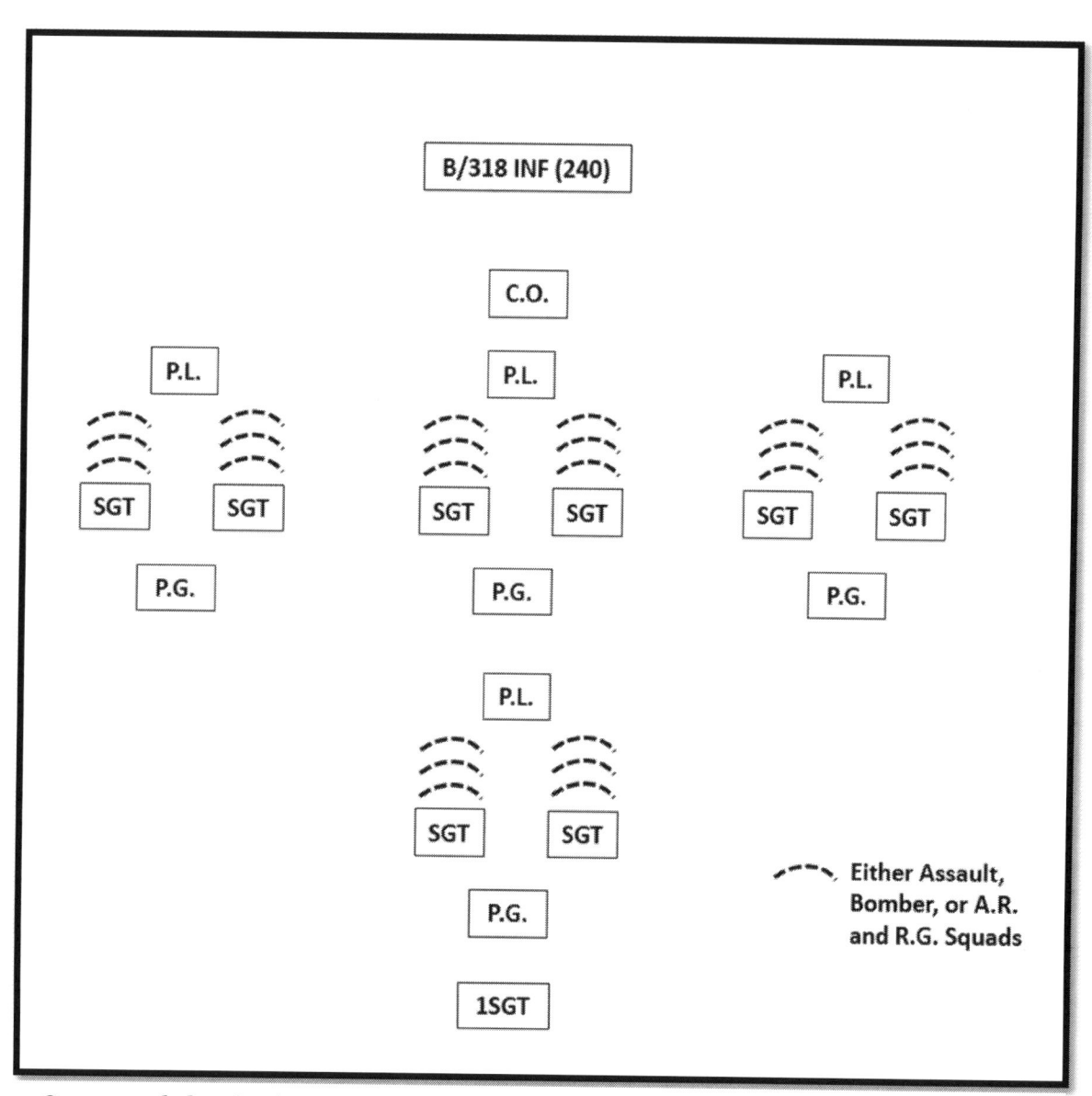

P.G.

1SGT

Conceptual sketch of B/1/318th Inf. on the attack, Nov. 1-9, 1918. We generally attacked three platoons up and one back. Each platoon had two equal combat groups with an assault, bomber, and A.R.-R.G. squad each. Usually, the bomber squad led.

"Over the Top at St. Georges. On their way to Immecourt, having captured St. Georges. 11-1-18" with the 319th Inf., (L) and "Battleground—Immecourt, 11-1-18." Photo of a squad from the 319th Inf. (R).

"An Austrian '88' captured at 8:30 a.m. and was used all afternoon on the former owners. Captured at *St. Georges*, 11-1-18 (L) and *Boche* M.G. squad moving into position (R).

"Boche Prisoners, 600 Strong. On their way to the rear. St. Georges, 11-1-18" (L) and "80th Div. troops passing through Imécourt, Nov. 3, 1918."

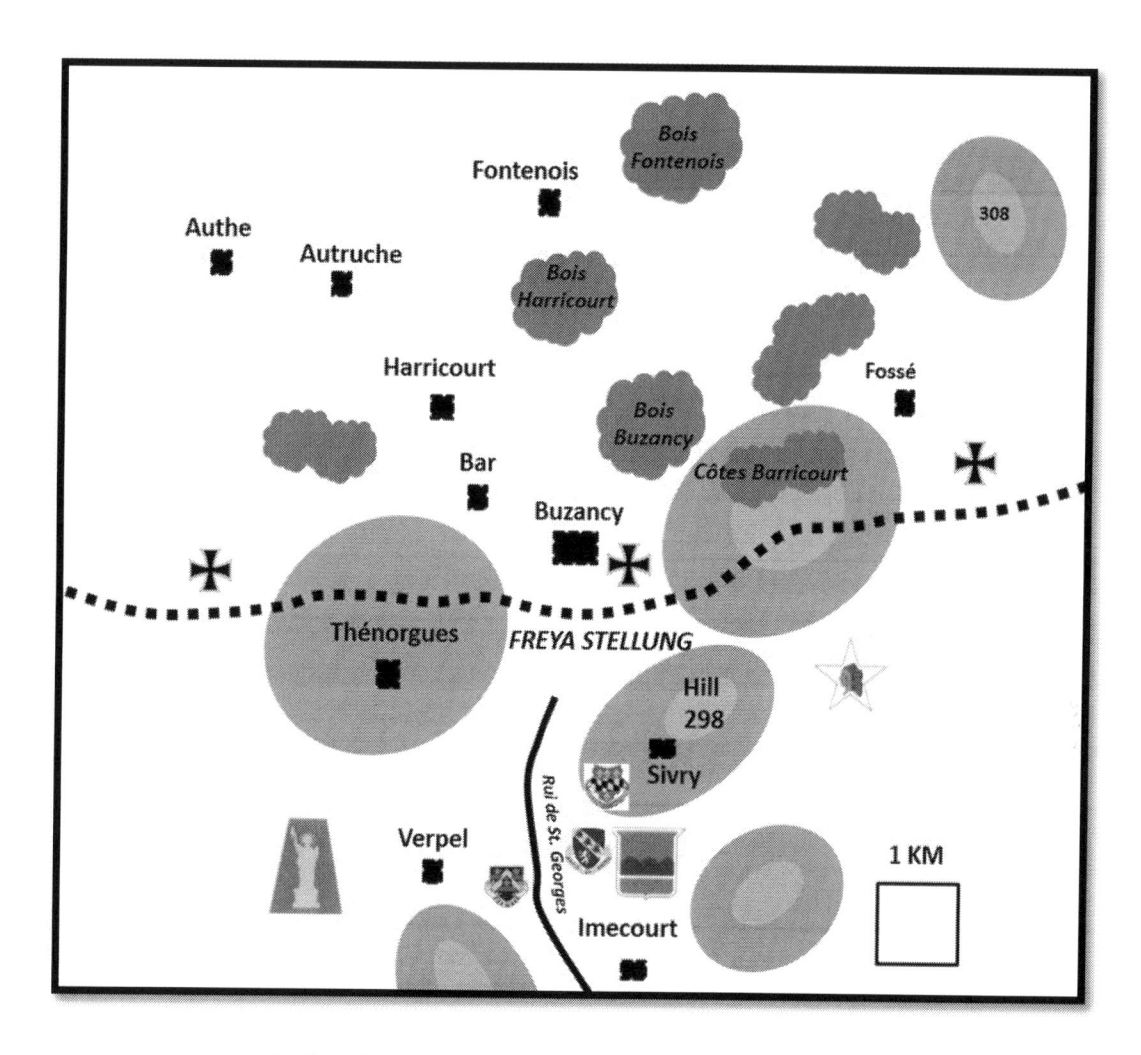

80th Inf. Div. Area of Operations, Nov. 2, 1918, A.M.

Attack axis of 320th Inf. between Verpel and Immecourt (L) and "First Transport across St. Georges, 11-1-18." This is where the 320th "Forward Regiment" got pinned down (R).

Doughs mving "Up the Line" (L). and Maj. Gen. Adelbert Cronkhite (R).

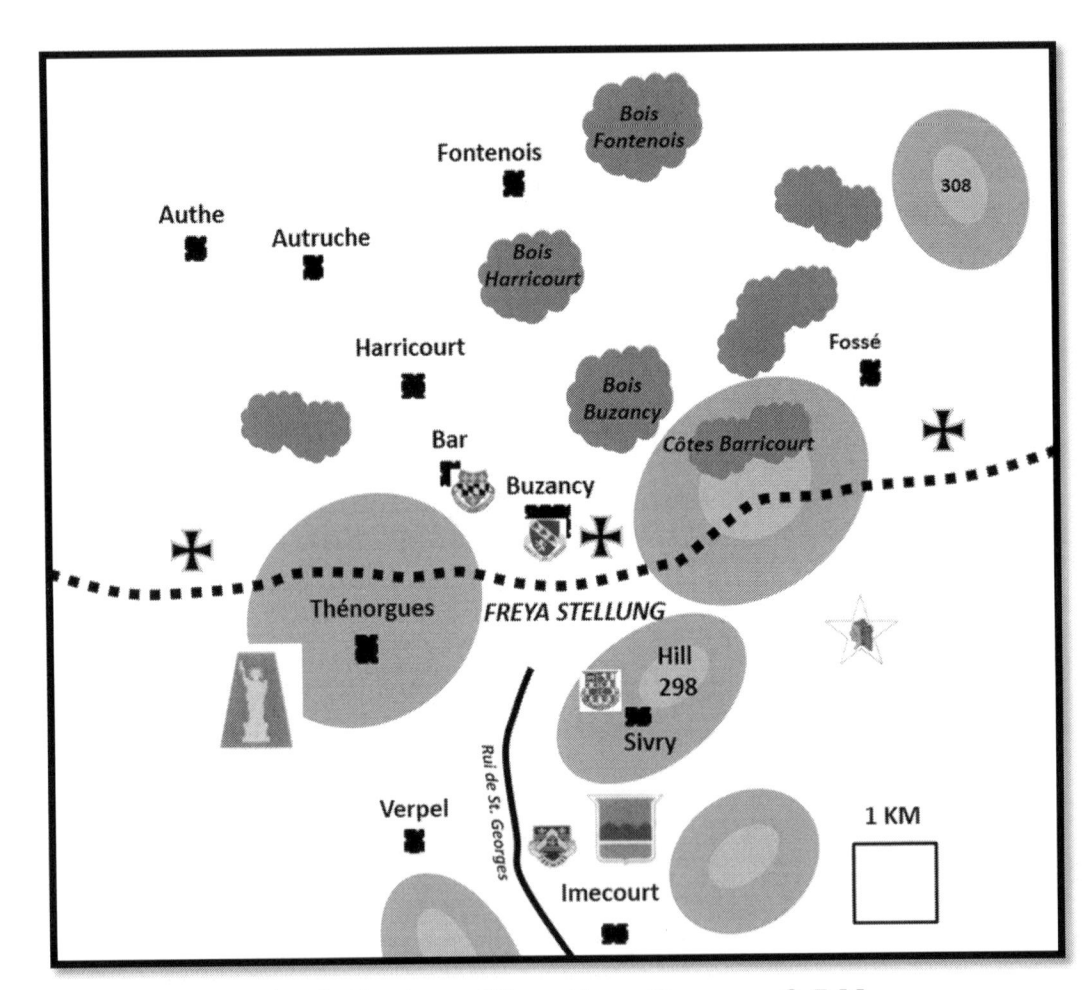

80th Inf. Div. Area of Operations, Nov. 2, 1918, P.M.

155mm howitzer firing under cover (L) and resupply in Verpel (R).

Another "Goat Rope" with the S.O.S.

"Soldiers' Home, Buzancy, 11-4-18. Used by the Germans as a recreation center."

Chapter 7
The Battle for Buzancy and *FREYA* (Nov. 1-2).

November 1, 1918.

Weather: Misty.

Roads: Good.

We in the 318th Infantry were awoken at 3:00 A.M., Nov. 1, 1918, to prepare for our great drive north, which we called the "Third Push." After remaining in a state of general uncertainty for nearly a week in *Forêt d'Argonne*, we received definite word that a *concerted* attack along the entire American First Army front was to be made in but a few hours. For us, we learned that the 159th Inf. Brig. was to follow our sister brigade, the "Golden Boys" of the 160th Inf. Brig. (319th Regiment on the right and the 320th Regiment on the left) up the division attack axis that was to run through Imécourt, Sivry, Buzancy, Vaux, the right (eastern) half of *La Petit Forêt*, and ultimately *Yoncq* and *Beaumont*, which were situated along the south bank of the Meuse.[293] In the 319th Infantry, it was Maj. James Montague's now-famous 2/319 as the attack battalion with Capt. Thomas Hooper's 3/319 in support and Maj. Wilfred's Blunt's 1/319 in reserve. In the 320th Infantry, Maj. Emory's 3/320 would be the attack battalion, Maj. Holt's 2/320 the support battalion, and Maj. Williams's 1/320 the reserve battalion. From Maj. Williams's command, Company D was detailed to be the regiment's moppers-up, Company C was the ammunition and ration carriers, Company A was to secure the regiment's left flank and act as a liaison with the 77th Division, and Company B was the regiment's dedicated reserve.

The twenty-four firing batteries of 313th and 314th Artillery were deployed just short of the L.D. among batteries from the All-American Divison. The heavy batteries of 315th Artillery were in firing positions just north of Sommerance, co-located with the division P.C. The division M.G. battalions, under the direction of D.M.G.O. Foley, were to fire "silent barrages" against enemy targets, complementing the artillery.[294] As a reminder, we could almost always hear artillery or *Minenwerfer* projectiles coming in—but almost never hear mortar or M.G. barrages coming in. Dickman's American I Corps fire support plan called for thousands of counter-battery gas rounds shot against known or suspected Hun artillery units in zone.

---

[293] *Imécourt* is pronounced "Im-ah-core," *Sivry* is pronounced "Cheev-ray," *Buzancy* is pronounced "Be-u-awn-see," *Vaux* is pronounced "Voe," and *Beaumont* is pronounced "Bow-mon."

[294] *314th M.G.*, 44.

Enemy forces to our front were reportedly from the 10th, 31st, 45th, 52nd, 115th, 240th, and 236th Prussian Divisions.[295] This meant two things to us: one, that the Germans were weakening other parts of their line to stop our advance (which we later found to be true), and two, we were really chewing up their units because there is no way that seven divisions should be operating in our narrow sector. Unlike before, when our divisions attacked with one infantry brigade up and one following in support, Pershing decided to attack with two infantry regiments up, followed by a "support regiment" followed by a "reserve regiment." What this means is that behind the 160th Inf. Brig. would come the 317th Infantry in columns of battalions, followed by we in the 318th Infantry, also in columns of battalions. While some in the 318th Infantry were disappointed that we were placed in divisional reserve, most, like the veterans, were elated. As for me, I really didn't care because either way, sooner or later, we were going "Up the Line." Also, being one of the last infantry companies in the division to attack, we would no doubt be the ones to deliver *le coup de grâce*. I was experienced enough to know that.

America's Blue Ridge Division, in conjunction with other A.E.F. divisions, would attack with a four-company front with forty-four companies in support (total of forty-eight infantry companies in each division), with two companies on line from the 319th Infantry on the right and two from the 320th Infantry on the left. For planning purposes, each soldier was to cover at least three meters of battle space, each squad 45 meters, each platoon 90 meters, each company, with two platoons (four combat groups) up an one back, 180 meters; each battalion, with two companies up and one back, 360 meters; each brigade/division with two battalions up, 720 meters. When one adds attached M.G.s, I.G.s, etc., that gave each division a little more than one km battle front. If every infantry squad of the division (768 of them) was in fact deployed on line, however, a division's frontage would have been almost 35 km! The armies of the Associated Powers long-ago decided to attack in depth and along a narrow front, however, in order to keep the attack moving forward.

The 77th (Metropolitan) Division, to our left, was to take *Verpel* and *Thénorgues,* break *FREYA* just south of *Harricourt,* and take the western edge of *Buzancy,* out-flanking *Côtes Barricourt,* which was the lynch-pin of *FREYA* in the American First Army's sector.[296] The 2nd (American Indian) Division, on our right, was to take *Landreville* and *Bayonville* and break

---

[295] *317th Infantry,* 76.

[296] *Verpel is* Pronounced "Vear-pel," *Thénorgues is pronounced* "Thee-norg," *Harricourt is pronounced* "Are-ree-core," and *Côtes Barricourt* is pronounced "Coats Barry-core."

FREYA at *Côtes Barricourt* once we in the 80th Division took *Buzancy*.[297] As our battalion officers looked over the map, they felt that we in the 318th Infantry would in fact be committed to the division's right, to support the attack of the 319th Infantry and the soldiers or marines of the American Indian Division.

We knew that every village or hilltop would be manned by at least a company of Hun infantry backed by several well-intrenched M.G.s. We knew that *FREYA* would be deep and reinforced. We knew that the Hun with the Gun had pre-planned artillery "kill boxes" established just for us. We knew that we would be under constant enemy observation, especially from Côtes Barricourt. But we also knew that our own artillery and M.G.s would plaster those same German strong-points into smithereens and, if properly supported, American infantrymen can take Hell itself. This was proven time-and-time again at Bois Belleau, Chateau-Thierry, Saint-Mihiel, and along Côtes Cunel here in the Meuse-Argonne. According to the Regulations, type of operation is called "Attack of Fortifications."

Attack of Fortifications

I.D.R. 481. Few modifications enter into the problem of attacking fortifications. Such as are to be considered relate chiefly to the greater time and labor of advancing, the more frequent use of darkness and the use of hand grenades to augment the fire.

I.D.R. 482. If the enemy is strongly fortified and time permits, it may be advisable to wait and approach the charging point under cover of darkness. The necessary reconnaissance and arrangements should be made before dark. If the charge is not to be made at once, the troops intrench the advanced position, using sand bags if necessary. Before daylight the foreground should be cleared of obstacles.

I.D.R. 483. If the distance is short and other conditions are favorable, the charge may be made without fire preparation. If made, it should be launched with spirit and suddenness at the break of day. (See Night Operations.)

I.D.R. 484. In siege operations troops are usually advanced to the charging point by sapping. This method, however, presupposes that an early victory is not necessary or that it is clearly inadvisable to attempt more direct methods.

---

[297] *Landreville et Bayonville* is pronounced "Lawn-dra-veal-ah ae Bay-yawn-veal-ah." The 2nd Division consisted of the 3rd and 4th Infantry Brigades; while the Infantry 3rd Brigade had the 9th and 23rd Infantry Regiments, the 4th Infantry (Marine) Brigade consisted of the 5th and 6th Marines.

During the dark, cold hours before dawn, the division M.G. battalions made their way forward to their firing locations. Ammunition and water cans were stockpiled. The M.G.s were dug-in and reinforced so their elevation settings wouldn't be affected by the backward vibration due to the firing. At about 2:00 A.M., all seventy or so of the new division Browning M.G.s were in position and ready to fire. At 3:30 A.M., the artillery and M.G. barrage opened up on different parts of the German line, each complementing the other. Of course, the Germans returned the favor, and the 80th Division suffered some casualties.[298] Maj. Ashby Williams, in command of the reserve battalion of the 320th Infantry remembered:

> *At 3:30 A.M. the heavies opened up a barrage and kept up their destructive fire for two hours, when they were joined by the 3-inch pieces. The 82nd Division was putting down the barrage for our attack, and it can be said for them that it was marvelously accurate and effective. The first wave of the front line companies formed behind this barrage and began their advance in liaison with the Marines, on our right and the 77th Division on the left.*[299]

Lt. Edward Lukens of I/3/320, whose platoon was in the assigned to the regiment's designated attack battalion, similarly remembered:

> *Early in the morning of Nov. 1 we were awakened by the most stupendous racket that ever smote on human ears. The whole sky ahead of us was aflame with the firing of the guns. The big guns just in front of us and the "75s" farther ahead roared and barked, while occasionally the sharper screech of an incoming shell trying to find our batteries varied the noise.*[300]

At 5:42 A.M., the great assault against the last line of the vaunted HINDENBURG STELLUNG was launched at *Imécourt* and *Verpel*, respectively, and as per S.O.P., the artillery and M.G. barrages rolled forward, churning up earth, barbed wire, and intrenched enemy positions. The 160th Inf. Brig., with the 319th Infantry on the right and the 320th Infantry on the left, followed by the 317th Infantry, passed through field guns, M.G.s, and infantry units of the 82nd (All-American) Division just north of KRIEMHILDE and attacked up the axis of advance toward FREYA and *Buzancy*. According to Capt. Charles Herr, commander of F/2/319th Infantry, the 319th Infantry's designated attack battalion remembered:

---

[298] *314th M.G.*, 46.

[299] As cited in *1/320th Infantry*, 159.

[300] As cited in *3/320th Infantry*, 116.

> *At 5:30 A.M. the barrage lifted and commenced to move forward one hundred yards every four minutes. The attack was on. F/2/319th Infantry moved forward at 5:42 A.M. through the 82nd Division, following H/2/319 at 500 yards. Some difficulty was experienced in getting through the German wire. Losses were heavy but the men continued the advance fighting their way to Immecourt. The company passed to the east of the village toward the hills beyond where heavy M.G. fire was encountered. The R.G.s and B.A.R.s immediately opened on the German position. The phosphorus grenades and the B.A.R.s struck terror to the hearts of the Germans, some 209 of them coming out of their trenches with hands in the air. Fifteen M.G.s were also surrendered as well as nine field pieces. The prisoners were sent to the rear under a small guard.[301]*

During the advance, elements of the 319th Infantry were able to out-flank and over-run a big Austrian 88mm "Whiz-bang" gun at around 8:00 A.M. For the rest of the day, a gun crew from Welsh's 155th Arty. Brig. fired it at enemy positions until they ran out of ammunition. Despite the success of Col. Love's 319th Infantry on the right, however, the attack of Lt. Col. Ephraim Peyton's 320th Infantry, which advanced on the left, turned into a disaster. Maj. German Emory's 3/320th Infantry (yes, his name was "German"), the designated attack battalion of the regiment, was literally cut to pieces in the open *Vallée De Rui Saint-Georges* between *Verpel* and *Imécourt* by heavy and accurate German M.G. and artillery fire.[302] Emory himself was killed. According to the officers of the 320th Infantry, the regimental and battalion commanders had already divined that the friendly artillery plan was inadequate—that they would in fact get chopped to pieces once they crossed the L.D. Well, they were right. Lt. Lukens of I/3/320th Infantry, a unit which felt the full bite of the enemy that day, remembered:

> *The American barrage, tremendous as it was, had at that point been too "long," and had left untouched a row of Boche nests between our men and the bombarded ground, so that when "H" hour came the battalion was met with as murderous a fire as though the barrage had never fallen. The major and the colonel had known the of this defect in the artillery plans the previous night and had appealed frantically to have them changed, but it was a corps plan, and someone on the staff, way back in safety, had "known it all," and refused to*

---

[301] As cited in *2/319th Infantry*, 13.

[302] *Vallée De Rui Saint-Georges* is pronounced "Val-lee day Rew San Jay-oarg," *Champigneulle* is pronounced "Chawm-peeg-nee-yell," and *Imécourt* is pronounced "Eem-a-core."

amend the orders of the batteries. It was no more the fault of the artillery line officers than of the infantry; like most blunders, it was made higher up, or, at least, farther back.[303]

Lt. Englar Rouzer, Maj. Emory's adjutant, reported:

We knew enough of the general situation to realize that we were about to take part in an attack of the greatest magnitude and importance. The Army objective was to destroy the German lines of communication by capturing the railroad from Metz through Sedan and Mezieres. This would force the withdrawal of the enemy from France. Our part of the proposed plan was to break through the last of the great German trench systems, which had been planned and constructed with their usually thoroughness and care, and seize the high-ground north of Buzancy. This contemplated an advance of eleven km on the first day...Maj. Emory had already reconnoitered the ground and his report was far from encouraging. We were to attack in a salient between St. Juvin and St. Georges subject to a flanking fire from our right. We knew that the preliminary barrage would not touch the enemy M.G. nests in our front and on our right flank, because of the salient and their proximity to our own outpost positions. Maj. Emory endeavored to have our outposts drawn back and their barrage line changed, but it was too late, and so we knew that our men would have to do the work of the artillery in over-coming this initial difficulty.[304]

Maj. Williams of 1/320, commander of the designated reserve battalion of the regiment, remembered:

In the front line, 3/320th Infantry came upon stubborn resistance immediately upon stepping off. For the purpose of safety, the barrage had been placed three hundred meters from the parallel to the departure. Enemy M.G.s had taken position in front of this barrage line, and upon the advance of our troops opened fire. Thus our front-line companies found themselves without artillery support and faced with the proposition of throwing personnel against material. After a splendid attack they broke through, but were again held up by M.G. fire from the north end of Rui Saint-Georges and [Thénorgues].[305]

---

[303] As cited in *3/320th Infantry*, 120.

[304] Ibid., 148.

[305] As cited in *1/320th Infantry*, 159.

As feared, the planned rolling barrage had not destroyed the enemy M.G. positions on the north slope of *Ravin Aux Pierres*, which ran perpendicular to *Vallée De Rui Saint-Georges*, and before the leading companies of Emory's 3/320th Infantry could cross it, the Huns opened up with full fury. It was, according to Lt. Rouzer, "a veritable hail of bullets."[306] As always, the Heinie positions were well-chosen and defended. Although K/3/320th Infantry, which was on the regimental right, was able to top the ridge of *Ravin aux Pierres*, M/3/320th Infantry, on the right, was literally cut in two by German M.G.s that were positioned in a wood at the head of the ravine.[307] From this position, the Krauts commanded the entire ravine and the valley beyond with deadly enfilade fire.

"Some days you get the bear and some days the bear gets you."

This day, the bear ate 3/320 Infantry. Lt. Rouzer remembered:

We had no accompanying artillery piece, our mortars and one-pounders were out of commission, and we had to depend on rifle fire and R.G.s to clean out the enemy nests. Owing to the severe shell fire, which had cut our telephone wire, we could communicate with regimental H.Q. only by runners, which was very slow, as the distance was about two km and the way most difficult. As soon as Maj. Emory saw that our advance was checked, he ordered me to fire a red parachute, which was the signal to hold advance of the artillery fire. The first was a fizzle, the second proved white, which had the contrary meaning (continue advance of the artillery) while the third was all right. The major and I were with Companies I and K. They finally gained the north slope of the ravine on the left of the sector and, through well-directed rifle and A.R. fire, were gradually advancing up the ravine to the assistance of Companies M and L.[308]

Pinned as 3/320th Infantry was, Maj. Emory was at the mercy of supporting weapons. When would they arrive? Could his command hold out long enough as retreating under fire, according to doctrine and proven by practice, was suicidal? When pinned, we Doughs were trained to dig-in until we could move forward or were ordered to withdraw during times of limited visibility. Maj. Emory knew that his men could neither stay in that ravine nor retreat. To advance was the only way to save what was left of his command. "Retreat forward!" as we'd sometimes say. To ready his men for a renewal of the attack, Emory, "though exposed to direct

---

[306] As cited in *3/320th Infantry*, 148.

[307] *Ravin Aux Pierres* or "Peter's Vale," is pronounced "Rah-veen ow Pee-air."

[308] As cited in *3/320th Infantry*, 149.

M.G. fire and in plain view of the enemy, calmly moved back and forth across his whole front, encouraging his troops."[309]

Like a heroic scene from any war, Maj. Emory rose and tried to lead his battalion forward out of Ravin aux Pierres, automatic pistol in hand. In so doing, however, he was cut down by Hun M.G. fire. His last words were: "My heart." Emory was later awarded the D.S.C. for his heroic actions. His citation reads:

> *On the morning of Nov. 1, 1918, the 3rd Battalion, 320th Infantry, had advanced under heavy enemy artillery and machine gun fire to the northern slope of RAVIN AUX PIERRES, north of the ST. JUVIN-ST. GEORES ROAD. The crest of the slope was being swept by a murderous machine gun fire and the advance of the battalion was momentarily checked. Without care for his personal safety and inspired only by the thought that his battalion must go forward, Maj. Emory, though exposed to direct machine gun fire and in plain view of the enemy, calmly moved back and forth across his whole front, encouraging his troops and personally directing the attack. While thus engaged, he was unfortunately killed. By his magnificent example of coolness and braver, he so encouraged and inspired the men of his command that they held this very exposed position and finally succeeded in overcoming the enemy resistance.* [310]

Lt. Rouzer, who was by Emory's side, remembered: "I at once reported the death of Maj. Emory to Lt. Col. Peyton and Maj. Holt, who was in command of the support battalion."[311] Peyton decided to move Holt's support battalion forward, allowing the now-battered 3/320th Infantry to extricate itself from the ravine, linking up with the 319th Infantry on the right and an Infantry battalion from the 77th Division on the left. With this hold-up on the left, the front line of the 80th Division was now "crooked," with the 320th and 319th Infantry forming a diagonal line, facing west, and not north.[312]

To better stabilize the front, Cronkhite judiciously ordered Col. Keller's 317th Infantry to advance to Sommerance and attach itself to Brett's jammed-up 160th Inf. Brig. We in the 318th Infantry were to remain as the division's reserve and as such, was ordered to march some five

---

[309] As cited in *3/320th Infantry*, 152.

[310] *Ibid*.

[311] *Ibid*, 149.

[312] *319th Infantry*, 37.

km east across the head-waters of *Rivière d'Aire* and into a ravine about 500 yards southwest of *Sommerance*.[313]

Due to the converging streams and the existence of but one available bridge in the vicinity of *Sommerance*, it was necessary to adhere to the road, in single file. Consequently, our horrid, mud-encrusted march to the front was only ended at 1:00 A.M. on Nov. 2, 1918, several hours being required to cover a scant five km. The days of traffic jams and "Goat Ropes" had not yet passed! As we weaved our way north through the "gypsy column," which consisted mostly of units from brigade or division-level ammunition or supply trains, we ensured that we were 100% "filled up" with rations and ammunition before going Up the Line, grabbing as many 30.06 bandoliers and cans of crackers or "corned willy" as possible. We also noticed that the supply train had already packed up several mules with ammunition, as the combat carts or ammunition limbers sometimes could not reach the front-line infantry units. But mules could! They can in fact go just about anywhere a Dough can. Their use during the war was widespread and because of this, many became carrion for the buzzards. We often debated which kind of carcass smelled worse: human or mule. I went with human, as the bile that is excreted from shot-up bellies is absolutely disgusting.

During our march north to eventually relieve a shot-up regiment from the 160th Inf. Brig. in the vicinity of *Sivry-Buzancy*, Cronkhite received glowing telegrams from our army group and corps commanders, Pershing and Dickman, respectively:

---

[313] *Rivière d'Aire* is pronounced "Reev-yare Dare."

> 1 November, 1918.
>
> From the Commanding General, A.E.F.:
>
> The Army Commander desires that you inform the Commander of the 80th Division of the Army Commander's appreciation of his excellent work during the battle of to-day. He desires that you have this information sent to all organizations of that Division as far as may be practicable this night. He fully realizes the striking blow your Division has delivered to the enemy this date.
>
> PERSHING

> 1 November, 1918.
>
> From the Commanding Brig. Gen., First Army Corps, A.E.F.:
>
> The Corps Commander is particularly pleased with the persistent, intelligent work accomplished by your Division today which has borne the brunt of the burden.
>
> DICKMAN

<u>November 2, 1918.</u>
Weather: Rainy.
Roads: Muddy.

To support Brett's 160th Inf. Brig., which currently held a diagonal front from *Imécourt* to *Sivry*, Cronkhite decided to replace the 319th Infantry with the 317th Infantry and ordered the 319th Infantry to attack due west across *Vallée Rui Saint-Georges* and into *Verpel*, flanking the enemy M.G. nests that commanded *Vallée Rui Saint-Georges*, enabling Peyton's 320th Infantry to "un-pin" itself.[314] Once completed, the 317th and 319th Infantry Regiments, reinforced by divisional M.G. units and accompanying artillery batteries, were to continue the attack north and breach *FREYA* near *Buzancy*. The 318th Infantry, still in divisional reserve, would be

---

[314] *317th Infantry*, 72 and *319th Infantry*, 37. We often used another term for "un-pin," but civil society dictates that I refrain from using such language.

brought forward to either help breach or exploit the breach of *FREYA* at or near Buzancy. Lt. Craighill of 2/317th remembered:

> *At 4:00 A.M. orders were received to attack in the direction of Buzancy. The 319th Infantry at that time in position on the general line from Hill 298 extending in a southerly direction was ordered to attack [west to relieve pressure from the 320th Infantry]. On the account of the unusual extent of our front and the fact that both flanks were in the air, it was deemed wise to attack with two battalions in line (1/317 and 3/317), and one in support (2/317). A/315th M.G. and the 317th One-Pounder Platoon were attached to 1/317. D/313th M.G. and one accompanying gun of the 320th Artillery [82nd Division] were attached to 3/317. The remaining artillery and regimental mortars were kept under regimental control and the above assignments did not change throughout the operation.*[315]

At 10:00 A.M., Nov. 2, the attack of the 160th Inf. Brig. commenced with the 319th Infantry attacking west across the valley and the 317th attacking north toward *FREYA* and Buzancy. As the 317th Infantry advanced closer to *FREYA*, however, almost on cue, they were "met by heavy fire from M.G.s organized in depth" on the ridge just south of the town. As such, Brett wisely ordered the 317th to hold its position before *FREYA* until the 319th Infantry pulled up on its left.

By noon, after suffering scores of casualties, the 320th Infantry had in fact been "unpinned" and Cronkhite ordered it back to Sommerance to recover while the 318th Infantry was brought forward to replace it. Once the 320th Infantry was extricated, the 319th Infantry turned north and adjoined with the left of the 317th Infantry. At this point, Cronkhite, like a master conductor, ordered the final attack to break *FREYA* and take Buzancy.

The subsequent sledgehammer assault of the 317th and 319th Infantry Regiments was legendary as it in fact broke *FREYA*, the last defensive band of the great *HINDENBURG STELLUNG*. Each regiment used their R.G.s, M.G.s, I.G.s, and mortars to full effect, smashing Hun defensive positions into dust, laying smoke with W.P. grenades, and then storming said positions with hand grenades, bullets, and bayonets.

Once *FREYA* was breached, the regiments established a defense in and around Buzancy. Lt. Craighill of the 317th Infantry remembered: "This defensive line was organized and held

---

[315] As cited in *317th Infantry*, 72.

despite heavy M.G. and artillery fire during the night of Nov. 2-3. Our M.G.s were echeloned in depth and placed on each flank."[316]

In breaking *HINDENBURG STELLUNG*, we knew that the campaign would rapidly become one of movement, just like in August-October, 1914, or along the mystical Eastern Front, but this time it would be us who would be doing the attacking and not the hated Hun with the Gun. The Army calls this type of operation a "Pursuit":

I.D.R. 476. To reap the full fruits of victory a vigorous pursuit must be made. The natural inclination to be satisfied with a successful charge must be overcome. The enemy must be allowed no more time to reorganize than is positively unavoidable.

I.D.R. 477. The part of the reserve that is still formed or is best under control is sent forward in pursuit and vigorously attacks the enemy's main body or covering detachments wherever found. The Artillery delivers a heavy fire upon the retreating enemy; the disordered attacking troops secure the position, promptly re-form, and become a new reserve.

I.D.R. 478. If the captured position is a section of the general line, the breach should be heavily occupied, made wider, and strongly secured by drawing on all reserves in the vicinity.

I.D.R. 479. After the pursuit from the immediate battle field, pursuit by parallel roads is especially effective where large commands are concerned. 480. Artillery and cavalry are very effective in pursuit.

In the meantime, we of the 318th Infantry marched some 12 km north from *Sommerance* through *Imécourt*, and on into *Sivry*. We arrived in the rain-soaked darkness at around 9:30 P.M., Nov. 2, 1918. Here we knew "foe shore" that we were well into the German "back areas" of the three years that had preceded "the American Drive," as it was now being called, as the country was much less desolate than the region of the old stationary front down near *Béthincourt*. Although there were a few ruined houses in the villages and shell holes in the fields, there was not the accumulated destruction of four years as we had previously witnessed. Villages were standing, fields were green, and the landscape overall was fair to the eye, almost bucolic. Signs of *les Boche* occupation were everywhere, and it was apparent that they had been comfortably situated and had expected the condition to be permanent. For example, in *Sivry*, we found a German hospital with an operating room fitted with glass sides like a sun parlor.

---

[316] *317th Infantry*, 72.

Buzancy must have been a center of importance in German scheme of things, for the signboards and the remnants of furnishings and equipment that we could see through the open doors and windows along the main street, gave evidence of the quartering of "Huns of High Degree." According to the men of the 317th Infantry, there was a *"Kommandantur"* of this or that unit advertised on the front of every prominent building, and over the gate of a chateau just beyond the town an enormous sign announced the *"Kommandantur"* of the "Ardennes Group" whom we thought was the equivalent of an army or at least a corps commander. A railroad station and train yards in a good state of repair between *Buzancy* and the adjacent town of *Bar* showed that the region had been far enough behind the danger zone for rail communications. There were no civilians in the town, although there were some in the villages further north (e.g., Sommerance). This region was also a paradise for "souvenir fiends," of which I was not one (I didn't want to carry it or was afraid of booby traps), for the vacated billets of *les Boche* officers yielded up many a *Stahlhelm*, *Pickelhaub*, weapon, or field gear.[317]

In the fields by the roadside, I saw burial parties from the sanitary corps at work, and already in places there were rows of rough board crosses that showed the cost of the victory. In my experience, places in which these detachments had not yet reached, we passed many American bodies as well as dead Germans or dead horses, mules, or donkeys. It is impossible to see a dead person, especially a fellow American soldier, without some sort of emotion, common as the sight might be in war. In my opinion, most did not look dead—they looked asleep. Some bodies were, however, contorted in haunting, gruesome poses, missing this or that, with blackened skin, etc. A dead German soldier, on the other hand, especially after a few days "Up the Line," incurred not one emotion from me. I neither celebrated nor condemned his death. He was simply dead—*hors de combat*—one less Son-of-a-*Boche* to kill.

Because our regimental P.C. (318th Infantry) was co-located in the bombed-out village of *Sivry* with those of Cronkhite's 159th Inf. Brig. , the 317th Infantry, and the 313th M.G. Battalion, all available shelter in such a small town was pre-empted and we Doughs were forced, once again, to tough it out in the open, forming a defensive perimeter of sorts around the town in the cold and driving rain, soaking us to the bone. We were told that the 319th Infantry was to our far-left-front at *Bar*, that the 317th Infantry was to our left-front in *Buzancy,* and that elements of the 2nd (American Indian) Division were to our right-front, atop *Côtes Barricourt*. To our rear, in the direction of *Immecourt*, was the shot-up 320th Infantry.

---

[317] The German *Stahlhelm* was fielded after 1916 and looks like a coal bucket, a *Pickelhaub* is the old leather helmet with a spike on it that the Germans had used from the 1860s up until 1916.

In moving forward, it became S.O.P. for us to bring only the company kitchen wagons, ration limbers, and water carts with us, leaving the other vehicles that were not essential to the feeding of the men. They would be brought along the next morning when the traffic congestion would probably be less severe. It was the smart choice, as it was far easier to get a short train through than a long one. In the Army, there were two general types of support trains, combat or field:

> *F.S.R. 275. Combat Trains.*—Combat trains include all personnel, vehicles and animals attached to organizations for transporting ammunition reserve and special equipment required during combat, including the mule or cart carrying

sanitary first aid equipment. To them are attached those vehicles required for the technical service of engineers and signal troops. Combat trains remain at all times with the unit to which attached and follow it into action.

F.S.R. 276. Field Trains.—Field trains include all personnel, vehicles, and animals attached to organizations or headquarters for the transportation of the authorized allowance of baggage, rations, and grain, and include rolling kitchens, if supplied... Field trains are assigned to regiments and independent battalions and are habitually divided into 2 sections: (1) A baggage section carrying baggage; and (2) a ration section carrying rations and grain exclusively, and include rolling kitchens, if supplied....

F.S.R. 278. Ammunition, Supply, Sanitary, and Engineer Trains.—The ammunition train includes all vehicles, animals, and personnel employed in transporting the divisional artillery and infantry ammunition reserve, or in bringing up the same from the refilling point to the combat trains of organizations.

The supply train includes all vehicles, animals, and personnel employed in transporting the divisional ration and grain reserve, or in bringing up the same from the refilling point to the distributing point. To it may also be attached herds of beef cattle, remounts, vehicles carrying reserve quartermaster supplies, and reserve transportation.

The sanitary train includes all vehicles, animals, personnel, and reserve sanitary material, not attached to organizations, employed in collecting and caring for the sick and wounded of the division pending their evacuation by the line of communication.

The engineer train includes all vehicles, animals, and personnel for transporting heavy entrenching tools, explosives, and other engineering equipment and material which, under ordinary circumstances, is required to accompany the division.

That night, Cronkhite issued the following attack for Nov. 3, 1917:

1-2

P.C. HAMILTON [80th Division], A.E.F.

2 November, 1918

FIELD ORDER NO. 31

MAP: BUZANCY, 1:20,000

1. The enemy on our front continues his retreat. The American First Army continues the advance tomorrow in conjunction with the Fourth French Army. The American V Corps, 2nd Division, advances on the right and the 77th Division on the left of the 80th Division.

2. This division will continue the attack at 5:30 A.M. tomorrow [Nov. 3, 1918] and push forward artillery, gain and maintain contact with the enemy and attack him vigorously whenever found.

(a) EASTERN BOUNDARY of the Division and of I Corps: SIVRY-LEZ-BUZANCY.

(b) WESTERN BOUNDARY of the Division: THENORGUES.

3. (a) The 159th Brigade, with attached artillery, will be the attacking brigade. It will push forward in its present area and gradually attain its proper position within the divisional boundary stated in para. 2. Combat liaison will be maintained with the units on the right and left.

2-2

(b) The 160th Brigade, less 2 battalions of the 320th Infantry and Machine Gun Battalion, will constitute the divisional reserve. Reorganization of units of the 160th Brigade will continue and it will be prepared to follow the attack on two hours' notice.

(c) The remaining units of the division will continue their present tasks and await further orders.

(d) The 157th Field Artillery Brigade [82d Division] will support the attack. Arrangements will be made with the Assistant Chief of Staff, G-3, at the forward P.C. as to the details of the initial supporting artillery fire. Batteries will be pushed boldly forward and support the infantry by direct fire whenever practicable.

4. No change to administrative arrangements.

5. P.C.'s of the leading Brigade and Regiments will be pushed forward as the troops advance. P.C. of the Division and 160th Infantry Brigade and the 157th Field Artillery Brigade will be at IMMECOURT.

A. CRONKHITE,
Major-General, Commanding.

As the reader hopefully already understands, planning a battle is a general officer's most important task (aside from being an expert platoon, company, battalion, regimental, and brigade commander). It's his job to identify the road to victory by developing the mission, the strategy, and the concept and then resourcing it. It's his job to come up with the "what" and not necessarily every minute detail of the "how," although he can and should provide some broad guidance. After that, a general officer's job is to ensure that the overall plan is in fact being executed through his assigned chain of command and, if necessary, to make alterations to the plan. Granted, a general officer has a staff of field grade officers (i.e., majors, lt. cols., and cols.) to help him, but in the end, it's his plan, it's his responsibility, it's his name. Everyone from the commanding general down to the lowliest private are supposed to help accomplish the defined mission.

Once an order is received from a division commander, a brigade commander is supposed to create his own orders, based upon the division commander's mission and concept. And once a brigade commander issues his orders, regimental commanders create their own orders, based upon the brigade commander's mission and concept, which is based upon the division commander's mission and concept, which is based upon the corps commander's mission and concept, which is based upon the army commander's mission and concept, etc.

Orders.

F.S.R. 84. The art of giving proper instructions and orders to troops is one of the most important features in the exercise of command. The expression of the will of leaders is conveyed in letters of instruction or by written or verbal orders.

Letters of Instruction.—At the beginning of operations and from time to time thereafter the plans of the superior leaders are communicated in the form of letters of instruction. These regulate movements over large areas and for considerable periods of time.

F.S.R. 85. Field Orders.—Field orders regulate the tactical and such strategic actions of troops that are not carried in letters of instruction. The filed orders of field army and division commanders are almost invariably written. When conditions demand the issuance of verbal orders, written orders follow. The field orders of brigade commanders are usually written. The field orders of regimental and smaller unit orders are usually verbal.

The object of field orders is to bring about a course of action, in accordance with the intention of the leader, suited to the situation and with full cooperation between all arms and services. They are issued for marches, halts, formation of camps or bivouacs, advance, flank and rear guards, outposts, combat, etc.

F.S.R. 142. The initial combat orders of the division and of all units higher than the division are almost invariably written. Troops may be put in motion in the desired direction, especially in a rencontre engagement, by verbal orders, but such verbal orders must be followed as soon as possible by written orders. After the action has begun the greater number of the orders given by the higher commanders will be fragmentary and verbal. In units higher than the regiment all such orders will, as far as practicable, be written out by a staff officer at the time they are issued, and a copy thereof be given the officer charged with the execution of the order, if possible at the time the order is delivered, otherwise as soon thereafter as it is possible to furnish it.

Troops deployed and under fire can change front only at the great risk of incurring heavy losses. When they are once committed to any line of action, change to another is costly both in men and morale. It is possible for the higher troop leaders to directly influence the course of an action once begun in any way except through the use of such reserves as may be at hand. Modern fire effect will not permit the higher leaders to change abruptly the course of action of troops already engaged by the mere sending of orders, verbal or written, to the commanders of such troops. These principles must be borne in mind in issuing combat orders.

Combat orders are the expression of a fixed decision and must definitely state the end in view, such as "To attack," or "To take up and defend" a position. Vague or ambiguous orders indicate vacillation and the absence of any definite decision on the part of the officer responsible for them. Troops have a right to be told, in terms that are direct and unmistakable, exactly what it is their leader wants them to do.

In my opinion, aside from platoon leaders, it was the brigade commander who had the most difficult job in the A.E.F. because it was he who had to synchronize multiple combat elements. In our instance, Cronkhite pretty much commanded the 159th Inf. Brig. in Jamerson's absence, with Lt. Col. Buchanan acting as his agent. To this day, we don't understand why there wasn't a brigadier assigned to the post after Jamerson was put on "medical leave," but whatever system Cronkhite came up with, it seemed to work. Brett's 160th Brigade H.Q., however, was considered to be a "well-oiled killing machine."

Attack axis of 320th Inf. between Verpel and Immecourt.

As we Doughs tried to sleep that night or performed sentry duty, the brigade and regimental commanders and their staffs created their own sets of mission orders of which I have included as examples. For us at the squad, section, or platoon levels, we never saw any of these documents. All we knew is that we were to attack in "that" direction and keep on going until we reached a "certain" point—we knew that we'd follow a pre-planned rolling barrage and that once we gained our objective, the artillery would send liaisons forward with field phones, establish O.P.s, and help us hold said position with artillery strikes by calling in targets on grids on a map sheet. Anyway, the following attack orders were issued by the 159th Inf. Brig. and the 318th Infantry Regiment for Nov. 3, 1917:

1-2

P.C. HAROLD [159th Inf. Brig.], A.E.F.

2 November, 1918.

FIELD ORDER NO. 15.

MAP: BUZANCY, 1:20,000.

1. SITUATION: Reports indicate enemy in full retreat. The First American Army continues its advance tomorrow, the 2nd Division advances on the right and the 77th Division on the left of the 80th Division.

2. MISSION: This division will continue its advance tomorrow.

(a) EASTERN BOUNDARY of the Division and of I Corps: SIVRY-LEZ-BUZANCY [00 Easting].

(b) WESTERN BOUNDARY of the Division: THENORGUES [96 Easting]

3. CONCEPT OF THE OPERATION: (a) The 159th Infantry Brigade will lead the advance and will push forward vigorously maintaining contact with the enemy at all times.

(b) The advance will be made with the regiments side by side in column of battalions, the 317th Infantry on the right, the 318th Infantry on the left.

(c) Regiments will be deeply echeloned, will maintain contact with adjoining units and will protect flanks by constant patrolling.

2-2

(d) The following troops are attached to the regiments:

-318th Infantry: Companies B and C, 313th M.G. Bn., Battery F, 321st F.A.

-317th Infantry: Companies A and D, 313th M.G. Bn., Battery E, 321st F.A.

-The above attachments will enable each battalion to be organized as a complete combat unit, similar distribution of auxiliary arms within the regiments is suggested.

(e) The rear battalion of each regiment will be subject to the orders of the Brigade Commander and will march as Brigade Reserve. (Battalions may be rotated in the advance but rear battalion will constitute reserve as above mentioned).

4. SERVICE AND SUPPORT:

(a) Combat trains will accompany units. Field trains will follow at suitable distances.

(b) Details of supply arrangements will be issued later.

5. COMMAND AND CONTROL:

(a) Axis of liaison: SIVRY LEZ BUZANCY-BUZANCY-SOMMAUTHE.

(b) P.C. Brigade: SIVRY

EDMUND A. BUCHANAN.
Lieut.-Col. Infantry, U.S.A., Commanding.

1-2

P.C. HAMMOND [318th Infantry Regiment], A.E.F.

2 November, 1918.

FIELD ORDER NO. 16.

MAP: BUZANCY, 1:20,000.

1. SITUATION: The 159th Brigade continues the advance to-morrow in conjunction with the 2d Division on the right and the 77th Division on the left.

2. MISSION: This regiment will advance on the western boundary of the 80th Division sector with the 317th Infantry on our right. The regiment's sector is about one half of the divisional sector.

3. CONCEPT OF THE OPERATION:

(a) The regiment, less 2d Battalion (in Brigade Reserve) will advance in column of battalions, 3d Battalion in advance, 1st Battalion in support. Each battalion with 2 companies side by side. The leading battalion will leave SIVRY by 5 A.M. The supporting battalion will follow 1,500 meters in rear of the advance battalion.

(b) Zone of advance (see Map).

(c) Battalions will be disposed in depth, each battalion will protect its own flanks by combat patrols, composed of a detachment of infantry and a section of machine guns.

2-2

4. ATTACHMENTS/DETACHMENTS:

(a) To the 3d Battalion: 2 Guns, Battery F, 321st F.A., Co. B, 313th Machine Gun Bn., 2 37-mm guns, 2 Stokes Mortars, ½ Pioneer Platoon.

(b) To the 1st Battalion: Co. C, 313th Machine Gun Bn., 1 37-mm gun, 2 Stokes Mortars.

(c) To the 2nd Battalion: Machine Gun Co., 318th Infantry, 2 Stokes Mortars.

(d) Detachments from the 2d Bn. attached to M.G. Co. and 37-mm. Platoon will report back to 2d Bn.

5. SERVICE AND SUPPORT: Combat trains of 3d and 1st battalions will follow in rear of supporting battalion. Field trains as indicated later.

6. COMMAND AND CONTROL:

(a) Axis of liaison—SIVRY LEZ BUZANCY-BUZANCY-SOMMAUTHE.

(b) Regimental P.C. at SIVRY until further notice.

JONES
Colonel, Commanding

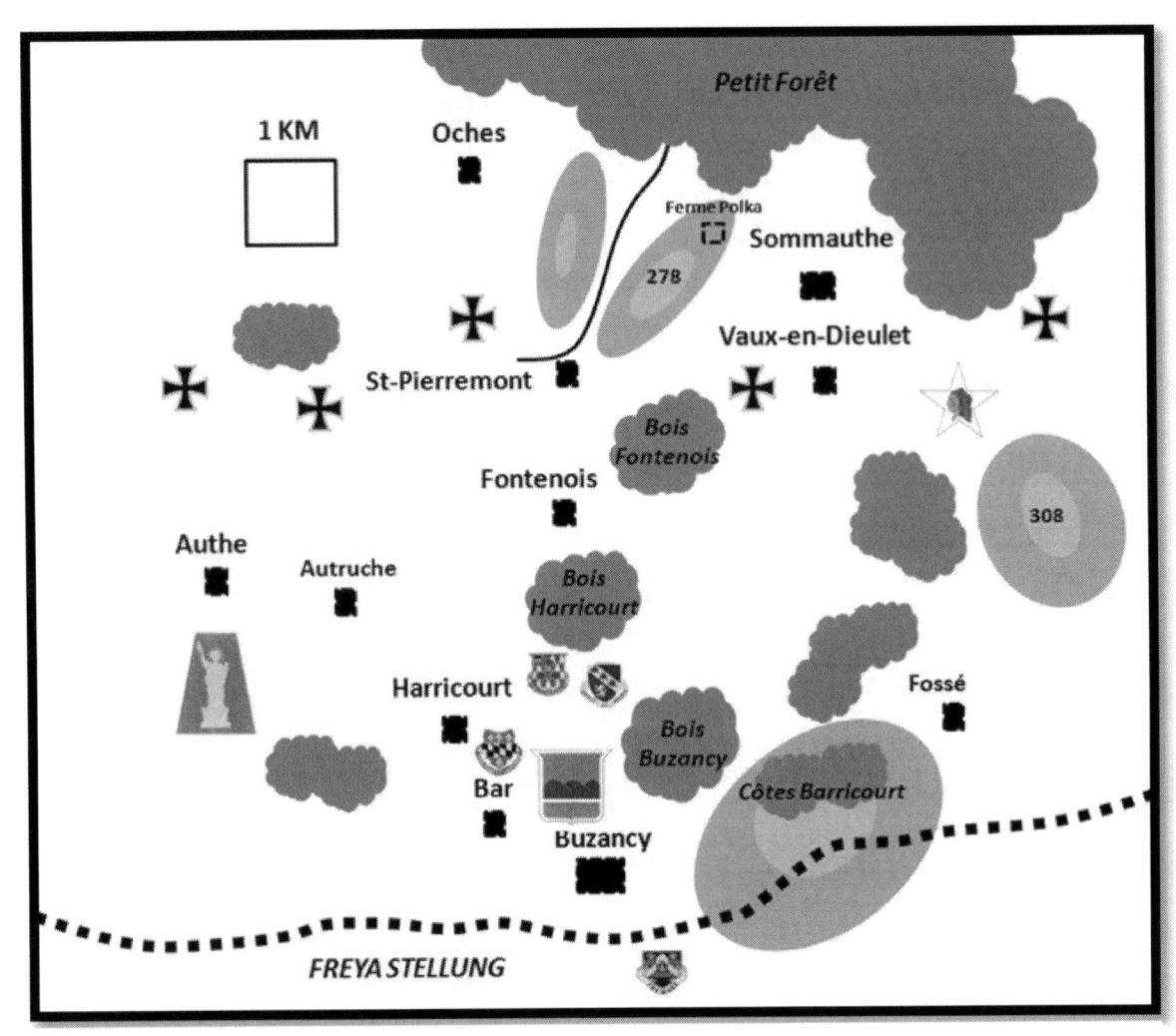

80th Division Area of Operations Nov. 3, 1918 A.M.

The 318th Inf. marching north through Buzancy toward Fontenois, Nov. 3, 1918.

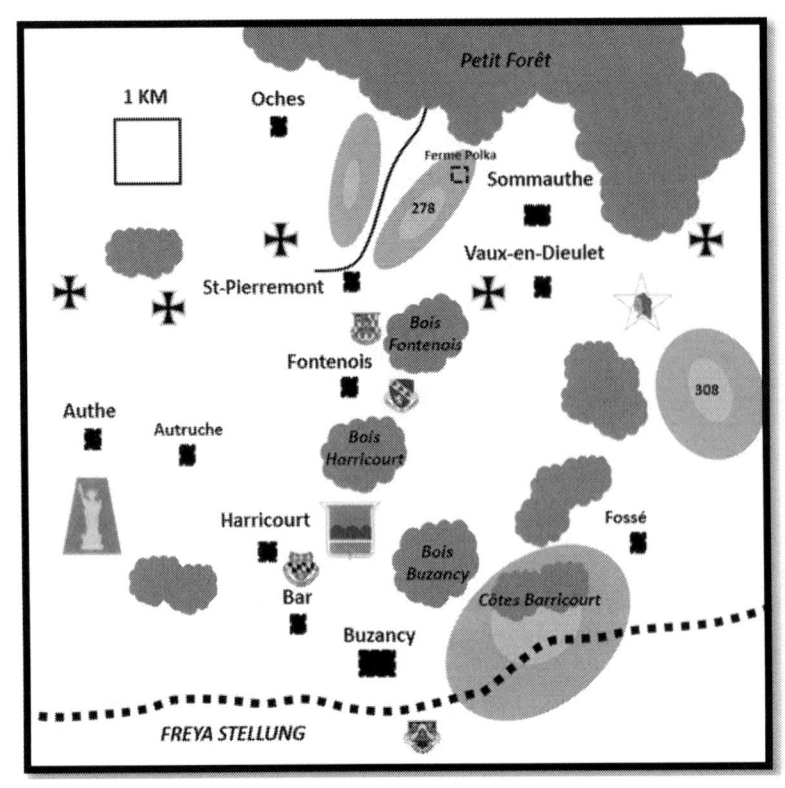

80th Division Area of Operations Nov. 3, 1918 P.M.

Lt. Col. Mitchell (L), X.O. of the 159th Inf. Brig. and Maj. Sweeny (R), commander of 1/318th Inf., finalize the attack plan before we advance.

"The effects of shellfire: Wilds at Grandpre, 11-11-18" (L). This is what Bois Harricourt and Fontenois also looked like to us. What's left of Vaux-en-Dieulet in the Meuse-Argonne (R). The 317th Inf. swept and cleared it of the Hun.

"Damage by shell fire, 7-28-18. It is claimed that the Germans put a shell a minute in this location" (L) and Destroyed train of cars at Harricourt, 11-6-18 (R).

"Machine gunners of the 80th Div. using a Browning M.G. to speed the departing Germans. The Browning heavy machine gun was pronounced by military experts the most effective weapon of its kind ever produced. Brig. Gen. Pershing refused to use the Browning gun until he had plentiful supply in Sept. 1918, because he feared the Germans might capture one and reproduce the type before America was fully equipped." Note the large flash arrestor.

Chapter 8
In the Open: The Battle for Fontenois (Nov. 3, 1918).

Nov. 3, 1918.

Weather: Rainy.

Roads: Muddy.

During the early morning hours of Nov. 3, 1918, while the 159th Inf. Brig. H.Q. and the 317th and 318th Infantry Regiments and their attachments were translating Cronkhite's attack order to take Hill 308 and Vaux, a wayward German H.E. round landed in the midst of our regimental P.C., killing Lt. Niven, the adjutant of 3/318th Infantry. The same round mortally wounded Lts. Coble and Robertson and wounded Capt. Talliaferro, Chaplain Brown, and Lts. Benson, Crutchfield, Kleinsturber, Morrison, Palmer, Turner, and Dillingham, all of whom were evacuated to the division field hospital except Chaplain Brown and Lts. Dillingham, Morrison, and Turner, whose wounds were relatively minor in nature. It was a heavy blow to the regiment to have so many officers taken out of action on the eve of a major attack.

In spite of the carnage, one amazing thing did happen during that dark, dreary, and deadly night: we actually received hot chow at about 3:00 A.M. from our loyal and stalwart company mess sergeants. As was already stated, we kept the (as we saw it) mission-critical kitchen wagons with us along with ration limbers and water carts. By combat groups, we rotated back to our blown-up P.C. for the hearty, warm victuals. It was the hot coffee with sugar that I remember the most from that unsettling night.

At 5:00 A.M., Maj. Burdick's 3/318th Infantry (reinforced by two 75mm guns from F/2/321st Artillery, 82nd Division, a platoon from B/313th M.G., two 81mm mortars, two 37mm I.G.s, plus a couple squads of Pioneers from the 305th Engineers), as the regiment's attack battalion, was ordered to pass through Col. Love's 319th Infantry at Bar and connect with the right of the 77th Division, which was reportedly operating in the vicinity of *Harricourt*. We in Maj. Sweeny's 1/318th Infantry (reinforced by C/313 M.G., one I.G., and two mortars) were to follow as the regiment's support battalion, followed by Maj. Wise's 2/318 (reinforced by the 318th M.G. Company and two mortars) as the regiment's reserve battalion. Per the order, we marched northwest through the rich rain-soaked farm fields between *Buzancy* and *Fontenois*.[318] As the regiment's designated support battalion, we were to provide flank security for the attack battalion with a rifle platoon on each flank, reinforced by M.G.s. The regimental P.C. was then to run wire back to brigade P.C., maintaining telephonic communications. If those

---

[318] *Fontenois* is pronounced "Font-en-nwah."

communications failed, then the regimental operations officer was to send runners and hope that they didn't get lost, killed, or captured going back-and-forth.

For this particular mission, my platoon, Lt. Ashby's 2/B/1/318th Infantry, was assigned to provide right flank security for Maj. Burdick's 3/318. We were given one M.G. section from C/313th M.G., which was commanded directly by Lt. Ashby and posted with our platoon guide, Sergeant Brown.

The Company Acting Alone.

I.D.R. 230. In general , the company, when acting alone, is employed according to the principles applicable to the battalion acting alone; the captain employs platoons as the major employs companies, making due allowance for the difference in strength. The support may be smaller in proportion or may be dispensed with.

I.D.R. 231. The company must be well protected against surprise. Combat patrols on the flanks are specially important. Each leader of a flank platoon details a man to watch for the signals of the patrol or patrols on his flank.

Combat Reconnaissance.

I.D.R. 389. Combat reconnaissance is of vital importance and must not be neglected. By proper preliminary reconnaissance, deployments on wrong lines, or in a wrong direction, and surprises may generally be prevented.

I.D.R. 390. Troops deployed and under fire can not change front and thus they suffer greatly when enfiladed. Troops in close order formation may suffer heavy losses in a short time if subjected to hostile fire. In both formations troops must be protected by proper reconnaissance and warning.

I.D.R. 391. The difficulty of reconnaissance increases in proportion to the measures adopted by the enemy to screen himself. The strength of the reconnoitering party is determined by the character of the information desired and the nature of the hostile screen. In exceptional cases as much as a battalion may be necessary in order to break through the hostile screen and enable the commander or officer in charge to reconnoiter in person. A large reconnoitering party is conducted so as to open the way for small patrols, to serve as a supporting force or rallying point for them, and to receive and transmit information. Such parties maintain signal communication with the main body if practicable.

I.D.R. 392. Each separate column moving forward to deploy must reconnoiter to its front and flank and keep in touch with adjoining columns. The extent of the reconnaissance to the flank depends upon the isolation of the columns.

I.D.R. 393. Before an attack a reconnaissance must be made to determine the enemy's position, the location of his flanks, the character of the terrain, the nature of the hostile field works, etc., in order to prevent premature deployment and the resulting fatigue and loss of time. It will frequently be necessary to send forward a thin skirmish line in order to induce the enemy to open fire and reveal his position.

Just a few kilometers short of *Buzancy*, 3/318th Infantry got hit by a Hun artillery strike, killing Lt. Turner and horribly wounding 1Sgt. Schutte of I/3/318. For his exceptional bravery and fortitude during the last couple of days, Lt. Turner was posthumously awarded the D.S.C. The citation read:

First Lieutenant James Turner, 318th Infantry (deceased). For extraordinary heroism in action near BUZANCY, France 2-3 November, 1918. After having been severely wounded during the night of 2nd November, 1918, Lieutenant Turner continued in command of his company. Despite his wounds he led his company in the attack the following day, when he was killed by an enemy shell. He sat an example of fearlessness and bravery to his men. [319]

After the artillery strike and just short of the *Buzancy* and *Bar* "road," and I use that term loosely, 3/318th Infantry had to work its way through a bone-chilling-arm-pit-deep swamp, followed by 1/318 and 2/318. As we passed through the swamp, we'd say things to each other like: "So, you wanted to join the Infantry, eh?" or "Greatest job in the world!" or "Just shoot me now!" or "Hey, this wasn't on the map!" or "What do we need water for, again?"

Once out of the swamp and into the flattened twin villages of *Harricourt-Bar*, contact was gained with the 319th Infantry on the right and the 77th Division on the left along the road. The 318th Infantry passed through the stalwart fighters of the 319th Infantry, cold, wet, and angry (just as planned!) in columns of companies. While K/3/318 was in the front line on the right, M/3/318 was in the front line on the left. Companies I and L were in support. Behind them was us, with C and D up and A and B in support (battalion commanders would often rotate the order of companies in the line—the front-right company being the "battalion guide" and numbered the "1st Company"), and behind us was 2/318. My particular combat group was still screening the

---

[319] As cited in *318th Infantry*, 82.

regiment's front-right flank with a section from C/313th M.G. Battalion. To our right, about 500 yards, was the flank combat group from the 317th Infantry Regiment.

Once the line was set, sometime around 8:00 A.M., Nov. 3, 1918, the order was given to renew the attack north, following the rolling barrage like "white on rice," with special emphasis on Bois Harricourt, which was two km to our front (the Germans established strong-points in the villages and the woods). This was the first time in four years that any of the Associated Powers were fighting "in the open" on the Western Front. Before, they were never able to break the third German line, let alone the fourth. In Nov. 1918, however, we finally did it. I don't exactly know how or why we did it, but we did. ("Joe Latrinsky" told us that German morale was sapped, as they were starving and we were not). In fact, I still don't understand why we weren't all killed with all of the lead, steel, or gas being thrown about like it was going out of style. The bottom line is that the German lines were finally broken and they were retreating back to "Hunland." The 318th Infantry's objective for Nov. 3, 1918, was to clear enemy forces from Bois Harricourt and take *Village Fontenois* while the 77th Division secured *Village Autruche* on our left and the 317th cleared Bois Buzancy on our right.[320]

As the rolling barrage tumbled forward, churning the farm fields to the north into muck and mire and on into Bois Harricourt, turning tress into toothpicks, the "battalion will advance" whistle was blown signaling the attack and up we rose, like spectres rising from the fog with our distinctive Brolie-Helmet-and-Enfield-Rifle-and-Bayonet silhouettes cutting through the thick gray horizon. While we "veterans" advanced with stoic precision, the "fresh fish" advanced in abject horror, waiting, just waiting, to get ripped into pieces by artillery or M.G. fire.

As Burdick's 3/318 approached to within five hundred yards of Bois Harricourt, the early morning fog lifted and as feared, enemy M.G.s opened fire upon them with a fury.

"Ra-a-tat-tat-rat-a-tat-tat!"

"Zing, zing, zing, splat!"

Caught in the open, 3/318th Infantry darted for newly carved-out shell holes or folds in the ground. Some tripped into the water-filled pits, landing head first (as opposed to "diving into second base," which was the preferred method). Some were hit. I heard men from 3/318 cry-out in agony, "I'm hit! Oh my God, I'm hit! I don't want to die! I don't want to die!" We were all paralyzed with fear and I, for one, didn't want to leave my particular shell hole. And then, just like clock-work, Hun artillery fire rained down upon us, almost dead nuts.

It was horrific.

It was shrapnel.

---

[320] *Autruche* is pronounced "Ooh-true-sh."

I saw a man cut almost in two, his feet going here and his hands going there. At this point, I was once again enraged and became an animalistic killer, seeking revenge.

Maj. Wise deployed 3/318 on line, positioned his attached M.G.s, I.G.s, mortars, and even 75mm field gun, and began to blast the wood line. The 75mm gun, hitched to a single mule, certainly did the job!

"Crack! Boom!"

Our flank platoon, which refused the regiment's right and faced east into Bois Buzancy, was reinforced, as was the platoon on the left flank, which refused the regiment's left and faced Autruche. My combat group fired only when we saw a target present itself between Bois Buzancy and Harricourt. With the direct fire cannon, I.G.s, and M.G.s pounding away, we felt very insignificant with our puny A.Rs, R.G.s, and rifles.

After about a half hour of intense firing, in which the combat groups of 3/318 leap-frogged forward using the field gun, I.G.s, and M.Gs to maximum use, Maj. Wise's 3/318 was able to take the wood-line with moderate casualties and move further into Bois Harricourt, driving the enemy north. We in 1/318 and 2/318 followed through the woods with two companies up and two back, kicking up an occasional German *Landser* rifleman with his "*Hände Hoch.*"[321] My platoon was still on flank guard duty.

By mid-afternoon, 3/318th Infantry cleared Bois Harricourt and captured an abandoned battery (four guns) of Hun "whiz-bang" 77mm artillery that lie tucked between Bois Harricourt and Fontenois. This battery no doubt helped bombard Sivry the night before, making minced meat of several of our officers, and we were glad to have it in our hands. The fact that the battery was simply left to be captured meant two things to us, and both were good. One, that the "Hun with the Gun" was in such a hurry—his lines in such disarray—that he did not have time to limber up and/or two, they plumb ran out of horses or mules, much like us. In fact, we hadn't received a new animal issue since the start of the "American Offensive" and were running low ourselves. But not so low as to abandon an entire battery of guns to the enemy!

With the German line broken in this sector, Cronkhite ordered 3/318th and 2/317th Infantry to advance as far north as Fontenois, securing the village by late-afternoon. Lt. Craighill of the 317th Infantry remembered:

The leading battalions advanced rapidly, at first encountering only slight M.G. fire which was speedily overcome. At about 11:00 A.M. the left battalion was held up temporarily by heavy M.G. fire from the Harricourt Woods and again at 1:55 P.M. by heavy fire from the heights southeast of Vaux. At 4:30 P.M. the

---

[321] *Hände Hoch* is German for "hands high" or "hands up"; it is pronounced "Hayn-da Hoak."

right battalion was definitely checked by organized M.G. resistance and severe artillery fire.[322]

1/318 and 2/318, meanwhile, were left to mop-up *Bois Harricourt*, sending out patrols, etc. Our regimental supply company was even—amazingly—able to come forward with its trucks and wagons to re-supply us. On our right, the 317th Infantry secured *Bois Buzancy*, and to our left rear, the 319th and 320th Infantry Regiments, as the division support and reserve regiments, moved north. In fact, the men of 2/319 boldly pitched their pup tents in a field just north of *Bar*, which was still burning (they did, though, judiciously dig-out little slit trenches just in case of an artillery strike or aerial bombardment). This proved to be a wise precaution as at around 9:00 P.M., some Hun aeroplanes dropped ten bombs within their camp. Many of their shelter tents were pierced and two men were W.I.A.[323]

The cries of wounded soldiers echoed across the valley that night and to this very day, some thirty years after the war, I still hear them, but only when I allow myself to think about it. Capt. Douglas decided to send twenty of us, led by Cpl. Shelton, on a patrol to get some of these guys out and bring them back to our lines. This night patrol was the most soldier-skill intensive mission that I executed during the war. I liked it, however, because it was all on us, the "small fries," as our officers stayed behind. We had to plan to not only navigate into the valley at night, but to also get back to our positions without getting shot-up by excited and exhausted Blue Ridgers.

It was decided that hand grenades would be our primary weapon as rifle shots would give away our position. Acting as Shelton's second, I headed to the rear looking for battalion's small supply depot that was about 200 yards away through the woods. Everyone was nervous as the Germans were known to send infiltration parties at night to light us up between artillery barrages and when I approached the depot, the supply guys went into a tizzy.

"Who goes there!?" they shouted.

"Riddle, Company B!"

"Where you from!?"

"Petersburg!"

"What's Petersburg known for!?"

"A big battle and pretty ladies!"

"Alright, come on up. What do you want?"

"I need hand grenades."

---

[322] *317th Infantry*, 74.

[323] *2/319th Infantry*, 13.

"Over there, take one crate only."

Needless to say, sleep depravation was really starting to kick in because I got lost on the way back to my company.

I in fact stumbled into the 2nd Battalion, had no clue where I was, and actually began to panic.

"Calm down, son," said an older soldier. "You're okay. Your battalion is that-o-way."

After I was sent me off in the right direction, carrying a heavy crate full of 20 hand grenades with my B.A.R. slung on my back, I delivered the cache and we prepared to move out. Shelton told us that the challenge was "Apple" and the password was "Green." This means that if we're stopped by anyone on our side, they'd yell "Apple" through the darkness. If we didn't answer "Green," they'd open fire. The scary part is that you had to yell it loud enough so they'd hear you but not too loud that you'd give away your position to the enemy. The supply guys never asked me for a password. As long as I knew that Petersburg had a battle, I was alright.

Because we were a casualty patrol, five of us carried canvas stretchers over our shoulders to bring the men out. The rest would act as guides and security. I was in charge of security with my B.A.R. We also agreed that because of the gas, we would stay out of the shell holes. To advance with masks on would be sure folly and to get into low-lying areas after a gas attack, even hours after one, would mean sure death or disfigurement without a mask on. There still wasn't any guarantee that we wouldn't breathe in some of the rot, but we felt so bad for those wounded men down there, suffering as they were, that we had to do something.

Soon after midnight, we moved out from the woods and headed down the hill toward the area where we heard the most screams or moans. On occasion, German or American flares would light up the sky, forcing us to take a knee. The hardest part was maneuvering through the chewed up barbed wire and shell craters. Some sharp wire in fact cut open my trousers just above my puddies and gave me a nasty cut, which later took weeks to heal due to infection.

Before long, near a road, we came upon our first group of wounded Blue Ridgers. As it was dark, we really couldn't tell who they were but knew that they had to be from 1/318th Infantry. One man seemed to me like he was hit in the stomach. To his left, was a gas attack victim who could hardly breathe. He was also hit in the leg. After finding five wounded men, we headed back up the hill and into the woods and then did it all over again, I think three times. On the third rotation, we ran into another patrol, some thought it was a German one while others, like me, thought it was one from 2/318th Infantry, and we opened fire on each other. Thank God nobody was hit, at least no one from our patrol. The other patrol fired their rifles and we hurled hand grenades. After that, all was quiet, and we evacuated three more wounded men on our last patrol.

Some keys to remember for a night patrol: stay close, but not too close, make sure everybody knows where they're going, never take the same route forward and back as the enemy may set up an ambush, and when carrying a stretcher, you must communicate with your buddy and, hopefully, will have four men carrying the litter as those bad boys get really heavy really fast. Of all the missions I was on during the famous Meuse-Argonne Offensive, this mission of mercy is my proudest. We saved lives and Corporal Shelton and the rest of us proved that we could conduct operations on our own volition.

At around 3:00 A.M., Maj. Cox of the 314th M.G. Battalion was summoned to the division P.C. and was instructed by the chief of staff, Col. William Waldron, "to form a skirmish line across the division sector, advancing northward, bringing in all stragglers and all men who could not show written authority for being where they were." This was an interesting order to give to a M.G. battalion: to "corral stragglers." As the duty was performed throughout the next day, scores of men were scooped from at least six divisions (!) and they were immediately put to work in "burying the dead horses and dead Germans in the vicinity."[324]

Entrance to a typical French *Ferme* or farm (L) and A.E.F. Medical Supply Cart in the Meuse-Argonne (R).

---

[324] As cited in *314th M.G. Battalion*, 48.

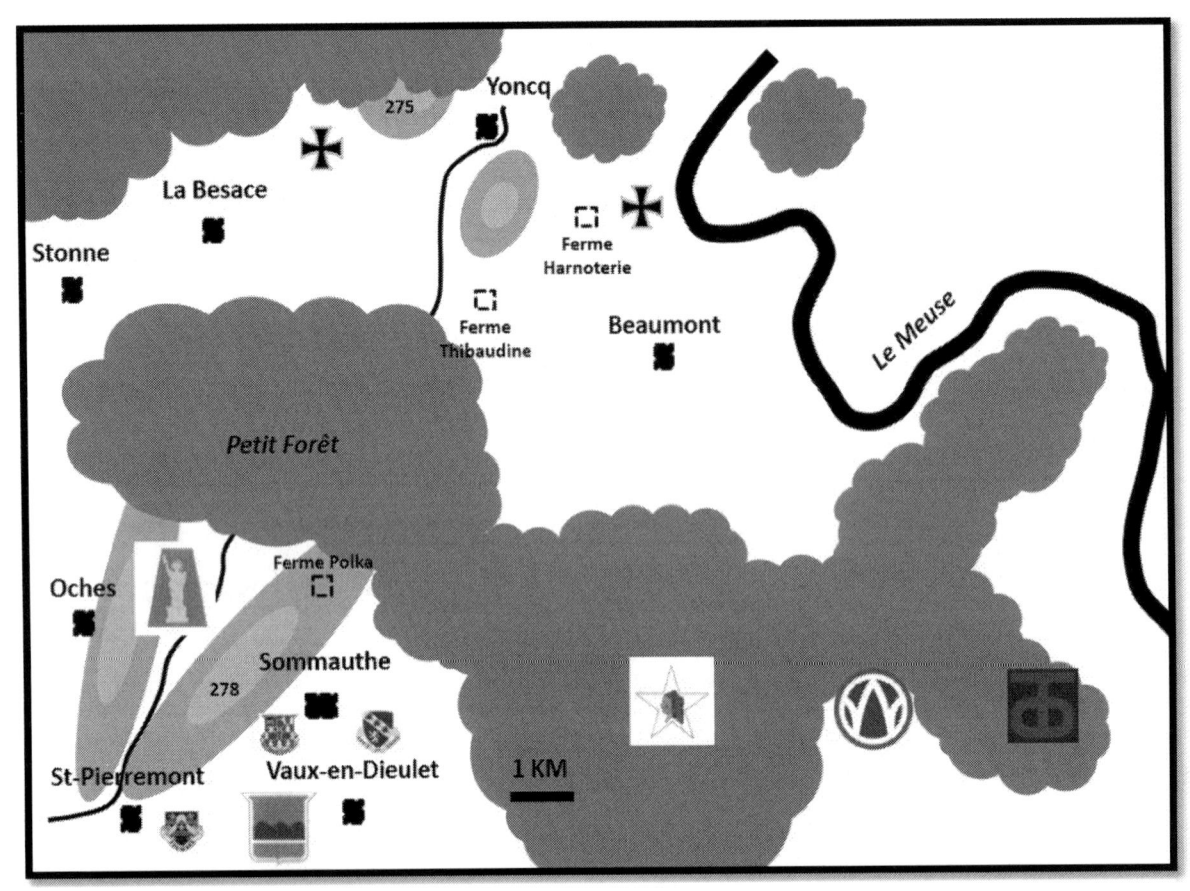

80th Inf. Div. Area of Operations, Nov. 4, 1918. The 317th and 318th Inf. Regts. lead the division attack while the 320th Inf. follows in support.

Infantry veterans with a captured Hun Maxim M.G. (L) and the monster 210mm "Hog Mortar" that we captured near Vaux-en-Dieulet, Nov. 4, 1918.

"On the Trail of the Hun" by Wilson Aylward (L) and "Infantry Sergeant" by Harry Everett Townsend.

"Jerry Kitchen, *Vaux*, 11-7-18." Our company kitchen wagons looked very similar and they were our most prized possessions (L) and "Effects of a 'Dud.' Beaumont, 11-7-18" (R).

Chapter 9
The Battle for *Ferme Polka* (Nov. 4, 1918).

November 4, 1918.

Weather: Misty.

Roads: Muddy.

At 6:00 A.M., Nov. 4, 1918, Cronkhite ordered the 159th Inf. Brig. to attack north from *Bois Harricourt* to *Ferme Polka*, which was along *Côte 278, via Bois Fontenois*, with the 317th Infantry on the right and the 318th Infantry on the left.[325] While 1/318th Infantry was assigned as the attack battalion (reinforced by C/313th M.G., two mortars, and two I.G.s), 2/318 was the support battalion, and 3/318 was the reserve battalion. In 1/318th Infantry, Companies B, C, and D were in front and Company A followed in support. As per S.O.P., the support battalion, in this case, 2/318th Infantry, was to provide flank support to the attack battalion with rifle platoons reinforced by M.G.s. These platoons would patrol on the flanks, refusing the line. It was very important, but dangerous duty—duty that we all wanted, yet all avoided (one has very contradictory emotions while engaged in combat). We wanted it because we were basically "on our own," away from the main unit, which would surely get plastered by enemy artillery and M.G. fire, but we were also repelled by it because we were on our own and could get overwhelmed by a counter-attacking company of enemy infantry.

Also per S.O.P., as one of the companies assigned to the designated attack battalion, we in B/1/318th Infantry were deployed with two platoons up and two platoons back. My platoon, Lt. Ashby's 2nd Platoon, was positioned on the left-front of the regimental advance, our flank "in the air." To our right was the 1st Platoon and to our rear, about 100 yards, was the 3rd Platoon. In the 2nd Platoon itself, we advanced in two combat groups, one on the left, and one on the right. Our platoon's 1st Combat Group, commanded by "Fightin' Bill," was on the left. It was led by the bombers, followed by the bayonets, followed by the A.R. and R.G. squad. To our right was Sergeant Murray's 2nd Combat Group, with the other bomber squad leading. Behind us and between the two combat groups was our trusted P.G., Sergeant Brown, and his attached medics.

Lt. Ashby was up front, between the two bomber squads of the combat groups (a P.L. commanded two combat groups). Ahead of him, further to the right front, was our company commander, Capt. J.S. Douglas, who I am shocked did not get killed during the war. And ahead of him, even further to the right front, was our intrepid battalion commander, Maj. Sweeny. Trailing the company, was 1Sgt. Baldwin C. Hewitt, who was in the center rear with a platoon

---

[325] *Ferme Polka* or "Farm of Polka" or "Polka Farm" is pronounced "Ferm-ah Pole-ka."

from C/313th M.G. (two sections of Browning M.G.s), one mortar, and one I.G. He would help bring them forward on the captain's orders.

About 300 yards south of *Bois Fontenois*, we began the familiar dance with the Germans opening up on us with rifle, M.G., and mortar fire. Once we were down, returning fire as best we could, "Fightin' Bill," who was behind us, ordered the bombers to advance by the low crawl with their wire cutters. The assault team followed them and in the meantime, we looked hard for the enemy M.G.s that were clattering away. Once we found them (or thought we found them) we maneuvered to the flank of the bombers and started to suppress the Hun M.G.s with automatic weapons fire and rifle grenades. Without the latter two weapons, there is no way we would have taken any ground.

None.

I remember laying down suppressive fire through the high grass in the kneeling position for several minutes and feeling that we weren't gaining fire superiority.

The P.L. didn't think so, either.

He therefore sent a runner to find a M.G. crew to bring it forward.

After about five minutes under intense fire, an M1917 Browning M.G. came up alongside my B.A.R. team. Before they "unleashed the beast," they coaxed us to pull back a few yards and to guard their flanks. We did so, at the low crawl. Once we lined up around to the M.G., it belched fire like a dragon, squirting its cone of bullets into the tree line in conjunction with another M.G. that had been set up behind one of the other combat group's B.A.R.s. They were firing into the tree line like a convex "vee."

"Rat-a-tat-a-tat!"

"Rat-a-tat-a-tat!"

"Rat-a-tat-a-tat!"

The tracer rounds from each M.G. were seen streaming into the woods and ricocheting into the air about fifty yards until they went out.

"Rat-a-tat-a-tat!"

"Rat-a-tat-a-tat!"

"Rat-a-tat-a-tat!"

Remember, the longer a M.G. fires, the less accurate it gets as the barrel heats up and expands. As such, after several belts, the cone of a M.G. really opens up. The same is true for B.A.R.s, although our rate of fire is about half of that of a M1917 Browning M.G.

As the M.G.s reloaded, we B.A.R. men really lit into the enemy, trying to maintain our suppressive fire against the enemy.

As the M.G.s and B.A.R.s fired, the R.G. teams also fired their tromblons, their special W.P. greanades filling the area with a thick, bullous white cloud that would hopefully mask our advance once the order was given.

Just then, we heard a "C-crupp! Boom! Crunch!"

Somehow the Red Legs had pulled up a 75mm gun and fired directly into the wood line!

Wow!

Combined arms at its best!

"With all guns a-boomin," the P.L. ordered the bomber and assault squads of the combat groups to "Charge!"

He actually used that word.

I'm glad he did. It may seem a little dated, but the term is noted in the *I.D.R.* and everyone knows it means: "Attack!"

Our training and experience had taught us to advance by bounds in teams or "clumps" and not *en masse*. That means that while the "guns were a-boomin," the bomber and bayonet squads moved forward by bounding about ten yards at a time: "Yankee Doodle Dandy!" or "I'm Up, I'm Seen, I'm Down!" They did this to our left. I remember it as clear as day, just like it happened yesterday. The W.P. smoke screened their movement forward and the B.A.R.s, M.G.s, and the big ole field gun keeping the Huns' heads down.

Once the bombers got to within twenty yards of the tree line, they took a knee and threw their hand grenades at the enemy, pulling them from their satchels, sandbags, or whatnot.

"Boom! Boom! Boom!"

"Boom! Boom! Boom!"

"Boom! Boom! Boom!"

After that, the assault squad zipped through the bomber squad and dove into the enemy, using their rifles and bayonets *á la gymnastique*. On their heels followed the bombers and then us in the B.A.R. and R.G. squad.

I remember rolling into the position just like we had before, in the wake of dead or dying Germans. This time, I noticed that Pvt. Asa Greathouse was wounded—he had taken a bullet in the gut. Because I had a B.A.R., I was not authorized to render first aid. Getz and I therefore moved forward through the platoon and set up a defense in the woods in case of a Heinie counter-attack.

After ten or so minutes, we were ordered to advance farther into *Bois Fontenois*, with what was left of the bombers once again leading. This was ordered for two reasons: one, you don't want to hang around too long lest you'll get hit by an artillery strike. Two, once you have the "enemy on the run," keep him on the run. This will be hard, as you'll be utterly exhausted. Every drop of water from your body will be gone.

Your canteen will be empty.

But do it!

We were about halfway through the woods when the absolute worst weapon combination of all hit us: artillery mixed with mustard gas. First came in the H.E. shells, which crashed through the canopy, scattering our men and causing serious injury to some, and killing others, like my good friend, Albert Getz.

That's right, my brother-in-arms, P.F.C. Albert Getz from Norfolk, Virginia, was killed by a Hun artillery shard that cut half of his head off, splitting his skull in two. His brains and bone were smattered upon me.

But I had no time to mourn or even go into shock because just then came the mustard gas. I remember being amazed by how quiet the gas was, even when its shell burst on the ground. There was no hissing—no nothing. There was just a thick cloud of yellow smoke that billowed up from the earth. It actually didn't look deadly at all. Corporal Reese was the first one to yell, "Gas!" and boy did we move quickly.

From our respirator bags, which were generally worn across our front or side at the "ready position," we ripped out our gas masks in sheer terror, dropping our weapons. The worst part of wearing the mask, aside from the heat, claustrophobia, and lack of peripheral vision, were the nose pinchers. Those British gas masks clamped one's nostrils totally shut—and it hurt—especially after an extended amount of time.

With our masks on, most of us grabbed our weapons and bolted to the rear. It seems like every time we dealt with a new threat, we'd panic and run to the rear. "They got Getz! They got Getz!" I yelled to myself in the mask.

It just then started to sink in.

As we reassembled in a small hollow, we noticed that some had forgotten their weapons. Jim Bruce was one of them. Although we weren't supposed to, we had dropped our weapons while he put on our masks. In the fear and confusion, Jim forgot to pick up his rifle and simply took off—running with the rest of us. It was decided to go back to where the artillery strike had taken place to try to get the weapons back, which was a good call. No telling what the Germans were up to.

When we got there, the gas was still creeping among the undergrowth like wispy yellow snakes, looking macabre but not overly dangerous. After men like Bruce found their rifles and I recovered Getz's dog tags, letters, and shelter half, the P.L. decided to continue the advance with our masks on.

I thought it was suicidal.

How are we going to spot M.G.s when they open up?

What if we hit the dirt and jarred off our mask? What if, what if…

"What if," if done too much in a combat zone, will lead to inaction and inaction will lead to death or disfigurement a sure defeat. Remember, only the offensive wins battles and won battles win wars. Sure, we could have fallen back and assumed a defensive posture, but what would have prevented the enemy from hitting us there? Nothing. And that was already proven. Our P.L. was a brave man. He didn't know everything—none of us did—but he knew enough when to listen and when to step up and lead the way.

This was one of those times.

Upon our next contact, a "what if" did happen when Pvt. Ott's mask jarred off and some of the gas got into his eyes. Of course he screamed over the din of the battle and was later taken to the rear. At least he didn't breathe in the nasty stuff, which would have burnt out his lungs, suffocating him with his own blood. So there you have it: automatic weapons fire, massed artillery of massive caliber and killing potential, poison gas, barbed wire, trenches, shell craters, aeroplanes, and disease.

That's the face of modern war.

It is a far cry from the Spanish-American War or the Philippine Insurrection that the Army had fought was just twenty years before.

We were wet, cold, hungry, exhausted, and scared out of our wits. When would it all end?

"When we're all dead," said Henry Adkins.

And then I wailed, "Poor Getz! Poor Getz! Those Sons-of-*Bosches* got Getz! I'll take ten of them for him! Ten!"

Henry quickly wrapped his arm around me really tight, wiped my face of Getz's blood, and said: "We'll help you, brother, we'll help you. Let's go. Let's get up there. Let's show 'em! Give 'em a what fer!"

As we exited the woods (I was still in a daze of rage) and into the cleared fields between Bois Fontenois and *Village Sommauthe*, we became the leading unit across the entire American First Army's front and soon paid for it.[326] We encountered Hun M.G. fire from both flanks—from positions within the sectors of adjacent units. In order to protect ourselves, it was decided to cross into the 77th Divison's zone and take *Village Sommauthe*. Trust me when I tell you that

---

[326] *Sommauthe* is pronounced "So-moath-ah."

we would have preffered to have left it to the Metro Boys, but due to the situation, we felt that we had no choice. During this attack, we captured a huge Hun 210mm "hog-mortar" that had been abandoned between Faux and Sommauthe. It was the division's biggest trophy of the war.[327]

Three Doughs from the 159th Inf. Brig. were later awarded the Distinguished Service Cross for conspicuous gallantry during this day's battle: Corporal John N. Berg of C/1/317, Private Edward Chaney of C/1/317, and Private "Bill" Tignor of D/1/318. Their citations read:[328]

Corporal Berg led his squad under heavy M.G. fire in an attack on a M.G. nest, capturing two M.G.s, killing the gunners and driving off the remainder of the crews. With his squad he held the position for one hour until the arrival of the rest of his company.

Private Chaney crawled in front of the line under heavy M.G. fire and carried a wounded soldier to safety.

Acting as a scout, Private Tignor repeatedly went forward and by calling and making noises, drew machine gun fire upon himself in order to locate machine gun nests, which were subsequently put out of action.

At about 10:00 A.M., we in 1/318th Infantry turned *Sommauthe* over to 1/317th Infantry, and the 318th Infantry continued its attack northwest toward *Ferme Polka*, which was situated atop a low-lying but dominating ridge. Slow but steady progress was made throughout the rest of the day and toward nightfall, our regimental line of attack, as well as that of the 317th Infantry's, which was to our right, generally ran east-west and few hundred yards southeast of *Ferme Polka*. Mortars, rifles, and hand grenades were our initial defensive weapons, as we reserved fire for the I.G.s, M.G.s, and B.A.R.s, only in an emergency so as not to give up their position. Remember, "the M.G. is a weapon of emergency."

While holding this defensive line, we in the 159th Inf. Brig. were plagued by extremely heavy and accurate indirect M.G. fire from the southwest, which came from the American Indian Division's zone of operations. To make it stop, 2/317th Infantry sent patrols into that section of Petit Forêt to locate targets for the artillery.[329]

Things fared no better to the left with the 77th (Metropolitan) Division, as it was having trouble taking the wooded high ground to the west of *Ferme Polka*. This height dominated our

---

[327] *Vaux-en-Dieulet* is pronounced "Voo-awn Due-let."

[328] As cited in *317th Infantry*, 91 and *318th Infantry*, 82.

[329] *317th Infantry*, 74; *Petit Forêt* or "Little Forest," is pronounced la Pay-teet Fore-et."

sector, and by means of direct M.G. fire, the Huns controlled the situation to our front as long as he had observation from this particular hill.

Sometimes patience on the battlefield saves lives. Other times not. On this occasion, it was best for us to stop and wait for the situation to develop. Our battalion had already suffered several casualties, including Lt. Davidson, K.I.A. and Capt. Winant, W.I.A. In this case, we waited for the Metropolitans to swing around *Ferme Polka*, and they did, allowing us to walk into it without firing a shot.

That night, H.Q. and Supply Companies/318th Infantry, moved the regimental P.C. just north of Fontenois to provide the rifle companies with even better support. We hooked up with the 317th Infantry on our right, along the southern wood line of Petit Forêt. It rained all night and it was cold, too. We had nothing but our light packs (and some didn't even have that) with a slicker or shelter half and the suffering was intense. I was one of those who kept a slicker in my pack and Getz (R.I.P.) carried a shelter half. Together, we were able to stay relatively warm and dry.

But with Getz gone, all I had was a slicker and a shelter half. But at least I was alive.

For now.

Back with the 160th Inf. Brig., the 319th and 320th Infantry Regiments had established a bivi near *Vaux-en-Dieulet*. The division P.C., meanwhile, located in *Buzancy* along with the P.C. of Welsh's 155th Arty. Brig. and they were protected by mobile sections from the 314th M.G. Battalion.

We later learned that on Nov. 4, while we were fighting our way north toward *Ferme Polka*, the Austro-Hungarian Empire had dissolved and asked the Allies for an armistice based on Wilson's Fourteen Points. The Austro-Hungarian emperor, Franz, had abdicated and Austria and Hungary split in two and declared themselves republics, based upon the French model.

"80th Div. marching through St. Juvin after relief from the front line."

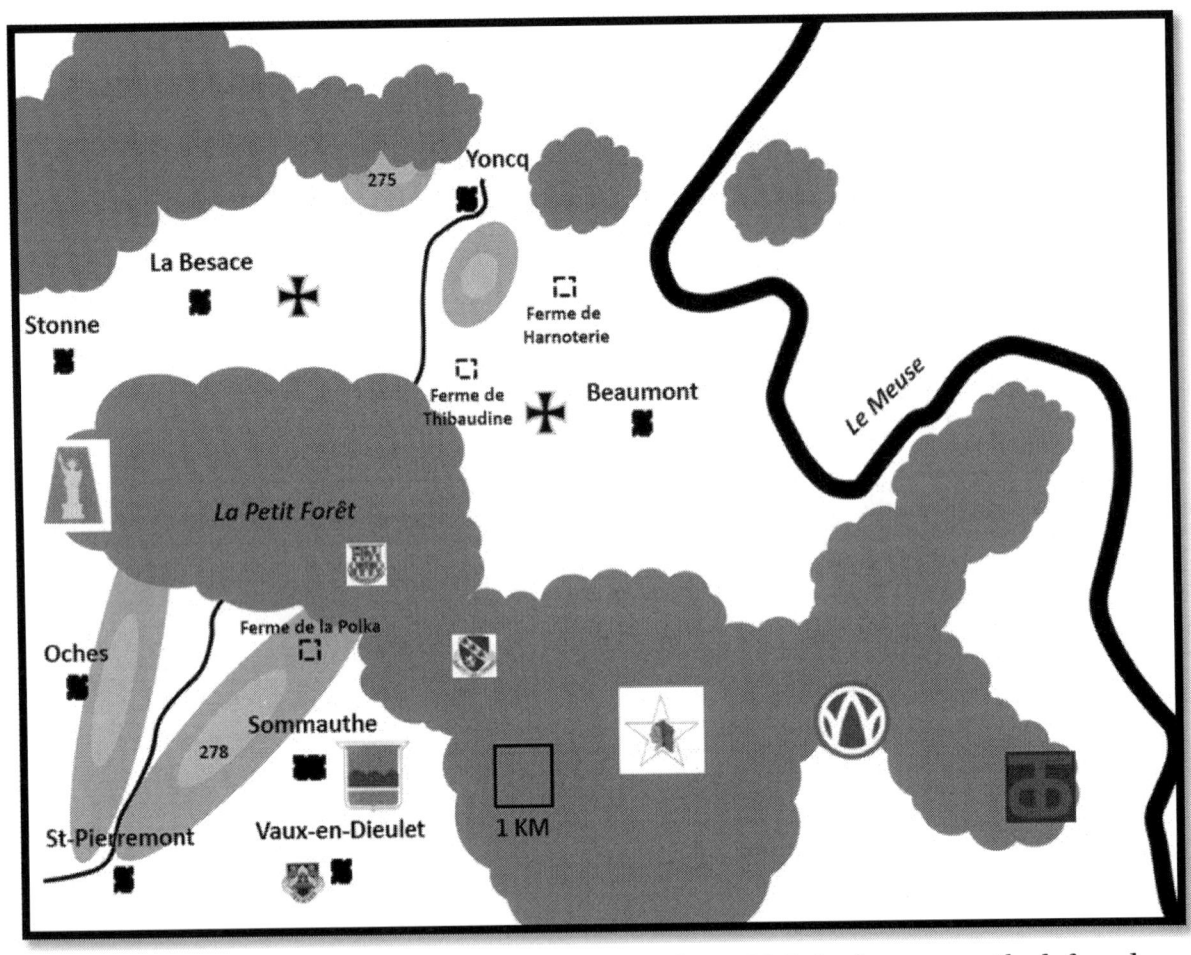

Operations in La Petit Forêt, Nov. 5, 1918, A.M. The 318th Inf. advances on the left and the 317th Inf. advances on the right.

Der Kaiser ist Kaput! Germany is declared a federal republic, which directly leads to the armistice (L). "The Last Shot in the Great War, 11:06 A.M. 11-11-18" with one of the howitzers of the 315th Artillery (R).

With the 80th Div. near Ferme Madelaine (L). The soldier to the left is filling a canvas "lister bag" with water while members of the division's Sanitary Corps check for potability. "Jerry Ammunition Truck, Beaumont, 11-9-18.

This photo went national: Blue Ridgers assemble around a bombed-out alter in the Meuse-Argonne.

"Ruins at Grandpre, 11-11-18" (L) and "Grandpre, 11-10-18" (R).

Staff of the 319th Inf. in La Chalade. "It's almost over, over there!"

Chapter 10
The Final Drive, Relief, and Cease Fire (Nov. 5-11, 1918).

November 5, 1918.

Weather: Rainy.

Roads: Muddy.

At 5:30 A.M., Nov. 5, Maj. Wise's 2/318 was ordered to push through our lines at the southern edge of Petit Forêt, pick up the M.G. sections, the 81mm mortars, and the 37mm I.G.s that had been attached to us, and lead the regiment's attack through the woods onto *Plaine Yoncq-Beaumont* in the vicinity of *Ferme Thibaudine*.[330] 3/318th Infantry would be the support battalion and 1/318th Infantry, still recovering from the previous day's fight, would be the reserve battalion. 3/318, as the support battalion, was responsible for sending out rifle platoons, reinforced by M.G.s, to protect the flanks of the attack battalion. In the 317th Infantry's zone, on the right, the attack was led with two battalions up and one behind. Advancing on the right was 2/317, on the left, connecting with 2/318, was 1/317, and following in support was 3/317.[331]

2/318th Infantry advanced north into *Petit Forêt* with E/2/318 on the left and G/2/318 on the right with F and H Companies in support. Surprisingly, the Germans had left only a small rear-guard in the woods, which consisted of elements of dismounted cavalry from the Mecklenburg Dragoons. 2/318 traversed some four km, coming upon *Plaine Yoncq-Beaumont* in the vicinity of *Ferme Thibaudine* by 9:30 A.M., along with companies from the 317th Infantry, which were deployed to our right. During this movement, 2/318 hooked four P.O.W.s from the Mecklenburg Dragoons and they stated that the days of "*der Kaiser und das Deutsche Reich*" were finished. To our left, on the other side of a creek, continued the advance of units from the 77th (Metropolitan) Division.

As we secured the plain, the support and reserve battalions near Vaux were once again strafed by elements of the Hun air fleet. To put a stop to it, Cronkhite ordered D.M.G.O. Foley to assign at least one company from the 314th M.G. Battalion (Mot.) to perform "Archie" missions along the road to better protect the all-so-important S.O.S. units. Capt. Donald Hand's B/314th M.G. was chosen for said duty and his Ford "Specials" established aerial interlocking fields of fire to at least deter Heinie air attacks.[332]

---

[330] *Plaine Yoncq-Beaumont* is pronounced "Plan Yonk Bow-mon" and *Ferme Thibaudine* is pronounced "Firm-ah Tee-bow-dean."

[331] *317th Infantry*, 74-75.

[332] *314th M.G.*, 49.

Seeing that the Germans were pulling back closer and closer to the Meuse and our ultimate objectives, Sedan and Namur, Cronkhite ordered the division, led by the 159th Inf. Brig., to advance to *Village Yoncq* and into the bottom lands of the Meuse north of Beaumont.[333] The battalions of the 160th Inf. Brig. would be held in reserve in the vicinity of Sommauthe.

By mid-afternoon, we of the 318th Infantry in fact took Yoncq, linking up with the 77th Division's right, and the 317th Infantry took *Ferme Harnoterie* and *Village Beumont*, connecting with the left-most companies of the Indian Head Division. Lt. Craighill of the 317th Infantry remembered:

> *1/317 was held up in a ravine west of la Harnoterie Farm by heavy M.G. fire from well-concealed emplacements. The fire became so intense that the battalion was forced to withdraw. Vigorous patrolling toward the Meuse was carried out through the night by both battalions and a small detachment of corps cavalry rendered very valuable service by definitely locating hostile M.G. emplacements.*[334]

There was still a German company dug-in to our left-front, however, atop Hill 275, and we and a battalion from the 77th Division would have to deal with the next day

Or so we thought.

November 6, 1918.
Weather: Rainy.
Roads: Muddy.
At 6:30 A.M., Nov. 6, 1918, instead of receiving the order to attack Hill 275, advance to the Meuse, and push on to Sedan, unhinging the entire German line in France and Belgium (!), we were instead told that the American 18th Infantry (Vanguards) Regiment, 1st (Big Red One) Division was going to replace us on the line and that the 42nd (Rainbow) Division was going to replace the 77th Division.

This may sound strange, but we were actually infuriated by this "relief" because we knew what it meant: it meant that Pershing's "Fair-haired Boys," at least the 1st Division, who had fought the "longest and the mostest," was given the "position of honor" with our "glorious advance" upon Sedan. I was in fact so upset that I insulted several Big Red Ones, calling them

---

[333] *Yoncq* is pronounced "Yunk" and *Beaumont* is pronounced "Bow-mon."

[334] *317th Infantry*, 75.

unpleasant things that would match up with male body parts ("Big red one this, blank-blank, etc.").

Fights actually broke out.

Can you believe it?

We were being relieved and we were upset!

I was still extremely upset about the death of Getz, so that was part of it, too. My blood was up, so they say, and to be pulled out of the line in that condition is unnatural.

We had only been "Up the Line" for 36 hours, had had three days' rest and had suffered very light casualties on our drive up to *Yoncq*. The morale of the division was never higher during our time in the Meuse-Argonne. It was like they pulled the carpet right from under us just because our "number was too high." We later learned that "no division had advanced farther or suffered fewer casualties from November 1st to 6th than had the 80th Division" and that the 318th Infantry Regiment *was the farthest A.E.F. unit to advance* into German lines up until that date.[335]

That's something to be proud of, no matter what the Big Red One says.

Still in a state of disbelief and betrayal, we marched back through Petit Forêt and by noon were encamped in the woods and ravines about *Ferme Polka*. Once settled, we received news that the 80th Division was to hold in place and conduct recovery operations for forty-eight hours, after which we should be ready to resume offensive operations. I have to admit, once I curled up in my slicker and shelter half soon after dusk, I was no longer angry at the Big Red Ones. I was, in fact, thankful.

---

[335] *318th Infantry*, 81.

During the fighting from Nov. 3-6, from *Sommerance* up through *Immecourt, Sivry, Buzancy, Fontenois, Ferme Polka, La Petit Forêt*, and on to *Yoncq*, the 318th Infantry suffered the following casualties: 25 killed, 93 wounded, and 1 missing. The 80th (Blue Ridge) Division reported taking 38 enemy officers and 793 E.M. as P.O.W., including an entire battalion staff. We captured 55 Hun artillery pieces, 22 *Minenwerfers*, 507 Maxim M.G.s (the Germans really loved their M.G.s!), 1,160 Mauser Rifles, eight anti-tank rifles, and vast amounts of ammunition, wagons, limbers, motor trucks, armored motor cars, field kitchens, telephones, wire, steam shovels, railway, etc.[336] Below is the official "Report of Operations of the 318th Infantry Regiment, November 3-6, 1918":

---

[336] *317th Infantry*, 77.

1-3
Report of Operations of the 318th Infantry Regiment.
November 3-6, 1918.

Attention is invited to detailed report of operations of this regiment from Nov. 3-6, 1918.

The attack ordered by Field Order No. 16 of these headquarters started at 5:20 A.M., Nov. 3, 1918, with the movement of the leading battalion (3rd Battalion, Major Burdick commanding). About 8 A.M. the battalion moved forward on its objective, on the left of the 317th Infantry and right of the 77th Division.

The attack continued during Nov. 3, 4, and 5, the front line being relieved by the 1st Battalion (Major Sweeny commanding) on Nov. 4, and by the 2d Battalion (Major Wise) commanding on November 5.

The attack started from the HARRICOURT-BAR ROAD (Map BUZANCY, grid squares 66 and 76) and progressed (Map LA POLKA FARM) until the regiment was passed through by the 18th Infantry, 1st Division, at 6:15 A.M., Nov. 6, 1918 (Map YONCQ), after which the regiment was assembled at La Polka Farm.

The enemy's resistance consisted of fire from machine guns and 77's, and at the end, some 155s. It was moderately strong at many points during the advance, but the progress of the advance was retarded at only 2 points, HILL 278 (west of SOMMAUTHE) and the front of the woods in squares 94 and 04 and (Map LA POLKA), and the advance of the 2nd Battalion from LA BAGNOLLE-WARNIFORET ROAD (squares 21 and 30 on Map YONCQ) to the point at which it was relieved by the passage of lines executed by the 18th Infantry, 1st Division.

At the first mentioned points, squares 94 and 04 and HILL 278, the resistance from machine gun nests was sustained and very rigorous and necessitated the use of the supporting artillery. At the last mentioned point, LA BAGNOLLE-WARNIFORET ROAD, the enemy resisted vigorously from Hill 275 and the woods south of the same, and this point was reduced by direct fire from our accompanying guns and battalion artillery. There was delay in getting the accompanying guns into action on Nov. 4, due to the failure of these guns to report to duty in time to be of service. After this the support of the artillery was excellent throughout.

CASUALTIES.

	Killed.	Wounded.	Missing.	Strength in Action.	%.
Off.	5	9	0	73	19%
E.M.	20	84	0	2879	3%
Total	25	93	0	2952	4%

PRISONERS TAKEN.
4 from the Mecklenburg Dragoons (Prussian Army).

2-4

CAPTURED MATERIAL.
9 Field Guns.
1 Field Gun.
2 Trench Mortars.
70 Heavy Machine Guns.
150 Light Machine Guns.
200 Machine Gun Carts.
15,000 Rounds Artillery Ammunition.
2,000 to 3,000 Rifles.
Many thousands of rounds of ammunition.
1 Engineer dump of lumber and construction material.
15 Hospital Wagons.
10 Transports Wagons.
1 Complete Railroad Station (YONCQ).
2 Cavalry Mounts.

TOWNS TAKEN OR OCCUPIED.
BAR, HARRICOURT, FONTENOIS, SOMMAUTHE.

CONCLUSIONS.
The work of all the units of this regiment was executed with commendable skill and speed, but our leading troops were many times delayed by the flanking elements not keeping up with our advance (i.e., 317th Infantry and 77th Division). Combat liaison was maintained throughout by the use of combat patrols from the supporting companies and support battalion, the line being practically continuous at all times.

Liaison from the front to rear was excellent and the Regimental Commander was never at any period of the attack without control of the advancing troops. Weather conditions were deplorable and increased by arduous work of maintaining liaison, the advance being very rapid throughout and it being impossible to maintain wire communication forward. In this connection the Commanding Officer calls attention to the necessity of providing wire connection from Brigade to Regiment.

The Regimental personnel being insufficient to work both to front and rear, all our wire was used constantly in keeping connection with brigade and left none for service forward to battalions. Attention is invited to the fact that the mission given this regiment was accomplished with comparatively light casualties, considering the nature of the operation.

This is attributed not only to the excellent judgment displayed by unit commanders, but to the employment of formation of companies in half-platoons, and the equalization and coordination of the arms of each half-platoon unit, which insured proper distances and intervals.

3-4

RECOMMENDATIONS.

The Regimental Commander desires to express his appreciation of the zeal and spirit of the officers and men of this regiment without exception during every phase of the action. Orders were promptly and intelligently executed, and the high degree of initiative and spirit shown by all ranks was very gratifying. The following officers and men are, in the opinion of the Regimental Commander, deserving of special mention and the divisional citation, for the efficient performance of duty during the progress of the operation:

LIEUTENANT-COLONEL CHARLES L. MITCHELL.
Regimental Executive Officer.
This officer was especially zealous in seeing that the orders of the regimental Commander were carried out by the leading and support battalions. He accompanied the advance and established the advanced Regimental P.C. and by his example and influence aided materially the successful consummation of the operation.

MAJOR CHARLES SWEENY.
Commanding First Battalion.
This officer displayed rare tactical ability in handling his battalion. He met with strong opposition at one point in his attack, and the fact that he gained ground with as few casualties as he had reflects great credit on his ability and judgment.

MAJOR HENRY H. BURDICK.
Commanding Third Battalion.
This officer must be particularly commended, not only for his good tactical judgment in the advance of his battalion, but for the excellent control exhibited, which enabled him to maintain contact by putting in combat patrols when ordered by the Regimental Commander and establishing liaison with our flanks.

CAPTAIN EDWARD H. LITTLE.
Regimental Operations Officer.
This officer was of invaluable assistance to the regimental Commander. He showed rare tactical ability during the action, and maintained a grasp of the situation that was of material assistance to the success of the operation.

4-4

CAPTAIN JOHN MCBRIDE.
Regimental Supply Officer.
This officer, by his indefatigable zeal, was able to keep the regiment supplied during the advance, notwithstanding insufficient transportation, bad road conditions, and the extreme rapidity of the advance. It is an extreme comfort to me as regimental Commander to know that the Supply Company of this regiment is in such able hands.

FIRST LIEUTENANT MARION S. BOISSEAU.
Regimental Intelligence Officer.
This young officer's services were of great value. His initiative and zeal were responsible for the prompt receipt and dissemination of information and intelligence, and his functions were excellently performed.

FIRST LIEUTENANT JEFFERSON E. BROWN.
Regimental Signal Officer.
This officer was in charge of one of the most important functions of our advance, the duty of keeping the advancing troops in touch with the regimental and Brigade Commanders. I recommend him for special consideration for duty excellently performed, often under fire and throughout under immeasurable difficult conditions.

H.C. JONES.
Colonel, Infantry, U.S.A., Commanding.

As far as the 80th Division goes, the Third Phase or Push of the Meuse-Argonne Offensive (i.e., Buzancy to Yoncq) cost us 1,305 men (278 K.I.A. and 1,027 W.I.A.):

317th Inf.: 40 K.I.A. and 158 W.I.A.
318th Inf.: 25 K.I.A. and 91 W.I.A.
319th Inf.: 94 K.I.A. and 294 W.I.A.
320th Inf.: 93 K.I.A. and 343 W.I.A.
313th M.G.: 5 K.I.A., 18 W.I.A.
314th M.G.: 1 K.I.A., 6 W.I.A.
315th M.G.: 1 K.I.A. and 24 W.I.A.

The 305th Engineers lost 12 K.I.A. and 67 W.I.A. before going on detached service on Nov. 6. Other units of the Blue Ridge Division, exclusive of the artillery serving with the III Corps, were 7 killed and 26 wounded. The 320th Infantry had the heaviest total casualties of any unit in the 80th Division during the Third Push with 379 K.I.A and 1,235 W.I.A., a total of 1,614 which was exactly 50% of the greatest strength it ever had: 3,228. We in the 80th Division believe our record is evidence of efficiency and of able, wise, and acutely conscientious leaders who not only accepted that although casualties are unavoidable to reach an assigned objective, but who also refused to waste one man in order to create mere "prestige" for the division or an individual.

For this, we thank God we had Adelbert Cronkhite for division commander.

There were divisions with far less active service who suffered far more casualties. The 80th Division stood twentieth on the list, yet it lost almost as many men killed as did any ten divisions ahead of it and even more than one of the ten. In these eleven divisions, the wounded in three were almost double and, in three others, were from one-half to two-thirds greater than the number of wounded in the 80th Division. And this in spite of the fact that some of them never even had their own artillery in line with them.

Although the 80th Division has never boasted about its relatively low casualties, it does take pride in the fact that it performed three separate major attacks with so few and that for every man killed there were fewer than five wounded or gassed, while many divisions ahead of it in the list of casualties had as many as seven or eight wounded for every man killed. In the 80th Division, as in other "first class" divisions, the proportion of killed and wounded was about the same—less than five wounded for each battle death. In two of the 80th Division's Infantry regiments the proportion was one killed to three wounded.

Despite efforts to spend its men in the most frugal fashion and only for value received, it was not always possible to avoid losses if an objective was to be obtained, as it always was, on some of the most costly fronts. For us, the 80th Division's lower casualty rate was not due to engagement in soft spots on the line. For example, the fighting of Oct. 4-12 and Nov. 1-2 was against positions desperately defended by the Germans. Army-wide casualties pretty well show where the heaviest fighting took place on Nov. 1 and 2: in the center, the brunt being borne by the 90th (Tough Hombres), 89th (Rolling W), 2nd (American Indian), and 80th (Blue Ridge) Divisions, from right to left. For five days, Nov. 1-5, the 5th (Red Diamond) Division and attached units on the extreme right suffered only 677 casualties. On the 80th Division's left, Nov. 1-2, the 77th (Metropolitan) Division suffered 291 casualties. The American Indian Division, including attached units, suffered 1,446 casualties, and the 80th Division, including 35 in its attached artillery from the 82nd (All-American) Division, suffered 866 casualties in two days. But this does not quite tell the whole story since the 2nd Division attacked with four battalions abreast on a four km front while the 80th Division attacked with two on a two-km front. In the 2nd Division's three attacking regiments were 10,800 men—in the 80th Division's two were 5,200. The 2nd Division also had the additional assistance of two extra artillery brigades and an extra M.G. battalion.

While we rested and refitted at *Ferme Polka*, Capt. John McBride's Supply Company/318th Infantry got us up to 100% and we were once again ready for action. Then, to everyone's pleasant surprise, orders arrived directing the regiment to march some 50 km (!) south to *La Chalade,* which was in *Forêt d'Argonne* just north of *Islettes Les Petites*. [337] There we were to occupy an old French resort in which the Germans had used as a rest area for the last two years, after the great 1916 Battle of Verdun.

"Was the war that close to being over?" we asked ourselves. We knew we had hammered the Hun, but believed that they still had some fight left in them. Nevertheless, the march south was once-again accompanied with Lord Alfred Tennison's famous stanza: "Forward, the Light Brigade! Was there a man dismayed? Not though the soldier knew. Someone had blundered: theirs not to make reply, *theirs not to reason why; theirs but to do and die: into the valley of death rode the 600.*"

---

[337] *La Chalade* is pronounced "La Sha-laad."

During the night of Nov. 7-8, 1918, we marched some 20 km southwest from *Ferme Polka* through Fontenois and Harricourt and on to *Briquenay*, which was the scene of some heavy fighting between the Metropolitan Men and the Hun in October. [338] Due to the flurry of activity, roads in the Meuse-Argonne were packed, and traffic moving toward the front was given priority on the best roads, of course. As such, we were shunted down back roads. Horses were scarce in those days, and we never got any replacements for the animals lost in the first drive until long after the armistice, and went through the Argonne offensive without a spare animal. If a single one had been disabled, we would have had to abandon a wagon. The division movement orders for Nov. 8 was as follows:

---

[338] *Briquenay* is pronounced "Bree-cue-nay."

1-2

P.C. Hamilton, A.E.F.

7th November, 1918-22 hours.
Field Order No. 34.

1. The 80th Division will proceed by marching to the area BUZANCY-LA CHENERAY-MARCQ-ST. JUVIN-IMECOURT-SIVRY-LES-BUZANCY, all inclusive.

2. The movement will commence at 7 hours 8th November, and will be completed by 19 hours 9th November.

3. (a) ORGANIZATION ROUTE BILLETING AREA:

-160th Brigade: March off road CHAMPIGNEULLES-ST.JUVIN- MARCQ.

-159th Brigade: March off road BUZANCY-THENORGUES-BRIQUENAY.

-157th F.A. Bde: ST. PIERREMONT SIVRY-LEZ-BUZANCY-AUTRUCHE-IMECOURT-BUZANCY.

-305th Engineers: March off road, BEFFUET LE MORT-HOMME-LA CHENERAY.

-305th Fd.Sig.Bn.: March off road, VERPEL.

-Hq. Troop: BUZANCY-THENORGUES-VERPEL.

-Cavalry Detachment: No restrictions, ALLIEPONT.

-Co.E, 1st Gas Regt.: March off road, ALLIEPONT.

-314th M.G.Bn.: Foot troops marchoff road, CHAMPIGNEULLES.

(b) All motor transport and artillery will move by way of ST. PIERREMONT-AUTRUCHE-BUZANCY, or ST. PIERREMONT-AUTRUCHE-BRIQUENAY to destination. Horse transport will march by way of ST. PIERREMONT-FONTENOY-HARRICOURT to destination.

(c) All other elements of the Division will march under the direction of G-1.

(d) All elements except the 159th Brigade will march at 7 hours November 8th. The 159th Brigade will march at 7 hours November 9th. Transport will march in the following order on November 8th:

2-2

-314th Machine Gun Bn.

-305th Fd. Sig. Bn.

-160th Brigade.

-Co. E, 1st Gas Regiment.

-157th F. A. Bde. will follow the transports.

(e) Foot troops will not march on roads used by horse and motor transport, except where no other road is practicable, such as bridge crossings and through villages. Brigade trains will each be under the command of a Field Officer. Troops may stage on the night of November 8/9 at points within the Division area.

4. All artillery ammunition will be collected in one dump, located on the north side of the BEAUMONT-STONNE Road, and the location reported to G-1, 1st Army Corps. Infantry combat wagons will be carried filled.

5. P.C. 159th Brigade: BUZANCY.

160th Brigade: ST. JUVIN.

157th F. A. Bde.: IMECOURT.

CRONKHITE

Maj. Gen.

Maj. Ashby Williams, commander of 1/320, 160th Inf. Brig., recalled the southward march in this way:

> *We passed through the woods and over the fields as far as Buzancy, the roads being cluttered up with artillery and troops travelling in trucks trying to overtake the fleeing Boche. As we passed through Buzancy, we moved by the roads on to Marcq, a distance of twenty-two kilometers. Everywhere there were the ever-present evidences of a great struggle—equipment, dead horses, captured artillery, and great quantities of German ammunition piled like cords of wood everywhere. Indeed, on this one road over which we passed I estimated on the one day's march that we passed a million rounds of German artillery ammunition piled along the roadside...At Marcq the men bivouacked in an orchard, and my officers and I billeted in an abandoned residence that was partly torn down by shell fire. The chimney was intact, however, and we built a roaring fire in the fireplace and I slept in a French bed without coverlet or any other thing to keep me warm except the clothing I wore. The town of Marcq had evidently been a German H.Q. of some sort as Boche signs were everywhere... On the morrow we continued the march southward through the muddy roads to the Bois d'Apremont, which we reached about 1:00 in the afternoon. Here we rested that night and the next day, which was Sunday, the 10th of November. The men were sheltered in a deep ravine in the woods in shacks that had long been occupied by the Boche. My officers and I were housed in one large one-room shack under the hill that had a stove and a large number of chicken-wire cots in it. Sunday was a day of reminiscences around the stove, and the warm fireside made them pleasant to relate and pleasant to listen to...The preliminary conferences between the Allies and the Germans had already taken place, the German delegates had gone back to announce the terms that had been laid down by General Foch, and there was much speculation as to whether the Boche would accept the terms. Of pleasant and happy recollection to me will always be the mock conference my officers held in that shack that Sunday night between the Allies and the Germans.*[339]

---

[339] As cited in *1/320th Infantry*, 166.

As instructed in the order, on Nov. 9, we in the 159th Inf. Brig. marched eleven km southeast from Briquenay to Saint-Juvin.[340] As we hoofed it, Marshal Foch sent telegraphic instructions to all Associated commanding generals-in-chief indicating that he was not certain regarding the outcome of the negotiations and wished to let the enemy know that there could be no further delay in asking for an armistice. The telegraph said: "The enemy, disorganized by our repeated attack, retreats along the entire front. It is important to co-ordinate and expedite our movements. I appeal to the energy and the initiative of the commanders-in-chief and of their armies to make decisive all results obtained."[341]

The next day, Nov. 10, we marched four km southwest from Saint-Juvin to Cornay, which was the same place we encamped on our march up on the night of Oct. 31. The men of the 155th Arty. Brig., however, maintained their positions at the front (as always), providing fire support for the "Fair-hared Boys" of the Big Red One ("If you have to be one, you may as well be a big red one!") During these operations, on Nov 10, two soldiers from C/314th Artillery, 1Sgt. Lawrence Brown and Pvt. Walter Roach, were cited for bravery:

1Sgt. Brown, at Mouzay, Nov. 10, 1918, although under heavy M.G. fire from the enemy, dragged a wounded comrade to a place of safety, extricated a working detail of which he was in charge, from a very hazardous position and although armed with a revolver succeeded in holding his position until reinforcements came to his assistance.

Private Roach, at Mouzay, Nov. 10, 1918, volunteered to bring up food to his comrades through an area which was being continually swept by the enemy's M.G. fire. He continued to perform this duty until severely wounded.[342]

At around 9:00 A.M. on Nov. 11, as we marched south from Cornay to the small wooded resort town of La Chalade, we heard that the warring powers had formally agreed an armistice and that the war, at least for now, was over. I remember this as clear as if it happened yesterday because soon after 11:00 A.M., we passed a number of French *Poilu* who were capering about joyously and shouting: "*La guerre est finie!*"[343] Jim Stewart answered in his normal Virginia drawl (I've heard that we have drawls): "Well, for the Law'd sake, don't start another one unless you can finish it yourself!" Maj. Gen. Harbord remembered:

---

[340] *Saint-Juvin* is pronounced "San Jew-vahn."

[341] As cited in Harbord, 460.

[342] As cited in *314th Artillery*, 44.

[343] *La guerre est finie* is French for "The war is finished!" and is pronounced "La gare Ace Fee-knee."

By the 11th of November the 81st, 26th, 79th, 32nd, and 5th Divisions were pressing forward east of the Meuse... The American Second Army was pushing in the general direction of Briey... The Artillery of the III Corps had the German line of supply under interdiction fire after November 8th. Of the V Corps, the 2nd and 89th Divisions were over the Meuse and the enemy communications within range of their guns. The whole First Army had been responding in those days last days like a racing car with Pershing's foot on the accelerator.[344]

We marched into *La Chalade* soon after noon and were welcomed by the most comfortable billets we had seen since being in the Army. It felt like we were at an actual resort, being rewarded for a job well-done. We had electric lights and even indoor plumbing (!) as the area had been practically undisturbed during four years of war, save for occasional long-distance shelling and occupation by German troops on rest, as the town was entirely hidden by dense foliage. The resort was situated in a beautiful wooded vale along a fast-flowing creek (Rui Blesme) along a saucer-shaped wooded hill. The clap-board buildings were arranged in five tiers, all connected by steps and paths, and both Infantry brigades, some 16,000 men, were bivouacked in and around *La Chalade*. The men took it as a good omen that we had reached such a haven on Nov. 11, 1918: Armistice Day. Maj. Gen. Harbord remembered:

General Pershing, commanding America's armies in the field, had not been asked by his government as to the advisability of granting an armistice. He did not even know the president's own attitude on the matter, though he probably guessed it with some accuracy. In my reading of the history of wars, I remember no other case where a government acted on granting an armistice to an enemy without ascertaining the views of its own commander—except possibly where the government and the commander were the same, as in the Wars of Napoleon.[345]

As has already been stated, just before our Third Push up the Meuse-Argonne, there was a rumor that, due to our advance on Sedan—the lynchpin of the Hun line in Belgium and France—the Germans were looking to call it quits. On Sept. 27, Bulgaria, an ally of Germany and the Austro-Hungarian Empires, had surrendered to the Allies on the basis of Wilson's Fourteen Points (the U.S. was only at war with Germany and Austro-Hungary)—this was soon after followed by the surrender of Austria and Hungary to the Associated Powers.

---

[344] As cited in Harbord, 455.

[345] *Ibid.*, 527.

On Sept. 29, 1918, while we were fighting in *Bois Septsarges*, *Generalfeldmarschall Paul von Hindenburg*, the Supreme Commander of the Imperial German Army, informed his emperor and king, Wilhelm II, and his *Reichskanzler* (prime minister) *Graf Georg von Hertling*, that Germany's military situation was hopeless.[346] Hindenburg, probably fearing a breakthrough in both the British and the American areas of operation (i.e., the Somme and the Meuse-Argonne), said that he could not guarantee holding the front for much longer and pleaded with the German Emperor to ask for a cease-fire or an armistice with the Associated Powers, based on Wilson's Fourteen Points.

Faced with this crisis, *der Kaiser* fired von Hertling as *Reichskanzler* and replaced him with Prince Maximilian von Baden ("Prince Max") on Oct. 3, 1918. Baden, a leading member of Friedrich Ebert's majority Social Democratic Party (S.P.D.), was to begin negotiations with the Associated Powers. For the next three weeks therefore, while the Allies and the Americans drove toward Sedan utilizing the combined arms concept, the Crown Prince of Baden worked tirelessly to achieve an "honorable peace" with the Associated Powers. On the night of 29-30 Oct., 1918, when several crews of the German Navy mutinied at the northern seaports of Kiel and Wilhelmshaven, refusing to deploy out to sea to fight "the final (losing) battle," however, Prince Max saw the writing on the wall.[347]

This rebellion, inspired by members of Baden's very own S.P.D., quickly spread south like a wild-fire into the Prussian Westphalia and the Ruhr, which was Germany's industrial heartland, and into the ultra-conservative Kingdom of Bavaria, even forcing the King of Bavaria, Ludwig II, to abdicate. On Nov. 9, 1918, as we were marching south to Saint-Juvin, the Prussian King/German Emperor, Wilhelm II ("Kaiser Bill"), also abdicated (!) and Ebert of the S.P.D. proclaimed Germany a *Bundesrepublik* (federal republic). Hindenburg subsequently resigned and Ebert replaced him with *Reichsfeldmarschal Wilhelm Groener*.[348] Ebert quickly sent a German delegation headed by Matthias Erzberger to Sedan where they were loaded aboard Ferdinand Foch's private train that took them to a quiet railway station in *Forêt Compiègne*.

It is my understanding that *Maréchal de France* Foch appeared only twice during the three days of negotiations: on the first day, to ask the German delegation what they wanted, and on the last, to see to the signatures. The Germans were handed the list of Allied demands and

---

[346] *Reichskanzler* is German for "Imperial Chancellor" and is pronounced "Ryks Kaan-zel-ler."

[347] *Deutsches Kriegsmarine* or "German Navy" is pronounced "Doitch-es Kreegs Mar-ee-nah," Kiel is pronounced "Keel," and *Wilhelmshaven* is pronounced "Vill-helms-haav-en."

[348] *Bundesrepublik* or "Federal Republic" is pronounced "Boon-des Reap-ub-lick," *Generalfeldmarschal* Wilhelm Groener is pronounced "Gen-er-awl-feld-marsh-awl Vil-helm Grew-nahr," and *Forêt Compiègne* is pronounced "Fore-et Cawmp-ee-en-ee."

were given but three days to agree lest offensive operations would renew. After much mashing of teeth, a formal armistice (cease fire in preparation for a peace treaty) was agreed to at 5:00 A.M. on Nov. 11, 1918, while we were on the march to *La Chalade*. The official cease-fire came into effect at 11:00 A.M. Paris time (noon Berlin time), for which reason the occasion is sometimes referred to as "the Eleventh Hour of the Eleventh Day of the Eleventh Month."

As part of *l'Armistice*, the Associated Powers were allowed to outright annex Alsace-Lorraine and occupy the Rhineland of Germany—the areas between France and the Rhine—to act as a "security buffer."[349] I couldn't believe the Germans actually allowed this, as they probably would have given us a good fight in 1919—if they didn't eat sawdust, that is. I also thought that the cease fire would simply stop the fighting and let Germany keep what it had won in the war. If the war would have lasted into 1919, the A.E.F. would have had three field armies in Lorraine, and we would have born the lion's share of the fight, with our French and British partners operating to our north.

But make no bones about it—we would have beaten the Germans in 1919.

I know that many Germans today, through their President-Chancellor, Adolf Hitler, deny this, but it's true.

Soon after we settled in at *La Chalade*, we naturally started to celebrate that the war, at least for now, was *"finis."* The division band was assembled and included in its normal show were the national anthems of the U.S., Britain, France, and Italy in order to show tender tribute to the fallen. A memorial service was also facilitated by the various chaplains of the division. Truth be told: there wasn't a dry eye. Soon after, almost on cue, "somebody found" a stash of pyrotechnics and lit up the sky around La Chalade, hoping not to catch the Argonne Forest on fire (which would have been almost impossible with all of the rain over the past month). It's actually a good thing that we only had one bottle of *Vin Rouge* or *Vin Blanc* on us or else things would have gotten out of control, placing the officers in a horrible position.

As for me and quite a few others, however, we mourned the losses of our pals, especially those who had been lost in the recent fighting (like my friend P.F.C. Albert Getz, B/318th Infantry, 80th Division, A.E.F.). It just didn't feel right to celebrate anything without him. I was robbed! Poor Getz, may he R.I.P.!

Once all was said and done, B/318 suffered nine killed and sixteen wounded (twenty-five total) in our third and final push up the Meuse-Argonne from Nov. 1-11, 1918. I'm actually shocked that all two-hundred or so of us weren't killed, considering what we were up against:

---

[349] *L'Armistice* is pronounced "Larm-as-tees."

CASUALTY REPORT.

NOV. 1-11, 1918.

B/1/318th Infantry, 80th Division, A.E.F.

K.I.A.(9).

1Lt. Frank G. Coble, 1Lt. Joe M. Davidson, Sgt. John P. Clingempell, Sgt. Curtis R. Hood, Pvt. Albert M. Getz, Pvt. Frederick W. Hetzel, Pvt. Curtis R. Hood, Pvt. Herbert L. Mauch, Pvt. Clifton L. Perkins, Pvt. Frank L. Smith.

W.I.A.(16).

2Lt. Arthur Benson, Sgt. Chester Schuyler, Corporal Kemp R. Rush, Pvt. Clarence W. Arnold, Pvt. Elmer L. Barkley, Pvt. William M. Brinkley, Pvt. William D. Cash, Pvt. Nelson D. Easterline, Pvt. Percy B. Edwards, Pvt. Jacob G. Prilliman, Pvt. Henry B. Rediern, Pvt. George M. Rollins, Pvt. Edmund J. Roth, Pvt. Rush S. Young.

Douglas,
Captain, Infantry, A.U.S.

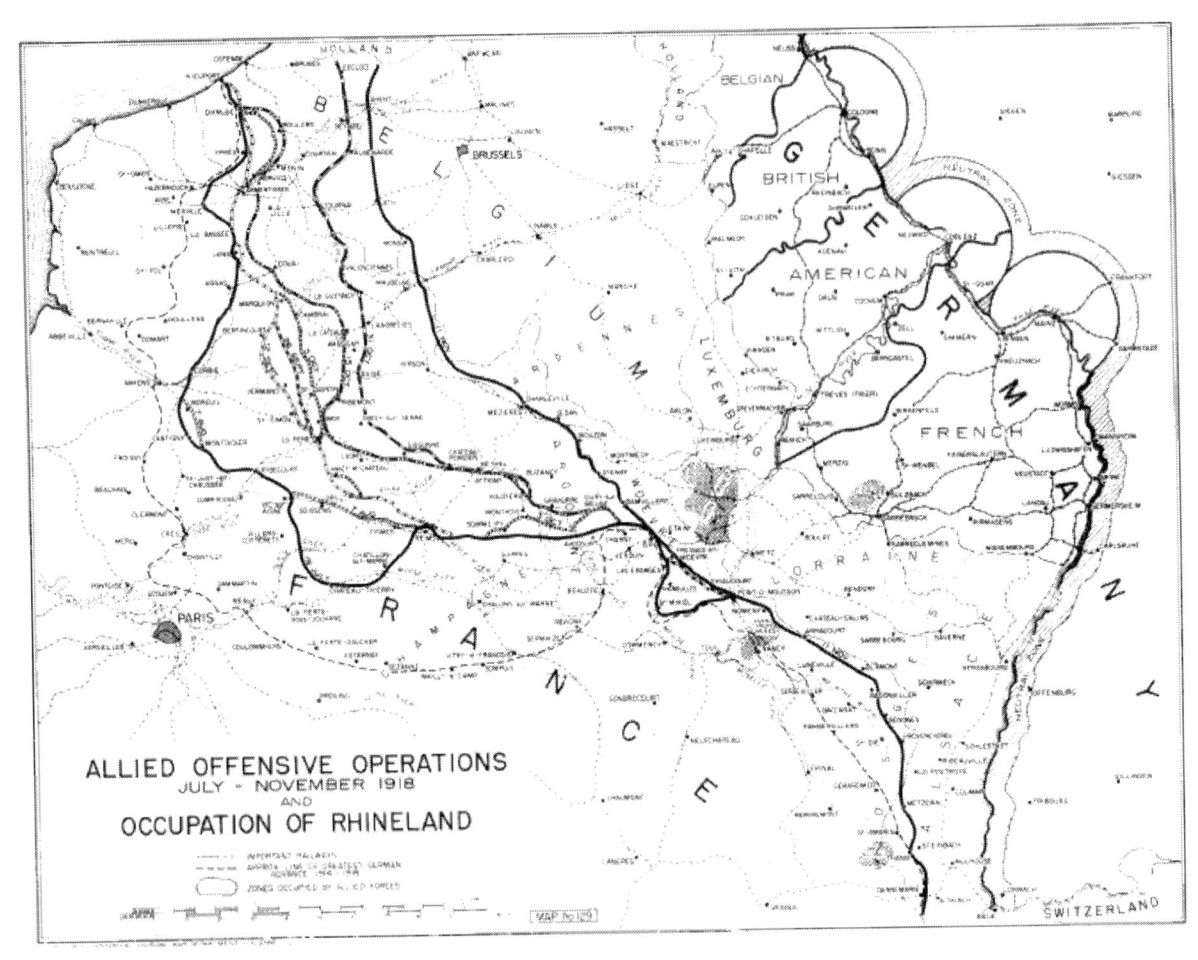

Victory and Associated Powers' Zones of Occupation. *A.B.M.C.*

"Battalion H.Q.; Sandbag dugout in the Argonne Forest, 11-17-18" (L) and "Ration Dump. Levigny, 11-26-18" (R).

"Near Fleville, 11-30-18" (L) and "Top of tree cut off by barrage, Grandpre, 11-11-18" (R).

"Q.M. Dump, *Cuisy*, 12-12-18" (L) and "Thanksgiving Dinner 1918 On the March" with 319th Inf. (R).

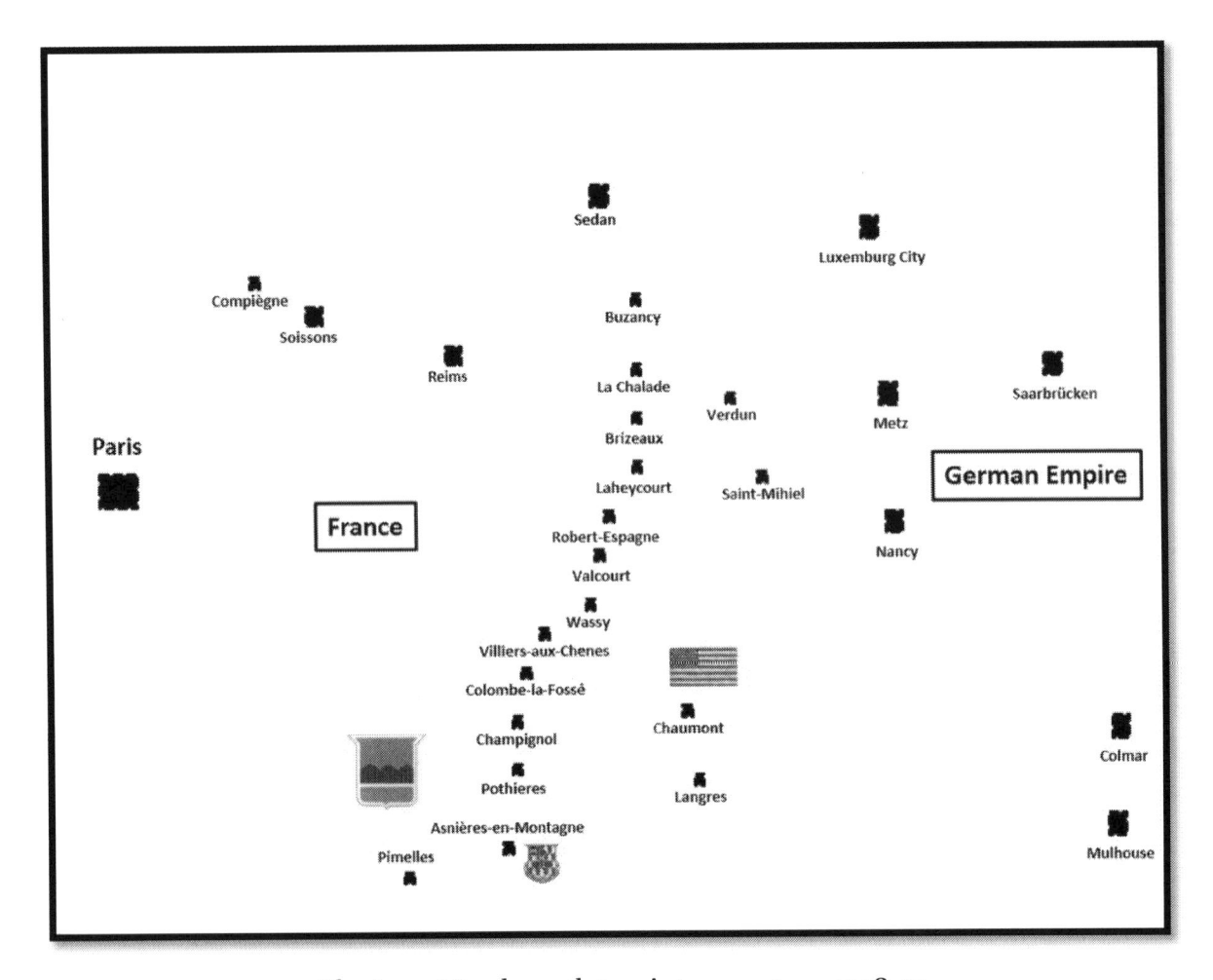

The Long March south to winter quarters, 1918-19.

"14 Day Hike. 11-30-18." Soldiers from the 319th Inf. march south in "column of fours" (L) and "Napoleon Gun. Villiers-en-Lieu, 11-22-18" (R).

"Cootie Hunt, Aisny, 12-1-18" (L) and "*Fulvy*, 12-7-18; A Ceasar [sic.] Army camp 2,500 years ago."

DISTINCTIVE INSIGNIA
AMERICAN EXPEDITIONARY FORCES

GENERAL HEADQUARTERS

ARMIES

FIRST ARMY   SECOND ARMY   THIRD ARMY

CORPS

I CORPS   II CORPS

III CORPS   IV CORPS   V CORPS

VI CORPS   VII CORPS   VIII CORPS   IX CORPS

349

DIVISIONS

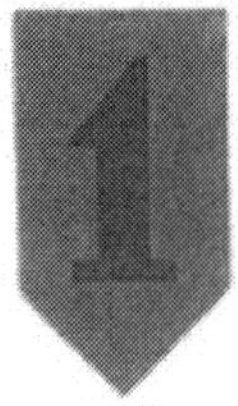

1ST DIVISION	2D DIVISION	3D DIVISION

4TH DIVISION	5TH DIVISION	6TH DIVISION	7TH DIVISION

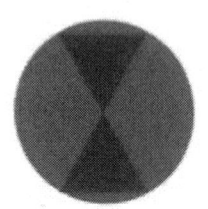

8TH DIVISION	26TH DIVISION	27TH DIVISION

28TH DIVISION	29TH DIVISION	30TH DIVISION	31ST DIVISION

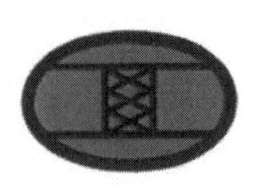

32D DIVISION	33D DIVISION	34TH DIVISION

DIVISIONS

35TH DIVISION

36TH DIVISION

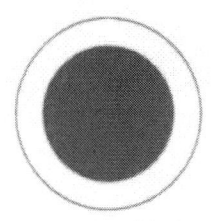

37TH DIVISION

38TH DIVISION

40TH DIVISION

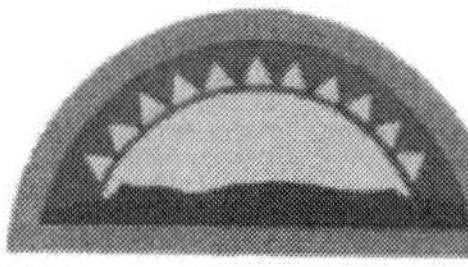

41ST DIVISION

42D DIVISION

76TH DIVISION

77TH DIVISION

78TH DIVISION

79TH DIVISION

80TH DIVISION

81ST DIVISION

82D DIVISION

83D DIVISION

84TH DIVISION

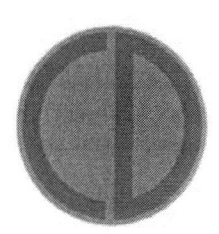

85TH DIVISION

DIVISIONS

86TH DIVISION	87TH DIVISION	88TH DIVISION	89TH DIVISION
90TH DIVISION	91ST DIVISION	92D DIVISION	93D DIVISION

SPECIAL UNITS

- SERVICES OF SUPPLY
- ADVANCE SECTION S. O. S. 
- CHEMICAL WARFARE SERVICE 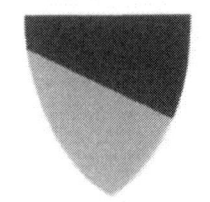
- DISTRICT OF PARIS 
- AMBULANCE SERVICE 
- RESERVE MALLET 
- TANK CORPS 
- RAILHEAD 
- A. E. F. NORTH RUSSIA 
- REGULATING STATION

Different manufacturers in France made our division patches during the winter of 1918-19. It would have been nice if we had them during actual combat.

314th Arty. Band in France (L) and 317th officers in France (R).

One of our G.S. wagons from Supply/318th Inf. Regt. with "Old Virginia Never Tires" (L) and a captured donkey that we called "Jerry" pulls an ammunition caisson with an M1917 Rifle (standing straight up) labeled "Anti-Aircraft Gun" (R).

Another cold formation, winter of 1918-19 (L) and platoon from 319th Inf. in France (R).

Portraits of various Blue Ridge Doughboys.

"Panorama of Forwarding Camp at Le Mans" (L) and "Relay Race at Le Mans" (R).

"Gen. Pershing Inspecting 80th Div. 4-26-19."

"80th Div. review 4-26-19" (L) and "Le Mans" (R). Maj. Gen. Adelbert Cronkhite is in the reviewing stand wearing the Overseas Service Cap.

One of the last decoration ceremonies at Brest before our return home (L) and Camp Pontanezen—Brest, 6-28-19" (R).

"Good-bye France—Port of Brest" (L) and "The Great War for Civilization Service Ribbon" with campaign bars (R).

The final leg home (L) and "Ferry-Brest. Taking troops to transport" (R).

The U.S.S. *Maui* (L) and the U.S.S. *Zeppelin* (R) transported the 159th Inf. Brig. and other 80th Division units from from Brest to Norfolk.

The S.S. *Graf von Waldersee* transported men from the 160th Inf. Brig. from Brest to N.Y. (L) and 318th Inf. Baseball Team on way home (R). I'm bottom left.

Welcome Home! 80th Division troops parade through Richmond, 1919.

Chapter 11
The Long Walk Home (Nov. 12, 1918-June 9, 1919).

The day after *l'Armistice* went into effect, Nov. 12, 1918, General Pershing issued the following *communiqué* to the "officers and soldiers of the A.E.F.":

> *The enemy has capitulated. It is fitting that I address myself in thanks directly to the officers and soldiers of the A.E.F. who by their heroic efforts have made possible this glorious result. Our armies, hurriedly raised and hastily trained, met a veteran enemy, and by courage, discipline, and skill always defeated him. Without complaint you have endured incessant toil, privation, and danger. You have seen many of your comrades make the supreme sacrifice that freedom might live. I thank you for the patience and courage with which you have endured. I congratulate you upon the splendid fruits of victory which your heroism and the blood of our gallant dead are now presenting to our nation. Your deeds will live forever on the most glorious pages of American history...*[350]

As for the overall "cost" of the war, at the time of the Armistice there were over *two million* American troops in France. Napoleon took an allied army of about one quarter this amount into Russia in 1812. According to Maj. Gen. James Harbord, the commander of the American S.O.S.: "For the period of twenty-five months, from April, 1917, through April, 1919, the war cost the U.S. considerably more than $1 million an hour...a sum of $22 billions [or] twenty times the pre-war national debt...In addition to this huge expenditure loans were advanced to the Allies at the rate of nearly $500,000 an hour. Congress authorized for this purpose $10 billions and there was actually paid to various governments the sum of $8 billions. The U.S. had the best fed, the best clothed, best shod, and most carefully looked after soldiers in the Great War."[351] As of this writing, an estimated *ten million people lost their lives* because of the war (and not just during—but because of). In approximate numbers, France suffered the most of the Associated Powers with 1,737,800 deaths (4% of the population) and 4,266,000 wounded, Great Britain suffered around one million deaths (2% of the population) and 1.7 million wounded, Russia suffered three million deaths (2%) and four million wounded, Serbia suffered one million deaths (2%) and 133,148 wounded, Belgium suffered 140,000 deaths (1.5%) and 44,686 wounded, and the U.S., including my good friend Albert Getz, suffered 117,465 deaths (or less than one percent of the population) and 204,002 wounded. Of the Central Powers, Turkey suffered three million deaths (15.36% of the population) and 700,000 wounded,

---

[350] As cited in Harbord, 465.

[351] Harbord, 467.

Germany suffered 2.8 million deaths (4.32% of the population) and four million wounded, Austria-Hungary suffered two million deaths (4% of the population) and 3.6 million wounded. During the early 1930s, I once heard a young person say, "Those casualty figures don't seem so high." Yes, on paper, 0.13% for the U.S. does not seem very high. But to the affected families, it is. To the soldiers who served, especially in the infantry outfits where the casualty rates sometimes topped 50%, the casualty rate was high. And also remember that many of the wounded who made it home were permanently disfigured. Some cities even passed so-called "Ugly Laws" where it was a crime for disfigured veterans to venture out into public without wearing a mask.

Being drafted—the gift that keeps on giving.

Over the next several days, we were tasked to salvage all surplus property in the area, clear off mud and dirt from clothing and equipment, and to get everything in good shape in accordance with the high standard of the regiment. For the evening battalion formation, we were read Maj. Gen. Adelbert Cronkhite's General Order 19, which famously coined the phrase: "The 80th Division Always Moves Forward," effectively replacing our tentative divisional motto *Vis Montium* (To Draw Strength from the Mountains):

1-2

HEADQUARTERS EIGHTIETH DIVISION.

AMERICAN EXPEDITIONARY FORCE.

France, 11 November, 1918.

GENERAL ORDER No. 19.

To the Members of the 80th Division:

The 80th Division Only Moves FORWARD.

It not only moves forward against the Enemy, but it moves forward in the estimation of all who are capable of judging its courage, its fighting, and its manly qualities.

In the operations for the period of November 1-5, the Division moved forward fifteen and five-eighths miles in an air line.

It always led.

It captured two Huns for every man wounded.

It captured one machine gun for every man wounded.

It captured one cannon for every ten men wounded, besides large quantities of munitions and other stores.

It accomplished these results of vast importance to the success of the general operation, with a far smaller percentage of casualties than in any other Division engaged.

It has learned from hard training and experience.

The appreciation of the Corps and the Army Commanders is expressed in the following:

Telegram from the Commanding General, First Army (dated Nov. 1):

"The Army Commander desires that you inform the Commander of the 80th Division of the Army Commander's appreciation of his excellent work during the battle of to-day. He desires that you have this information sent to all organizations of that Division as far as may be practicable this night. He fully realizes the striking blow your Division has delivered to the enemy this date."

2-2

Letter from the Commanding General, First Army Corps, A.E.F. (dated Nov. 11):

"The Corps Commander desires that you be informed and that those under your command be informed that in addition to other well deserved commendations received from the Army Commander and Corps Commander, he wishes to express his particular gratification and appreciation of the work of your division from the time it has entered under his command."

It is necessarily a great honor to be allowed to command an organization which earns such commendation.

It is likewise a great honor to belong to such an organization.

I do not know what the future has in store for us.

If it be war, we must and shall sustain our honor and our reputation by giving our best to complete the salvation of our country.

If it be peace, we must and shall maintain our reputation and the honor of our Division and the Army, as soldiers of the greatest country on earth, and as right-minded, self-respecting men.

The 80th Division Only Moves FORWARD.

CRONKHITE, Major-General.

As best we can figure, the 80th Division suffered 6,101 casualties (1,232 K.I.A. and 4,869 W.I.A.) out of around 30,000 assigned (20% casualty rate). The infantry battalions, of course, suffered the most casualties. In Maj. Emory's 3/320th Infantry, the one that got shot to hell near Immecourt, for example, suffered 600 casualties out of 840 men (71%). By operation, the numbers are as follows:

Somme, 1918: 427 casualties (7 K.I.A., 420 W.I.A.).
Meuse-Argonne (Phase I): 1,064 casualties (27 K.I.A., 1,037 W.I.A.).
Meuse-Argonne (Phase II): 3,551 casualties (1,154 K.I.A., 2,397 W.I.A.).
Meuse-Argonne (Phase III): 1,059 casualties (44 K.I.A., 1,015 W.I.A.).

The reader will note that America's Blue Ridge Division suffered the most during its fight for *Bois d'Ogons*, with 3,551 casualties or 18%. It was in that hated wood that every unit of the division was engaged. We didn't worry so much about getting killed, as that would have been that. We were far more concerned about getting severely wounded, especially if we were blinded, had a leg severed, suffered severe gas burns, etc. How would we live after the war? Who would take care of us? Would we ever fall in love? Get married? Have children? Would we be a burden on our families? It must remembered that most of us had been drafted into service—we did not volunteer. To some of us, it was a form of indentured servitude. (But at least we weren't "Slackers" or "Y.M.C.A. Tools"). What will we do when the Army releases us, as it will? What then? Some states had "veterans' homes" for we wash-ups, but would they be able to handle all of us with permanent disability? We did not expect the government to take care of us, as it had not with our fathers after the War with Spain, nor with those from the Great War Between North and South. Granted, during the War with Spain, soldiers were all volunteers and during the Blue-Grey War, most veterans from my state, Virginia, had fought against the U.S. government. But with this war, we were forced by the U.S. government, by law, to join the Army, suffer, and kill the enemy or be killed.

And not every person is suited to be a soldier, let alone an infantryman.

And I know some infantrymen who shouldn't be infantrymen, either—including me.

As for awards and decorations, the 80th Division received a total of 619, as follows:

Distinguished Service Crosses: 59

Distinguished Service Medals: 20

General Headquarters, A.E.F. Citation: 41

War Dept. Citations: 31

Division Citations: 35

Brigade Citations: 345

Meritorious Service Certificates: 34

Foreign Citations and Awards: 54

Speaking for many, Lt. Lukens of I/3/320th Infantry summed up his impressions of "the war" in his memoirs this way:

It is with mingled feelings that we look back on the days of the war. Truly it was the greatest time in our lives, and no one would have wanted to miss it, but none of us would want to go through it again for a million dollars. Each man has his own individual experience, not identical with that of any other man, yet similar to that of millions of men in all the allied countries. To be one of the great body of war veterans is something that a man will treasure all his life...The exhaustion, the hunger and thirst, the feeling of being shot at and of having shells bursting around you, the fear that all know though almost all control and conquer, and the horror of seeing comrades killed and mangled and human flesh blown to pieces—these things will remain vividly in our memories for years to come. But with them there will be other memories as lasting and more precious—the singing of the platoon on the march, the thrill of success when a M.G. nest was cleaned out, the deeds of sacrifice and devotion that we have witnessed, the friendships formed and tested by fire, and the feeling of carefree abandon—the great American "don't give a damn" spirit, which really means trust in Providence—with which we went forward in attack...The monotony, the petty annoyance, and the impatience to get home after it was over will soon be forgotten, but the real events of the "Great Adventure" will remain always fresh in our minds, and whenever in future years two or three old 320th men are gathered together, pipes will be filled, the old light will come back to our eyes and the hard look will return to our jaws, and the wet "Bois" and shell-torn fields northwest of Verdun will be dragged back from the pages of history and fought over once more.[352]

Maj. Gen. Harbord, in command of the American S.O.S., summed up the operations of the American First Army during the Meuse-Argonne Offensive, the greatest battle ever fought by the U.S.:

Between Sept. 26 and Nov. 11, twenty-two American and six French divisions with an approximate fighting strength of half-a-million-men on a front extending from southeast of Vedun to the Argonne Forest, had engaged and decisively beaten forty-three German divisions, with an estimated strength of 470,000 men, in perhaps the strongest fortified defensive position, outside of the Verdun-Douaumont [defensive lines of] 1915-16, that was taken by troops of either contestant during the World War. The enemy suffered an estimated loss of over 117,000 casualties; the American First Army about 117,000. The total strength of the First Army, including 135,000 French troops fighting under its command, reached 1,031,000 men. It captured 26,000 prisoners, 874 cannon, 3,000 M.G.s, and great quanities of material. Seven French and twenty-six American divisions, with hundreds of thousands of Marine and Army troops, moved in and out of the American zone. A total of 173,000 men were evacuated to the rear, and more than 100,000 replacements joined during the battle. The supply problem had been a tremendous one.[353]

The next week or so was spent in the pleasant surroundings of *La Chalade,* continuing to conduct recovery operations, our favorite type of military operation. This time reminded us of our halcyon days at Fort Lee, which seemed to us to have been some three centuries before. To make our time at *La Chalade* even more delightful, the sun decided to shine benignly and the air had just the "tang" needed to put everyone in "fine fettle."

On Nov. 14, 1918, our battalion was inspected by our division commander, a man none of our replacements had ever seen, as well as the division chief of staff, Col. W.H. Waldron, and Lt. Col. E.A. Buchanan, the executive officer of the 159th Inf. Brig. Most of us liked Cronkhite, but could care less for the staff officers. To us, our officers were our platoon leader, our company commander, and our battalion commander. Anything above that may as well have been God, the

---

[352] As cited in *3/320th Infantry*, 139

[353] As cited in Harbord, 462.

Devil, or the President of the U.S. We only got hostile with a field-grade officer if he acted like he knew us. Generally, we'd simply say, "Sir, please talk with our company commander."

On Nov. 15, 1918, official sanction was given for 20% of the officers to treat themselves to a well-earned seven days' leave (exclusive of time of travel). The allotted quota departed, including our very own Lt. Ashby, a man who we all respected (as well as Lt. Myers, who was released from the hospital and reassigned). It was the first leave most of the officers had had in a year or more and was therefore most welcome, the more so in that the signing of the Armistice marked the successful completion of the job which had called them from their civil pursuits.

On Nov. 18, 1918, the 159th Inf. Brig. was ordered to march 220 kilometers (137 miles) south from *La Chalade* to *Asnières-En-Montagne*, which is southwest of *Chaumont* and Langres, the A.E.F.'s center-of-gravity, to billet in the "15th Training Area" at *Asnières-En-Montagne* for the winter (the entire 80th Division was to winter just southwest of *Chaumont*).[354] It would take us nine days to accomplish this feat. Most of us were in fact glad that we went on our "long walk," as it was therapeutic—it gave us time to assimilate the horrors of the war, it gave us time to calm down, it exercised our minds, bodies, and souls back into top shape, and it kept us out of trouble. There are two essentials with which an infantry soldier, whatever his other qualifications, must be able to do. First and foremost is the ability and eagerness to fight—the second is the ability to get anywhere on his own motive power. The regiment, having already demonstrated its possession of the first essential, was now given the opportunity to show what it could do on a real continuous march:

> 18: La Chalade to Brizeaux (20 km).
> 19: Brizeaux to Laheycourt (19 km).
> 20: Laheycourt to Robert-Espagne (26 km).
> 21: Rest at Robert-Espagne.
> 22: Robert-Espagne to Valcourt (30 km).
> 23: Valcourt to Wassy (15 km).
> 24: Rest at Wassy.
> 25: Wassy to Villiers-aux-Chenes (19 km).
> 26: Villiers-aux-Chenes to Colombe-la-Fossé (17 km).
> 27: Colombe-la-Fossé to Champignol (19 km).
> 28: Champignol to Pothieres (31 km).
> 29: Pothieres to Asnieres-en-Montagne (34 km). [355]

---

[354] *Asnières-En-Montagne* is pronounced "Awn-yeyr Awn-Mawn-tawn."

[355] *Brizeaux* is pronounced "Bree-zoo," *Laheycourt* is pronounced "La-eh-core," *Robert-Espagne* is pronounced "Roe-bear Es-pan-ya," *Valcourt* is pronounced "Val-core," *Wassy* is pronounced "Va-see," *Villiers-aux-Chenes* is pronounced "Vil-ee-air lew Chen," *Colombe-la-Fossé* is pronounced "Column-bee la Fose-ah," *Champignol* is pronounced "Chawmp-an-yol," and *Pothieres* is pronounced "Poit-tee-airs."

The march started under almost ideal weather conditions, which continued for several days. Once we reached *Villiers-Aux-Chenes* on Nov. 26, however, our luck changed as a cold and driving rain set in and continued until Nov. 29. In other words, those last three or so days were rather trying.

One bright spot was that the division's S.O.S. functioned admirably throughout the march in rationing and supporting the troops. The 159th Inf. Brig. dispatched advance parties to find the exact billeting possibilities of all towns to be occupied by its units. Each day at 4:00 P.M., for example, a representative of the regiment reported to brigade P.C., receiving the march order for the next day, with the names of all towns to be occupied and the billeting possibilities of each. The only thing definitely known throughout the march was that we were headed for the 15th Training Area at Asnieres-en-Montagne and that division P.C. would be in *Ancy-Le-Franc.*

On Nov. 21, 1918, while at *Robert-Espagne*, 583 replacements were assigned to the 318th Infantry, representing every degree of training from a year to a month and every branch of the service from infantryman to balloon observer. While some came fully equipped, others lacked nearly everything save the clothing on their backs. No service records arrived with any of them. It was an unfortunate deluge to arrive at such a time. In our platoon, we received eight new privates, four going to each combat group. There was but one serious defect to be noted in the arrangements for the march: no provision had been made for a resupply of shoes, and the 220 km march over metalled roads played havoc with the shoes, which had already seen hard service "Up the Line." As a result, many men finished the hike with their feet practically on the ground.

During our "Long March," private benevolent organizations like the Y.M.C.A, the American Red Cross, and the Knights of Columbus, really helped us out. They provided us with smokes, candy, games, and reading material to help pass the time. Each town had a building or a tent for at least one of these organizations, and when one considers the size of the A.E.F., the scope of these private relief agencies is stunning. Truth be told, however, some Doughs hated, and I mean hated, the male members of the Y.M.C.A. They saw them as "draft dodgers," as "slackers," as "war profiteers." I didn't feel this way, because they were at least here with us as "private S.O.S. troops." They were mostly looked poorly upon, in my opinion, because the Y.M.C.A. over charged the troops for said smokes, donuts, etc. The American Red Cross, however, did not. My attitude was, if you didn't want to pay for it, then don't. They weren't Army issue and if they wanted or needed to make a profit from one's urges, then that was the Dough's problem because nobody forced him to buy from the Y.M.C.A. (unlike those Libery Bonds we had to buy at Camp Lee).

The last leg of our "Long Walk," *Pothieres* to *Asnieres-en-Montagne*, was also our most strenuous (34 km or 21 miles). We arrived totally spent during the late-afternoon of Nov. 29 and pretty much collapsed in our billets, not waking up until around noon of the next day.

Our stay in *Asnieres-en-Montagne* during the winter of 1918-19 was as pleasant as it could be because we were treated better than in any other place while in the service and came to know almost every person in the town. After the first few days of our stay, during which time we managed to get washed up and into clean clothes, we had a few days of leisure in which to look around and investigate the town that was to be our home for the next several months. Let it be said that Western European towns, like those found in France, are not like those found in Virginia. In some ways they are nicer, in other ways, not. They're nicer, in my opinion, because they're older and they make more sense. In each town there is an open square, a market, a church, and several wooden and stone buildings that date back hundreds of years. Surrounding the square are houses and barns, which also date back hundreds of years, and beyond that are the farmsteads or *Ferme,* which some men of the regiment were used to at home.

In this setting, everyone, from regimental commander on down (and rank does have its privileges while in garrison), was busy trying to make himself as comfortable as possible. A few soldiers, men who we shall not name, had a wonderful system to make their stay very comfortable. They're found in every company, and they all network. In general, the system was to spot a lonely (or desperate) *madamoiselle,* find out where she lived, and call on her frequently with gifts of *chocolate,* etc. The next step was to coax the girl into giving up the room that was usually reserved for a visiting relative. Once the details of rent were settled, the soldier had a very nice (and private) setting that sometimes included visits from *la madamoiselle*.

Without going into too much detail, this was the time and place where V.D. once again became an issue for some of the women of the town and for some members of the 318th Infantry (and for the A.E.F. *writ large*). Our commanders came down hard on those who contracted the stuff (extra cleaning, guard duty etc.) and because of the "delicacies" of this type of disease, I will not discuss it farther than I already have.

On a more pleasant note, we had a wonderful Thanksgiving Dinner in *Asnieres-En-Montagne* with *beaucoup Vin Blanc ou Rouge* that we acquired from our new French friends who were more than willing to part with some of their wine and food in exchange for our money. As some French soldiers (hollow shells of men) started to trickle back, however, tension grew. A first, there was a feeling of *camaraderie*. But then, the longer we stayed, the more resentful they felt, especially when it came to females and money.

On Nov. 21, Maj. Gen. Cronkhite was assigned to command the IX Corps of Bullard's American Second Army and was replaced by Maj. Gen. Samuel D. Sturgis. Needless to say, the was not happy to see him go, but as long as *l'Armistice* held, we thought we'd be alright. Sturgis was a graduate of the U. S. Military Academy Class of 1880 and an officer of "mature experience" when the war came. An artillerist, he had served 1907-1911 on the general staff and had commanded an artillery brigade during the Meuse-Argonne Offensive. On Nov. 28, again fit for duty, Brig. Gen. George H. Jamerson resumed command of the 159th Inf. Brig., with H.Q. at Stigny.

On Dec. 6, 1918, our regimental commander, Col. Harry Jones, was transferred after a job well done and was replaced by newly-minted (but battle-tested) Col. George D. Freeman. Soon after, Lt. Col. Mitchell, our regimental executive officer, was transferred to the 92nd (Buffalo) Division, and our very own battalion commander, the ever-popular Maj. Charles Sweeny, was finally promoted to lt. col. and transferred to H.Q., American I Corps. He was replaced by newly-promoted Maj. Louis Koch. Maj. John C. Wise, commander of 2/318, was transferred to Pershing's H.Q. and he was replaced by newly-promoted Maj. Edward H. Little. We also saw the return of many officers and men who had been wounded as well as the arrival of several newly-minted lieutenants from the O.T.C. at *Langres*. Because many of these new officers had in fact missed the last great push as E.M. or young officers, they were looked down upon with scorn by those of us who had participated. I'm not saying that it was right or fair—it's just the way it was.

On Dec. 13, 1918, President Wilson, the second U.S. president to ever leave American soil while in office (the first was Theodore Roosevelt), landed in France to ensure that his Fourteen Points were actually be implemented by the Allies. He was already starting to see things being handled in the "Old Way" (i.e., punitive) and by doing so, in his opinion, it would simply sow the seeds of a future war. This he could not endure, as he had asked us Doughs to participate in "one hell of a bloody mess" to ensure that a perversion like this would never happen again—that it would not simply be another war for the "profiteers and imperialists, etc.," but truly be a "War to End All Wars."

For the next four months, from Dec. 1918-March 1919, the division stayed in Training Area 15. This region of France differed in many ways from any area in which we had previously been stationed. Located in *le ministère de la Yonne* and overlapping on its eastern edge into *le ministère de la Côte d'Or*, it is essentially an agricultural region with little manufacturing. Forests cover considerable areas of the department. It embraces 2,880 square miles and in 1919 had a population of around 315,000. Its climate is temperate, except in the Morvan Hills, where the extremes of heat and cold are greater and where rainfall is more abundant. The nearby vineyards of Tonnerrois and Auxerrois produce some of the finest red wines of lower Burgundy, and those of *Chablis* the finest white.[356]

Throughout Training Area 15, there existed numerous examples of civilization dating back to the Roman conquest and colonization of Gaul. In addition to crumbling mementoes of that early era, nearly every town and village boasted of one or more historical links with centuries and events long past, notably during the Middle Ages. Among these was a Cistercian abbey at *Pontigny*, where Thomas A. Becket spent two years of his exile. Its church an excellent type of the Cistercian architecture of the 12th Century. As the various units of the division reached the area, they were assigned billets in the following towns and villages:

H.Q., 80th Division: Ancy-le-Franc.

305th Trains: Ancy-le-Franc.

80th Military Police Company: Ancy-le-Franc.

305th Field Signal Battalion: Ancy-le-Franc.

H.Q., 305th Sanitary Train: Ancy-le-Franc.

Ambulance Section: Pimelles.

Field Hospital Section: Gland.

305th Mobile Veterinary Section: Cusy

H.Q., 305th Engineers: Aisy-sur-Armancon.

1/305: Aisy-sur-Armancon.

2/305: Etivey.

Engineer Train: Perrigny.

305th Motor Supply Train: Cusy et Pacy.

313th M.G. Battalion: Sennevoy-le-Bas.

314th M.G. Battalion: Sennevoy-le-Haut.

315th M.G. Battalion: Gigny.

H.Q., 159th Infantry Brigade: Stigny.

H.Q./M.G./A/317th Infantry: Les Forges.

Supply/317: Sennevoy-les-Bas.

B/C/317: La Main.

D/317: La Loge.

E/F/317: Fontaines-les-Seches.

G/H/317: Planay.

---

[356] *Le ministère de la Yonne* is pronounced "Lay mean-ees-tair day la Yon" and *la Côte d'Or* or "the Golden Coast," is pronounced "La Coat Door."

K/L/M/317: Savoisy.

I/317: Etais.

H.Q./Supply/A/B/C/318th Infantry: Asnieres-en-Montagne.

M.G./D/318: Verdonnet.

2/318: Stigny.

L/M/318: Arrans.

I/K/318: Etais.

H.Q./160th Infantry Brigade: Fme. de Maulnes.

H.Q./Supply/M.G./319th Infantry: Cruzy-le-Chatel.

B/C/319: Villon.

A/319: Cruzy-le-Chatel.

E/F/319: Arthonnay.

G/H/319: Quincerot.

K/I/319: Villiers-le-Bois.

L/M/319: Balnot-le-Grange.

H.Q./A/B/320th Infantry: Molesme.

Supply/M.G./320: Griselles.

C/320: Vertault.

D/320: Villedieu.

2/320: Nicey.

K/I/320: Channes.

L/M/320: Bragelogne.

My platoon was billeted in the rooms of a large house in Asnieres-en-Montagne. Although we lacked electricity (which many of us did not have in Virginia anyway), we were under a roof, had three hot meals a day, a latrine, relatively warm bunks, and a small wood stove. It wasn't bad, especially considering conditions "Up the Line." Our biggest enemy, in fact, was homesickness, drunkenness, "the disease," or boredom. For me, it wasn't so bad. For the married men with children, however, it was very difficult—probably the most difficult time of their entire tour because all they wanted to do was to go home. But because peace was not formally agreed to yet (there was simply a cease fire in place), several American divisions, in conjunction with French and British divisions, were occupying the German Rhineland just in case hostilities resumed. The 80th was not one of those divisions but if hostilities resumed, we would no doubt be one of the first sent across the Rhine into the heart of Germany.

On Dec. 5, as other units of the division had scarcely completed the occupation and organization of their billets, the 155th Arty. Brig. began to arrive to the training area. Its subordinate units were assigned as follows:

H.Q./155th Artillery Brigade: Nuits-sous-Ravieres.

H.Q./313th Artillery: Argenteuil.

Supply/313: Pacy.

1/313: Argenteuil.

2/313: Ancy-le-Libre.

H.Q./Supply/314th Artillery: Lezinnes.

A/C/314: Argentenay.

B/314: Vireaux.

E/F/314: Saint-Vinnemer.

D/314: Lezinnes.

H.Q./315th Artillery: Nuits-sous-Ravieres.

Supply/315: Aisy.

1/315: Nuits-sous-Ravieres.

2/315: Aisy.

3/315: Etivey.

305th Ammunition Train: Cusy.

305th T.M.: Villiers-les-Hauts.

Formal negotiations among the Associated Powers started on January 18, 1919, in the *Salle l'Horloge* at the French Foreign Ministry, on the *Quai d'Orsay* in Paris.[357] Initially, seventy delegates from twenty-seven nations participated in the negotiations. Having been defeated, Germany and her allies were excluded from the negotiations. Russia was also excluded because it had negotiated a separate peace with Germany in 1918, in which Germany gained a large fraction of Russia's land and resources. If Germany, Austria, and Hungary did not agree to the terms that the Associated Powers were ginning up, then the armies of said powers would cross the Rhine and invade the heart of Germany.

That's what we were preparing to do.

Our training consisted of three types: maneuver and terrain exercises, sports and other physical activities, and classroom. It was apparently like what it was to be in the peacetime Regular Army, of which most of us had little or no interest in belonging. We wanted to fight the war, win it, and go home. Although we were a little frustrated that the war was not yet officially

---

[357] *Salle l'Horloge* is pronounced "Sal-day Lorge" and *Quai d'Orsay* is pronounced "Kay Door-say."

over, we kept telling ourselves that it was far better being where we were than being "Up the Line." Let the politicians talk and threaten and debate in gay Paris while we stayed nice, warm, and safe in *Asnieres-en-Montagne*. But we would not give them forever and a day to complete the negotiation.

Clearly, the most demanding of our training was the field exercises. Higher H.Q. ordered that all combat troops in the reserve areas should pursue a "vigorous course of training" between the signing of *l'Armistice* and their eventual return to the U.S. The reasons were two-fold: to prepare the Army for possible resumption of hostilities and to keep the troops occupied during the trying months of a French winter. Our biggest task was to assimilate the new additions with the old hands and to build an unbreakable combat team of infantry soldiers.

The maneuvers and terrain exercises were held under all sorts of weather conditions. Snow, rain, or mud—it didn't matter. Staff officers often longed for an opportunity to fight out the problems around a table over a large map, with the chance thereby to form a mental picture of the situation of the involved units. The system of having the staffs on the ground had an advantage of making them get their "heads off their desks" and various signal units of the division also obtained excellent practice in rapid communication.

Before the four months of winter were concluded, we had practiced every conceivable kind of mock battle, from the defense of a well-organized sector to the escort of a convoy through hostile territory. As far as my platoon, combat group, squad, and team went, we were on it. We were confident, we worked well with the new officers who were smart enough to work with us and not against us, and we quickly assimilated the "fresh fish" who were in awe of our nonchalant but very direct and intense combat experience.

We were most interested in rehearsing "hasty attack" or "deliberate frontal assault," as they were the missions we'd most likely have to execute if the war resumed. We stressed the importance of laying down suppressive grazing fire by the B.A.R.s, laying out a smoke screen by the R.G.s, and rapid and intense movement to the flank by the bomber and assault squads while attached M.G.s provided suppressive plunging or grazing fire upon the target for the maneuvering squads.

But not all of our time was devoted to close and extended order drill. Efforts were also made with the limited facilities on hand to get and keep as many men as possible interested in all forms of athletics. Football teams were organized in all companies and after a few weeks of practice, intra-battalion games were played to determine the battalion champions. Those having been selected, the regimental championship was fought out. In the final game for the 318th Infantry, A Company defeated I Company after a grueling contest of 13 to 10.

After football came track and field. Two track meets were held at *le Village Cry* on Feb. 12 and March 12, 1919, with entries from all units. For these meets, a provisional H.Q. team, composed of the headquarters, supply, and machine gun companies of the regiment was organized and its representatives competed with teams from the three line battalions. In both of these regimental meets, the H.Q. team carried off the honors and won the banner donated by the regimental commander.

Speaking as a member of one of the line battalions, we really didn't care about the sports matches. We felt that we had already proven enough of our "manliness" to the world and were pretty beat up for it. To the members of H.Q. team, however, they apparently felt that they had something more to prove and the track and field match helped them gain some sort of a weird feeling of "manliness."

It's hard for me to explain, but there it is.

I'm glad that the "H.Q. clique" won their little matches if it helped them feel a little better about themselves. As for us in the rifle companies, however, we already knew that we were not only top dog, but also at the very bottom, in the mud and the blood.

While we were billeted at *Asnières-En-Montagne*, we had some local French tailors fabricate cloth 80th Division shoulder patches that were to be worn on the upper left sleeve of our tunics. This was an Army-wide movement. Because the patches were crafted by different makers, there were literally hundreds of different styles. The 80th Division's patch consists of a shield with white trim and three "azure blue" peaks of the Blue Mountains, which represents Virginia, West Virginia, and Pennsylvania. These patches, of course, brought a feeling of pride and quiet contemplation, as we would always remember those who were left behind in the great Meuse-Argonne Offensive of Sept. 26 to Nov. 11, 1918.

I was told that the patches idea came from the Civil War when each division in the Yankee Army had its own color-shaped patch. We were proud of our division patches but many of us, especially those from the infantry or artillery regiments, also wanted a scroll for our regimental number because we were even prouder of our regiment. But the Army wouldn't allow it, so those few of us who had regimental scroll made, kept them in our pockets and that was that.

The American 1st Division adopted a red "1" for its symbol, the 2nd Division an "Indian Head" and the two Marine regiments that belonged to it, the 5th and 6th Marines, adopted the same symbol into their regimental crests. The 3rd Division adopted blue and white diagonal stripes to commemorate its battle along the Marne River at *Chateau-Thierry*, the 4th Division adopted a Four-Leaf Clover, the 5th Division a red diamond, and the 6th Division, which saw no combat, a red Hebrew Star of David.

For the National Guard divisions, which performed yeoman service in the war, the 26th Division adopted a "YD" for "Yankee Division," the 27th Division adopted an "NY" and the stars of the Orion belt to commemorate its state and its commander, Maj. Gen. John O'Ryan, the 28th Division adopted a red keystone, the 29th Division adopted a blue and grey swirl to represent the states of Virginia, Maryland, Delaware, and New Jersey who fought on different sides during the Civil War, the 30th Division of North Carolina and Tennessee adopted a hickory nut to commemorate Andrew Jackson, and the 31st Division of Florida, Georgia, and Alabama adopted a "DD" for "Dixie Division." The 32nd Division of Wisconsin went with a red arrow; the 33rd Division, a great division from Illinois, adopted a yellow cross on a black background; the 34th Division of Minnesota and Iowa, a red bull; the 35th Division of Missouri and Kansas, a white wagon wheel for the Sante Fe Trail; the 36th Division, an arrowhead with a "T" for Texas; the 37th Division of Ohio, a red circle for "Buckeye"; the 38th Division of Indiana as "CY" for "Cyclone," the 39th Division of Arkansas, Mississippi, and Louisiana a triangle with a "D" for "Delta"; the 40th Division of California a full sun, the 41st Division of Oregon and Washington a setting sun, and the famous 42nd Division, one of the A.E.F.'s best formations, a rainbow.

For the National Army divisions, which proved their mettle and utility time-and-time again, the symbol of the 76th Division has a weird kind of crest that is interesting, but hard to describe, the 77th Division, which slugged its way up through the nasty Argonne Forest, adopted the Statue of Liberty, the 78th Division has a white lightning bolt with a red background, the 79th Division, which took Montfaucon, has a white Cross of Lorraine on a navy blue shield, the 80th Division you already know, the 81st Division has a black cat, the 82nd Division has an "AA" for "All-American" as its recruits were drawn from across the United States (like the 42nd), the 83rd Division has an upside down black triangle with the letters "OHIO" written atop one another, the 84th Division has an ax with "LINCOLN" written above it, the 85th has "CD" for "Custer Division," the 86th Division has a goofy black falcon, the 87th Division has an acorn, the 88th Division has a dark-blue four foil, the 89th Division had a "W," the 90th Division has a "TO" placed upon the other for "Texas and Oklahoma," the 91st Division, from the Pacific Northeast, has a pine tree, the 92nd Division, an all-black division with white officers, has a buffalo to commemorate the Buffalo Soldiers of the Indian Wars, and the 93rd Division, another all-black division, has a French Adrian Helmet because it served directly under the French, much like African colonial units.

One of the organizations that helped us pass the time in our winter cantonment was the "159th Inf. Brig. Amusement Troupe," which was headed by Capt. Raymond. The troupe performed as a Vaudeville act and it consisted of soldiers from various units of the brigade. They usually put on a one-hour show that included singing, dancing, joke telling, etc. They actually did an outstanding job and to this day, I don't get near the joy from the radio shows or from the movies shown at local theaters as I did with them. Other regimental, battalion, or even company-level performing troupes were also created to help pass the time and they would travel throughout the division to entertain the soldiers in conjunction with *troupes* that came in from the States. The troupe of the 319th Infantry, for example, wrote and performed the comedy "A Night in an Orderly Room," which had about fifteen speaking parts. It was directed by Sergeant Charles I. Friedberg and Pvt. William H. Mayhew played the Minstrel part (Minstrel shows were *en vogue* at the time).

Dances for the E.M. and the officers also occupied an important place in the schedules of the men. Officer and N.C.O. clubs were established in all towns. One was called the "Cu-Bru" to commemorate our toughest fight along the Cunel-Brieulles Road near *Bois d'Ogons*. The regimental band travelled continuously from one town to another giving concerts. Many of the men were on leave at one time or another during these four months. In other words, everything was done with the means at hand to help make the winter pass more agreeably.

On Christmas Day, the units in each town, forgetting or suppressing their own homesickness, tried to make the day one to be remembered by all the French youngsters. Enormous and well-decorated Christmas Trees brought the holiday touch and presents were lavishly distributed among the children. Company funds were drawn upon freely to make the day a pleasant one for all the men and it was a peculiar genius who was a grouch on that day, in spite of his absence from home.

Hand-in-hand with training, athletics, and amusements went formal classroom instruction. The Old Army Regulars knew that once the guns fell silent, soldiers could neither drill nor play football all of the time, and that a large percentage of the troops, myself included, would welcome the opportunity to improve their formal studies. Schools were therefore established in every town, books were obtained, and instructors were interviewed, vetted, and selected. Interest was so great that our division reportedly outnumbered the other eight American First Army divisions in the number of participating students. Working on the adage that "A little learning is a dangerous thing," we certainly did embrace "the danger."

In January, the Blue Ridge Division began a series of horse shows that I found especially interesting (command had to find ways to keep us busy). These "horse and pony shows" (no pun!) gave the Blue Ridge Division the opportunity to prove to the entire A.E.F. that, in care of animals and transport (as well as fighting prowess), we were second-to-none. On Jan. 21, 1919, after preliminary battalion shows, the regimental horse shows were held, followed by the division horse show, which was held on Feb. 1, 1919 in Ancy-le-Franc. For whatever reason, the 318th Infantry won the horse competition (we all thought it would be the 317th Infantry) and Col. Freeman was presented with a locally-manufactured silver cup. The 314th Artillery came in a close 2nd Place.

The best entries, however, were comical in nature. For example, a little *Boche* donkey who had been taken along *FREYA*, now named "Jerry," was resplended with a wooden German Cross around his neck and German field cap between his ears. Behind him he carried a small cart which had a sardonic "anti-aircraft rifle," which was a M1917 Enfield Rifle sticking straight up into the air.

On Feb. 8, 1919, our horse team, representing the entire 80th Division, competed in the American I Corps horse competition and won against the 36th (Arrowhead) and 78th (Lightning) Divisions. On March 5, 1919, we again won at the American First Army's competition. I don't know why—we just did. Many people attributed it to our time with the British in Artois.

And all the while, I thought about poor Getz and the others who were killed or horribly wounded.

Why did I make it out?

Why was I here?

On March 5, 1919, Capt. John U. Hussey's D/2/314th Artillery, representing the I Corps, participated in the American First Army's "Best Battery Competition" at Bar sur Aube and took first place, beating the "Regulars" of F/2/3rd Artillery of Maj. Gen. Charles P. Summerall's V Corps. This match-up, even after all we had been through together, caused quite an uproar among some of the "Old Regular" officers of the American First Army. In their mind, there was no way a "Selectee unit" could ever nor should ever beat a Regular Army unit!

Silly.

The day before the competition, for example, Summerall inspected all of the batteries in competition and declared that "his" precious Regular Battery F was "unbeatable."

The next day, we Blue Ridgers proved him wrong.

The competition consisted of hitching up the gun to its limber, driving 75 yards, going into action, and firing one shot while the limber went back to the starting point. Then, on signal from the chief of section, the limber again went forward, the gun carriage was limbered, and the entire gun squad returned to the starting point. The most amazing feature of the contest was the fact that the Blue Ridge gun section had completed its work before the limber of that much vaunted Regular Army section had left the scratch. General Summerall, who had commanded the 1st Division's artillery brigade early in the war, "was nowhere to be found after the event." So the 80th Division holds the enviable title of having the "fastest battery" of the entire American First Army.[358]

Whatever that means.

The Army never wanted there to be division among the divisions that were created around Regular Army, National Guard, or National Army regiments. We were supposed to be one army—the Army of the United States. But invariably, there is unit competition and pride and part of that competition and pride rolls into the various components of the Army. It may get tiresome—but that's just the way it is.

On March 18, 1919, we got our first real hint of going home when the 80th Division was officially transferred to Harbord's S.O.S. effective March 20. We had a tentative date of "sometime in May" to return to the states for demobilization. Just before our transfer to S.O.S., Maj. Gen. Wright, commander of the American I Corps, thanked us for our service:

---

[358] *314th Artillery*, 62.

1-2

HEADQUARTERS FIRST ARMY CORPS, A.E.F.

France, 18 March, 1919.

GENERAL ORDERS NO. 12.

The 80th Division, having been instructed to prepare for return to the United States, will pass from the command of this Army Corps on 20 March, 1919.

The 80th Division arrived in France about June 5, 1918. This Division trained with the British Troops and was on active duty with them in the PICARDY SECTOR near ARRAS in July. The Division was in reserve at the battle of ST. MIHIEL, except the 320th Infantry and 315th Machine Gun Battalion, which took part in the operations of the II French Colonial Corps. From September 26 to 29, inclusive, the Division attacked at BETHINCOURT with the III American Corps and advanced 9 kilometers in 2 days. The division was withdrawn from the line for five days and again attacked on October 4 at NANTILLOIS. In 9 days of heavy fighting through the BOIS DE OGONS an advance of four kilometers was made. The Division was withdrawn from the line October twelve for re-equipment and replacements. The division moved forward on October 29 and 30 and re-entered the line at ST. JUVIN.

The 80th Division passed under the orders of the I Corps on October 23. On November 1, the Division attacked as the right division of the I Corps and in six days advanced a depth of 24 kilometers. The division was relieved from the line on November 6, with its patrols on the west bank of the MEUSE.

2-2

From 18 November to 1 December, the division marched 221 kilometers to the 15th Training Area at AUEY-LE-FRANC. The artillery of the division was part of the time detached from the division and was in action at all times from September 26-November 11. The division has remained in the 15th Training Area until its present order to prepare from embarkation to the United States.

The 80th Division was given the difficult tasks on the front line and in accomplishing them made a splendid record. The Corps Commander desired particularly to express his appreciation for the soldierly achievements of this division during the time it served with the I Army Corps. After returning to the Training Area where living conditions were not easy and often difficult the spirit of the division has been excellent and has been manifest at all times. The Division leaves on the first part of its journey with the Corps Commander's congratulations for its excellent record and his wishes for a speedy return to the United States and a successful future.

By command of Major-General Wright.
W.M. FASSETT.

Chief of Staff.
OFFICIAL.
Lt.-Col. A.G.D. Adjutant.

On March 20, 1919, the men of the 319th Infantry assembled at 9:00 A.M. on the drill field southeast of *Pimelles* to participate in their "Athletic and Military Meet." The real draw, however, was the barbecue. For two days previous, two trenches had been dug in preparation for the grand American tradition, claimed to be the "largest barbecue seen in that section of France."

Not bad for a bunch of Yankees!

When mess call was sounded by the top sergeants, it was a virtual stampede into the company mess halls, many of which had been laboriously decorated with pine and cedar branches in the rafters (mostly to mask the smell). After two hours, everyone had their fill and the games renewed, including boxing. A *troupe* of Red Cross entertainers were even brought in and good times were had by all. The evening was finished with a band concert and a fireworks display for all to see.

On March 26, 1919, America's Blue Ridge Division was assembled at *Pimelles* and inspected by none other than the commanding general of the A.E.F., John "Black Jack" Pershing. A more impressive scene could not have been imagined and it was the only time I saw the entire division assembled together on a parade field. Most of us even had our shoulder patches on!

Perhaps the most impressive event of the day (I was in the second rank and could see most of it) was the bringing together of all the regimental colors before "Black Jack" who affixed our battle streamers. While the infantry regiments received four, the artillery regiments received three as they only participated in the Meuse-Argonne:

SOMME OFFENSIVE, 1918. France, July 23 to Aug. 18, 1918.
MEUSE-ARGONNE OFFENSIVE (I). France, Sept. 26 to Sept. 30, 1918.
MEUSE-ARGONNE OFFENSIVE (II). France, Oct. 4 to Oct. 12, 1918.
MEUSE-ARGONNE OFFENSIVE (III). France, Nov. 1 to Nov. 6, 1918.

On March 31, 1919, the men of Brett's 160th Inf. Brig. were ordered to roll-up their packs, say good-bye to their French friends, and to once again load aboard 40 or 8s and head for *Le Mans*, which was the great clearing house of the A.E.F. in France to go home.[359] Just about every American Dough went through *Le Mans*. The same held true for Jamerson's 159th Inf. Brig. on April 2, 1919. For this trip, which took two days, straw was provided for the floors of the cars and only thirty men were loaded aboard each car, allowing everyone to "sit pretty."

---

[359] *Le Mans* is pronounced "Lay Mawn."

At *Le Mans*, we de-trained and marched 12 km south to *Depôt Le Mans*. Upon arrival, we were served hot chocolate, cake, and cigarettes at the Red Cross canteen ("fo' free"!). From there, we were sent out to our billets, which were stuffed to the gill. We shared the depot with the 305th Engineers, the division M.G. battalions, the division S.O.S. battalions, as well as members of the 28th (Red Keystone) Division, most of its men coming from Pennsylvania, like our very own 160th Inf. Brig. Over the next two weeks, we turned in all of our heavy equipment and prepared for overseas movement home.

In order to better pass the time at *Le Mans*, we started regimental-level baseball and basketball leagues in which at least one game was played per day. Passes to *Le Mans* were liberally given. Nice town, *Le Mans*, for what we saw of it. I think for every ten Doughs in town, there was one M.P.

About the middle of April, a movement began to form a fraternal association for the veterans of the 80th Division. Capt. R.P. Williams, Jr. and Sergeant William V. Moseley represented the 318th Infantry at the organizational meetings. The proposed constitution met with great enthusiasm throughout the division and units vied with each other for the highest enrollment percentage. An executive committee was selected to serve until October 1920 and it consisted of two representatives from each brigade and two from divisional troops. Our recently-returned division commander, Maj. Gen. Adelbert Cronkhite, was elected as the "80th Division Association's" first President; Col. W.H. Waldron, division chief of staff, was elected as the Association's first vice-president, Capt. Frederick Hickman, the Adjutant of the 319th Infantry, was elected as the Association's first secretary, and Capt. Reuel W. Elton, 318th Infantry, was selected by the executive committee to serve as the Association's first treasurer.

Pittsburgh was selected for the Association's ceremonial H.Q. and the site of the first reunion. By the time we got back to the States, the 318th Infantry had enrolled six life members and 2,254 annual members.[360]

On May 8, 1919, the 318th Infantry was inspected and reviewed for the last time by General Cronkhite. I remember it was a perfect spring day, one filled with happiness and excitement in "getting ready to get ready to get home." As of yet, the Germans, who were still in a state of disarray, had not officially surrendered to the Associated Powers. As such, many American divisions continued to be posted in the Rhineland, poised to cross into the heart of Germany in case the power-broker class decided that the war should resume to achieve whatever political or economic end state they had in mind. But whatever that might be, it apparently would be done without the 80th Division (good!).

---

[360] The 80th Division Association still exists and has an annual reunion.

From May 13-15, the regiment was moved by rail from *Le Mans* to the great American embarkation point at *Brest*. This time we were put aboard an American passenger train with luxurious Pullman Cars! A kitchen car was even attached to the train and at the appointed hour the train halted and hot meals were served! On all former train trips in France we were accustomed to opening a can of cold Corned Willie or sharpening our teeth on hard tack. Our train passed through *Laval, Rennes, Saint-Briem, Mortaix,* and *Landermear* and after a day and a night of travel, we pulled into *Brest*. I still remember smelling the sea when we pulled in. Home! The smell of home! We were so close to getting home that we could all literally taste it!

Newspapers from the States were had reported about the horrible conditions at *Brest* and "Camp Pontanezen," much like Frazier Hunt's stories about the new American soldiers from the 77th (Metropolitan) Division at Camp Upton in Yaphank, N.Y. in 1917.[361] Fortunately for us, conditions at Camp Pontanezen had been remedied long before our arrival and we found it to be in fact the best organized camp in France. A hot meal, for example, was served as soon as we alighted from the train. The up-hill march to the camp, which was commanded by the famous Brig. Gen. Smedley Butler, U.S.M.C., was very trying but the cleanliness and organization of the camp made up for its location.[362]

A section of the tent area was assigned to us. Everything was clean and the chow was up to Army standards. Wool Army blankets were furnished "a plenty" and we actually had cots to sleep on, the first we had seen of anything like a bed since leaving Camp Lee!

Here, at our last stop before the much awaited ocean crossing, we were issued brand new wool uniforms and every effort made to send each man back to the States as sharp-looking as possible (and for some Doughs—it was impossible). We were also given a physical examination to ensure that we weren't carrying any contagious diseases, especially "the Spanish Flu," which had already killed thousands of people in the States—the camp delouser worked over-time.[363] It's my understanding that the first outbreak of the flu had occurred in Germany, hastening their surrender, and then spread to troops of the Associated Powers. The distemper was then spread to the States by returning Doughs from France. Joe Latrinsky surmised that it was a biological weapon created by the Germans that lost its containment, but that has never been proven

---

[361] Hunt, Frazier: *Blown in by the Draft: Camp Yarns Collected at One of the Great National Army Cantonments by an Amateur War Correspondent. Forward by Col. Theodore Roosevelt.* (New York: Doubleday, Page, and Company, 1918). Passim.

[362] Marine Brig. Gen. Smedley Butler earned two Medals of Honor while fighting enemies of the U.S. in China, the Philippines, Central American and the Caribbean since 1898. In 1931 he retired from the Corps and in 1935, wrote the polemical *War is a Racket*, which argued that too much of America's foreign policy is based on protecting American business interests. Butler comes from a Quaker family just outside of Philadelpiha.

[363] All told, the "Pandemic of 1918-20" took the lives of some 75 million people, or 4% of the world's population at the time.

(which is usually the case with Joe). All that I can say is that I'll never, ever forgive the Hun for being the first to use chemical weapons (e.g., mustard gas) on its enemies. Being gassed is just a whole new level of terror in war, further dehumanizing us.

Although we had to provide work details to the various departments of the camp (when would it end?) we still fielded baseball teams and our teams did well. In fact, one of our teams from the 319th Infantry beat one of the Marine teams that was posted as permanent station at the camp. Three different afternoons were called out to parade for the final presentation of medals to some member of the division. Finally French *Francs* were exchanged into American Dollars and everyone realized that home sweet home, the good old U.S.A. was not far off.

Finally, on May 17, 1919, we in Jamerson's 159th Inf. Brig. were loaded aboard the U.S.S. *Maui* for home and freedom. The *Maui* was an oil-burning vessel of some 17,000 tons that used to haul goods between San Francisco and the Hawaiian Islands before it was purchased by the U.S. Navy.[364] At 4:45 P.M., the *Maui* sailed out of *Brest* in a convoy that was headed for Norfolk, Virginia. The 80th Division H.Q. and special troops, meanwhile, were loaded aboard the U.S.S. *Zeppelin*, which had been recently been taken from the Germans by the terms of *L'armistice*. It departed Brest on the morning of May 18, 1919. It too was headed for Norfolk. Troops from the 160th Inf. Brig. were loaded aboard the *Graf von Waldersee*, which had also been ceded by the Germans, and it departed Brest on the morning of May 20, 1919, headed for N.Y. Harbor.[365]

The "Old Timers" of the 80th Division had been in France for almost a year and it was with mixed emotions that we watched as the coast of Brittany slowly receded into the eastern horizon. Although every man wanted to "go home," many were also saddened by the violent loss of our comrades-in-arms whose lives were taken from them far too early.

We also worried about what life would be at home, esp. after what we had been through. We wondered if "the war" had really been worth it, too. We really did. Although we came to hate "the German," or "*les Boche*," or "the Hun," or "the Heinies," we also understood that they were, in large part, men just like us. In fact, we soon realized that we Doughs had far-more in common with the steel helmeted, jack-booted Hun than we did with "Slacker Bill-Down-The-Street" who was somehow able to avoid service in the A.E.F.

In retrospect, I guess that it is best that Germany lost the war and that its empire collapsed in 1918. If it would have won the war, it was posited, Belgium (including its African colonies), Luxembourg, Poland, and parts of the Ukraine and the Baltic States would have been added to its empire, France would have been forever cowed, and, one day, the German Navy

---

[364] The *Maui* was reverted back to the Matson Navigation Company at the end of 1919 and is still in service.

[365] *Waldersee* is pronounced "Val-dare zay."

would engage the British Navy in a fight to the finish. What would that then mean for us in the United States?

There is no doubt that Wilson made a strong case for war and I was all for it in 1917, but when all was said-and-done, I wasn't so sure.

Was it really worth Albert Getz's life?

The lives of all the others?

As soldiers, we mostly focus on two things: accomplishing the mission and survival. Most of us achieved both. Not only did the U.S. play a decisive role in winning the war (remember what it was like before we entered the lines in 1918?), but also, through it all, the vast majority of us survived without shirking our duty. For the rest of my life, I'd have nothing else to prove to anybody because if I could survive the Great Meuse-Argonne Offensive (Phases I, II, and III), which was Gettysburg times one hundred as an A.R.-man with the now-famous 318th Infantry Regiment, 80th Blue Ridge Division, I could survive anything—or so I thought.

It took us ten long days to cross the North Atlantic, even through a nasty storm, which forced most of us to spend the first five of those days above decks puking our guts out from seasickness. I was one of them. We of course cursed the Army one last time, blaming it for the nasty weather. "Damned Army!" we'd yell when we could between vomits. I know that it doesn't make sense, but when you're put under inordinate stress, like we were, little releases like this do help. Trust me, "the Army" can take it.

The worst duty aboard ship, especially during the storm, was kitchen patrol (K.P.), at least on the *Maui*, as the assigned Navy cooks proved themselves to be totally unable to supply we Army dogs with anything like livable chow. Quite naturally, everyone was in a cross frame of mind. The American Red Cross and Y.M.C.A. did what they could to alleviate our pangs by offering supplemental snack food items and those Doughs who had money made furious onslaughts on their canteens.

The food situation was in fact so bad on the *Waldersee* with the 319th Infantry that the ranking Army commander on the ship took control of the kitchen and handed it over to Mess Sergeant Jesse Honse of F/2/319. Honse, from Homestead, Pennsylvania, the place of the infamous steel worker uprising against Henry Frick and Andrew Carnegie in 1892, totally revolutionized the mess. Bread ovens were used to roast the meat, eggs were found in the ship's larder, and various other things were unearthed that made everyone wish that Honse had been given charge of the mess on Day One. The other mess sgts. assisted Honse in any way possible. For example, each night, twenty men peeled potatoes. The kick about the chow on the *Waldersee* quickly ceased and smiles began to take the place of frowns.

By May 22, the seas calmed, as did our stomachs (thank God!), and at 3:00 o'clock in the afternoon on May 27, 1919, the *Maui* pulled into the U.S. Navy Yard at Norfolk, Virginia. From there, we were ushered aboard motor trucks and sent to Camp Stuart, Virginia (near Williamsburg), and then onto Richmond, Virginia, to be paraded as "Richmond's Division." The U.S.S. *Zeppelin*, with Cronkhite aboard, pulled into Norfolk a day later, and those troops were also sent to Richmond for the official "Welcome Home" ceremony. One reporter noted:

Marching in triumph through the rose-colored streets of their capital city, swinging proudly along dense lines of madly cheering friends, returning the salutes of high chieftains of another time and the honors of great American leaders of their own army, Virginia's veterans reached the last objective of a world struggle…Booming cannon saluted them as train and boat hove in sight on the city's eastern edge; happy loved ones, rising with the sun, stood with swelling hearts to catch a first glimpse of the incoming veterans as the guns heralded their approach, and back of the early morning welcomers was an expectant city covered with the flags they had fought for. It was a Memorial Day of mixed emotions. While tender memories came to the cheering thousands of the many gallant soldiers who fell too soon to hear the shouting of victory, pride in the achievements of those who marched and love for the heroic qualities they exhibited in the time of stress, held sway in the hearts of Richmond. [366]

Overall, the parade in Richmond was nice, if you're into that sort of thing. Although I do think it is important for the soldiers and the nation to share such an activity, I also feel like it is an esoteric if not cheap remembrance for what we had experienced. What about those who were left behind? What about after the cheering is done, etc.?

After the parade, we were transported to Camp Lee, where we received our last pay and were formally discharged from the Army of the United States.

And just like that, our great adventure was over.

Meanwhile, soldiers from Brett's 160th Inf. Brig., on the *Waldersee*, pulled into New York Harbor on June 2, 1919. Capt. Charles Herr of F/2/319th Infantry remembered:

The morning was bright and clear and breakfast was served early. The pilot came aboard and we realized that we were soon to greet those for whom we fought. Quiet reigned aboard the ship as we slowly steamed up N.Y. Harbor. We

---

[366] As cited in Stultz, 654.

realized some of our number would never return and all that meant to their loved ones.[367]

The *Waldersee* docked at Pier 1, Hoboken, N.J. During roll call, the men answered with somber visage and then reported to the Red Cross mess for chow. After that, they were transported to Pennsylvania Station in Jersey City and loaded aboard a troop train that was headed for Camp Dix, which was just outside of Wrightstown, New Jersey, between New York and Philadelphia.[368] At Camp Dix, the men were once again housed in large tents and slept on Army canvas cots. Capt. Herr continued:

A short hike in the hot afternoon sunshine brought us to the camp's tented area. Cots were drawn and everyone made himself as comfortable as the high grass about the tents would allow. Rations were drawn and by dark, supper was ready. Ice cream, the first many of us had seen since leaving the States, was procured from a nearby canteen. The next morning found us at the bathhouse getting new clothes and cleaning up generally. A few of the men were fortunate enough to have relatives in the nearby towns, who came to see them. The end was rapidly drawing nigh. Many hearts were sad at the thought of parting from friends found as true as steel when tested in the heat of battle, but all realized that our work was finished, and the quicker we resumed our places in the world, the better off we would be.[369]

On June 4, after a week or so at Camp Dix, most of the men of the 160th Inf. Brig. were sent to Camp Sherman, Ohio (*via* Pittsburgh, "The Steel City") for final demobilization. Before his brigade departed Camp Dix, General Brett said to them:

The thing I'm most proud of is that my men did so much and lost so little. Now that I am back in America, I do not have to hang my head in shame in the fear that lives were lost needlessly...I think our record of killed considering the character of the fighting, was lower than any other units in the American Army. The fighting in the Argonne was the heaviest of the war...Our brigade was like a big family. We have been together now for almost two years. We were united and this was our strength...The officers interested themselves in the men, and I know the men had the interests of their officers...It is with deep regret that I am

---

[367] As cited in *2/319th Infantry*, 16.

[368] Named after Civil War Maj. Gen. John Adams Dix who is known for securing Maryland for the Union cause.

[369] As cited in *2/319th Infantry*, 18.

going to part from these men. I have been in the Army nearly forty-five years... I have never had better or more intelligent troops...They were clean morally— they were real red-blooded Americans. I love every one of them... I have tried to take the best care of them. The confidence I had in them was not misplaced.[370]

On June 5, those sent to Camp Sherman arrived in the Steel City where they were ecstatically greeted by family, friends, and even wounded members of the brigade who had been sent home to convalesce. After their last Red Cross meal, they were lined up and paraded down the crowd-engorged streets of the city, just like what we had experienced in Richmond. The men of the 160th Inf. Brig., 80th Division, were led by Brig. Gen. Frank S. Cocheu, who was the commander of the 319th Infantry up until Oct. 1, 1918, and were reviewed by none other than Maj. Gen. Cronkhite, Brig, Gen. Brett, and city officials. Lt. Col. Ashby Williams, the commander of 3/320th Infantry, a person who was not from Pittsburgh (he was from western Virginia), remembered:

It was a royal, heartfelt welcome from the time we landed until the time we left...When we swung into the principal street that leads from the depot, the way was lined with beautiful young ladies who handed us flowers as we passed. We reached Syria Mosque at 10 o'clock, and the men stacked arms and fell out. As I passed into the beautiful mosque, General Brett was at the door and greeted me as I entered. He had come many miles to be there with the men and officers who had served under him and who idolized him. I recall as I went into the basement of the building that my eyes met a very beautiful and splendid scene—breakfast was set for 3,000 men. After breakfast, time was given for visiting among the men and their relatives.[371]

One soldier from the 319th Infantry remembered:
Starting at Fifth Avenue and Bigelow Boulevard, the [brigade] proceeded in platoon front down the avenue, to the Point, and onto the North Side. The automobiles carrying Gen. Cronkhite, Col. Sinclair, Col. Waldron, and Mayor Babcock, scurried out in front of the reviewing stand on lower Liberty Avenue, and the throng arose in tribute as they left the machines for their places in the stand. The head of the parade arrived in the downtown section at 6:00 o'clock and at 6:15 was passing the reviewing stand. As Gen. Cocheu and Lt. Col.

---

[370] As cited in Stultz, 646.

[371] As cited in *1/320th Infantry*, 196.

Montague came abreast the stand, their hands at salute, and their eyes rigidly turned to the right, a bouquet of flowers came out of the stand and dropped at their feet. Gen. Cocheu left the line at this moment and turned into the reviewing stand, while Col. Montague continued on with his men. His band was just behind him, with more than forty men playing the march.

Fifteen minutes of joy supreme—fifteen minutes of streets filled from curb to curb with marching men, their faces wet with perspiration, their rifles shining in the sunlight, their lines incredibly straight; fifteen minutes of cheering and music and glorious tumult—such a fifteen minutes was the thing that Pittsburgh had from the 319th Infantry Regiment, with only the presence of Gen. Brett, the brigade commander, and Col. James M. Love, the second of the organization's wartime commanders, needed to complete the inspiring spectacle.[372]

The next day, the soldiers of the 160th Inf. Brig. were loaded aboard yet another train and were sent to Camp Sherman, Ohio, where they were officially mustered out of the Army on June 10, 1919 (the families of course didn't understand why they just couldn't have been mustered out in Pittsburgh, after the parade). From that point, the brigade and its subordinate units ceased to exist until they were reconstituted as part of the Organized Reserve in 1921 with most of the rest of the division.

As for me, my parents met me at Camp Lee and my dad drove me home after I received my last pay and discharge papers. Let's just say that I returned to Petersburg a changed man. I was no longer the child that my mother sent off to war. I tried to live at home, but it didn't work out, so a few of us Blue Ridgers got an apartment and looked for work, which was impossible to find.

While we were off fighting in France, our economy boomed as industrial output hit a dizzying height. But once peace was declared, everything slowed down and there were hundreds of people out of work in Tidewater. Showing up after the fact, we veterans held a distinct disadvantage in the job hunt. Not only that, but a flu pandemic had swept across much of the world, including many of our own cities—killing millions—even more than the war itself. Petersburg got hit with some cases and we vets were blamed for spreading the disease, which was another reason why many people did not want to associate with us.

At least that's what I thought.

---

[372] As cited in Stultz, 654.

That, plus, we were arrogant buggers, still angry and haunted by the war. If you were a man who gave us problems or who acted tough and didn't serve, we scorned you—we thought that you were less-than-a-man. This of course is somewhat irrational as it takes an entire nation and not just its military to win a war, but that just shows you what our mindset was like—what the horror of war had done to us. Besides—if people treated each other kindly, we'd have far less problems in the world.

The next few years were therefore a little rough for me and many former Doughs until we were finally able to settle down. I worked at my dad's railroad yard but found the work very unrewarding, especially after what I had experienced in France. I therefore studied hard, saved up, and got accepted to the College of William and Mary in Williamsburg. In 1925, I graduated with an A.B. in Education and have taught in the Richmond Public School system ever since, taking the advice of Lt. Myers, my first platoon leader.

In 1926, I was able to talk Ms. Norma Wagner into marrying me.

By 1935, we had four children, three boys and one girl. We were happy, although she would get upset at my occasional outbursts. But we kept it under control, and the war seems more distant to me now, thanks to Father Time and Mother Norma.

Chapter 12
America's Blue Ridge Infantry Division Today (1938).

Every annual reunion (our first was in Pittsburgh in 1920), members of the current 80th Division brief the A.E.F. veterans of the 80th Division Association on the "Current State of the 80th Division." Some of the members of the current division, who are now sergeant majors or colonels, were privates or lieutenants while we were in France in 1919.

The 80th Division was officially reconstituted on Sept. 1, 1921, at 1014 E. Main Street, Richmond, Virginia, as part of the Organized Reserve. It was assigned to the Army's XIII Corps (the country was divided into regions of field armies and corps, Regular Army, National Guard, and Organized Reserve units all falling under the *aegis* of corps and field army control, commanded by Regular Army major or lieutenant generals, respectively). In 1926, division H.Q. was moved to the Post Office Building in Richmond and in 1933, to the Broad-Grace Arcade Building at Third and Grace Streets. In 1935, it was again moved, this time to the Parcel Post Building in Richmond, and that's where it stands today.

During the mid-to-late 1920s, each regiment of the National Army units finally came up with its official distinctive unit insignia (D.U.I.) or "regimental crest." The crests for the infantry regiments of the division, some of which were later stationed in Maryland or D.C., are as follows:

The D.U.I of the 317th Infantry was approved by the Army on February 26, 1927. It has an dark blue shield with three raptors and a rampant lion with *Armis et Animis* scrolled across the bottom. The raptors represent the regiment's three drives up the Meuse-Argonne in Lorraine and the rampant lion represents the regiment's service in Picardy with the British (Lorraine has hawks on its coat of arms and Picrady has a lion). The Latin motto *Armis et Animis* translates to "By Arms and By Courage."

The D.U.I of the 318th Infantry was approved on March 27, 1926. It has a red background, white bell-shaped tents, three green oak trees, the 80th Division patch in the left canton, and "Virginia Never Tires" scrolled across the bottom. The white bells represent the bell tents at the marshalling camp in Pas de Calais (it was the first regiment of the division to be concentrated there) and the red background represents their partnership with the British in

Picardy. The three oak trees represent the regiment's three drives up the wooded Meuse-Argonne. The motto "Old Virginia Never Tires" was adopted by the men of the regiment while at Camp Lee.

The D.U.I of the 319th Infantry was approved by the Army on January 10, 1925. It has an infantry blue shield, a gold and black diamond checkered fess background, four *fleurs-de-lis*, and "*Volens et Potens*" scrolled across the bottom. The gold and black checkered fess is from Lord Baltimore's arms, which are the arms of Maryland, to which the regiment was allocated after the war (many of the Great War vets wanted the colors of Pittsburgh, but lost out to the Army), The four *fleurs-de-lis* represent the regiment's participation in the Somme Offensive with the British in Picardy and three offensives in the Meuse-Argonne. The French motto *Volens et Potens* translates to "Willing and Able."

The D.U.I for the 320th Infantry was approved on July 9, 1925. It has a field of *azure et semée-de-lys*, which was taken from the coat of arms of Picardy, *fleur-de-lis*, a "broken silver chevron," two red bars, and "Forward" scrolled across the bottom. The *fleur-de-lis* represent the regiment's service in Picardy and in the Meuse-Argonne. The "broken silver chevron" and the two red bars are taken from the coat of arms of Washington, D.C., to indicate the current home of the regiment. The motto "Forward" is taken from Cronkhite's famous, "The 80th Division Always Moves Forward!"

Today, the division is a skeletal or "cadre" organization with all of the H.Q. units down to battalion. The subordinate units stretch from Richmond, in the south, up through Washington, D.C., and into Baltimore, Maryland, in the north. There are no units posted in either Pennsylvania or West Virginia. Volunteers of the division "drill" four times a month, usually one night a week, from 6:00 to 10:00 P.M. Emphasis is placed on the "School of the Soldier" or the "School of the Squad." The men wear pretty much the same uniforms and use the same equipment and small arms as we did in 1919, including M1917 Enfield Rifles and M1918 B.A.R.s.

Reserve duty is okay. Will the current members of the division be ready for combat if war is declared? No. Will they be farther ahead we were in 1917? Yes. I chose to rejoin the division and take a commission mostly because I didn't want my experiences from the war to rot away to nothing and because I wanted the money. I could also pass along at least some of the hands-on things that I learned during the war to new officers or E.M. and buy my wife and kids a few extra things. It has also helped me handle my grief over Getz.

A day does not go by that I don't think about "ole Getzey" and the rest of the platoon and continued service with America's Blue Ridge Division helps me deal with the trauma of the war. For others, it's best that they stay a mile away from all of it: no celebration of Armistice Day, no commemoration of Memorial Day, etc. The T.O. of the 80th Infantry Division (1938) is as follows:

<u>80th INFANTRY DIVISION</u>
<u>80th Div. H.Q. and H.Q. Company: Richmond, VA</u>
305th Med. Regt., Richmond, VA
305th Engineer Regt., Richmond, VA
80th Div. Q.M. Company, Richmond, VA
80th Div. Air Service Company, Richmond, VA
305th Ord. Company, Richmond, VA
80th Tank Company, Richmond, VA
80th Motorcycle Company (Recon.), Richmond, VA
80th M.P. Company, Alexandria, VA
80th Signal Company, Washington, D.C.
<u>155th Artillery Brigade, Washington, D.C.</u>
313th Arty. Regt., Baltimore, MD
314th Arty. Regt., Richmond, VA
305th Ammo Train, Washington, D.C.
<u>159th Infantry Brigade, Richmond, VA</u>
317th Inf. Regt., Lynchburg, VA
318th Inf. Regt., Richmond, VA
<u>160th Inf. Brigade, Baltimore, MD</u>
319th Inf. Regt., Baltimore, MD
320th Inf. Regt., Washington, D.C.

During summer, 80th Division soldiers have the opportunity to attend a voluntary two-week "training camp" at Camp Meade, Maryland, that pays well. There, soldiers of the brigades or the specialty troops train alongside Army Regulars, many of whom are far too long to have experienced combat. While there, they focus primarily on the "School of the Company." The regimental, brigade, and division staff officers meanwhile practice the jobs they will be expected to perform during the first months of mobilization, God-forbid. The goal is not to have a fully-trained division ready for combat. The goal is to have a sort-of-kind-of-trained skeleton organization that is ready to get ready to absorb, equip, and train selectees for combat and not to simply start from scratch like we did.

The division T.O. remains similar to what it was in 1917, except for four salient points: first, the Army made each fourth company of an infantry battalion (D, H, and M) a heavy weapons company; second, it added a cannon (artillery) company to each infantry regiment, armed with 75mm field guns; third, it assigned tank and motor reconnaissance companies directly to the division; and forth, it added a division air reconnaissance unit. Each new heavy weapons company is supposed to have several of sections of new air-cooled M2 .50 cal. M.G.s (similar to the French Hotchkiss, just bigger and far better) and water-cooled M1917 Browning 30.06 cal. M.G.s that are mounted on armored motor cars, and not mules. It's supposed to also have several sections of 81mm mortars, which are to be mounted on armored motor cars. These sections would be parceled out to the rifle companies as the battalion commander saw fit. The division's new cadre tank company has three platoons of American-built Renault-style tanks that can move as one unit or be parceled out to the infantry brigades.

In our experience, the critical concepts of battle are: offensive operations, supporting arms, and aggressive action of infantrymen schooled in the use of the rifle, bayonet, and hand grenade. One does not win a battle or a war by staying on the defensive. The defensive should only be a temporary condition in order to prepare for offensive operations. One must pound the enemy and keep the pressure on him with over-whelming and integrated combined arms fire. As such, we fully support the tenants that were taught to us in the *F.S.R.*:

> *122. Combat is divided into two general classes, the offensive and defensive. The defensive is divided into purely passive defense and the temporary defense, which has for its object the assumption of the offensive at the first favorable opportunity. DECISIVE RESULTS ARE OBTAINED ONLY BY THE OFFENSIVE. Aggressiveness wins battles. The purely passive defense is adopted only when the mission can be fully accomplished by this method of warfare. In all other cases, if a force be obliged by uncontrollable circumstances to adopt the defensive, it must*

be considered as a temporary expedient, and a change to the offensive with all or part of the forces will be made as soon as conditions warrant such change.

We also learned that Pershing was only half-right. He believed that a highly trained and motivated infantryman, armed with rifle and bayonet, was the key to victory. We quickly learned, however, thanks to the British in Artois and Picardy and real-life experience in the Meuse-Argonne against the adept Hun, that infantrymen also need supporting arms in order to *Always Move Forward*. What worked best for us was in getting the A.R.s and R.G.s up front as soon as possible. They would lay down suppressive fire into the targeted enemy embrasures and wait for the supporting arms to expand the front—the attached field guns, the I.G.s, and the M.G.s. The R.G.s, A.R.s, and supporting heavy weapons, backed by mortars, would then blast the designated enemy position to hell while the bomber and bayonet squads, armed with grenades, rifles, and bayonets, screened by W.P. fired by the R.G.s, stormed the objective.

As such, we only moved as fast as our supporting weapons.

I have recently learned that the Army is currently fielding wireless radio sets to artillery forward observers and with this new communication, the artillery can do far more "adjust fire" missions for the infantry. In my opinion, this will revolutionize maneuver warfare. Pre-planned rolling barrages were nice, but having an artillery forward observer call in a map grid to his fire direction center to suppress an enemy target in conjunction with other supporting weapons, will be the most deadly weapon on the battlefield. As they correctly say: "Field Artillery is the King of Battle." This statement is true but only partially so. The fact is that the integrated infantry-artillery team trumps all, as it is not only the King and Queen of Battle, but also the Rook, the Bishop, and the Knight.

As for tanks, we found them to be utterly useless. The few we saw were either abandoned, broke down, or stuck in the mud or in a ditch or in a shell hole. Given the current firepower of artillery—churning up the battlefield into deep craters—tanks cannot keep up with the infantry, which, if properly trained, can traverse almost any obstacle like rainwater running downhill during a thunderstorm.

We heard that the British, especially during the last few months of the war, used the infantry-artillery-armor-aeroplane team well to break the German lines in Flanders. That's all well and good but I wonder how far forward their tanks actually got. In humble my opinion, the Army should get rid of tanks and add six more artillery battalions per division, pairing an artillery battalion with an infantry battalion. But the Army has chosen to keep the same infantry-to-artillery ratio that we had during the Great War for Civilization: twelve infantry battalions and six artillery battalions per division. Granted, the Army has several independent artillery brigades in its T.O., which can be attached to a division by a corps H.Q., but we still feel that the Army needs to double its artillery quota as it is "The King of Battle."

A few contemporary European military theorists like British Col. John Frederick Charles Fuller, who wrote *Provisional Instructions for Tank and Armoured Car Training* (1927) or German *Generalmajor Heinz Guderian* who just published *Achtung Panzer!* (1937) see tanks or "armored fighting vehicles" (*Panzerkampfwagonen*) as being used *en masse* to exploit a breakthrough in the line with the help of aeroplanes, which would drop bombs to protect their flanks. The tanks would get into the enemy's rear and destroy his S.O.S. capabilities, just like pursuit cavalry of old.

In my view, the biggest problem with Fuller's and Guderian's exciting theory is that the only thing that is going to be broken is the tank itself. It will either break down mechanically, get shredded into scrap metal by opposing artillery, fall into a gaping engineer trap or shellhole, or get strafed by one of the new and better-armed aeroplanes. It would be better if the cavalry or mounted arm in fact remained mounted on horses, as horses can at least keep up with the infantry under battle conditions. Granted, the horses or mules assigned our artillery batteries or M.G. platoons suffered high casualty rates during the Meuse-Argonne Offensive, but at least those that did survive performed their assigned duties.

To close, I will never forget those great, brave men of America's 80th (Blue Ridge) Division and the A.E.F. during the Great War for Civilization, the War to End All Wars. In all, the 80th Division received 619 awards and decorations, seized twenty-three miles of enemy-held territory, captured 1,813 enemy soldiers, and suffered 6,232 casualties, including 1,232 killed.

The 80th Division Always Moves Forward! See you at the next reunion.

Bibliography.

"*313th Artillery*": Irving, Thomas and Edward Crowell. *A History of the 313th Artillery, U.S.A.* (New York: Thomas Y. Crowell Company, 1920).

"*314th Artillery*": *History of 314th Artillery* (314th Artillery Veterans' Association, N.D.).

"*314th M.G.*": *314th M.G. Battalion History, Blue Ridge (80th) Division. Published as a Matter of Record by the Officers and Men of the Battalion* (N.P., 1919).

"*317th Infantry*": Craighill, Edley, *History of the 317th Infantry Regiment, 80th Division* (N.P., N.D.).

"*318th Infantry*": *History of the 318th Infantry Regiment of the 80th Division, 1917-1919* (Richmond, Virginia: William Byrd Press, N.D.).

"*319th Infantry*": Peck, Josiah C. *The 319th Infantry A.E.F.* (Paris, France: Herbert Clarke Printing, 1919).

"*2/319th Infantry*": Herr, Charles Ryman. *Company F History, 319th Infantry* (N.P., 1920).

"*1/320th Infantry*": Williams, Ashby. *Experiences of the Great War: Artois, St. Mihiel, Meuse-Argonne* (Roanoke, Virginia: Press of the Stone Printing and Manufacturing Company, 1919).

"*3/320th Infantry*": Lukens, Edward C. *A Blue Ridge Memoir* (Baltimore, Maryland: Sun Print, 1922).

"A.D.R.": *Drill and Service Regulations for Field Artillery, 1917* (Washington, D.C., Government Printing Office, 1917).

"A.B.M.C.": *American Armies and Battlefields in Europe: A History, Guide, and Reference Book* (Washington, D.C.: Government Printing Office, American Battle Monuments Commission, 1938).

"B.M.G.M.": British General Staff. *Infantry Machine-Gun Company Training Manual, 1917*.

"Bullard": Bullard, Robert Lee, Maj. Gen. (U.S.A., ret). *Personalities and Reminiscences of the War* (Garden City, N.Y., 1925).

"F.S.R.": *Field Service Regulations, U.S. Army, 1914. Text Corrections to December 20, 1916.* (New York: Army and Navy Journal, 1916).

"Harbord": Harbord, James. *The American Army in France, 1917-19* (Boston: Little, Brown, and Company, 1936).

Hunt, Frazier: *Blown in by the Draft: Camp Yarns Collected at One of the Great National Army Cantonments by an Amateur War Correspondent. Forward by Col. Theodore Roosevelt.* (New York: Doubleday, Page, and Company, 1918).

"I.D.R.": *Infantry Drill Regulations, 1917.* (Washington, D.C.: Government Printing Office, 1917).

"I.N.C.O.M.": *Manual for Noncommissioned Officers and Privates of Infantry of the Army of the United States, 1917, to be used by Engineer companies (dismounted) and Coast Artillery companies for Infantry instruction and Training* (Government Printing Office, 1917).

"Mitchell": Mitchell, Lt. Col. William A. *Outlines of Military History* (Washington, D.C.: National Service Publishing Company, 1931).

"M.G.D.R.": *Drill Regulations for Machine Guns: Infantry, 1917* (Washington, D.C., Government Printing Office, 1917).

"M.M.T.": Moss, Col. James. *Manual of Military Training* (Menasha, Wisconsin: Army and College Printers, 1917).

"M.S.T.": *Drill and Service Manual for Sanitary Troops, U.S.A., April 15, 1917.*

"N.C.O.M.A.": *Manual for N.C.O.s and Privates of Field Artillery of the A.U.S., 1917* (Washington, D.C., Government Printing Office, 1917).

"Pershing": Pershing, John Joseph. *My Experiences in the World War* (New York: F.A. Stokes, 1931), 2 volumes.

"P.M.": Ellis, O.O. and E.B. Garey, Majors, U.S. Army Infantry. *Plattsburg Manual: A Handbook for Military Training* (New York, The Century Company, 1917).

"Stultz": Stultz, Sergeant Russell Lee. *History of the 80th Division, A.E.F.* (80th Division Veterans' Association, 1923).

"T.O.E., 1914": *Tables of Organization Based on the Field Service Regulations of 1914* (Washington, D.C., War Department, 1914).

Young, Rush, S. *Over the Top with the 80th, by a Buck Private* (N.P., 1933).

About the Author

Author, historian, and Army Major Gary Schreckengost (ret.) is a life member of the 80th Division Association (80thdivision.com). A Cold War, Homeland, Bosnia, and Iraq War veteran, Schreckengost is the author of *Wheat's Tigers: The 1st Louisiana Special Battalion in the Civil War* and has been published in *America's Civil War Magazine, World War II Magazine, Field Artillery Journal,* and *Armor Magazine.*

The four books in this series, found on Amazon.com, are:

The 80th Division in World War I, Volume 1: Camp Lee to Saint-Mihiel.
The 80th Division in World War I, Volume 2: Meuse-Argonne to Homecoming.
The 80th Division in World War I: Into the Meuse-Argonne, Sept.-Nov. 1918.
The 80th Division in World War I: The Battle for Bois d'Ogons, Oct. 4-6, 1918.

Other 80th Division Books on Amazon.com

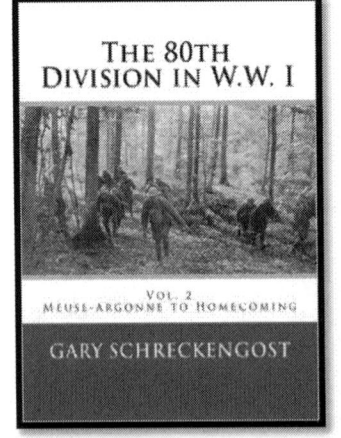

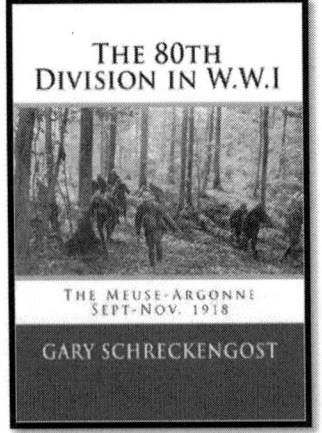

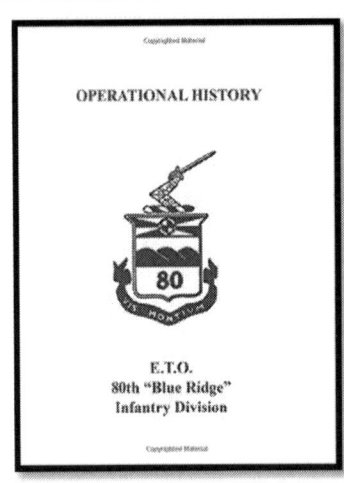

Made in the USA
Middletown, DE
08 October 2018